THE HAMPTON ROADS COMMUNITIES IN WORLD WAR II

Virginia Division of Ports

"The dominant geographic characteristic of the region is its location on a protected harbor only a few miles from the open sea and with easy access to the populous centers of the eastern seaboard. This strategic situation has largely accounted for its importance as a war center." (The waterfront and business section of Norfolk, Hampton Roads' largest population center.)

THE HAMPTON ROADS COMMUNITIES IN WORLD WAR II

BY

THE HAMPTON ROADS-PENINSULA WAR STUDIES COMMITTEE
College of William and Mary

CHARLES F. MARSH, Editor

JAMES E. PATE W. WARNER MOSS
R. WAYNE KERNODLE JOHN A. McGUIRE

THE UNIVERSITY OF NORTH CAROLINA PRESS
Chapel Hill

PREFACE

Few sections of the United States have presented such an array of wartime and postwar problems as the Hampton Roads-Peninsula area of Virginia. As early as October, 1942, faculty members of the College of William and Mary at Williamsburg, situated on the edge of the area, initiated studies of the impact upon their own community of the establishment of army and navy posts and other war activities in the vicinity. In December, 1943, the Division of the Social Sciences at the college formed the Hampton Roads-Peninsula War Studies Committee in the hope of expanding these studies to cover the whole area. A three-year grant in 1945, totalling $31,500, from the Rockefeller Foundation and supplementary funds from the General Education Board and from local sources, together with substantial assistance from the college in the form of office space, equipment, and reduced teaching loads made this expansion possible. This book is the direct outgrowth of these studies.

The establishment of a record of the impact of the Second World War upon the Hampton Roads communities and the rendering of assistance to them in understanding and meeting their war problems, in making postwar adjustments, and in developing long-range plans have been prime objectives of these studies. It has been hoped also that they would shed light on how war activities affect communities throughout the nation to which heavy war duties are assigned and, perhaps, contribute to the development of new techniques for research in the social sciences.

From its outset to its completion, this project has been a cooperative venture. While the five authors prepared their respective chapters as independent studies, they have worked together closely and harmoniously. The active encouragement, advice, and numerous forms of practical assistance offered by John E. Pomfret, President of the College of William and Mary, have been major factors in making this book possible. The general plan of the studies and the provision of research facilities were worked out by the War Studies Committee, consisting of James Ernest Pate, Sharvy G. Umbeck, and the editor, and were reviewed by the faculty of the Division of the Social Sciences. Ruth Lynch Kernodle prepared most of the charts and tables, supervised the preparation of the manuscript for publication, and made important contributions to the organization of the entire book. While the studies of Mary Hudson Robinson, George T. Kalif, and A. J. Mapp, members of the Committee's research staff, have been noted in footnotes at appropriate places in the text, special acknowledgement should be made of their contributions.

Many officials of local, state, and federal government agencies, businessmen, heads of social agencies, ministers, judges, labor leaders, officers of the armed forces, and other individuals have given generously of their thought, time, and facilities in assisting the authors in their field studies. Particularly significant assistance has been rendered by Commander Raymond B. Bottom, publisher of the Newport News *Daily Press;* Homer L. Ferguson and A. Albert Geise, Newport News Shipbuilding and Drydock Company; John S. Alfriend and S. T. Northern, National Bank of Commerce of Norfolk; Anna R. Thomas, Bureau of Vital Statistics, Virginia Department of Health; Lorin M. Thompson, Bureau of Population and Economic Research, University of Virginia; and Captain J. M. Hetherington, Hampton Roads Port of Embarkation. Commander Richard Velz, U.S.N., and members of the staffs of the Maritime Museum of Newport News, the Norfolk Advertising Board, and the Virginia Division of Ports, Department of Conservation and Development, provided the photographs used in this book.

Among the research and clerical assistants, including students of the college, who have aided in this project, special mention should be made of Frances Whitehead, Gretchen Erb, Jacqueline Fowlkes Harrod, John Reid, and Wallace Lemon. The Richmond Area University Center, through its grants-in-aid policy, has made a substantial contribution towards the publication of this book.

Williamsburg, Virginia CHARLES F. MARSH
July, 1950

CONTENTS

ILLUSTRATIONS

FIGURES

TABLES

I

THE AREA AND THE WAR'S IMPACT

Norfolk Advertising Board

"The demands of World War II were so heavy that naval expansion could not be contained within the immediate vicinity of the Naval Operating Base at Norfolk." (The men and supplies being loaded aboard naval vessels at the base indicate the extent of these demands.)

CHAPTER I

THE HAMPTON ROADS-PENINSULA AREA—ITS GEOGRAPHY AND PREWAR POPULATION*

FROM THE SETTLEMENT of Jamestown in 1607 to the present, war has been a potent factor in shaping the lives of the people living along the shores of Hampton Roads and the peninsula formed by the James and York rivers. Indian warfare, Cornwallis' retreat and surrender at Yorktown, and such events in the War Between the States as McClelland's Peninsular Campaign as he retreated from Richmond and the Monitor-Merrimac battle in the waters of Hampton Roads have given the region a battlefield heritage matched by few parts of the United States. The impact upon the region and its people, however, of the First and Second World Wars, though fought in distant lands and waters, was probably even sharper than the earlier campaigns. The building and repair of ships; the training, embarkation, and debarkation of soldiers and sailors; and other war activities absorbed, especially in World War II, most of the existing human and other productive resources of the region, brought in thousands of migrants from other parts of the country, and necessitated the construction of vast military and industrial plants, public works, and housing.

This study represents an attempt to discover some of the more significant phases of the impact of the Second World War upon the social, economic, and governmental life of the Hampton Roads-Peninsula area. Essential first steps toward this end include (1) an inventory of the geography, population, and social and economic structure of the region before it was transformed by war, and (2) identification of the channels through which the war came to the region. These steps are taken in Part One, and the balance of the volume is concerned with tracing the major social, economic, and governmental changes during and after the war and appraising their long-run significance.

*By Charles F. Marsh, Professor of Economics and Business Administration, College of William and Mary.

GEOGRAPHIC CHARACTERISTICS

The Hampton Roads-Peninsula region is the southeastern portion of what geologists term "The Coastal Plain Province of Virginia." Its center lies approximately 200 miles southeast of Washington, D. C. and 80 miles from Richmond. It extends, roughly, from the Chickahominy River about halfway between Richmond and Newport News, the York River, and the Blackwater River on the north and west to the North Carolina line and the Atlantic Ocean on the south and east. Its area comprises about 1800 square miles or 4.5 per cent of the total area of Virginia. A map of the region is shown in the end papers of the book.

Hampton Roads itself is the drowned mouth of the James, the Nansemond, and the Elizabeth rivers as they flow into the Chesapeake Bay and thence, between the twin capes, Henry and Charles, into the Atlantic. The harbor of Hampton Roads is thus doubly landlocked. A total shore frontage of approximately fifty miles, a tidal range averaging less than three feet, and freedom from ice throughout the year make it one of the finest natural harbors in the world.

The waters of the harbor divide the area into two parts. The south side includes the cities of Norfolk, Portsmouth, South Norfolk, and Suffolk, and the counties of Norfolk, Princess Anne, Nansemond, and Isle of Wight. The northern shore is the end of the peninsula between the James and York rivers upon which lie the cities of Newport News, Hampton, and Williamsburg, and the counties of Elizabeth City, Warwick, York, and James City. The traditional Hampton Roads area as delimited by the Bureau of the Census includes only the cities of Norfolk, Newport News, Portsmouth, Hampton, and South Norfolk, Elizabeth City County, and the more populous sections of Norfolk, Princess Anne, and Warwick counties. The broader area embraced by this study, which is the same as that used by the War Manpower Commission,[1] reflects the realities of World War II, during which the pressures of expanded war activities for land, labor, housing, and public works burst the traditional boundaries of the Hampton Roads area. In spite of this, the relatively greater impact of the war on the larger core communities and the fact that some statistical data have not included the outlying portions of the region have

1. This commission defined the area "in terms of commuting accessibility to the closely contiguous industrial centers of Newport News, Norfolk, and Portsmouth."—War Manpower Commission, Historical Report, Hampton Roads Area, World War II (mimeographed), September, 1945, p. 1.

necessitated confining certain parts of this report to the more restricted area.

The dominant geographic characteristic of the region, obviously, is its location on a protected harbor only a few miles from the open sea and with easy access to the populous centers of the eastern seaboard. This strategic situation has largely accounted for its importance as a war center. Its topography, climate, geology, soil, and natural resources are also of significance, however, in providing an understanding of the region's problems in war and peace.

Like the rest of the lowland part of the Coastal Plain, the Hampton Roads-Peninsula area consists of a gently sloping lowland, broken by sluggish tidal rivers and their tributaries, which rises gradually from the sea to a maximum of about one hundred feet above sea level. The heart of the area around Norfolk and Newport News scarcely exceeds twenty-five feet in elevation and contains considerable mud flats and marshlands.[2] The Great Dismal Swamp, with Lake Drummond, Virginia's largest fresh water lake in its center, lies in Norfolk and Nansemond counties and adjacent portions of North Carolina. These marshes and swamplands, together with the rivers and their tributaries, Hampton Roads, Chesapeake Bay and the Atlantic itself, have restricted the land available for expansion incident to wartime growth of the crowded urban centers. They have also complicated land transportation to much the same degree that they have facilitated water transportation. Bridges, ferries, and land-fills for highways and railroads have had to be provided at considerable expense to general taxpayers and users, and travel routes are still roundabout and congested.

Climate

The climate of this southeastern portion of Tidewater Virginia[3] is mild and even with an abundance of sunshine and well-distributed precipitation. While relatively high humidity sometimes produces more oppressive summer heat and more penetrating winter chill than

2. C. K. Wentworth, *Sand and Gravel Resources of Virginia*, Virginia Geological Survey, Bulletin No. 32, 1930, pp. 7-9; also S. Sanford, *The Underground Water Resources of the Coastal Plain Province of Virginia*, Virginia Geological Survey, Bulletin No. 5, 1913, pp. 7-11, 159-295.

3. Sources of factual data on climate include C. W. Newman's "Climate," in *Virginia: Economic and Civic*, Virginia Polytechnic Institute and Virginia State Chamber of Commerce, 1933, pp. 70-81; *Handbook of Virginia*, Virginia Department of Agriculture and Immigration, 1937, pp. 17-19; and U. S. Department of Commerce, Weather Bureau, Richmond, Virginia.

actual temperatures would suggest, cool breezes in summer and warm sunshine in winter make it a generally healthful and pleasant climate in which to live.

The region has an average of about 258 days of sunshine per year and a ratio of actual to possible sunshine of more than 60 per cent. A long growing season of 200 to 230 days or more and the mild winters make it possible to grow truck crops almost the year around. Average total snowfall is less than 10 inches a year, and there is snow on the ground, normally, fewer than 10 days per year.

Rainfall is abundant throughout the year, ranging from a monthly average of 2 to 2½ inches in November to 5 to 6 inches in July, with annual precipitation averaging about 45 inches.

While wind velocities are somewhat higher in Tidewater Virginia than in the western part of the state, winds of destructive velocity seldom develop. The tropical storms which sometimes move up the Atlantic seacoast in late summer do not often reach the Hampton Roads region and when they do it is with diminished strength.

Geology and Soils

The geologic structure of the Hampton Roads-Peninsula area is simple. Beds of sedimentary rock, derived chiefly from the waste of Piedmont rocks, dip toward the sea under the younger formations of the Coastal Plain. Crystalline rocks which come to the surface in the Piedmont region form a basement 2,246 feet below the surface at Fort Monroe. They are overlain by unconsolidated sands, clays and cobbles, gravels, shells and marls. Ordinary hard rocks are virtually nonexistent in the region.[4]

While soil surveys have identified thirty or more different soil types in the Hampton Roads region, they may be grouped into (1) light-colored well drained soils; (2) light-colored poorly drained soils; (3) dark-colored poorly drained soils; and (4) miscellaneous land types.[5] For the area as a whole, the light-colored well drained soils are predominant. Inherently, these soils are not as fertile as some of the poorly drained soils, as they are acid, low in organic matter, and subject to leaching. They warm early in the spring, however, respond readily to fertilizer and lime, and are easy to cultivate. They

4. See Wentworth, *op. cit.*, pp. 25-29; Sanford, *op. cit.*, pp. 10-29.

5. M. Whitney, *Soils of the United States*, U. S. Bureau of Soils, Bulletin No. 55, 1909, p. 233; *Soil Survey*, U. S. Department of Agriculture in cooperation with Virginia Agricultural Experiment Station, Nansemond County (Series 1932, No. 6), Isle of Wight County (Series 1937, No. 1), and Princess Anne County (Series 1939, No. 3).

are admirably adapted to vegetable crops for the early markets, when prices are higher. Some of the more poorly drained soils, notably in Princess Anne County, have produced with the aid of open drainage ditches higher crop yields than the better drained types, but much of this land is cultivated to only a small degree or left as forest land. The miscellaneous land types including dunesands, swamp, marsh, and peat are generally not arable and are devoted to sparse pastures, timber, homesites, and recreational activities, notably hunting and fishing. Artificial drainage, however, has reclaimed some swamp and marshland for agricultural purposes.

Other Natural Resources

More than half of the land of the Hampton Roads-Peninsula region is forested, largely in second-growth timber.[6] Loblolly and other yellow pines predominate but considerable stands of such hardwoods as gum, oak, locust, soft maple and poplar are present. Frequent clear cuttings often followed by fire have reduced the average diameter of the trees until sawing by large mills has become less profitable and large areas, particularly in the Dismal Swamp, have been so denuded that artificial reforestation has become necessary. Small scale lumbering, especially by farmers, is widespread. The rapidity with which trees grow to pulpwood size in the favorable climate of Tidewater Virginia has provided the basis for a substantial pulpwood industry in some parts of the region. Leaders in this industry have given increasing cooperation in recent years to the conservation efforts of the Virginia and United States Forest Services.

Each of the eight counties included in the region looks to seafood as an important natural resource. Their total catch in 1939 was estimated at 40,561,000 pounds, about 70 per cent of which consisted of finfish and the balance of such shellfish as oysters, crabs, lobsters and clams. Less than half, however, of the estimated value of the total catch of $1,277,000 was accounted for by the thirty-odd varieties of finfish because of the larger unit value of shellfish. These catch figures understate the importance of seafood to the region as they do not include receipts by seafood companies in such important markets as Hampton, Phoebus, and Norfolk, from catches in the waters of other Virginia counties and from Maryland.[7] Depletion of this important

6. J. E. Lodewick, "Forests and Forestry," in *Virginia: Economic and Civic, op. cit.*, pp. 142-55.

7. Fish and Wildlife Service, U. S. Department of Interior; see also M. L. Jeffries, "Commercial Fisheries," in *Virginia: Economic and Civic, op. cit.*, pp. 158-68.

resource, particularly the oyster branch, through lack of cooperative effort by members of the industry, absence of effective state control, and pollution of tidal waters by sewage and industrial wastes, has been observed for some years. In spite of efforts by the United States Fish and Wildlife Service and by such agencies as the Virginia Commission of Fisheries and the Virginia Fisheries Laboratory to learn more about the migration, habits, and propagation of fish in tidal waters and the conservation and expansion of this resource, much remains to be done before the problem of depletion can be considered as close to solution.

Except for minor deposits of low-grade iron ore on the peninsula, which may have provided the basis for the small colonial iron industry, no metallic minerals occur in the Hampton Roads region. No indication of either natural gas or petroleum of commercial importance has been found in the area. Only such non-metallic minerals as sand, gravel, clay, and marl are available. A considerable brick industry has developed on both sides of Hampton Roads because of the excellent deposits of clay. Shell marl from deposits in Nansemond and Isle of Wight counties have been manufactured into Portland cement in Norfolk and used in the manufacture of fertilizer.[8]

Perhaps the weakest feature of the resource pattern of the Hampton Roads-Peninsula area consists of limits upon expanding the supplies of fresh water for domestic and industrial use in the Norfolk-Newport News sections. Ample supplies are available for present use, but the problem of finding new sources of water for a vastly increased population and industrial development is far more serious than in many other sections of the country. Limited land masses hemmed in and penetrated by bodies of salt water restrict the extent to which additional reservoirs can be created from ponds, creeks, and lakes to serve as surface supplies. A minute analysis of experience with deep wells drilled before 1909 brought the conclusion that because of excessive mineral and salt content of the water they could not be viewed as good potential sources.[9] No evidence has come to light since then to contradict this conclusion. Newport News found it necessary to construct a pipe line approximately fifty miles long to the Chickahominy River to insure a supply of water for the greatly expanded population served by its waterworks during the war years. This chronic difficulty

8. W. M. McGill, *Outline of the Mineral Resources of Virginia*, Virginia Geological Survey, Bulletin No. 47, Ed., Series No. 3, 1936; see also Wentworth, *op. cit.*, pp. 119-34.

9. Sanford, *op. cit.*, pp. 97-295.

in obtaining new sources of water has caused the Norfolk Industrial Commission, a private agency concerned with attracting new industry, to discourage industries requiring large amounts of water from coming to the Norfolk area.

THE PREWAR POPULATION PICTURE

Understanding of the impact of World War II upon all phases of American life has been aided by the historical accident through which the 1940 Census was taken shortly before the United States became involved in the conflict. While war activity in Europe had been reflected in a slight upswing in shipbuilding activity in the Hampton Roads region before April 1, 1940, the census date, information provided by this census has yielded numerous prewar benchmarks from which the nature and extent of the war's impact upon the region may be measured. The more basic of these benchmarks are portrayed in this section and in Chapters II and III.

At the outset of the war, the Hampton Roads-Peninsula area was more densely populated and had experienced more rapid population growth during the previous fifty years than any other district of comparable land area in Virginia. Its 1940 population of 408,624 was 15.3 per cent of that for the entire state but its area was only 4.5 per cent of the state total. The population had increased 166 per cent since 1890 as compared with only 62 per cent for the state as a whole. The three major cities—Norfolk, Portsmouth, and Newport News—showed an increase of 341 per cent while the population of all urban centers in Virginia rose 234 per cent during the same half century. The periods of greatest growth were the decades 1890-1900 and 1910-1920, which reflected activity around Hampton Roads incident to the Spanish-American War and the First World War. Population growth slowed somewhat between 1900 and 1910. The sharp decline in shipbuilding and other war activity during the early twenties was accompanied by a decrease of 2.9 per cent in population during that postwar decade. Revival of shipbuilding after 1934, however, especially toward the end of the decade, and other economic activity brought an increase of 13.3 per cent between 1930 and 1940, in spite of the depression.

Distribution within the Area

The distribution of population among the cities and counties of the Hampton Roads-Peninsula region from 1890 to 1940 is shown in

TABLE 1. POPULATION OF COUNTIES IN THE HAMPTON ROADS-PENINSULA AREA OF VIRGINIA, 1890 TO 1940

	1890	1900	1910	1920	1930	1940
ENTIRE AREA	153,610	219,400	268,293	371,349	360,580	408,624
North Side	36,057	57,197	61,566	86,446	84,735	102,202
Newport News[a]	4,449	19,635	20,205	35,596	34,417	37,067
Warwick Co.[a]	2,201[e]	4,888	6,041	11,417	8,829	9,248
Hampton	2,513	2,764	5,505	6,138	6,382	5,898
Elizabeth City Co.[a]	13,655[e]	16,696[e]	15,720[e]	19,111[e]	19,835	32,283
York Co.[b]	7,596	7,482	7,757	8,046	7,615	8,857
Williamsburg[b]	1,831	2,044	2,714	2,462	3,778	3,942
James City Co.[b]	3,812[e]	3,688[e]	3,624[e]	3,676[e]	3,879	4,907
South Side	117,553	162,203	206,727	284,903	275,845	306,422
Norfolk[c]	34,871	46,624	67,452	115,777	129,710	144,332
Portsmouth	13,268	17,427	33,190	54,387	45,704	50,745
Norfolk Co.[c]	28,899	50,780	52,744	57,358	30,082	35,828
South Norfolk[c]					7,857	8,038
Princess Anne Co.	9,510	11,192	11,526	13,626	16,282	19,984
Suffolk[d]	3,354	3,827	7,008	9,123	10,271	11,343
Nansemond Co.[d]	16,338[e]	19,251[e]	19,878	20,199	22,530	22,771
Isle of Wight Co.	11,313	13,102	14,929	14,433	13,409	13,381

a. Parts of Warwick County annexed to Newport News in 1920 and 1921. Parts of Elizabeth City County annexed to Newport News in 1921, 1926, and 1938.

b. Parts of James City and York counties annexed to Williamsburg in 1925.

c. Part of Norfolk County annexed to Princess Anne County in 1921, and part to Norfolk in 1923. The 1920 figure for Norfolk County includes population of South Norfolk (7,724), which became an independent city in 1921 and for which separate population figures were not reported prior to 1920.

d. Parts of Nansemond County annexed to Suffolk in 1926 and 1928.

e. In order to show population trends in Newport News, Hampton, Williamsburg and Suffolk before they became independent cities, the figures for the counties of Warwick, Elizabeth City, James City and Nansemond during the indicated years exclude these towns, even though they were parts of the respective counties during these years.

Source: U. S. Census.

Table 1. Throughout the period, approximately three-fourths of the people in the entire area lived south of Hampton Roads, though the north side communities have shown a slightly greater rate of increase.

In 1940, approximately four-fifths of the population was concentrated in the metropolitan area including Norfolk, Portsmouth, Newport News, and urban portions of surrounding counties. The three central cities themselves comprised between 55 and 60 per cent of the total population in 1920, 1930, and 1940 as compared with only 34 to 45 per cent in 1890, 1900, and 1910. Norfolk, the largest city, was home for 31 to 36 per cent of the people of the entire region, according to the last three censuses, in contrast to 21 to 25 per cent in the

1890, 1900, and 1910 enumerations. It is apparent that population had tended to become concentrated increasingly in the major cities and their environs with relatively smaller portions of the people living in the outlying parts of the area. The relative density of population in 1940 is indicated in the end paper map referred to in the previous section of this chapter.

Every community, according to Table 1, except Williamsburg and the counties of Nansemond and Isle of Wight, increased in population under war pressure between 1910 and 1920. Warwick County, adjacent to Newport News, showed a gain of 89 per cent with Newport News, Norfolk, and Portsmouth registering increases of 76, 72, and 64 per cent, respectively. These same communities, less Norfolk but with Norfolk County added, showed the greatest population losses as war activity declined during the twenties. The fact that the city of Norfolk showed an increase and Norfolk County a decrease of almost 50 per cent between 1920 and 1930 should be considered in the light of the latter's loss of population through annexation to the former and to Princess Anne County and the creation in 1921 of South Norfolk, formerly a part of Norfolk County, as an independent city.

Every city and county, except Hampton and Isle of Wight County, experienced population growth during the thirties. These two localities showed slight decreases. Elizabeth City County, adjacent to the cities of Newport News and Hampton and the military posts Fort Monroe and Langley Field, the latter the home of the expanding laboratories of the National Advisory Committee on Aeronautics, led the field with a 63 per cent increase in population. The rate of increase of the other localities did not deviate greatly from the 13.3 per cent increase for the entire area during the decade.

CHAPTER II

THE PREWAR SOCIAL STRUCTURE*

THE HAMPTON ROADS region, before the war, presented an example, though somewhat exaggerated and unique, of the social paradox that is Virginia. Truly Southern in its emphasis upon the importance of ancient traditions and of friendly, gentle living, its agricultural economy and rural society, its large Negro and small foreign-born population, and its predominantly Protestant religious tendencies, the border state of Virginia has been influenced over the years, to a greater degree than most of its sister Southern states, by its neighbors to the north and west.[1] Increasing industrialization with the aid of northern capital and management, military expansion incident to World War I, and the ease of migration of both white and Negro youths from the state have had their inevitable effects upon Virginia's social structure. The maritime location and shipping interests of the Hampton Roads-Peninsula area have always made it particularly subject to outside influences which have tended to differentiate its social pattern from that of other parts of Virginia. This has been accentuated by such major developments as the construction by Collis P. Huntington of the Chesapeake and Ohio Railway down the backbone of the peninsula and his establishment of the Newport News Shipbuilding and Drydock Company, the construction and expansion of various military and civil establishments on both sides of Hampton Roads by the federal government, the expansion of Virginia Beach into a nationally known summer resort, and the thirty-million dollar restoration of colonial Williamsburg by John D. Rockefeller, Jr. By 1940, ancient traditions and leisurely habits had tended to give way to new ideas and activities, industrialization and urbanization had pushed the traditional agricultural and rural society into the outlying sections of the area, and the rising flood of visitors from other sections, with their dollars and their mores, had irreparably breached the dikes behind which many residents had been able to maintain their traditional attitudes and ways of life.

*By Charles F. Marsh, Professor of Economics and Business Administration, College of William and Mary.

1. See J. B. Gittler, *Virginia's People, A Cultural Panorama*, Population Study Report No. 5, Virginia State Planning Board, 1944, Chapters 1-2.

URBAN-RURAL CHARACTER

According to the 1940 Census, almost two-thirds of the population of the Hampton Roads-Peninsula area lived in cities or towns of 2,500 or more inhabitants and were thus classed as urban, as compared with only a little more than one-third in the state of Virginia as a whole. The trend toward urbanization of the area during the past fifty years is indicated in Figure 1.

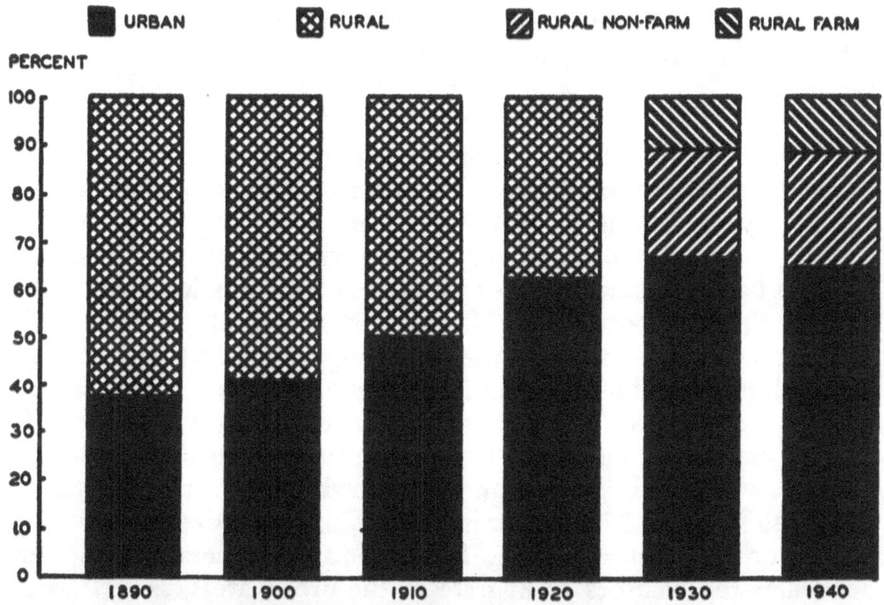

FIGURE 1. PERCENTAGE DISTRIBUTION OF POPULATION BY URBAN AND RURAL, HAMPTON ROADS-PENINSULA AREA, 1890-1940

Source: U. S. Census.

The extent to which the agricultural pattern of life had been departed from before the Second World War is further indicated by the relatively small portion of the rural population which was classed by the census as "rural farm." Only in Isle of Wight and Nansemond counties did as many as half of the rural inhabitants live on farms in 1940. The bulk of the rural population, classed as "rural non-farm," lived just outside the limits of incorporated cities and towns or in towns and villages with less than 2,500 inhabitants, many of which were suburbs of the larger cities rather than true rural towns. This was particularly true of Elizabeth City, Norfolk, Warwick, and York counties, which had very small farm populations.

Of the total population of the entire area, both urban and rural, only 10.9 per cent lived on farms in 1940 and 12 per cent in 1930. These figures contrast sharply with the farm population percentage for Virginia of 36.7 per cent in 1940 and 39.2 per cent in 1930. It is apparent that even before World War II activities concentrated population in the urban sections of the Hampton Roads region, its dominant pattern was already that of an urban society, with the distinctive rural society of Virginia being compressed into two counties—Isle of Wight and Nansemond—and the more remote districts of the other counties in the region.

RACIAL COMPOSITION

Negroes comprised an important but steadily decreasing portion of the total population in the Hampton Roads-Peninsula area during the fifty years ending in 1940. Of the persons living there in 1890, slightly more than one-half, or 78,878, were Negroes. While their number had increased by 1940 to 145,831, this was less than 36 per cent of the total population. Native whites, with 62 per cent of the total, accounted for most of the remaining population with foreign-born whites contributing about 2 per cent, and Chinese, Japanese, and Indians just a trace. Throughout the period, Negroes constituted a larger part of the Hampton Roads population than in Virginia as a whole,[2] where their percentage of the total was about 38 per cent in 1890 and less than 25 per cent in 1940. This emphasizes the predominantly urban character of the former and the generally recognized tendency for Negroes to migrate to the urban areas, as well as the traditionally heavier colored population in Tidewater than elsewhere in Virginia.

Migration of Negroes out of both the Hampton Roads area and the entire state was the major factor accounting for the smaller rate of increase in the Negro population than in the white population. The former increased approximately 85 per cent between 1890 and 1940 in the coastal area and only 4 per cent in Virginia as a whole, whereas the white population increased more than 250 per cent in the Hampton Roads region and 100 per cent in the entire state.

The tendency for the Negro population to decline in relation to the total population was rather general throughout the area. Only Newport News, with a gradual increase in the percentage of Negroes, ran completely counter to this tendency. Portsmouth, after a sharp

2. See Gittler, *op. cit.*, for analysis of population trends in the entire state.

rise in the relative number of Negroes through 1920, experienced during the next twenty years much the same downward trend as the rest of the Hampton Roads area. The somewhat different trend in Portsmouth and Newport News than in other localities was attributable in part to the expanding employment opportunities for Negroes in the shipbuilding industries of those two cities. The development of Newport News as a shopping and social center for Negroes and the tendency for many white people to move to suburban Elizabeth City and Warwick counties, particularly during the thirties, were additional factors which tended to increase the relative size of the colored population in that city. Such rural areas as Nansemond, Isle of Wight, and James City counties, however, still exceeded Newport News in 1940 as regards the relative percentage of Negroes in the total population, in spite of the latter's consistent increase.

In terms of absolute numbers, approximately 55 per cent of the 145,831 Negroes living in the Hampton Roads region in 1940 were concentrated in the three central cities of Norfolk, Portsmouth, and Newport News.

SEX COMPOSITION[3]

As is generally the case where heavy industry is important, the number of white males in the Hampton Roads-Peninsula area during the years 1890-1940 exceeded the number of females. According to the Census of 1940, there were more than 112 white men to every 100 white women in the area in that year. The presence of such establishments as the shipyards in Newport News and Portsmouth, army and navy posts on both sides of Hampton Roads, the National Soldiers Home and the laboratories of the National Advisory Committee on Aeronautics, each with predominantly male personnel, was primarily responsible for this condition.

For Negroes, however, except in 1920, all census enumerations from 1910 to 1940 showed an excess of women over men. In 1940, the ratio of Negro men to women was 95.7 per cent. Employment of Negro men in shipbuilding, apparently, was not sufficient to offset the normal tendency for women to be more numerous than men in urban communities. Moreover, few Negroes were stationed at the military posts in the Hampton Roads region before 1940, Negro men had

3. See *Population in Flux, A Study of Population Trends in the Hampton Roads Area,* 1890-1942, Virginia State Planning Board, 1942, p. 17, 32-36, for a more detailed analysis than is presented herein.

migrated from the region in considerable numbers, particularly after 1920, and opportunities for Negro women in domestic service and commercial occupations grew as the urban population increased.

Sex ratios for the individual cities and counties in the area, while following the same broad tendencies as those for the region as a whole, showed some significant differences. Elizabeth City and Warwick counties, adjacent to the shipyards in Newport News, and Newports News itself showed the greatest predominance of males. The coming of Langley Field and the National Advisory Committee on Aeronautics increased the sex ratio for Elizabeth City County to 189.3 in 1940, which was far higher than that for any other city or county. The cities of Norfolk, Suffolk, Hampton, and Williamsburg, with little or no heavy industry of their own, had sex ratios consistently below the averages for the area as a whole. The more rural counties in the Hampton Roads area, like other rural communities in the United States, consistently showed more males than females, for Negroes as well as whites.

AGE STRUCTURE

Like most other sections of the United States, the population of the Hampton Roads-Peninsula region in 1940 was showing signs of increasing age. Census figures indicate that a smaller proportion of the total population of the region was under twenty years of age in 1940 than in 1930 and that the middle-aged and oldest groups had become relatively more numerous. Breakdowns of the census for the Hampton Roads communities according to sex and race showed the same tendency for the younger age groups, male and female, white and colored, to decline and the older groups to increase. The implications of the coming of an older population for school authorities charged with providing adequate and economical educational facilities; for those concerned with problems of old-age relief and assistance; for businessmen with products and services to sell to children, those in middle years, and elderly people; and for many other groups are obvious. As will be noted in Part II, the phenomenal increase in war marriages and births and in number of in-migrants after 1940 revolutionized the age structure at least temporarily, but it is important to recognize that the prewar trend was toward an older population.

A comparison of the age structure in the Hampton Roads region with that of Virginia as a whole yields significant evidence of basic differences in their social structures. Both in 1930 and 1940, a substantially larger part of the people living near Hampton Roads were in the productive years of twenty to fifty-four and a smaller portion were under twenty years and over fifty-four years than was true for the rest of the state. The predominantly urban character of the Hampton Roads region as compared with the relatively great importance of the rural population in other parts of Virginia, which was noted earlier in this chapter, is the chief explanation for those age differentials. In rural communities, particularly rural-farm communities, children and old people generally comprise larger proportions of the total population than in cities. Young adults tend to migrate to the cities where more varied employment opportunities exist. Less than half of the population of the predominantly rural counties of the area were in the age group of twenty-five to fifty-four in 1940 as compared with 54.6 per cent for the entire Hampton Roads-Peninsula area and 55 to 60 per cent for the urban localities. Persons under twenty years of age, similarly, comprised 36 to 43 per cent of the total population of the rural counties as compared with an area average of 33.5 per cent and only 30 to 32 per cent for the larger cities.

EDUCATION LEVELS OF THE POPULATION

By asking each person interviewed to give "the last full grade of school completed," the Census of 1940 provided for the first time an index of the educational levels attained by the population of the United States. The median school years completed by males 25 years old and over in the cities and counties of the Hampton Roads-Peninsula region ranged from 4.8 in Isle of Wight County to 9.6 in Hampton. The cities of Norfolk, Portsmouth, and Newport News showed completions of 8.4, 8.1, and 7.9 respectively. For females over 25 years, the range was from 6.0 years in Nansemond County to 10.7 in Hampton, with the three major cities showing 8.7, 8.5 and 8.3 median school years.

For most of the Hampton Roads communities, median school years completed were lower than in comparable classes of communities for Virginia as a whole. The major factor accounting for these lower educational attainments was probably the relatively large Negro population in the Hampton Roads region. This is supported by the fact that the communities in the region with the highest educational levels are, in general, those with the smaller Negro populations.

RELIGIOUS STRUCTURE

Church people in the Hampton Roads-Peninsula area before World War II, as in the rest of Virginia, were predominantly Protestant, though Roman Catholics and Jews were relatively more numerous in these tidewater localities than in the state as a whole. In 1936, both in Virginia and the Hampton Roads region, the three largest Protestant denominations—Negro Baptists, Methodists, and Southern Baptists—accounted for more than one-half of all church members and Roman Catholics and Jews for less than one-fifth of the total.[4] Roman Catholics, however, comprised 8.4 per cent and Jews 9.2 per cent of total members reported in the Hampton Roads region as compared with only 4.0 per cent and 2.3 per cent, respectively, in Virginia as a unit.

Similarly, the three largest Protestant bodies included only 50.6 per cent of the Hampton Roads total and 62.1 per cent of the state total.

Figures on church membership, inadequate though they are, thus present additional evidence of the tendency for the social structure of the Hampton Roads area to be affected by outside influences to a somewhat greater degree than the rest of the state. Urbanization, industrialization, and in-migration from northern states generally tend to be associated with rising proportions of Roman Catholics and Jews. This is borne out by the church membership figures for urban as compared with rural communities within the Hampton Roads region. Roman Catholics accounted in 1936 for 11.4 per cent of total church members in Norfolk, 11.9 per cent in Portsmouth, and 8.2 per cent in Newport News. Jewish membership in the same cities amounted, respectively, to 15.3 per cent, 8.4 per cent, and 10.3 per cent. On the other hand, no Roman Catholics or Jews whatsoever were reported for the agricultural counties of Nansemond and Isle of Wight.

VOTING PARTICIPATION

An important test of the social health of a state or region in a democracy is the degree to which the potential voting population actually uses the ballot.[5] Judged by this test, neither Virginia nor the Hampton Roads-Peninsula area appears to have been particularly healthy in the prewar years. In the 1940 presidential election, only

4. *1936 Census of Religious Bodies.* See Vol. I, pp. 20-22 for the Bureau of the Census statement as to the limitations of the 1936 figures. No comparable figures for a later date are available, according to a letter from Leon E. Truesdell, Chief, Population Division, Bureau of the Census, August 18, 1948, because the failure of Congress to provide funds prevented completion of the 1946 Census of Religious Bodies.

5. The facts in this section have been drawn largely from Gittler, *op. cit.*, pp. 98-104.

21.9 per cent of potentially qualified voters in Virginia went to the polls as compared with 61.8 per cent in the United States and 28.5 per cent in the eleven southeastern states. Every city in the Hampton Roads region except Hampton was below the average for the state. Among the counties of the region, only in Warwick and Norfolk counties did as many as 20 per cent of the potential voters exercise their franchise in 1940. In no city or county in the area did the actual voters exceed 30 per cent of potential voters.

Virginia and the Hampton Roads communities, before World War II, showed an even smaller degree of voting participation in state and local elections. Only 8.6 per cent of Virginia's potential voters went to the polls in the gubernatorial primary election August 5, 1941. All Hampton Roads cities except Newport News, where only 4 per cent of potentially qualified voters exercised the franchise, exceeded the state average but only in Hampton, where 32.7 per cent voted, did the proportion of voters exceed 20 per cent. The percentage of actual to potential voters in the 1941 primary was less than 15 per cent in all counties in the Hampton Roads-Peninsula region and dropped below 5 per cent in Elizabeth City and Warwick counties.

The large Negro population and the poll tax have probably been important factors in explaining the relatively low degree of voting participation in Hampton Roads and the state as a whole. Of greater importance, however, has been the lack of a vigorous two-party system and, except infrequently, the mildness of contests within the predominant Democratic party. A special reason for the exceptionally small vote in Newport News and the adjacent counties of Elizabeth City and Warwick in 1941 was the fact that the war boom in shipbuilding had already begun in Newport News by the summer of that year, even though the United States was not yet at war, and many of the potential voters were transients who had not yet established voting residence and had little interest as to who became governor of Virginia.

HOUSING CONDITIONS

Inadequate housing has generally been associated with the existence of personal and social disorganization as evidenced by broken families, juvenile delinquency, crime, disease, and similar conditions. Low rates of owner-occupancy, similarly, have tended to accompany poor housing conditions. Accordingly, consideration of some of the basic housing characteristics of the Hampton Roads-Peninsula area in 1940 should be helpful in portraying its prewar social structure. Census figures relating to several of these characteristics are summarized in Table 2.

TABLE 2. SELECTED HOUSING CHARACTERISTICS, HAMPTON ROADS-PENINSULA AREA, AS COMPARED WITH VIRGINIA AND THE UNITED STATES, 1940

Place	Vacant, for sale or rent[a]	With occupancy of 1.51 or more persons per room	Needing major repairs[c]	Without private bath[c]	Over 30 years old[c]	Owner-occupied[b]
	(Percentage of Dwelling Units)					
United States						
Urban and rural	5.0	9.0	18.3	43.8	40.8	43.6
Urban only	4.2	5.8	11.5	22.5	42.2	37.4
Virginia						
Urban and rural	4.0	12.4	23.3	63.9	39.8	48.9
Urban only	2.8	6.8	15.4	36.3	41.0	36.2
Hampton Roads-Peninsula Area						
Entire Area	3.2	7.1	24.5	44.1	38.1	38.2
North Side[d]	3.2	6.3	29.6	43.0	32.0	48.0
South Side[e]	3.2	7.3	23.0	44.4	39.9	35.2
Central Cities						
Norfolk	3.0	6.1	19.8	34.1	40.1	28.4
Portsmouth	2.6	5.3	29.0	45.4	57.8	30.8
Newport News	2.6	5.8	30.7	42.1	42.8	29.9

a. Percentage is of total dwelling units.
b. Percentage is of total occupied dwelling units.
c. Percentage is of total dwelling units reporting state of repair, bathing facilities, and age.
d. Includes cities of Newport News, Hampton, and Williamsburg, and counties of Elizabeth City, Warwick, York and James City.
e. Includes cities of Norfolk, Portsmouth, South Norfolk, and Suffolk and counties of Norfolk, Princess Anne, Nansemond, and Isle of Wight.

Source: U.S. Census of Housing, 1940.

It is clear from these figures that prewar housing in the Hampton Roads communities, particularly in Portsmouth and Newport News, was generally inferior to that in Virginia and the United States. The vacancy rate of 3.2 per cent of total dwelling units compares with rates of 4.0 per cent for the entire state and 5.0 per cent for the country as a whole. The region's margin of available housing to care for the thousands of war workers and camp followers who were soon to appear was slim. When it is realized, furthermore, that approximately one-fourth of the existing housing was in need of major repairs and that upwards of one-half was lacking in such essentials for decent living as private bathing facilities, the area's capacity in 1940 to provide decent housing for additional population disappears completely.

The fact that the Hampton Roads-Peninsula communities compared a bit more favorably with other parts of the country as to age of structure and extent of overcrowding, as measured by the percentage of occupied dwelling units with more than 1.5 persons per room, than as to vacancies, state of repair, and plumbing facilities does not alter the general conclusion that housing facilities were grossly inadequate for the people already living there in 1940. The national and state levels themselves were recognized by anyone familiar with the essentials of decent housing as being well below these essentials.[6]

In view of the poor housing conditions in the area, it is not surprising to find that only 38.2 per cent of all occupied dwelling units in the Hampton Roads communities were owner-occupied in 1940, as compared with 48.9 per cent in Virginia as a whole and 43.6 per cent in the entire country. The cities of Norfolk, Portsmouth, and Newport News, with their relatively large Negro and transient populations, had particularly low rates of owner occupancy. Only exceptionally high ratios in suburban Warwick, Elizabeth City, and Norfolk counties and in the relatively stable rural counties of York and James City kept the owner-occupancy percentage for the entire area from being much lower.

PERSONAL AND SOCIAL DISORGANIZATION

War demoralizes individuals and communities to such a degree that it is essential to include in this inventory of the prewar social structure of the Hampton Roads communities some indexes of the extent of social and personal disorganization already in existence before the impact of the Second World War became evident. Divorce, juvenile delinquency, and crime, the measures of disorganization in Virginia used by Gittler,[7] are useful for the purposes of this study, though it is recognized that other measures might be just as helpful.

6. See A. B. Handler, L. N. Bloomberg, and H. G. Brunsman, "Housing," in J. Frederick Dewhurst and Associates, *America's Needs and Resources*, Twentieth Century Fund, 1947, pp. 141-71.

7. Gittler, *op. cit.*

Divorce

If divorce rates are an index of social strain, the Hampton Roads region was certainly in relatively bad shape in 1940. Divorce rates in that year were higher than in any other part of Virginia. Norfolk's rate of 63.9 divorces per 10,000 white population and Newport News' rate of 56.9 per 10,000 colored population were not even approached by other cities in the state. Portsmouth also ranked relatively high as to the incidence of divorce among both whites and Negroes. While divorces were relatively more numerous in the cities of the area than in the counties, in harmony with national tendencies, the counties of Princess Anne, Elizabeth City, and Norfolk, with rates in excess of 20 per 10,000 white population were among the seven Virginia counties with the highest rates of divorce; and Warwick, York, and James City counties were in the top half of the state's counties. Leaders in divorce rates among colored people included Warwick and Elizabeth City counties, with rates approximating 30 and York, James City, and Princess Anne counties were included among the highest 36 counties according to Negro divorce rates.

The high incidence of divorce in the Hampton Roads region reflects not only the general tendency for divorces to be more frequent in urban, industrial areas but also the social instability associated with seaports and communities near military and naval establishments. The poor housing conditions described in the preceding section were also a contributory factor.

Juvenile Delinquency

No adequate statistical measure of juvenile delinquency exists as much of the anti-social conduct of youngsters is never recorded. Probably the best index is the number of cases per 100,000 population ten to seventeen years of age heard by juvenile courts, though it should be emphasized that such an index does not include cases of delinquents who avoid arrest or which are handled by school authorities or social agencies. On the basis of such data for the Hampton Roads cities for the two years 1939-1941, as summarized in Table 3, juvenile delinquency appeared to be less serious in that region than in some other parts of Virginia. While Newport News ranked among the leaders, its rates were considerably below such cities as Danville and Roanoke for colored juveniles and, for white youngsters, below

Charlottesville and Richmond also. Norfolk, Portsmouth, and Suffolk ranked with the middle group of cities and were well below the leaders.

TABLE 3. DELINQUENT CASES HEARD BY JUVENILE COURTS, HAMPTON ROADS-PENINSULA CITIES,[a] 1939–1941

	Delinquent cases per 100,000 population aged 10–17 in 1940		Rank among Virginia cities reporting[b]	
	White	Colored	White	Colored
Norfolk	2,552	7,512	8	10
Portsmouth	2,083	8,376	11	6
Newport News	3,647	10,334	5	3
Suffolk	2,130	7,853	10	8

a. No data available for Hampton, Williamsburg, and South Norfolk.

b. Seventeen cities reported white delinquent cases and 16 reported colored delinquent cases.

Source: Annual Reports of Virginia Department of Public Welfare, as interpreted by Gittler, *Virginia's People*, pp. 115–118.

No counties in the Hampton Roads-Peninsula area were included in the six Virginia counties with highest rates of white juveniles in court, though Elizabeth City and James City counties were among the twelve highest and Princess Anne, Nansemond, and Warwick were in the top half of the state's one hundred counties. Elizabeth City, James City, and Nansemond were ranked among the nine counties with highest Negro delinquent rates and Warwick rated in the highest one-fifth of the total number of counties. Norfolk, Isle of Wight, and York counties had relatively low rates of juveniles in court, both white and colored.

Subject to the limitations of juveniles in court as an index of delinquency, it is reasonable to conclude that prewar juvenile delinquency was probably no more serious in the Hampton Roads-Peninsula region than in many other parts of the state. It should be noted that the rate of juveniles in court was consistently higher for Negroes than for white children in all Hampton Roads and other Virginia communities.

Crime

Crime rates for 1940 provide the most startling evidence of prewar personal and social disorganization in the Hampton Roads area. On the basis of number of offenses known to police per 100,000 inhabitants, as reported to the Federal Bureau of Investigation, murder, robbery, aggravated assault, burglary, and larceny were all considerably more prevalent in Norfolk, Portsmouth, and Newport News than in the average city of comparable size throughout the United States. The same was true for automobile thefts in Norfolk and Newport News, but Portsmouth had a slightly lower rate for this type of offense than the average city of its size. With a few exceptions, the incidence of these crimes was greater in each of these cities than in all cities in excess of 25,000 population in Virginia, the South Atlantic states, and the entire country. Table 4 gives the detailed comparisons.

TABLE 4. NUMBER OF OFFENSES KNOWN TO THE POLICE PER 100,000 INHABITANTS, HAMPTON ROADS CITIES, AS COMPARED WITH OTHER CITIES, VIRGINIA, THE SOUTH ATLANTIC STATES, AND THE UNITED STATES, 1940

City or Group of Cities	Murder, Non-negligent Man-slaughter	Robbery	Aggravated Assault	Burglary, Breaking, or Entering	Larceny, Theft	Auto Theft
United States*	5.4	52.5	45.8	348.4	926.3	174.6
Virginia*	13.6	64.8	171.1	451.7	1428.3	227.2
South Atlantic States	15.2	72.0	135.6	430.3	1175.7	222.2
Norfolk	12.5	93.5	88.7	603.5	1568.6	367.2
55 cities 100,000 to 250,000 pop.	6.5	50.8	53.7	418.4	1069.1	208.9
Portsmouth	23.6	72.9	346.8	478.9	1816.9	145.9
100 cities 50,000 to 100,000 pop.	5.7	37.8	63.8	364.8	993.3	168.1
Newport News	5.4	94.4	279.9	766.2	1154.7	272.5
191 cities 25,000 to 50,000 pop.	3.4	32.2	35.7	313.5	953.3	158.2

*Includes only cities of 25,000 or more population.

Source: Federal Bureau of Investigation, *Uniform Crime Reports*, 1940.

This index, while generally accepted as the best measure of the occurrence of crime, has been criticized on the ground that local police departments use different systems of reporting and classifying crimes. It has also been suggested that some departments may suppress some information as to offenses known to police in order to avoid making a poor showing if such offenses exceed the number of arrests and convictions by any great margin.[8] The F.B.I., itself, urges caution in comparing crime data for individual cities. In particular, it emphasizes the fact that "the amount of crime committed in a community is not solely chargeable to the police but is rather a charge against the entire community, and that it depends upon such diverse factors as the composition of the population, climate, economic structure, educational, recreational and religious facilities, and the attitude of the public toward law-enforcement problems."[9]

The maritime location of the Hampton Roads cities, proximity to military and naval establishments, large Negro and transient populations, relatively low educational levels, and poor housing conditions are all factors that must share with law enforcement agencies and public attitude toward law-enforcement problems the responsibility for the exceedingly high crime rates even before wartime congestion and confusion accentuated crime in these communities.

SUMMARY

The details presented in the foregoing pages as to the social structure of the Hampton Roads-Peninsula area before the Second World War fit into a rather consistent pattern. This pattern is characterized by a high degree of urbanization; a large but decreasing Negro population; an age-sex structure made up predominantly of males and the vigorous middle-aged; relatively low educational attainments, except in some communities; Protestant religious tendencies but with relatively more Jews and Roman Catholics than in Virginia as a whole; low degree of voting participation in national and state elections; poor housing conditions; and high degree of personal and social disorganization as measured by divorce and crime rates.

Two significant conclusions can be drawn from this summary. One is that the Hampton Roads region, even before World War II arrived, was somewhat less Virginian than Virginia in much the same way that Virginia, as a border state, had become less Southern than the South. In other words, traditional social structures both in Hampton Roads and Virginia had already been modified extensively by outside influences. A second and closely related conclusion is that there was little about the social structure of the Hampton Roads area in 1940 which could provide a cushion for absorbing the impending

8. National Commission on Law Observance and Enforcement, *Report on Criminal Statistics*, (Washington, 1931), pp. 52ff., as quoted in Gittler, *op. cit.*, p. 105.

9. F.B.I., *Uniform Crime Reports*, 11:4 (1940), p. 178.

shocks of the Second World War. The fluid in its social shock absorbers had already been largely forced out by the events of the First World War and the postwar and depression years and had not been replenished before the defense activities of the summer of 1940 and 1941 and the more serious business following Pearl Harbor confronted the region.

CHAPTER III

THE PREWAR ECONOMIC STRUCTURE*

THE DOMINANT POSITION of shipbuilding, army and navy establishments, transportation and shipping, and trades and services tributary to these activities in the economic life of the Hampton Roads-Peninsula region since the 1890's has already been suggested. It is the function of this chapter to look more fully into the role of these and other activities in the economy of the region and to portray, through analysis of data relating to the labor force and its employment, to each of the major economic activities, and to the income derived therefrom, the economic structure existing in the region before the Second World War began to reshape it.

THE LABOR FORCE AND ITS EMPLOYMENT

The proportion of the population of working age in the labor force, the percentage of this force actually employed, and its distribution by occupations and by types of employment are significant indices of the nature and extent of a region's economic activities and its capacity to enlarge the scope and intensity of such activities if circumstances require. In view of the wartime pressures destined to make their appearance in Hampton Roads in the early forties, it is particularly appropriate that data on each of these factors for 1940 be presented in this study.

Nature of the Labor Force

Approximately 180,000 persons, or 56 per cent of the population fourteen years of age and older in the Hampton Roads-Peninsula communities, were either at work or able and willing to work in 1940 and were thus included in the labor force. (See Figure 2.) This percentage was somewhat larger than that for the entire state of Virginia and for the United States, as would be expected in view of the urban character of the region and the inclusion in its labor force of the approximately 22,000 men in the armed forces stationed there.

While women comprised a somewhat larger percentage of the

*By Charles F. Marsh, Professor of Economics and Business Administration, College of William and Mary.

labor force in the Hampton Roads region[1] (23.9 per cent) than in all of Virginia (23.1 per cent), their proportion was considerably below the 32.8 per cent for Virginia urban areas with more than 30,000 population, largely because of the men in the armed forces and the few women employed in shipbuilding. The proportion of women was only 19.8 per cent in the North Side communities, dominated by these two fields of employment, as compared with 25.5 per cent on the South Side of Hampton Roads, with its somewhat more diversified trades and services and smaller reliance upon shipbuilding.

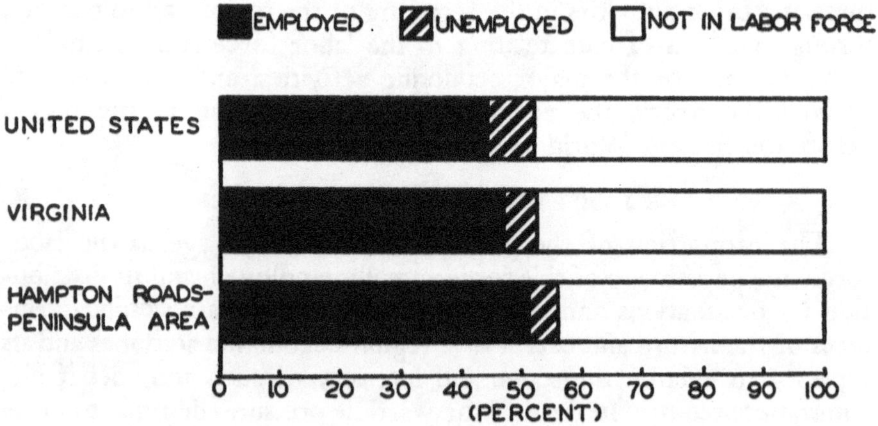

FIGURE 2. EMPLOYMENT STATUS OF POPULATION 14 YEARS OF AGE AND OVER, UNITED STATES, VIRGINIA, HAMPTON ROADS-PENINSULA AREA, 1940

Source: U. S. Census.

Nonwhites, chiefly Negroes, comprised approximately 34 per cent of the Hampton Roads labor force in 1940 as compared with approximately 33 per cent of the population.[2] Almost one-third of this work force was engaged in personal services and more than 80 per cent of all workers in this field were colored. The following tabulation shows the major fields in which Negroes were employed in

1. U. S. Bureau of Labor Statistics, *The Impact of War on the Hampton Roads Area*, Industrial Area Study No. 23, December, 1944 (mimeographed), pp. 8-9. The area included by the Bureau is somewhat smaller than that covered by this study, and embraces the cities of Norfolk, South Norfolk, and Portsmouth, and Norfolk County on the South Side and the cities of Newport News and Hampton and the counties of Elizabeth City, Warwick, and York on the North Side of Hampton Roads.

2. *Ibid.*, pp. 9-10.

the Norfolk-Portsmouth-Newport News Metropolitan District and their relative importance in the total employment in each field:

	Per cent of Negroes[a] in each industry	Negroes[a] as a per cent of total employment in each industry
Total, all industries	100.0	31.8
Personal services	32.1	80.1
Manufacturing	19.3	26.7
Shipbuilding[b]	9.2	21.1
Other manufacturing	10.1	35.3
Trade	12.0	23.8
Transportation	12.0	34.4
Government[c]	3.5	6.1
All other	21.1	35.6

a. Includes 365 colored persons of other races than Negroes.
b. Includes employment at Norfolk Navy Yard.
c. Does not include employment at Norfolk Navy Yard, which is included under shipbuilding.

Extent of Employment

The 1940 labor force of the Hampton Roads area, according to Figure 2, was more fully employed than that of either Virginia or the United States as a whole. Only 8.6 per cent of the total labor force was unemployed as compared with 9.5 for the entire state and 14.4 per cent for the country in general. That this was largely attributable to the revival of shipbuilding in the late thirties and the presence of men in the armed forces is suggested by the relatively low percentages of unemployed in Newport News (7.8), the site of the large private shipyards company, and Elizabeth City County (4.0) with its two major military establishments. The influence of these two factors is seen, also, in the higher percentages of unemployment for women (13 per cent) and Negroes (16 per cent), neither of which were members to as great a degree as white male workers of the labor forces attached to shipbuilding and the armed forces.[3]

It is apparent from these figures that the Hampton Roads-Peninsula region, unlike many other sections of the country which had not fully emerged by 1940 from the industrial unemployment of the thirties, had little surplus white male labor available to meet the vastly expanded demands which the wartime boom in shipbuilding, camp construction, and other war activities was soon to bring to this region.

3. *Ibid.*, p. 10.

Even the proportion of the population of working age not already in the labor force was smaller than that for the rest of the country. It is obvious, therefore, that, in spite of the availability of some unemployed white women and Negroes of both sexes, the impending increases in demand for war workers would have to be met from shifts of white male workers from their regular employment or through inmigrants from outside the region.

Distribution of Employed Workers by Occupations and Types of Employers

The prewar occupational structure of the Hampton Roads-Peninsula area, according to Table 5, differed from that of Virginia and the United States in general in that craftsmen and foremen, service workers, and domestic servants comprised considerably larger elements of the work force and that farmers, farm laborers, and operatives were somewhat less important.

TABLE 5. PERCENTAGE DISTRIBUTION OF EMPLOYED WORKERS BY OCCUPATION, HAMPTON ROADS-PENINSULA AREA, 1940

	United States	Virginia	Hampton Roads-Peninsula Area
Professional	6.4	5.2	4.9
Semi-Professional	1.0	0.8	1.5
Farmers, Farm Managers	11.4	13.8	3.0
Props., Mgrs., Officials	8.3	6.6	7.7
Clerical, Sales	16.6	12.4	14.3
Craftsmen, Foremen	11.2	10.1	15.2
Operatives, etc.	18.3	16.8	13.6
Domestic service	4.7	6.5	8.0
Other service workers	7.7	7.6	14.9
Farm Labor (wage)	4.3	6.7	4.2
Farm Labor (unpaid)	2.6	3.1	0.4
Labor (except farm)	6.8	9.7	11.5
Occupation not reported	0.8	0.7	0.8
TOTAL	100.0	100.0	100.0

Source: U.S. Census, 1940.

The relatively important place of craftsmen and foremen and the somewhat smaller number of operatives in the Hampton Roads area reflect the dominance in the region of shipbuilding, which uses many highly skilled craftsmen in comparison with manufacturing industries which get along with semiskilled machine operators.

The important role of service workers in the total occupational structure of the Hampton Roads region is explained, in part, by the inclusion by the Bureau of the Census of members of the armed forces in this category. This largely accounts for the fact that almost one-third of all employed workers in Elizabeth City County in 1940 were "service workers." The naval establishments in Norfolk and Portsmouth, similarly, helped to swell the size of this group for those cities, although many other persons were employed in a variety of service enterprises catering to sailors and other transients.

The urban character of the region plus the large Negro population account chiefly for the relatively numerous domestic servants, as compared with the state and the country as a whole. The fact that the population of the area, except for the counties of Isle of Wight,

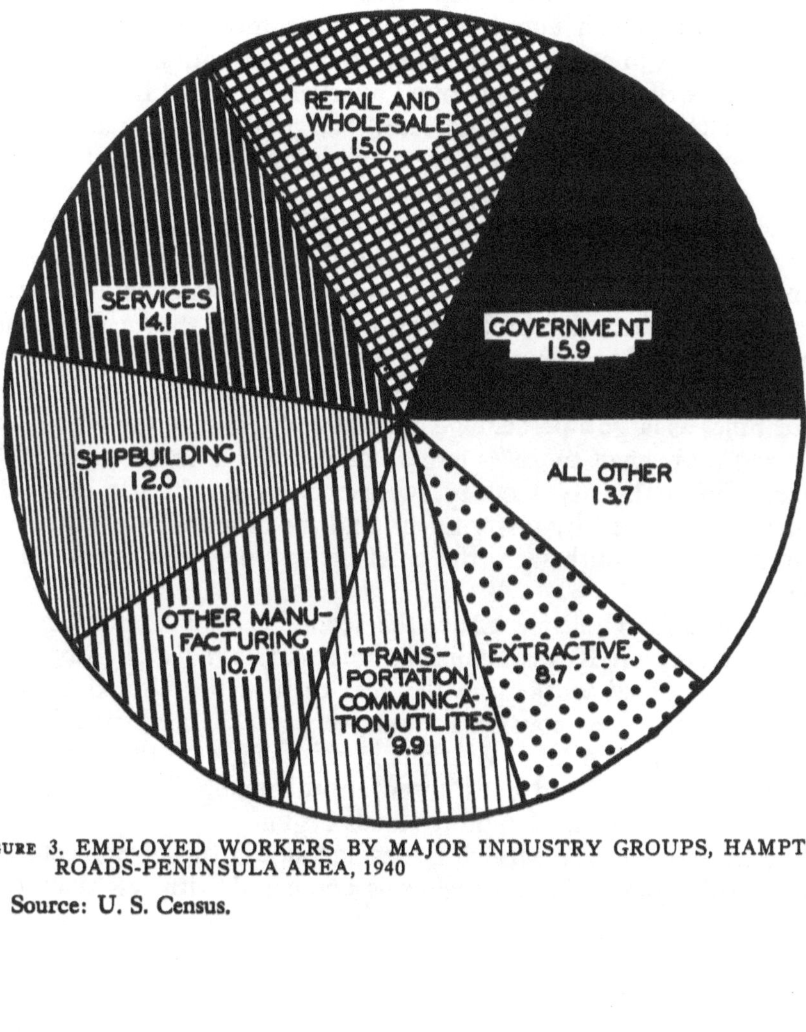

FIGURE 3. EMPLOYED WORKERS BY MAJOR INDUSTRY GROUPS, HAMPTON ROADS-PENINSULA AREA, 1940

Source: U. S. Census.

Nansemond, Princess Anne, and James City, was largely urban or rural non-farm in 1940 explains the relatively small proportion of farmers and farm laborers.

One other interesting fact revealed by Table 5 is that both the Hampton Roads-Peninsula region and Virginia in general had relatively more unskilled non-farm laborers than the rest of the country. The large Negro population was probably the chief explanatory factor. The fact that these laborers comprised especially large percentages of the total employed workers in the predominantly agricultural counties of the region may indicate either that they were former farm laborers or that they lived in rural communities because of lower housing costs and the possibility of producing part of their own food supply. At any rate, these non-farm laborers represented a floating labor supply which could be available to meet the wartime labor demands soon to appear in the Hampton Roads cities.

The distribution of employed workers in the Hampton Roads region, shown in Figure 3, indicates that government, trade, services, and shipbuilding were the major employing groups in 1940, with other manufacturing, transportation, communication, utilities, and extractive industries following in that order. Table 6 relates the percentages of employed workers in each industrial group to comparable percentages for Virginia and for the United States and shows the percentage distribution by these groups in each of the localities within the Hampton Roads-Peninsula region.

For the region as a whole, government employees comprised about four times as large a percentage of total workers as in the whole country and more than twice as large a percentage as in the state of Virginia. Elizabeth City County, with more than 50 per cent of its workers employed by government, and the cities of Norfolk, Hampton, and Portsmouth were the chief centers of government employment.

Retail and wholesale trade, the second largest employing group in the Hampton Roads-Peninsula area, employed a slightly smaller proportion of all workers in the area than in the United States but its 15 per cent was considerably above the 12.4 per cent of all Virginia employed workers. Workers in this field were the largest single group in Norfolk and constituted approximately half of all tradespeople in the entire Hampton Roads region.

Employees in the service trades accounted for 14 per cent of all employed workers in the region as compared with less than 12 per

TABLE 6. PERCENTAGE DISTRIBUTION OF EMPLOYED WORKERS BY INDUSTRY GROUPS, HAMPTON ROADS-PENINSULA AREA, 1940

Area	Total	Extractive	Construction	Mfg.	Transp., Commun., Utilities	Trade	Finance, Insurance, Real Est.	Services	Professional	Govt.	Industry not reported
UNITED STATES	100.0	20.8	4.6	23.4	6.9	16.7	3.2	11.7	7.3	3.9	1.5
VIRGINIA	100.0	27.2	5.2	20.1	6.9	12.4	2.0	11.9	5.9	7.1	1.3
HAMPTON ROADS-PENINSULA AREA	100.0	8.7	4.4	22.7	9.9	15.0	2.2	14.1	5.7	15.9	1.4
Norfolk City	100.0	0.7	4.5	14.7	13.6	19.8	3.3	16.7	5.9	19.7	1.1
Portsmouth	100.0	0.7	3.3	32.3	12.8	13.8	1.9	13.7	5.1	14.8	1.6
South Norfolk	100.0	1.0	4.4	42.7	13.1	18.9	2.2	9.6	3.6	3.2	1.3
Norfolk Co.	100.0	20.3	5.8	33.1	8.4	11.2	1.2	9.1	2.9	6.9	1.1
Princess Anne Co.	100.0	37.1	6.0	8.5	6.0	10.7	1.7	17.4	3.7	7.2	1.7
Suffolk	100.0	0.8	5.9	33.5	7.2	20.8	3.9	16.5	7.1	2.9	1.4
Nansemond Co.	100.0	44.3	2.8	29.4	3.1	6.0	0.4	8.7	2.6	1.7	1.0
Isle of Wight	100.0	53.8	3.1	15.5	3.3	8.8	0.7	9.5	3.3	1.2	0.8
Newport News	100.0	0.7	4.1	41.2	10.3	16.1	2.0	16.0	5.6	2.8	1.2
Hampton	100.0	2.0	5.0	18.1	6.5	16.0	2.3	16.8	13.1	17.2	3.0
Elizabeth City Co.	100.0	3.0	2.8	14.4	3.4	7.7	1.2	7.8	5.8	52.9	1.0
Warwick Co.	100.0	7.2	4.2	46.3	6.6	12.6	2.4	11.1	5.1	3.7	0.8
Williamsburg	100.0	0.8	3.0	1.8	2.5	11.0	1.1	32.2	43.3	3.5	0.8
James City Co.	100.0	27.7	8.5	10.2	4.6	8.9	0.4	17.8	16.8	4.0	1.1
York Co.	100.0	28.3	9.1	13.9	2.7	9.3	1.0	10.5	4.4	9.5	11.3

Source: U.S. Census, 1940.

cent in the entire country and in Virginia. The presence of relatively large numbers of soldiers and sailors, even before war began to swell these numbers materially, had created a special need for a variety of personal and amusement services in the cities of the area. Norfolk, with 44 per cent of the region's service workers, was again the chief center for these service industries, although Hampton, Newport News, and Suffolk were also important. Williamsburg and James City County, with their relatively large institutional and tourist populations, and Princess Anne County, including the summer resort town of Virginia Beach, topped all other localities with respect to the percentage of total workers engaged in the service trades.

While the percentage of total workers engaged in manufacturing in 1940 was less in the Hampton Roads area than in the United States in general and only moderately larger than in the entire state, more than half of all manufacturing employees and 12 per cent of all employed workers were employed in shipbuilding. More than 90 per cent of those employed in Newport News and adjacent counties and 70 per cent in Portsmouth built and repaired ships for a living. Other types of manufacturing were sufficiently important in Norfolk and other southside communties, however, to cut the proportion of shipbuilding workers to 45 per cent in Norfolk County, 33 per cent in the city of Norfolk, and still smaller percentages in the other localities. Prewar shipbuilding employed more workers than any other employing group in Newport News, Warwick County, Portsmouth, and Norfolk County, but was exceeded in the city of Norfolk by trade, government, services, transportation, and utilities, other types of manufacturing, and professional and related services.

The fact that almost 10 per cent of all employed workers in 1940 were engaged in transportation, communication, and public utilities as compared with less than 7 per cent in the United States and in Virginia reflects the shipping activities of the Port of Hampton Roads as well as the importance of Norfolk and Newport News as railroad centers. More than half of this group of workers were resident in Norfolk, Portsmouth, and South Norfolk, and Newport News also exceeded the percentage of all employed workers accounted for by this group in the region as a whole.

While the Hampton Roads area is predominantly urban in nature, more than one-twelfth of all employed persons in the area worked in extractive industries. They were the chief source of employment in all of the counties except Elizabeth City and Warwick. Except in

York County, where approximately half of those employed in the extractive industries were fishermen, most of this group were agricultural workers.

The relative size of such employing groups as the professions, construction, and finance, insurance, and real estate in the Hampton Roads-Peninsula region did not differ materially from the norms for the United States as a whole and for Virginia. Except for unusually large percentages of professional workers in Williamsburg, James City County, and Hampton, because of the presence of educational institutions and hospitals, the percentages for each of these groups remained fairly near the averages for the state and nation.

MANUFACTURING CHARACTERISTICS

Manufacturing in the Norfolk-Portsmouth-Newport News Metropolitan District, according to the Census of Manufactures for 1939, was carried on by 18,254 wage earners in 317 establishments, exclusive of the government owned Norfolk Navy Yard at Portsmouth. Each establishment thus had an average force of 58 workers, as compared with 52 per establishment in Virginia as a whole and 43 in the entire country. The high figure for Hampton Roads is largely accounted for by the Newport News Shipbuilding and Drydock Company, with its average work force during 1939 of almost 8,000,[4] as most of the other manufacturing concerns in the region were comparatively small.

Because other census data on the characteristics of manufacturing in the region fails to cover not only the Navy Yard but also the Newport News company[5] and because of the dominant position of shipbuilding, the latter will be discussed separately from other manufacturing.

Shipbuilding

Since the establishment of the Norfolk Navy Yard in 1834, the repair and construction of ships has been an integral part of the economic life of the Hampton Roads area. Its significance was heightened considerably with the establishment in the late 1880's, by the vigorous Collis P. Huntington, of what has been known since 1890

4. According to the Company's records, the number of employees rose steadily from 6,179 in January, 1939, to 9,765 in December.

5. In accordance with customary census procedure whereby data for particular localities is withheld from publication in order to avoid disclosure of confidential information which might be identified with particular companies.

as the Newport News Shipbuilding and Drydock Company.[6] Several other companies have been active in repairing ships and, during World War I, in shipbuilding, but their role has been so insignificant that it is reasonable to consider the Hampton Roads shipbuilding industry as having consisted primarily of the government yard at Portsmouth and the Newport News company. While activity in these two yards has waxed and waned in somewhat parallel fashion with changes in naval policy and business conditions, the characteristics of the two establishments have been sufficiently different to warrant separate treatment.

Newport News Shipbuilding and Drydock Company. Since a few years after its formation in 1886, the Newport News Shipbuilding and Drydock Company has ranked as one of the two or three largest private shipyards in the United States. During its first half century, it built 327 ships and did a business of 382 million dollars. While only 71 of these ships were built for the Navy, they cost 184 million dollars or almost half of the total business of the yard through 1936. At the outset of the First World War, approximately one third of the Navy's ships of war had come from its ways and its working force had risen to include approximately 5,800 workers.[7]

While the company had experienced its first war boom in connection with ship repair and conversion activities during the Spanish-American War, the 1917-1921 period brought such heavy demands for its services that unprecedented expansions of plant facilities and reorganization of managerial procedures, especially with respect to personnel, were necessitated.[8] While the company concentrated on naval construction during this period, nineteen merchant vessels were completed for the Emergency Fleet Corporation and approximately one thousand repair orders, ranging in duration from one to fifty days, were executed. The battleships *Mississippi* and *Maryland* and twenty-five destroyers were completed before the end of 1921. The battleship *West Virginia*, 70 per cent completed by January 1, 1922, was the only one of two battleships and two even larger battle cruisers on the Newport News ways to survive the axe wielded by the Washington Disarmament Conference. The others were cut up for scrap. Contracts for six destroyers had been cancelled in 1919. Employ-

6. See E. O. Smith and L. D. White, "A History of the Newport News Shipbuilding and Drydock Company," *Newport News, 325 Years*, 1946, pp. 35-47.

7. U. S. Bureau of Labor Statistics, *op. cit.*, p. 16.

8. Smith and White, *op. cit.*, pp. 43-44.

ment had reached a peak of 11,369 workers in May, 1919, just before that cancellation. Naval construction occupied about 60 per cent of the company's shipbuilders in the winter of 1918-1919, with the remainder almost equally divided between repair work and the construction of merchant ships. Early in the war, almost as many workers were engaged in repair activities as in naval construction. After February, 1919, not more than 2 per cent of all shipbuilders were assigned to building merchant ships.[9]

The action of the Disarmament Conference and decreased demand for merchant tonnage during the early twenties resulted in drastic curtailment of yard activities. In spite of the high degree of industrial statesmanship demonstrated by the management of the Newport News company in developing the construction and repair of railroad cars, the manufacture of hydraulic turbines, and other non-shipbuilding work, and in obtaining important contracts for the conversion and construction during the late twenties of passenger and cargo vessels, employment from 1921 through 1938 was seldom more than half its 1919 peak.[10] The depression of the thirties added to the company's difficulties. Yet it did build, during the 1929-41 period, forty-seven ships, including ten naval vessels, thanks to some revival of naval shipbuilding after 1934 and the adoption in 1936 of a new shipbuilding program by the United States Maritime Commission. Included in this group were such World War II stalwarts as the *America*, luxurious transatlantic liner converted to serve as a troopship, and the famed quartet of pioneer aircraft carriers, the *Ranger*, *Yorktown*, *Enterprise*, and *Hornet*. The depression period was utilized by the company not only to provide these vital naval weapons and to acquire "know-how" in building these new types of warships but also "to regroup its forces and equipment" through streamlining its material control system, reducing inventories, and training employees in more than one shipbuilding occupation. It was thus able to "convert a misfortune into an asset which had much to do with the unequalled records set for turning out ships during World War II."[11]

Norfolk Navy Yard. The prime function of the Norfolk Navy Yard, since its establishment in 1834, has been the repair of naval vessels. It is, however, one of the three United States Navy yards

9. Caroline Buck Reeves, *Impact of World War I on the Hampton Roads Area*, U. S. Bureau of Labor Statistics Historical Study No. 69, 1944 (mimeographed), pp. 2-7, 13-16.

10. U. S. Bureau of Labor Statistics, *op. cit.*, p. 16.

11. Smith and White, *op. cit.*, pp. 44-45.

equipped to build battleships and has increasingly become more important in ship construction in recent years. In 1939, it ranked third in employment among the six major Navy Yards.[12] As a naval establishment, it did not participate directly to any great degree in the construction and repair of merchant ships before World War II. Fluctuations in its activities, accordingly, have been related almost entirely to changes in naval policy rather than to cyclical economic variations which have affected the construction of private cargo and passenger ships. It has thus been unable to emulate the Newport News company in cushioning the shock of curtailed naval construction and repair by providing employment through the manufacture of turbines and other "landlubber" products and through bidding for private shipbuilding jobs. Its employment, therefore, has tended to vary between greater extremes than that of the private company.

The Navy Yard, like the Newport News plant, expanded greatly during the 1917-21 period. At the outset of the First World War, it had three drydocks for ship repairs and one way for the construction of new vessels. By the end of 1921, three new drydocks and one new and vastly larger way for the construction of battleships were in operation. Employment rose from 7,247 in June, 1917, to a peak of 11,234 in February, 1919, and receded below the early 1917 level by the end of 1920. Workers engaged in building the new drydocks as well as those repairing and building ships were apparently included. The relatively small part played by ship construction in contrast to repair is indicated by the fact that the Norfolk Yard, with approximately the same work force as the Newport News company, completed only four destroyers between 1917 and 1921 as compared with the latter's two battleships, twenty-five destroyers, and nineteen merchant ships. Similarly, the suspension order from the Disarmament Conference February 8, 1922, found the Navy Yard with only the battleship *North Carolina* 36.7 per cent completed and the practically complete *Langley*, aircraft carrier converted from a collier, on its ways as compared with three battleships and two battle cruisers at Newport News.[13]

The complete dependence of employment at the Yard on national naval policy is evidenced by layoffs after the cancellation of the *North Carolina* contract and accompanying reductions in appropriations for naval repairs which cut employment in 1923 to 2,400, approximately

12. U. S. Bureau of Labor Statistics, *op. cit.*, p. 17.
13. Reeves, *op. cit.*, pp. 11-16.

the 1899 level,[14] and by developments since then. The number of workers increased gradually until 1936, when the effects of the new policy of naval expansion was instituted. By January, 1939, approximately 6,500 persons were at work[15] and by the end of that year the World War I peak of more than 11,000 had been reached.[16]

From this brief survey of the prewar status of the two major shipyards in the Hampton Roads-Peninsula region, it is apparent that the industry, even before Hitler's fateful march into Poland, to say nothing of Pearl Harbor, was, by World War I standards, operating under boom conditions. The Second World War's cry for more ships and more and faster repairs was to fall, therefore, upon the ears of shipbuilders in this region who were already working their yards at "capacity" and who could heed the cry only by expanding capacity manyfold and carving out new frontiers in shipbuilding techniques.

Other Manufacturing

Of the 18,254 privately employed manufacturing workers reported for the Norfolk-Portsmouth-Newport News Metropolitan District by the Census of Manufacturers for 1939, more than 10,000 were engaged in other types of manufacturing than shipbuilding.[17] In the entire Hampton Roads-Peninsula region other manufacturing firms employed 17,627 workers in 1940, or about 2,000 less than the total workers in shipyards including the Norfolk Navy Yard. Most of them worked in the cities of Norfolk, Portsmouth, and Suffolk, south of Hampton Roads.

Chemicals, food products, the Ford assembly plant at Norfolk, and printing and publishing employed more than half of the 1940 southside workers with the balance distributed chiefly among small clothing and textile mills, foundries and machine shops, and the manufacture of lumber products, furniture and mattresses, cement and concrete products, and agricultural implements.[18] Twenty-five of Virginia's thirty-four fertilizer plants and the Proctor and Gamble cottonseed oil mill at Portsmouth were the chief chemicals manufacturers. Food processing consisted chiefly of meat packing, seafood and fruit

14. Virginia State Planning Board, *Population in Flux,* Population Study Report No. 2 (September, 1942), p. 22.

15. Richmond *Times-Dispatch,* February 19, 1946.

16. U. S. Bureau of Labor Statistics, *op. cit.,* p. 17.

17. Manufacturing in Newport News and Warwick County occupied 8,129 workers, most of whom worked at shipbuilding.

18. U. S. Bureau of Labor Statistics, *op. cit.,* pp. 17-19.

and vegetable canneries, peanut mills in Suffolk, and the making of flour, bottled beverages, dairy products, meat products and ice.

In general, manufacturing other than shipbuilding has been a stabilizing element in the economic structure of the Hampton Roads

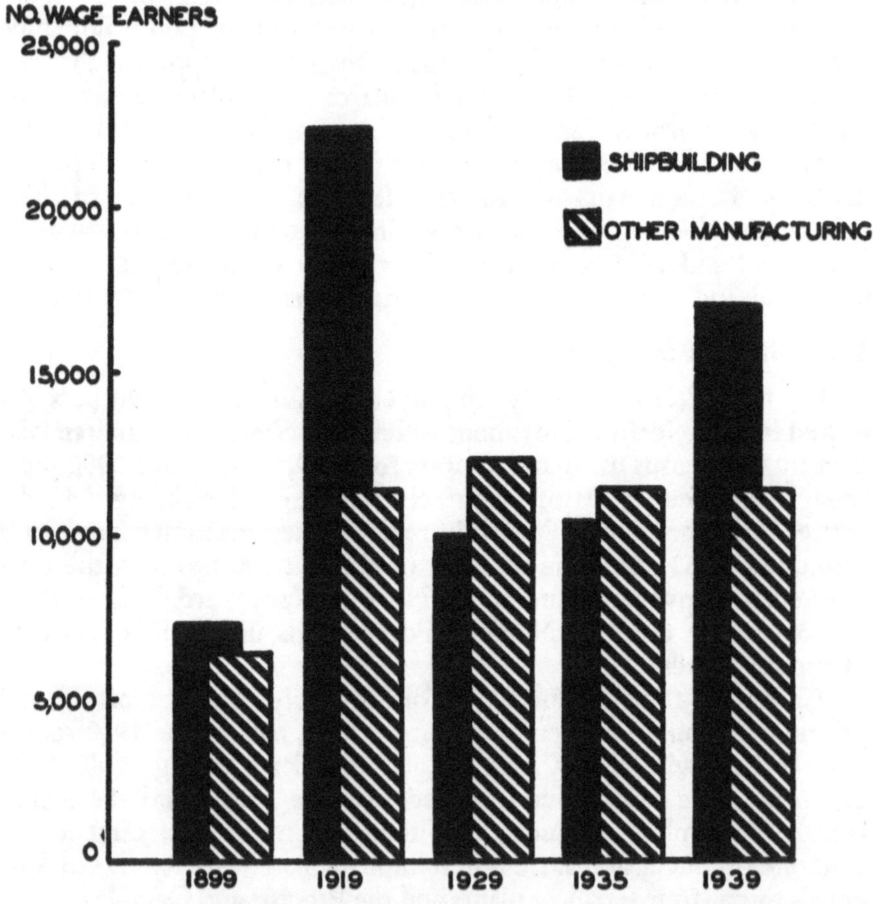

FIGURE 4. WAGE EARNERS IN SHIPBUILDING AND IN OTHER MANUFACTURING, FOR SELECTED YEARS, HAMPTON ROADS AREA

Source: Virginia State Planning Board, *Population in Flux in the Hampton Roads Area*, Appendix Table 5.

area. This is indicated by Figure 4, which shows that employment in shipbuilding fluctuated to a much greater extent than that in other manufacturing during the period from 1899 through 1939. The fact that the latter consisted largely of consumers goods was the chief explanation for its greater stability. Unfortunately, however, these other manufacturing activities were on too modest a scale to do more than partially offset the violent fluctuations in shipbuilding.

NON-MANUFACTURING GOVERNMENT ACTIVITIES

Government agencies in the Hampton Roads-Peninsula area employed in 1940 more than 25,000 persons, in addition to civilians working at the Navy Yard. Official records indicate that between 15,000 and 16,000 of this group were members of the armed forces stationed at the Naval Operating Base at Norfolk, the Navy Yard, Naval Hospital, and Naval Ammunition Depot at Portsmouth, Fort Monroe and Langley Field in Elizabeth City County, the Naval Mine Depot in York County, and several other small establishments. The remainder consisted of civilians employed at these posts, employees of the National Advisory Committee on Aeronautics at Langley Field and of other federal agencies, a few state employees, and a considerable number of city and county workers.

These government employees have provided an important part of the purchasing power upon which the economy of the Hampton Roads region has rested, even before the Second World War. Yet government activities, like shipbuilding, have been a mixed economic blessing to the region since they too have been subject to enormous expansion during wartime followed by severe curtailment in times of peace. Not only were there considerable fluctuations in the number of soldiers and sailors assigned to the Norfolk-Newport News-Portsmouth district during and immediately after World War I, but the impact of the war on the economy of the area was sharpened by great expansion and contraction of the number of civilian workers involved in the construction and operation of various war establishments. More new construction occurred during the war years in the Hampton Roads area than at any other place in the United States. The largest projects, other than expansions at the two shipyards, were the Army Supply Base and the Naval Operating Base at Norfolk, Camps Stuart, Hill, and Alexander—parts of the Newport News facilities for the embarkation and debarkation of troops—and various housing projects on both sides of Hampton Roads. While figures as to the total number of construction workers engaged on these projects are not available, the employment of 10,000 men on the Newport News camps in 1917, 9,000 workers on the Norfolk Army Base in 1918, and 3,000 in 1919 on the Portsmouth housing project alone gives some indication as to why the local labor market was drained and workers had to be brought in from distant states. One interesting aspect of World War I activities in the region was the fact that construction on several of these projects was not completed until long after the need for them had passed. While this appeared at the time to indicate an inexcusable delay in adjusting federal policy to peacetime conditions and to involve an unnecessary waste of public funds, it did cushion the economy of the Hampton Roads area against some of the difficulties resulting from immediate cessation of war activities which many other war centers experienced. Moreover, as will be noted later in this study, some of the facilities completed after the end of the First World War, notably portions of the Naval Operating Base and the Army Supply Base as well as the Hilton and Craddock housing projects, were available for use at the outset of the Second World War twenty years later. The blow eventually fell, however, as the demobilization of the armed forces, abandonment of some army and navy establishments, and cuts in naval appropriations after 1920, with their accompanying termination of construction and decrease in military and civilian complements at the permanent military posts, set in motion the outward trek of population during the twenties.[19] The Hampton Roads economy contracted severely as these war workers and military personnel moved elsewhere.

Transfer of a large part of the fleet and naval personnel from Norfolk to the Pacific Coast in 1931 brought further economic difficulties to the region. The New Deal legislation, however, and revival of interest in national defense gradually increased the number of governmental employees during the thirties until they had become, by 1940, the largest single employee group.

TRANSPORTATION AND SHIPPING

While the natural advantages of the harbor of Hampton Roads have made shipping an important economic activity since colonial times, the development of the modern port, ranking behind only New York and Philadelphia among Atlantic ports, had to await connection late in the last century through the three Pocahontas railroads and five other major rail lines with its rich coal, agricultural, and indus-

19. That the exodus had already begun before 1920 is indicated by estimates that Norfolk's population reached a peak of 220,000 in 1919 before dropping to 115,777 in 1920; and that Newport News had a population of 65,000 in 1918 before it settled down to its 35,596 population in 1920. *Ibid.*, p. 55.

trial hinterland. These eight major railroads and connecting belt line, approximately ninety steamship companies, including sixty overseas lines, and various auxiliary facilities[20] combined to make transportation and shipping a basic feature of the prewar Hampton Roads economy.

The general nature of the waterborne commerce in 1940 is shown in Table 7. Coastwise trade comprised more than 70 per cent of the total with foreign shipping and internal and local traffic each amounting to about 14 per cent. Except for the relatively small amount of intercoastal traffic, outbound shipments far exceeded receipts.

TABLE 7. WATERBORNE COMMERCE, HAMPTON ROADS PORTS, 1940

Type of Traffic	Total	Inbound	Outbound
	(In thousands of cargo tons of 2,240 pounds)		
Total Commerce	27,524	5,004	22,313
Internal	3,740	1,450	2,290
Local	207	—	—
Total exclusive of internal and local	23,577	3,554	20,023
Foreign	3,975	922	3,053
Intercoastal	154	94	60
Coastwise	19,416	2,530	16,886
Non-contiguous	32	8	24

Source: U.S. Maritime Commission, Division of Economics and Statistics; District Engineer, U.S.A., Norfolk, Virginia; and Hampton Roads Maritime Exchange, *The Ports of Greater Hampton Roads Annual*, 1946, p. 15.

In 1940, coal accounted for more than three-fourths of all outbound coastwise tonnage and more than 40 per cent of exports to foreign countries.[21] Hampton Roads has regularly shipped more coal than any other port in the United States. In addition, it has accounted for more than 60 per cent of all bunker coal supplied to foreign and domestic vessels along the Atlantic seaboard. In terms of value, coal exports have been second to leaf tobacco and tobacco manufactures. Other important exports before the war included corn and corn products, cotton manufactures and cotton mill waste, lumber, paper, iron and steel scrap, steel products, and chemicals.

More than 50 per cent of the exports from Hampton Roads went to Europe, with the balance going to the Far East, South America,

20. Hampton Roads Maritime Exchange, *The Ports of Greater Hampton Roads Annual*, 1946, pp. 30-63.

21. *Ibid.*, pp. 16-17, and Report of Chief of Engineers, Part 2, *Commercial Statistics*, Waterborne Commerce of the United States, 1941, U. S. War Department.

Oceana, North America, including Central America and the West Indies, and Africa, in that order.

Imports included fuel oil, canned meats, hides, fertilizer materials, food products, cane and other sugar, crude rubber, Quebracho extract, unmanufactured tobacco, textiles, fibres, wood, paper and pulp, newsprint and cigarette paper, and manganese and chrome ores, chemicals and related products.

Outward coastwise shipments, other than coal, consisted of cotton textiles, tobacco and tobacco products, and manufactured goods produced in the Southeast. Receipts consisted largely of petroleum products, sugar, and manufactures from New England and New York.

In the intercoastal trade, the westbound movement consisted chiefly of grain, fodder, fruits and vegetables, tobacco, textiles, paper, iron and steel products, and other metal goods. The eastbound movement was made up largely of animal, fish, and dairy products, fruits and vegetables, lumber and wood pulp, sugar and molasses, building materials and grain products.

In sketching this brief picture of Hampton Roads shipping before the war it should be noted that, except for coal, the port was not a full cargo port. Boats would pick up part of their cargo in Boston, Philadelphia, and Baltimore and finish it off with Hampton Roads shipments. The local population and industry and near-by hinterland were unable to develop sufficient export-import business to make it a full cargo port or to justify the successful operation of overseas steamship lines which had their headquarters in Norfolk or Newport News. All of the sixty steamship lines engaged in 1940 in overseas shipping were owned by interests in New York or some other port and have tended to regard Hampton Roads as of secondary importance.[22]

TRADES AND SERVICES

The extensive development of trades and services in the Hampton Roads-Peninsula area provides indirect evidence of the economic importance of military and naval activity, shipbuilding and shipping, and general manufacturing. As indicated in Figure 3 and Table 6, almost 30 per cent of all employed persons in the area in 1940 worked in these fields, and in Norfolk, the leading trade and service center,

22. Personal interview with J. H. Devereaux, a Norfolk foreign freight forwarder, and during the war, War Shipping Administration executive, August 20, 1945. Also, statement by E. O. Jewell, General Manager, Norfolk Port Authority, *Norfolk Virginian-Pilot*, February 22, 1949.

almost 37 per cent were so employed. The magnitude of Hampton Roads wholesale and service trades in 1940 is summarized in the following compilation of census data:

	Wholesale	*Retail*	*Service*
Number of establishments.	534	5,114	1,593
Volume of business (000)	$138,646	$128,778	$10,993
Number of employees	6,783	17,426	5,381
Wages paid	$7,487	$14,683	$4,574

The relatively great development of trades and services in the region is suggested by the fact that, with only 15 per cent of the population of Virginia, the Hampton Roads area accounted for 22 per cent of the state's wholesale trade, 21 per cent of its retail trade, and 25 per cent of the total service receipts in 1940. Similarly, with 3.1 per cent of the population of the entire country, the area did almost exactly that proportion of total retail trade in the United States and 3.2 per cent of the country's service business. Its wholesale trade, however, was only 2.5 per cent of the United States total.

Table 8 suggests that Hampton Roads trade and service establishments were larger, on the average, than in the rest of the state and

TABLE 8. TRADE CHARACTERISTICS, HAMPTON ROADS-PENINSULA AREA, VIRGINIA AND UNITED STATES, 1940

Trade Characteristics	Hampton Roads-Peninsula Area	Virginia	United States
Wholesale Trade			
Volume of business per establishment	$259,636	$258,072	$275,539
Employees per establishment	12.7	11.6	7.8
Wages per employee	1,104	1,203	1,680
Retail Trade			
Volume of business per establishment	25,035	21,215	23,748
Employees per establishment	3.4	2.5	2.6
Wages per employee	843	853	985
Per capita sales	315	235	319
Service Trade			
Volume of business per establishment	6,901	4,817	5,295
Employees per establishment	3.4	2.2	1.7
Wages per employee	850	729	971
Per capita receipts	27	17	26

Source: U.S. Census.

country, judged by comparative figures as to volume of business and number of employees per establishment. Only the United States figure for the volume of trade of wholesalers exceeded the comparable Hampton Roads figure. Wages per employee, however, were lower than the average for all three types of business in the United States and except for the service trades were also lower than average wages in Virginia. It is probable that the relatively large Negro population in the Hampton Roads region is the chief explanation for the lower average wages paid. Per capita retail sales of $315 and service receipts of $27 were considerably in excess of state averages and diverged only slightly from the national per capitas.

EXTRACTIVE INDUSTRIES

Agriculture, fishing, and forestry are the chief extractive industries of the Hampton Roads-Peninsula region. As has been noted, mineral resources other than sand, clay and gravel are almost nonexistent. Agricultural workers numbered 12,855 in 1940, or more than 90 per cent of all extractive workers in the region. The census classification "forestry other than logging and fishing" accounted for almost 9 per cent of the 14,176 extractive workers with the balance scattered among minor extractive activities. In view of the fact that forestry in this area has been carried on traditionally by small farmers rather than full-time forestry workers, most of the workers in the forestry and fishing group in 1940 were probably fishermen. Accordingly, agriculture and fishing are the only extractive industries whose prewar status will be considered separately in this section.

Agriculture

The large rural non-farm population of the Hampton Roads-Peninsula counties in 1940 kept the proportion of total acreage to farms relatively low in most of them. Agriculture in the area was characterized generally by relatively small farms whose value of land and buildings and gross farm income was, on the average, roughly equal to that for the entire country and above that for Virginia. Except for Nansemond and Isle of Wight counties, farm tenancy was considerably less prevalent than in the United States as a whole and somewhat below Virginia's tenancy rate. Owner-occupancy was particularly high in the four counties lying north of Hampton Roads. The variations in these factors relating to agricultural structure from county to county in the region, and as compared with the entire state and country, are indicated in Table 9.

TABLE 9. AGRICULTURAL STRUCTURE, UNITED STATES, VIRGINIA, NORFOLK-PORTSMOUTH-NEWPORT NEWS METROPOLITAN DISTRICT AND COUNTIES OF THE HAMPTON ROADS-PENINSULA AREA, 1940

Area	Proportion of Total Acreage in Farms	Average Size of Farm	Average Value of Land and Buildings per Farm	Average Approx. Gross Farm Income per Farm	Proportion of Farm Tenancy
	(per cent)	(acres)	(dollars)	(dollars)	(per cent)
United States	55.6	174.0	5,518	1,837	38.7
Virginia	64.4	94.0	3,860	863	26.9
Metropolitan District*	40.0	72.7	5,459	1,879	21.4
Counties					
Warwick	26.6	34.1	5,117	746	12.1
Elizabeth City	32.1	43.1	5,665	1,436	10.1
York	31.5	58.9	3,545	622	9.3
James City	46.2	135.9	7,146	1,311	11.7
Norfolk	35.6	74.9	4,874	1,945	25.4
Princess Anne	51.3	93.3	6,220	2,356	23.4
Nansemond	57.0	93.9	4,209	1,505	45.3
Isle of Wight	68.2	112.3	3,736	1,469	48.3

*Includes totals for the counties represented in the district, namely, Elizabeth City, Norfolk, Princess Anne, and Warwick.

Source: U.S. Bureau of Foreign and Domestic Commerce, *Virginia County Basic Data Sheets*, 1945; and *Metropolitan District Basic Data Sheets*, 1946.

As would be expected in a rural area adjacent to urban centers and with relatively large rural non-farm populations, field crops, livestock, and products used by farm households provided relatively smaller and dairy products and vegetables somewhat larger sources of farm income for the Hampton Roads-Peninsula region than in the rest of the state and in the United States. As indicated in Table 10, dairy products were particularly important income producers in Warwick and Elizabeth City counties and vegetable growing was particularly important in Princess Anne and Norfolk counties. Nansemond and Isle of Wight counties, on the other hand, depended to a very high degree upon field crops and received only small portions of total farm income from dairy products. These two counties had smaller rural non-farm populations and were less closely affected by their urban neighbors than other counties in the region. It should be noted, also, that poultry products and horticultural specialties, grouped in Table 10 under "all other sources," were relatively large income producers in such urban counties as Elizabeth City, Norfolk, and Warwick.

TABLE 10. SOURCE OF AGRICULTURAL INCOME, IN PER CENTS OF TOTAL, UNITED STATES, VIRGINIA, NORFOLK-PORTSMOUTH-NEWPORT NEWS METROPOLITAN DISTRICT AND COUNTIES OF THE HAMPTON ROADS-PENINSULA AREA, 1940

Area	Total	Livestock sold or traded	Dairy products sold or traded	Field crops sold or traded	Vegetables harvested for sale	Products used by farm households	All other sources
				(in per cents)			
United States	100.0	22.6	14.3	31.6	2.6	14.5	14.4
Virginia	100.0	14.3	9.4	27.0	3.2	28.2	17.9
Metropolitan District*	100.0	4.0	23.5	23.7	18.0	8.8	22.0
Counties							
Warwick	100.0	4.0	50.2	1.2	3.8	18.8	22.0
Elizabeth City	100.0	1.4	37.3	7.1	4.8	9.4	40.0[a]
York	100.0	14.4	20.6	23.5	3.8	27.7	10.0
James City	100.0	6.5	29.5	25.7	7.4	18.6	12.3
Norfolk	100.0	4.0	23.7	21.7	14.5	9.2	26.9[b]
Princess Anne	100.0	4.4	17.6	31.0	25.4	7.2	14.4
Nansemond	100.0	6.7	4.8	55.6	9.8	13.9	9.2
Isle of Wight	100.0	9.4	4.1	59.1	1.4	14.8	11.2

*Includes counties of Elizabeth City, Norfolk, Princess Anne, and Warwick.

a. Consisted largely of poultry products (20.4 per cent) and horticultural specialties (12.4 per cent).

b. Consisted largely of horticultural specialties (19.5 per cent).

Source: U.S. Department of Commerce. *Virginia County Basic Data Sheets*, 1945; and *Metropolitan District Basic Data Sheets*, 1946.

Fishing

Most of the 1,223 persons reported by the 1940 Census as being engaged in forestry and fishing were probably engaged in fishing. In addition, it is probable that an indeterminate number of persons classified as agricultural workers worked part time as commercial fishermen. More than one-third of the forestry and fishing workers lived in York County, but residents of each of the other Hampton Roads-Peninsula communities participated in these activities. While it is possible that a small portion of the forestry and fishing workers reported for some of the communities, particularly Nansemond and Isle of Wight counties, may actually be engaged in forestry, it is reasonable to believe that a minimum of 1,100 to 1,200 persons depended upon fishing for their livelihood.

The thirty-odd varieties of fin fish accounted for more than two-thirds of the 40,561 pounds of fish caught in 1939 in the waters of the eight counties of the region and almost half of the total value of $1,278,000. Oysters comprised about 15 per cent of the catch, in pounds, but more than 40 per cent in terms of dollars. The catch of crabs, lobsters, and clams, while amounting to 15 per cent of total pounds of all fish only produced 11 per cent of the total value. Crabs were the chief item in this group, though moderate amounts of clams were caught. Very few lobsters are caught in Hampton Roads waters. Table 11 summarizes the details as to the major classes of seafood caught in each of the Hampton Roads-Peninsula counties in 1939. Elizabeth City County yielded almost half of the fin fish, with York and Norfolk counties accounting for most of the remainder. Norfolk County, with its famous Lynnhaven oysters, was the leader in oyster production, followed by Elizabeth City and York. York County accounted for almost half of the crabs and other shellfish, with Elizabeth City and Norfolk counties again completing the top three. It should be emphasized that these catch figures understate the importance of seafood to the region as they do not include receipts by seafood packers in such important markets as Hampton, Phoebus, and Norfolk from catches in the waters of other Virginia counties and Maryland, and from deep sea fishing.

INCOME

The major test of the effectiveness of the economic structure of the Hampton Roads-Peninsula area or of any other region is the income realized by its inhabitants. It is appropriate, therefore, to conclude this picture of the prewar economic structure of the Hampton Roads communities with a summary of available data on total and per capita income and its distribution among the residents of these communities in 1940. Unfortunately, income statistics are too fragmentary to do more than provide rough estimates of money income. The most helpful of these estimates are: (1) those derived by the Bureau of Population and Economic Studies of the University of Virginia from the U. S. Department of Commerce estimates of income payments in Virginia; (2) estimates of "effective buying income" by the magazine *Sales Management;* and (3) analyses of the published summaries of state income tax returns.

TABLE 11. CATCH OF FISH, HAMPTON ROADS-PENINSULA COUNTIES, BY QUANTITY AND VALUE, 1939

	Quantity (in thousands of pounds)				Value (in thousands of dollars)			
Counties	All Varieties	Fin Fish	Oysters	Crabs, Lobsters & Clams	All Varieties	Fin Fish	Oysters	Crabs, Lobsters & Clams
All Counties . . .	40,561	28,282	6,193	6,086	$1,278	$616	$520	$142
Elizabeth City . .	16,339	13,683	1,617	1,039	418	257	134	27
Warwick	754	624	—	130	19	16	—	3
York	9,869	6,417	516	2,936	277	155	43	79
James City . . .	205	205	—	—	13	13	—	—
Norfolk	9,324	4,983	3,660	681	438	121	306	11
Princess Anne . .	2,653	1,973	80	600	57	38	10	9
Nansemond . . .	546	91	305	150	31	3	26	2
Isle of Wight . . .	871	306	15	550	25	13	1	11

Source: U.S. Department of Interior, Fish and Wildlife Service (Statistics Section).

According to the bureau's estimates,[23] the Hampton Roads-Peninsula localities, with 4.5 per cent of Virginia's area and 15.3 per cent of its population, received 21.3 per cent of total state income in 1940. Each Hampton Roads resident received, on the average, $655 as compared with a per capita income of $461 for Virginia as a whole. That the relatively large urban and rural non-farm population of the Hampton Roads region was a major factor in explaining the higher income of its residents is indicated by the higher per capita incomes for the cities and urban counties than for the more distinctly farming counties. The range was from $233 in the farming county of Isle of Wight to $1,053 in thickly populated Elizabeth City County. Of the cities, only Hampton and Norfolk were above the median of $760 for all Virginia cities. Only Isle of Wight and Nansemond counties, on the other hand, were below the county median of $249. All of the others ranked in the top twenty of Virginia's one hundred counties.

Effective buying income in the Hampton Roads communities in 1940 was estimated by *Sales Management* at $235,117,000, or 22.1 per cent of the income for Virginia as a whole. The distribution of this

TABLE 12. EFFECTIVE BUYING INCOME, TOTAL AND PER CAPITA, HAMPTON ROADS-PENINSULA REGION AND VIRGINIA, 1940

Place	Effective Buying Income (Gross) Total (000)	Per Capita
VIRGINIA	$1,063,312	$399
Hampton Roads-Peninsula Area	235,117	582
Norfolk Co.*	155,767	655
Norfolk City	105,595	737
Portsmouth	34,522	681
Princess Anne Co.	5,853	294
Nansemond Co.*	12,688	372
Suffolk	7,183	636
Isle of Wight Co.	3,571	266
Warwick Co.*	36,050	780
Newport News	29,410	797
Elizabeth City Co.*	14,943	431
Hampton	3,520	597
James City Co.*	4,528	509
York Co.	1,717	195

*Includes the independent city.

Source: "Survey of Buying Power," *Sales Management*, April 10, 1941.

23. John L. Lancaster, Bureau of Population and Economic Research, "Per Capita Income of Virginia Counties for 1940," University of Virginia *News Letter*, October 1, 1945.

income among the individual communities and the per capita buying income for each is shown in Table 12. While the relative position of the various localities, as estimated by *Sales Management,* differs somewhat from that indicated by the bureau's estimates, both estimates indicate that the residents of the Hampton Roads-Peninsula region as a whole enjoyed somewhat higher income in 1940 than did other Virginians, on the average, and that incomes in such essentially agricultural counties as Isle of Wight, Nansemond, Princess Anne, and York were below and those of city dwellers and of the other counties were above the state averages.

TABLE 13. INCOME VALUES AND RETURNS, VIRGINIA STATE INCOME TAX, INDIVIDUALS AND FIDUCIARIES, HAMPTON ROADS-PENINSULA REGION AND VIRGINIA, 1941 (INCOME YEAR 1940)

Place	Income Value (000)	Number of Returns	Average Income Value per Return
VIRGINIA	$120,371	107,979	$1,115
HAMPTON ROADS-PENINSULA AREA	21,422	23,185	924
Norfolk City	11,828	9,194	1,286
Portsmouth	1,761	3,631	485
South Norfolk	162	379	427
Norfolk Co.	820	1,537	533
Princess Anne Co.	835	516	1,617
Suffolk	600	711	843
Nansemond Co.	250	110	2,269
Isle of Wight Co.	147	204	720
Newport News	2,081	3,000	694
Warwick Co.	723	926	781
Hampton	343	542	633
Elizabeth City Co.	1,173	1,741	674
York Co.	94	203	461
Williamsburg	482	366	1,318
James City Co.	123	125	986

Source: Annual Report of the Virginia Department of Taxation, Table 13.

The third source of information on incomes—state income tax returns for the income year 1940—not only provides additional evidence that the Hampton Roads people were relatively better off than their fellow Virginians but also gives some indication that incomes were distributed somewhat more evenly than in the rest of the state. While the Hampton Roads localities, with 15.3 per cent of Virginia's population, accounted for 21.5 per cent of the total returns under the state income tax law and 17.8 per cent of total income values reported for 1940, the average income value reported was only $924 as compared with $1,115 for the state as a whole. That this lower income value per return reflects a somewhat greater equality in the distribution of income than in Virginia as a whole is suggested by the fact that 90.2 per cent of the Hampton Roads residents reporting income had taxable incomes $3,000 and under as compared with 89 per cent of all Virginia residents. Similarly, only 4.9 per cent of the Hampton Roads returns showed income values above $5,000 as compared with 5.6 per cent for the state. A similar correlation between income value per return and percentages of returns below $3,000, between $3,000 and $5,000, and over $5,000 is indicated for the individual counties and cities of the Hampton Roads-Peninsula region in Tables 13 and 14.

TABLE 14. INCOME VALUES AND RETURNS, VIRGINIA STATE INCOME TAX, INDIVIDUALS AND FIDUCIARIES, BY INCOME GROUPS, HAMPTON ROADS-PENINSULA REGION AND VIRGINIA, 1941 (INCOME YEAR 1940)

		Number Reporting Income					
		$3,000 or under		$3,000–$5,000		Over $5,000	
Place	Total	Number	Per cent	Number	Per cent	Number	Per cent
VIRGINIA	73,554	65,464	89.0	4,008	5.4	4,082	5.6
HAMPTON ROADS-PENINSULA AREA	15,341	13,833	90.2	753	4.9	755	4.9
Norfolk City	6,673	5,777	86.6	416	6.2	480	7.2
Portsmouth	2,048	1.955	95.5	56	2.7	37	1.8
South Norfolk	184	174	94.5	6	3.3	4	2.2
Norfolk Co.	882	832	94.3	30	3.4	20	2.3
Princess Anne Co.	380	315	82.9	38	10.0	27	7.1
Nansemond Co.	71	63	88.8	4	5.6	4	5.6
Suffolk	454	386	85.0	51	11.2	17	3.7
Isle of Wight Co.	88	74	84.1	5	5.7	9	10.2
Newport News	1,944	1,822	93.7	57	2.9	65	3.3
Warwick Co.	607	559	92.1	17	2.8	31	5.1
Elizabeth City Co.	1,145	1,080	94.3	35	3.1	30	2.6
Hampton	356	335	94.1	13	3.7	8	2.2
York Co.	105	101	96.2	1	1.0	3	2.8
James City Co.	83	77	92.8	4	4.8	2	2.4
Williamsburg	321	283	88.2	20	6.2	18	5.6

Source: Annual Report of the Virginia Department of Taxation, Table 13.

The somewhat smaller variation in income among Hampton Roads residents than among Virginia residents as a whole is probably related to the relatively larger proportion of manufacturing workers and smaller proportion of agricultural and professional workers noted earlier in this chapter. This relationship was particularly evident for particular localities. Communities with predominantly industrial populations, notably Portsmouth, South Norfolk, Newport News, and Norfolk County, tended to show smaller income values per tax return and larger percentages of total returns with values of $3,000 and under than such predominantly agricultural counties as Nansemond, Isle of Wight, and Princess Anne and such cities as Norfolk and Williamsburg, with relatively fewer manufacturing and more numerous professional workers.

SUMMARY

The economy of the Hampton Roads-Peninsula region in 1940 was operating at close to its capacity, due to the mild boom in shipbuilding during the previous year or two. A relatively high percentage of its population of working age was already in the labor force and unemployment was well below that of the rest of Virginia and the United States as a whole. Government, chiefly the army and the navy, was the largest employer. Retail and wholesale trade, services, shipbuilding, other manufacturing, transportation, communication, and utilities, and the extractive industries followed in that order.

Norfolk's economy was centered largely in government activity, chiefly at naval establishments, shipping, retail and wholesale trades, services, and manufacturing other than shipbuilding. The economic structure of Newport News and Portsmouth, on the other hand, and much of the surrounding territory, was dominated by shipbuilding, though these cities were also important shipping and transportation, trade and service centers. Suffolk depended upon non-shipbuilding manufacturing, trades and services; Hampton's residents were employed chiefly in shipbuilding and government activities; and Williamsburg looked primarily to the professions and services. Government accounted for more than half of all employment in Elizabeth City County. Agriculture was dominant in Isle of Wight, Nansemond, and Princess Anne counties and of considerable importance in James City, York, and Norfolk counties as well. Almost half of Warwick County's employed persons worked at the Newport News Shipbuilding and Drydock Company. Fishing was a major activity of York County workers and was carried on commercially to some degree by residents of each of the other counties and cities in the area.

While per capita incomes of Hampton Roads residents in 1940 were probably higher than those of Virginians as a whole and there were probably fewer extremely large and extremely small incomes than in the state as a whole, these people had suffered from unstable incomes. Government employment and shipbuilding, both of which had tended to fluctuate violently with changing national policies, had dominated the economic structure of the Hampton Roads region to such a degree that other types of manufacturing and other economic activities which might have had a stabilizing influence were unable to modify appreciably the sharp changes in employment and income experienced by the area during and after World War I and during the thirties.

Just as the region's social structure was unable to provide a cushion in 1940 for absorbing the impending shocks of World War II without serious strain, so its economy lacked the unutilized manpower and other productive resources to meet effectively the demands for war production and related services which were soon to be felt.

CHAPTER IV

CHANNELS THROUGH WHICH WAR CAME TO THE AREA*

An Essential Step toward understanding the impact of the Second World War upon the Hampton Roads-Peninsula area is the identification of the channels through which that impact was delivered. One of these channels was the expansion of military establishments in the area. A second was the increased volume of such major war activities as building and repairing ships, the embarkation and debarkation of troops and material, and the various production and service activities carried on by civilians at military establishments. Construction activities incident to the war effort constituted a third way through which war came to the region. Changes in the quantity and characteristics of the civilian population may be listed as a fourth channel, though such changes may more properly be considered as evidence of the impact upon the social structure of the Hampton Roads area. Accordingly, only the first three of these channels are dealt with in this chapter and population changes are discussed in Chapter V.

EXPANSION OF MILITARY ESTABLISHMENTS

Expansion of Hampton Roads-Peninsula military establishments during World War II occurred through enlargement of the functions, physical structures, and personnel of existing posts as well as through the creation of new ones. The Naval Operating Base at Norfolk, the Norfolk Navy Yard at Portsmouth, and Fort Monroe and Langley Field in Elizabeth City County were important parts of the prewar economic structure of the region. Other establishments operating in 1940 and facilities created or reactivated during World War II are shown in Table 15.

Physical Expansion

While each army and navy post in the Hampton Roads-Peninsula region could tell its own story of the taking over of private property

*By Charles F. Marsh, Professor of Economics and Business Administration, College of William and Mary.

for military use and of hasty, uneconomic erection of physical structures, the experience of the Fifth Naval District provides such a clear picture of the manner in which physical expansion affected the Hampton Roads communities that this discussion will be confined to that experience. The story of the Hampton Roads Port of Embarkation and of the Navy Yard will be summarized in a later section of this chapter.

The Naval Operating Base at Norfolk was both the situs of a considerable physical expansion and, as the headquarters of the Fifth Naval District, the nerve center for all naval activities in Virginia, Maryland, West Virginia, and North Carolina. By far the largest physical expansion during World War II of the base itself occurred at the Naval Air Station, which, by 1944, accounted for 2,165 acres out of the total acreage of 3,000 for the entire base.[1] Other major facilities at N.O.B. in 1944 were the Naval Training Station, the Naval Supply Depot, the Naval Base Hospital, the Marine Corps Barracks and Supply Depot, and, a short distance from the base itself, the Naval Receiving Station.

While World War I naval expansion occurred chiefly through the establishment of the Naval Operating Base itself, the demands of World War II were so heavy that naval expansion could not be contained within the immediate vicinity of the base at Norfolk, but, in effect, exploded and found new locations chiefly in the Little Creek section of Princess Anne County and near Williamsburg, thirty miles up the Peninsula across Hampton Roads from Norfolk. Norfolk proved too crowded for the newly established training school for naval chaplains, and professors and students at the College of William and Mary evacuated classrooms and offices to make room for this school. As naval supplies piled up in the Naval Supply Depot at Norfolk, it became necessary to construct in 1943 a few miles from Williamsburg the Cheatham Annex Supply Depot, whose giant storage facilities provided by 1945 more than two million square feet of floor space. Expansion of the Naval Mine Depot, established at Yorktown in 1918, and creation of the Naval Mine Warfare School required considerable land just east of Cheatham Annex. The construction on Williamsburg's doorstep in 1942 of Camp Peary, the largest single military facility in the Hampton Roads region, provided such a dramatic illustration of the revolutionary impact of military expansion upon a civilian community that it merits special attention.

1. Norfolk Advertising Board, *Know*, August, 1944, pp. 62-63.

Camp Peary was established to do the large-scale job of training Naval Construction Battalions or "Seabees" which had been begun in a small way at Camps Allen and Bradford on the Norfolk side of Hampton Roads. The unnecessarily ruthless eviction, in order to provide the 11,000 acres needed by the Navy, of more than one hundred farming and residential families from their homes of many years with only a few days notice, no provision for their resettlement in an already congested war center, and only vague suggestions as to the time and amount of financial compensation aroused the ire of local ministers and other citizens to such a degree that high naval officials hastened to Williamsburg to attempt to adjust these difficulties. These attempts were only partially successful as settlement dragged out for years and much friction continued to exist between the Navy and the community throughout the existence of the camp.[2] One dispute, for example, over the amount to be paid for a fifty-acre tract, which had been appraised by the government originally at $635, was settled almost three years after it had become a part of Camp Peary by a jury award of $2,775.[3] The diversion of private property to military uses elsewhere in the region was accomplished in most instances with less shock than in the Camp Peary area. The total amounts of land required at any one time were far smaller, much of the land was worthless marshland not used for residential or farming purposes, and many owners were business concerns or persons of means who were in a much better position to negotiate with the navy than the small landowners and tenants, many of whom were Negroes, who lived on the Camp Peary lands. The taking over by the Navy of such properties as the Ford Motor Company assembly plant and the Imperial Tobacco Company's pier in Norfolk and the Cavalier Hotel at Virginia Beach, Hotel Chamberlain at Old Point Comfort and other luxury hotels in the Hampton Roads area were, in general, handled in businesslike fashion with little difficulty to either the Navy or the owners.[4]

2. The writer, as a member of the Williamsburg War Board created by the City Council shortly after Camp Peary was established, worked with other citizens and naval personnel in attempting to adjust the many difficulties incident to the coming of Camp Peary and other military posts to the vicinity of Williamsburg and can testify as to the seriousness of the problems confronting a small town adjacent to new military establishments.

3. Newport News *Daily Press*, July 3 and 16, 1946.

4. See *Norfolk Virginian-Pilot*, February 14, 1945, and August 16, 1946; Newport News *Daily Press*, March 28, 1946.

TABLE 15. MILITARY FACILITIES ESTABLISHED BEFORE AND DURING WORLD WAR II, HAMPTON ROADS-PENINSULA AREA

Facility	Function	Location
Before World War II		
Naval Operating Base	Headquarters, 5th Naval District, Training, Supply, and other naval activities	Norfolk
Norfolk Navy Yard	Shipbuilding and repair and administrative and guard activities related thereto	Portsmouth
Naval Hospital	Care of sick and wounded	Portsmouth
Naval Ammunition Depot	Storage	St. Julien's Creek, Norfolk Co.
Craney Island Naval Fueling Station	Storage and Fueling Ships	Norfolk Co.
St. Helena Naval Facility	Berthing ships and crews during repair activities at Navy Yard	Norfolk
Naval Mine Depot	Manufacture and Storage of mines	Yorktown, York Co.
Naval Fuel Oil Depot	Storage	Yorktown, York Co.
Fort Monroe	Army training and coastal and harbor defense	Elizabeth City Co.
Langley Field	Army air base, communications, weather reporting, etc.	Elizabeth City Co.
Fort Story	Army harbor defense, training, convalescent hospital	Princess Anne Co.
Nansemond Ordnance Depot	Army Ordnance storage	Nansemond Co.
During World War II		
Camp Allen	Naval training	Near Naval Operating Base, Norfolk
Amphibious Training Camp	Naval training and amphibious operations	Little Creek, Princess Anne Co.
Camp Bradford	Army-Navy amphibious training	Little Creek, Princess Anne Co.
Camp Shelton	Armed Guard School and separation center	Little Creek, Princess Anne Co.
Naval Auxiliary Air stations	Naval aviation training	Oceana, Pungo and Creeds, Princess Anne Co.; Fentress, Norfolk Co.; Monogram, Nansemond Co.
Naval hospitals	Care of sick and wounded	Fort Eustis, Warwick Co.; Naval Operating Base, Norfolk
Hampton Naval Training School	Training Negro specialists in basic crafts	Hampton Institute, Hampton
Camp Peary	Training "Seabees" and other naval personnel	York Co. and James City Co., near Williamsburg

TABLE 15—Continued

Facility	Function	Location
Cheatham Annex	Naval supply depot	York Co., near Williamsburg
Naval Mine Warfare School	Naval training	York Co.
Naval Training School (Chaplains)	Indoctrination school	College of William and Mary, Williamsburg
Camp Pendleton	Army training	Princess Anne Co., near Virginia Beach
Camp Ashby	Prisoner of War Camp	Princess Anne Co., near Virginia Beach
Fort Eustis	Army anti-aircraft training	Warwick Co.
Hampton Roads Port of Embarkation	Headquarters and port operations	Newport News
Camp Patrick Henry	Staging area and debarkation center	Warwick Co.
Camp Hill	Negro labor battalions	Warwick Co.
Oyster Point Ammunition Depot	Storage	Warwick Co.
Army Supply Base	Cargo Storage and handling	Norfolk
A.S.T.P. units	Army and college training	College of William and Mary, Williamsburg; Hampton Institute, Hampton

Construction of nonmanufacturing army and navy establishments throughout the area from June, 1940, through November, 1944, amounted to more than 267 million dollars,[5] and created, along with other types of wartime construction, a building boom which brought thousands of workers from other parts of the country. The construction of Camp Peary, for example, between September, 1942, and April, 1943, brought 10,000 construction workers to a community with a prewar population of approximately 2,500, exclusive of the patients at the Eastern State Hospital. Similar conditions accompanied the construction of other military facilities in the region.

Increased Personnel

The most direct form of impact of military expansion upon the people of the Hampton Roads-Peninsula communities was the vast

5. War Production Board, *Summary of War Supply and Facility Contracts*, through December, 1944.

increase in the number of men and women in varicolored uniforms who roamed the streets and competed with civilians for scarce goods and services and even park benches. A study of available records of the various military establishments in the Hampton Roads area shows that the number of officers and men stationed at these posts increased from less than 10,000 in September, 1939, to approximately 168,500 in December, 1943, the peak month of the war.[6] This did not include the 1,687,000 men and women who passed through the Hampton Roads Port of Embarkation during the war nor the 3,000 to 10,000 sailors who comprised liberty parties from the ships anchored in Hampton Roads. Shortly after V-J Day, as many as 20,000 men were on liberty from their ships in the Hampton Roads cities, chiefly Norfolk, at particular times.[7] The distribution of the military personnel among the major establishments is indicated in Table 16.

TABLE 16. ESTIMATED MILITARY POPULATION, HAMPTON ROADS-PENINSULA AREA, SEPTEMBER, 1939, WORLD WAR II MAXIMUM, AND AUGUST, 1945

Branch of Service	September 1939	Wartime Peak		August 1945
Total Armed Forces	9,600	168,500	(December, 1943)	104,500
Total Navy	5,600	121,500	(December, 1944)	77,000
Camp Peary	—	55,150	(June, 1944)	21,300
Other	5,600	66,350	(December, 1944)	55,700
Total Army	4,000	60,500	(June, 1943)	27,500
Fort Monroe and Harbor Defenses	1,000	20,000	(May, 1943)	6,900
Fort Eustis	—	22,700	(February, 1943)	1,900
Langley Field	3,000	10,000	(February, 1945)	8,800
Hampton Roads Port of Embarkation	—	12,200	(September, 1943)	9,900
A.S.T.P.	—	487	(October, 1943)	—

Source: Official files of and correspondence with the various military establishments.

INCREASED VOLUME OF WAR ACTIVITIES BY CIVILIANS

The major types of war activities in the Hampton Roads-Peninsula region other than the receiving and training of military and naval personel and related functions at regular military establishments were shipbuilding and ship repair, the operations at the Hampton Roads

6. See Chapter V for further details as to the size of the military population in relation to the total population of the area before and during the war.

7. *Norfolk Virginian-Pilot*, September 27, 1945.

Port of Embarkation, and such civilian activities at some of the military posts as the assembling, processing, storing, and shipping of naval supplies and miscellaneous clerical and service activities.

Shipbuilding and Ship Repair

Shipbuilding and ship repair have been carried on chiefly by the Newport News Shipbuilding and Drydock Company and the Norfolk Navy Yard (renamed the Norfolk Naval Shipyard in December, 1945). Several smaller private companies, the largest of which were the Welding Shipyard and Norfolk Shipbuilding and Drydock Company, also participated in this activity but represented a relatively small fraction of the total shipbuilding and repair work.

According to officials of the two major yards, the best index of the volume of shipbuilding and ship repair activity is the number of employees. Figure 5 shows that the total number of persons employed

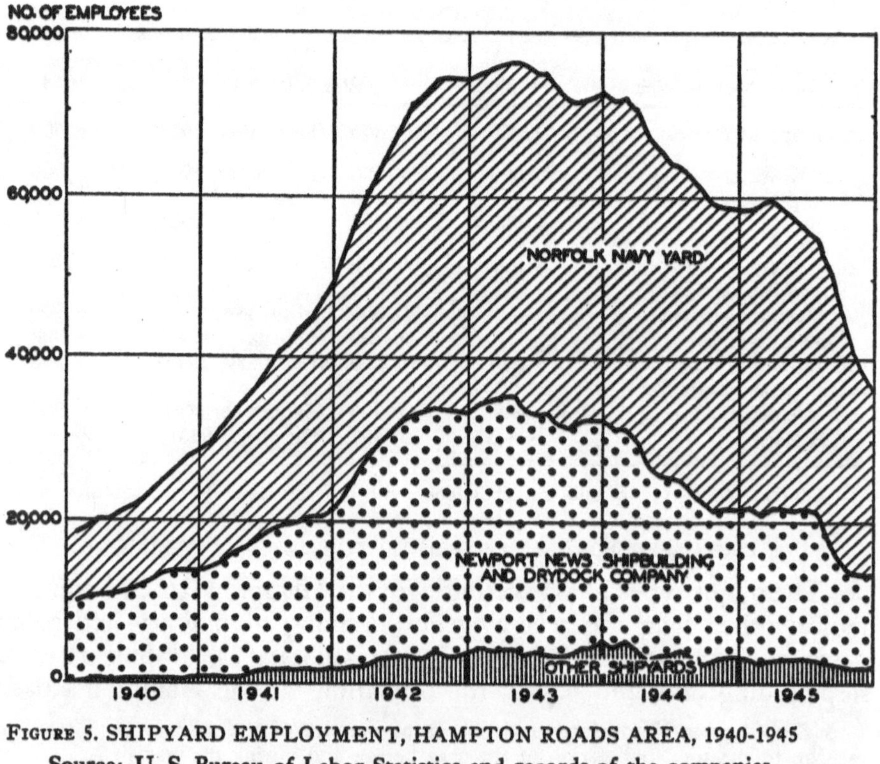

FIGURE 5. SHIPYARD EMPLOYMENT, HAMPTON ROADS AREA, 1940-1945
Source: U. S. Bureau of Labor Statistics and records of the companies.

in all yards, large and small, increased from approximately 19,000 in January, 1940, to a high point of 76,300 in April, 1943, and declined thereafter to less than 25,000 in December, 1945. The Newport News Shipbuilding and Drydock Company alone increased its workforce from 6,179 in January, 1939, to a peak of 31,016 in April, 1943.[8] In addition, it employed at one time approximately 21,000 persons through a subsidiary established during the war at Wilmington, North Carolina. The Norfolk Navy Yard went from 6,520 workers in January, 1939, to almost 43,000 in March and April, 1943.[9] Smaller firms engaged largely in ship repair and the production of small craft increased their employment from a few hundred to nearly 5,000 in May, 1944, and about 6,500 at the end of the war.[10]

It should be noted that both major yards continued to have a large volume of business until the end of the war and that the shrinkage in number of employees after April, 1943, resulted from loss of employees to the armed forces and through voluntary resignations rather than through lay-offs because of insufficient work. In this connection, turnover at the Norfolk Navy Yard was so high that it hired during the years 1939-1945, inclusive, 105,802 workers and lost 80,552 workers.[11] A major reason for the loss of workers by the Newport News Yard, according to its president, Homer Ferguson,[12] was the army's unexpected establishment in Newport News of the Hampton Roads Port of Embarkation. It had been generally understood by shipyards officials that Hampton Roads was to be essentially a naval and shipbuilding center in World War II in order to avoid the confusion which had prevented either shipbuilding or embarkation activities from being handled efficiently in 1917-1919. The shipyards not only lost workers directly to the Port of Embarkation but the additional pressure upon housing helped to send dissatisfied workers back home to North Carolina and to deter the Newport News Company from bringing in new workers.

Contracts awarded to the Newport News Company and the Navy Yard comprised most of the approximately $1,800,000,000 of war supply contracts and project orders awarded to establishments in the Hampton Roads area through November, 1944. These contracts

8. Figures supplied by the Newport News Shipbuilding and Drydock Company.

9. Official Navy records.

10. U. S. Bureau of Labor Statistics, *The Impact of War on the Hampton Roads Area*, p. 55; *Norfolk Virginian-Pilot*, February 6, 1949.

11. Richmond *Times-Dispatch*, February 19, 1946.

12. Personal interview, September 12, 1945.

amounted to more than five times the value of the products of the entire shipbuilding and repair industry in the United States in 1939.[13] A clearer picture of the tremendous importance of shipbuilding as a channel through which World War II came to the Hampton Roads communities is presented by the fact that the Newport News Yard during the years 1939-1945, in addition to repairing, converting, and reconditioning more than 700 ships, launched 33 warships (including the battleship *Indiana*), 8 cruisers, 11 aircraft carriers, and 13 amphibious vessels, and 18 private vessels all of which found their way into war service; and the Navy Yard during the same period, in addition to performing its major task of repairing and overhauling 7,283 ships of war, built 42 new naval vessels. The value of this construction at the Navy Yard for the seven-year period has been officially estimated at almost one billion dollars, and the total payroll for the same period was more than $500,000,000.[14] Small wonder that to many residents of the Hampton Roads communities, especially Newport News and Portsmouth, the "impact of the war" means just one thing—shipbuilding!

Hampton Roads Port of Embarkation

The Hampton Roads Port of Embarkation, with headquarters at Newport News, was activated June 15, 1942,[15] after about six weeks of preliminary study and preparation to provide for the embarkation of troops and supplies for service overseas. The impact of this activity was probably the sharpest and most dramatic of any of the various war activities in the region. The problems incident to building up a personnel organization, obtaining office, warehouse, cargo-hauling, and dock facilities, and providing living quarters for military and civilian employees in communities already swollen by expanded shipbuilding and military activities had many ramifications. Yet, between June and the end of October, 1942, when the port's first big job of sending men and material in connection with the first invasion of North Africa was largely completed, the total number of port personnel had risen from 569, only 2 of which were civilians, to 2,418, of which 1,491 were civilians.

Activities of the port for the entire period until its formal closing

13. War Production Board, *op. cit.*
14. Richmond *Times-Dispatch*, February 19, 1946.
15. This discussion is based largely on the two-volume work edited by Major W. R. Wheeler, *The Road to Victory*, New Haven: Yale University Press, 1946.

in January, 1946, can be summarized as follows: outbound cargo, 12,927,865 measurement tons; inbound cargo 1,761,447 measurement tons; number of personnel embarked, 772,133; number of personnel debarked, 915,350; number of ships handled, 4,059; and peak personnel at any one date, 26,202 (March, 1945), of which almost 12,000 were civilians.[16]

Changes in the volume of activities of the port are indicated in Figures 6 and 7. The high point as to total number of embarkees for any one month was reached in March, 1944, when 57,818 went aboard ship. Outbound cargo reached its peak in April, 1945, with 399,492 long tons or 664,428 measurement tons. Personnel debarked, naturally, was largest after the end of hostilities, with the tide rising to the high level of 107,033 in December, 1945.

Other War Activities

While the shipyards offered Hampton Roads civilians the greatest opportunity for direct participation in the war effort and the Port of Embarkation was the most dramatic illustration of an activity which mushroomed to major proportions during World War II only to disappear shortly thereafter, the war's impact was felt through other types of civilian employment as well. Naval establishments in the area experienced a ten-fold increase from the less than 2,500 civilians in their work force in 1939. Army posts, similarly, expanded nonmilitary personnel from a few hundred to between 3,500 and 4,000. The National Advisory Committee on Aeronautics, the civilian agency whose research contributed so heavily to wartime aviation, grew from approximately 450 workers to more than 3,500. Table 17 summarizes the best available estimates as to the number of civilian workers at these establishments prior to the war, at the wartime peaks, and on V-J Day.

Increases in civilian employment resulted largely from continuous expansion during the war years of production and service functions of the various facilities. As the military situation became more serious overseas, however, women and men not eligible for military service were used increasingly to release soldiers and sailors for combat duty in foreign theaters. Women comprised, for example, nearly three-

16. Excluding the Baltimore Cargo Port of Embarkation, which was a part of Hampton Roads Port of Embarkation, the peak personnel was 23,189 (August, 1944) of which 9,691 were civilian. Source: Statistics and Progress Branch, Hampton Roads Port of Embarkation, January 21, 1946.

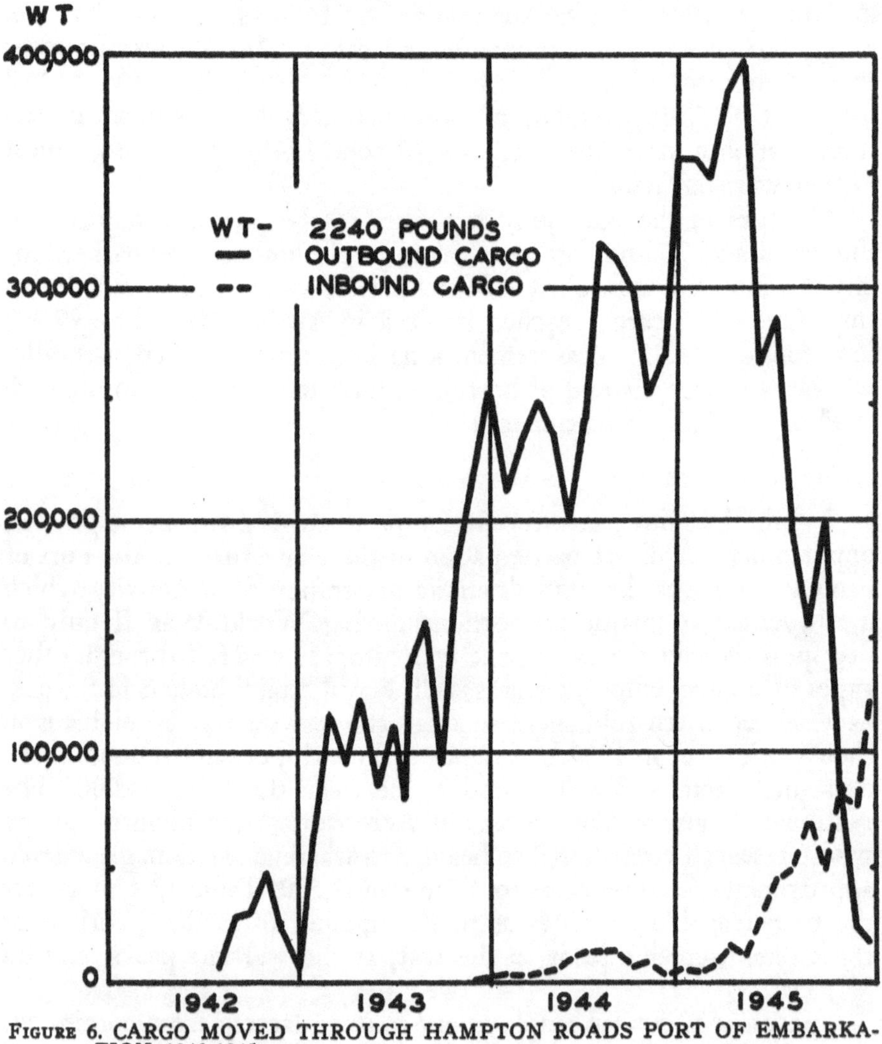

FIGURE 6. CARGO MOVED THROUGH HAMPTON ROADS PORT OF EMBARKATION, 1942-1945

Source: Official Records of Statistics and Progress Branch, Hampton Roads Port of Embarkation.

fourths of the staff of the National Advisory Committee on Aeronautics during the final phases of the war.[17] Civilian employment, accordingly, reached its height in some establishments in 1945 in contrast to the military population stationed in the region, which generally declined after 1943 as men were shipped overseas.

17. Newport News *Daily Press*, March 25 and May 10, 1945.

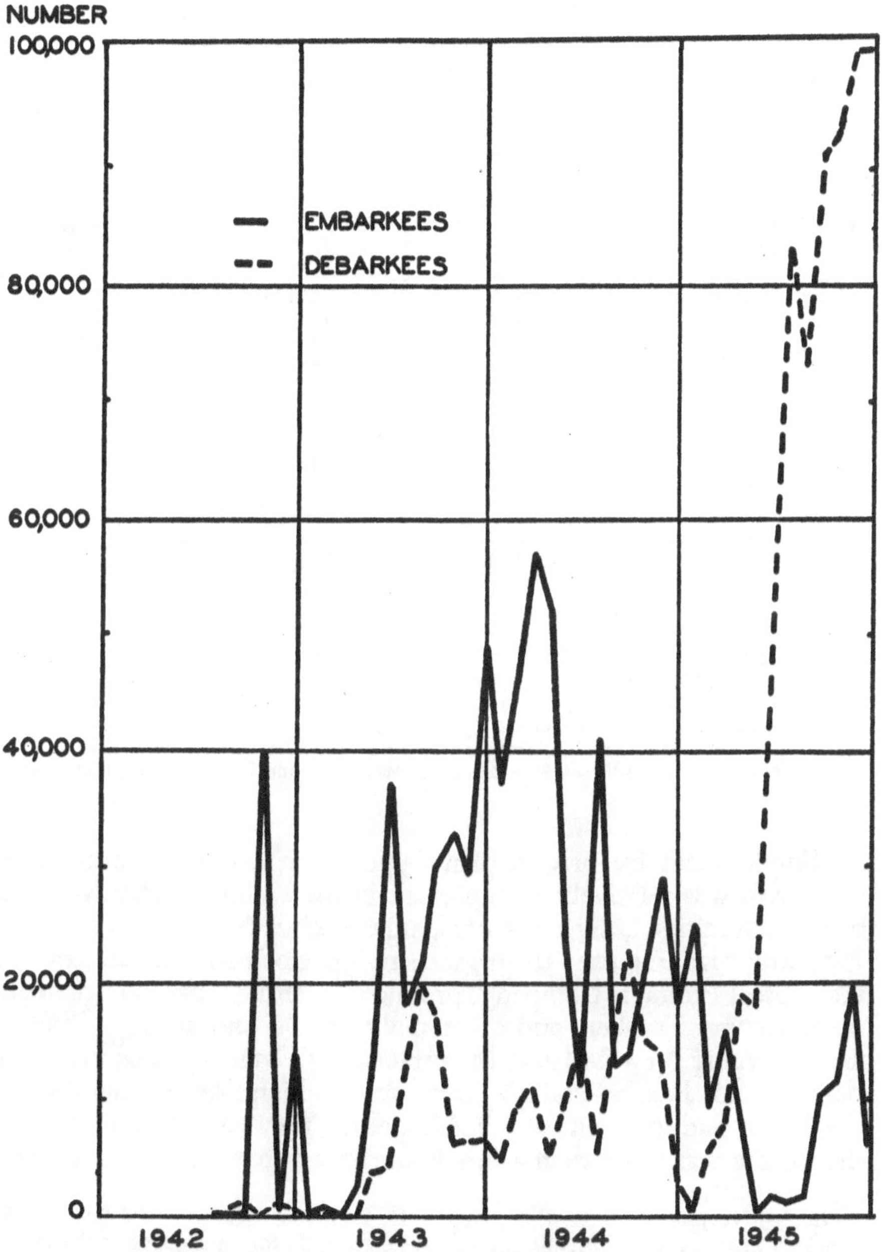

FIGURE 7. PERSONNEL MOVED THROUGH HAMPTON ROADS PORT OF EMBARKATION, 1942-1945

Source: Official Records of Statistics and Progress Branch, Hampton Roads Port of Embarkation.

TABLE 17. ESTIMATED CIVILIAN EMPLOYMENT, GOVERNMENT WAR ACTIVITIES,* HAMPTON ROADS-PENINSULA AREA, SEPTEMBER, 1939, WORLD WAR II MAXIMUM, AND AUGUST, 1945

	September 1939	World War II Maximum		August 1945
All Activities	3,473	36,784		30,247
Total Navy	2,450	27,989		23,175
Naval Operating Base	1,260	5,514	(July, 1944)	4,800
Naval Air Station	100	8,029	(March, 1944)	6,372
Naval Supply Depot	375	7,593	(August, 1945)	7,593
Naval Mine Depot	217	2,480	(August, 1942)	2,060
Naval Ammunition Depot	348	3,910	(May, 1943)	2,350
Naval Hospital	150	463	(May, 1946)	375
Total Army	488	5,542		3,833
Langley Field	100	1,612	(June, 1943)	1,318
Fort Eustis	—	1,411	(July, 1943)	500
Fort Monroe, Fort Story, etc.	248	2,050	(March, 1945)	1,625
Nansemond Ordnance Depot	100	469	(Sept., 1944)	390
National Advisory Committee on Aeronautics	575	3,253	(July, 1945)	3,239

*Exclusive of Norfolk Navy Yard and Hampton Roads Port of Embarkation.

Sources: Official files and correspondence with the various establishments; Federal Reserve Bank of Richmond, *Economic Effects of the War on the Hampton Roads Area;* and newspaper reports, especially *Norfolk Virginian-Pilot*, August 18, 1945, and March 22, 1946; and Newport News *Daily Press*, May 14, 1939, March 25, and May 10, 1945, and January 16 and July 11, 1946.

Employment by private plants under war contracts, other than shipyards, was relatively unimportant in the Hampton Roads-Peninsula communities. Only a few companies, such as Norfolk's Aberfoyle, Inc., first manufacturer to produce nylon cloth for parachutes; the Gary Steel Products Company, producer of anti-submarine net floats, components of tankers and other navy vessels, and artillery shells;[18] and Newport News' Mason Manufacturing Company, making truck bodies, and Benson-Phillips Company, which loaded bombs for the Navy, had war contracts.[19] Altogether, they employed at no time during the war more than a few hundred workers. Indeed, it became

18. See *Norfolk Virginian-Pilot*, August 17, 1945, and "The Story of Gary Steel," *Southern Machinery and Metals*, August, 1948, pp. 15ff., for an account of the reconversion of these two plants to civilian production.

19. World War II History Commission, *Newport News During the Second World War*, Newport News, 1948, pp. 62-65.

generally recognized that shipbuilding and ship repair, navy and army activities, and essential private businesses engaged in servicing shipyard workers, soldiers, and sailors needed all available labor in the Hampton Roads area and that the awarding of war contracts to other types of manufacturing in the area was contrary to national policy. One Norfolk manufacturer of men's clothing, for example, was refused a contract for uniforms on the ground that such contracts should be awarded to firms located elsewhere than shipbuilding centers and ports.[20]

CONSTRUCTION

Construction activities provided a channel through which the Hampton Roads communities received one of the earliest impacts of World War II. New construction at the shipyards, the building of barracks and other facilities at army and navy posts, erection of housing for war workers and the families of military personnel, and the construction of public works, public utilities and buildings to house businesses to serve the swollen population were needed in order that ships might be built and soldiers and sailors be trained. Unlike the First World War, when most of the essential construction was not completed until after the need for it had passed, the Second World War lasted long enough and the construction industry was sufficiently well organized to wind up most of the essential construction by the end of 1942. In accomplishing this, however, the entire Hampton Roads area was converted during the three years 1940, 1941, and 1942 into a giant construction camp manned by people of widely varying experience and skills hastily recruited from other parts of Virginia, from North Carolina, and from more distant places.

Employment and payrolls in contract construction increased more rapidly from 1939 to 1942 than in any other industry in the Hampton Roads communities, according to the files of the Virginia Unemployment Compensation Commission.[21] The average employment during the last half of 1942 of 34,135 persons was more than fifteen times the 1939 level of 2,175 persons. Payrolls were about 35 times as high in 1942 as in 1939. As contracts were completed in 1943, average employment dropped to less than 9,500 and construction payrolls de-

20. See Chapters IX and X for discussion of the impact of the war on this and other companies not engaged directly in war production.

21. As analyzed by the Department of Research and Statistics, Federal Reserve Bank of Richmond, *Economic Effects of the War on the Hampton Roads Area*, 1945, p. 17.

clined from 42 million dollars in 1942 to 11 million dollars. By late 1944, only 7,600 construction workers were employed.

In addition to the 257 million dollars worth of construction at nonmanufacturing army and navy establishments referred to earlier in this chapter, approximately 107 million dollars was expended in the construction of war manufacturing plants in the Hampton Roads-Peninsula region. Its distribution by industry and locality was as follows:[22]

	Total	*Shipyards*	*Other Plants*
		(in thousands of dollars)	
Norfolk, Portsmouth, Norfolk Co..	83,446	82,357	1,089
Newport News-Warwick Co. . . .	21,639	21,639	—
Elizabeth City Co.	25	—	25
York Co.	1,601	—	1,601
All Communities	106,711	103,996	2,715

The value of building permits issued in Norfolk-Portsmouth increased from 3 million dollars in 1939 to nearly 42.5 million in 1942 and declined to 13 million in 1943 and only 10 million in 1944. The variation during these years was even greater in Newport News, as the value of permits rose from less than half a million dollars in 1939 to almost 14 million in 1942, but dropped to just under two million in 1943 and 1.5 million dollars in 1944. Most of this construction was new nonresidential construction. New residential construction was less than one-fourth of total construction in Norfolk-Portsmouth in 1942 and about one-eighth of the total Newport News construction in that year.[23]

SUMMARY

The Second World War came to the Hampton Roads-Peninsula area largely through the expansion of naval and army facilities and shipyards and the accompanying flood of sailors and soldiers, shipyards and construction workers, and their families from all parts of the country. The ten prewar military establishments grew by 1945 to twenty-six; military personnel stationed at these posts increased approximately seventeen-fold from the 1939 complements of less than 10,000; and civilian war workers at these camps, shipyards and other

22. *Norfolk Virginian-Pilot*, July 22, 1945, and Newport News *Daily Press*, January 16, 1946.

23. U. S. Bureau of Labor Statistics, *op. cit.*, pp. 127-28.

war plants, and the National Advisory Committee on Aeronautics rose in number from about 16,000 to a maximum of more than 100,000. War projects swelled the prewar force of approximately 2,000 construction workers to more than 34,000 at the peak of construction late in 1942.

The Norfolk Navy Yard, with 43,000 workers early in 1943, and the Newport News Shipbuilding and Drydock Company, with its 31,000 employees at the same period, dominated the employment picture. The greatest turmoil was probably created by the Hampton Roads Port of Embarkation, with its mushroom growth superimposed upon a community already swollen by war pressures and with its varied activities incident to handling hundreds of thousands of men and millions of tons of cargo enroute to and from the battlefields of the world. Unlike most other war centers, war industries other than shipbuilding were of little significance in the Hampton Roads region.

With this outline of the channels through which the impact of the Second World War was delivered upon the prewar social and economic structure, it is now appropriate to proceed to an analysis of the nature of this impact and to appraise postwar developments and what the future may hold for this unique region.

II

IMPACT OF THE WAR UPON THE SOCIAL STRUCTURE

Norfolk Advertising Board

"The most direct form of impact of military expansion upon the people of the Hampton Roads-Peninsula communities was the vast increase in the number of men and women who roamed the streets and competed with civilians for scarce goods and services and even park benches."

CHAPTER V

POPULATION CHANGES*

The Great Population Changes which occurred in the Hampton Roads-Peninsula area during World War II are of basic importance to the understanding of the changes which took place in the social, economic, and governmental life of the region. With the great increases in shipbuilding activities and the expansion of the military installations in the area, the Hampton Roads area became one of the most congested regions in the entire nation.

In discussing wartime population changes in the region several types of population must be considered. These are: (1) civilian resident population, (2) army and navy personnel stationed in the area, (3) fleet personnel on liberty in the area, and (4) such transient elements as members of the merchant marine from ships in the harbor, relatives visiting service personnel stationed in the area, civilians seeking work, military personnel on leave, and camp followers.

TOTAL POPULATION

It is estimated that the total population of the area, including the civilian, military, and fleet population, reached the three quarter of a million mark during the war. (See Table 18.) The figures in Table 18 include only those persons in the area at a given time and do not begin to give the picture of the enormous flow of population into and out of the area. The personnel of the various military establishments changed so rapidly that many thousands passed through the camps and bases in the area during the war period. Not included in these figures are the 1,687,000 men and women of the armed forces who passed through the Hampton Roads Port of Embarkation during the war. The civilian population was probably not as much in a state of flux as the military population, but here too there was great movement not only into and out of the area but within the area. Not measured at all were the thousands of transients who were undoubtedly in the population but not actually counted in any of the population estimates.

*By R. Wayne Kernodle, Associate Professor of Sociology, College of William and Mary.

TABLE 18. TOTAL POPULATION OF THE HAMPTON ROADS-PENINSULA AREA, 1940–1944

	April 1, 1940	May 1942	November 1, 1943	May 1944
Civilian Population	392,909*	510,884	576,075	576,379
Military Population	15,715	66,190	158,024**	141,131
Fleet on Liberty†	unknown	3,400	5,000	7,720
TOTAL POPULATION	408,624	580,474	739,099**	716,230

*Military population subtracted from the census figure.

**Peak military population came in December, 1943, which brought the total close to the three quarter million mark.

†Estimated by assuming that approximately one-fourth of the complement of ships in harbor will be on shore liberty at a given time.

Source: Civilian population figures taken from census releases of the given dates. Military population computed from data furnished by the military establishments in the area. Fleet population on liberty estimated from reports of ships in harbor furnished by the Fifth Nava District Headquarters.

CIVILIAN POPULATION

The influx of civilian in-migrants began before the actual declaration of war in December of 1941. The shipyards began to increase production in 1939 and many workers were needed to construct the new military installations and enlarge the old ones in the area in 1940 and 1941. Some of this early in-migration is reflected in the 1940 Census figures.

The civilian population of the area, as shown in Table 19, increased 25 per cent in the two years between 1940 and 1942 and 40.7 per cent between 1940 and 1943. Between 1943 and 1944 there was a slight decrease in population. On the whole, the largest population increases occurred in the counties surrounding the cities rather than in the cities themselves. The three major cities of the area, Norfolk, Portsmouth, and Newport News all had a large increase between 1940 and 1942 but lost population between 1942 and 1944. This is undoubtedly because early in the war there was little extra housing available and it was in the cities that the in-migrant war workers crowded up in rooms, trailers, and other such temporary arrangements. By 1943 and 1944 considerable housing was available in the surrounding counties in the form of federal housing projects such as Copeland-Newsome Park located in Warwick and Elizabeth City counties and Broad Creek Village outside Norfolk. From Table 19 it appears that there was a great deal of internal movement between 1942 and 1944.

TABLE 19. CIVILIAN POPULATION OF THE CITIES AND COUNTIES, HAMPTON ROADS-PENINSULA AREA, 1940, 1942, 1943, 1944 AND PERCENTAGE INCREASE 1940–1944

	April 1, 1940[a]	May 1942[b]	Nov. 1, 1943[c]	May 1944[d]	Percentage Increase 1940–1944
ENTIRE AREA	408,624	510,884	576,075	567,379	38.8
North Side	102,202	139,493	159,513	155,709	52.3
Newport News	37,067	52,449	52,940	43,694	17.9
Warwick Co.	9,248	17,366	27,158	33,950	267.1
Hampton	5,898				
Elizabeth City Co.	32,283	49,000	55,281	54,964	44.0
York Co.	8,857	9,853	10,567	10,663[e]	20.4
Williamsburg	3,942	6,330			
James City Co.	4,907	4,495	13,567	12,433[e]	40.5
South Side	306,422	371,391	416,562	411,675	34.3
Norfolk City	144,332	171,812	343,849	167,944	16.4
Portsmouth	50,745	62,288		59,472	17.2
South Norfolk	8,038	9,583			
Norfolk Co.	35,828	54,634		110,502	151.9
Princess Anne Co.	19,984	24,744	25,891	26,264	31.4
Suffolk	11,343		12,815	12,932[e]	14.0
Nansemond Co.	22,771	34,794	20,889	21,320[e]	−6.4
Isle of Wight Co.	13,381	13,536	13,118	13,241[e]	−1.0

a. Includes 15,715 military personnel stationed primarily in Norfolk and Elizabeth City County.

b. Hampton and Elizabeth City are combined; also Suffolk and Nansemond County.

c. The following city-county combinations occur: Hampton and Elizabeth City County; Williamsburg and James City County; Norfolk City, Portsmouth, South Norfolk and Norfolk County.

d. The following city-county combinations occur: Hampton and Elizabeth City County; Williamsburg and James City County; South Norfolk and Norfolk County.

e. Census data not available. Figures taken from Virginia Bureau of Vital Statistics estimates.

Source: U.S. Census releases.

The heavy increase in the population of the area is further emphasized when compared with that for Virginia as a whole. Between 1940 and 1944 civilian population in Virginia increased only 4.3 per cent while that of the Hampton Roads-Peninsula area increased 38.8 per cent. Also, whereas in 1940 this area had 15.3 per cent of Virginia's population, in 1944 it had 20.3 per cent of it.

MILITARY POPULATION

At the same time that these increases were occurring in the civilian population, there was also a heavy increment in the military population in the area. Because there were several permanent military camps located in the area before the war there were already a number of service men in the population. However, in 1939 the entire service population did not exceed 11,000 and on April 1, 1940, numbered only 15,715 (see Table 18 and Figure 8). But with the imminence of war and the operation of Selective Service laws, the military population in the area began to rise in late 1940 and increased each year until early 1944, when it declined slightly, largely because of heavy embarkations.

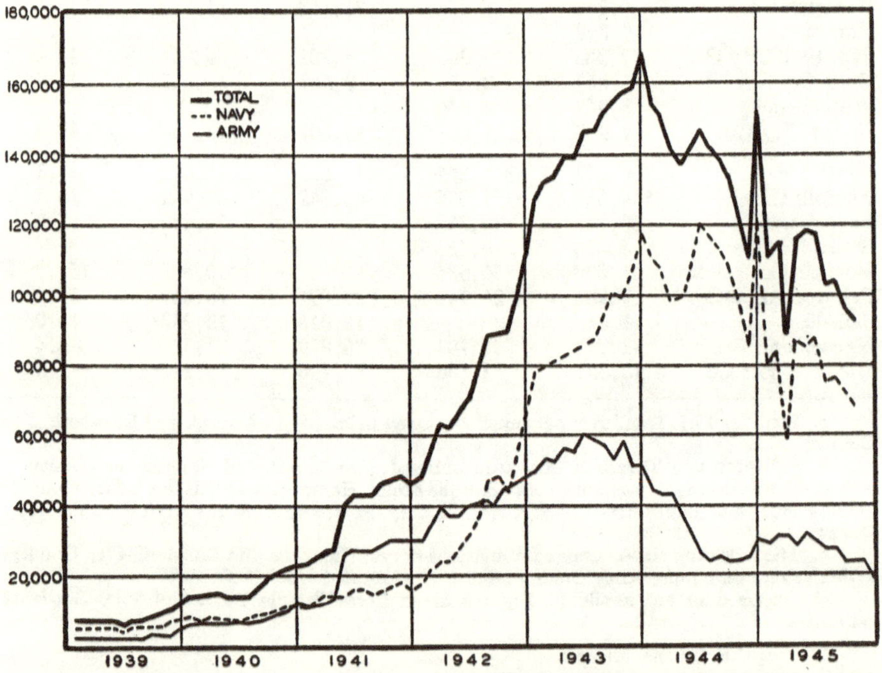

FIGURE 8. MILITARY POPULATION, HAMPTON ROADS-PENINSULA AREA, 1939-1945

Figure 8 shows that there were as many as 168,412 service personnel stationed in the area at one time during the war. This peak was reached in December, 1943, and was comprised of 117,323 navy and 51,089 army personnel. Between August, 1943, and February, 1944, a monthly average of over 150,000 service men were stationed in the area.

The peak of army strength was reached a year before that of the navy. During every month of 1943, with the exception of January, there were well over 50,000 army men stationed in the area; in June of the same year there were 60,552. The great majority of army personnel were stationed on the North side of Hampton Roads at four large establishments, Fort Eustis, Fort Monroe, Langley Field, and Hampton Roads Port of Embarkation. Fort Eustis, for example, the anti-aircraft replacement training center located in Warwick County, reached a peak of 20,722 men in September, 1942, and remained at this level until 1944 when the population of the camp began to decline rapidly. By June of 1945 there were only 3,250 men at this base. After the end of the war, however, this camp was designated as the permanent base of the Army Transportation Corps with a subsequent increase in personnel stationed there.

The peak of navy strength in the area did not come until 1944, with both June and December of that year being months when slightly over 120,000 naval personnel were stationed in the area. During 1941 and early 1942 the army population outnumbered that of the navy, but thereafter, with the expansion of prewar naval facilities and the activation of new naval camps and bases, the number of navy personnel increased sharply and greatly outnumbered that of the army throughout the war period. Beginning in 1943 and until the end of the war, there were always over 100,000 naval personnel stationed in the area.

FLEET PERSONNEL ON LIBERTY

Since Hampton Roads was a major fleet center, there were at all times a large number of naval ships in the harbor. When the men on these ships were given liberty they poured into the cities of Norfolk, Portsmouth, and Newport News, as well as into the surrounding towns and counties of the area. Because of wartime security measures it was difficult to measure this "floating population," but it has been estimated that the number varied from 3,000 to 3,700 during the early part of the war, from 6,500 to 10,000 during 1944 and early 1945, and as high as 20,000 after V-J Day. The number on liberty at any one time varied as to when the "fleet was in." More men were ordinarily on liberty during the week ends. Normally one-fourth of the ship's complement is on liberty at any one time when the ship is in port.[1]

1. Estimated from data furnished by the Fifth Naval District Headquarters, Norfolk, Virginia.

TRANSIENT POPULATION

An even more difficult type of population to measure was the transient population—wives, sweethearts, mothers and other relatives of service personnel and war workers who came into the area for a visit, camp followers, transient workers, service personnel from other parts of the country who took their "leaves" in the area, members of the Merchant Marine on ships in the harbor or getting ready to ship out, members of the navies and merchant marines of allied nations on ships in the harbor, and so on. As far as is known, no reliable estimate of the number of these people is available. Even though this segment of the population was not accurately counted, they were assuredly present in large numbers and added greatly to the congestion and problems of the area.

CIVILIAN IN-MIGRANTS

As indicated in Table 19, the civilian population of the Hampton Roads-Peninsula area increased 38.8 per cent from 1940 to 1944. In the Hampton Roads area proper[2] approximately one out of every three persons living in the area in May, 1944, had moved in since April 1, 1940. At this time (1944) in-migrants comprised 33.4 per cent of the total population. The special census of 1944 showed 165,760 in-migrants. All children under four years of age and all persons who lived in the area on April 1, 1940, were regarded as nonmigrant.[3]

Of the total in-migrants to the area during the period, only 13.4 per cent of the total were nonwhite. Chiefly as a result of the relatively large number of whites among the in-migrants, the proportion of Negroes and other colored persons in the population of the area dropped from 33.2 per cent in 1940 to 28.3 per cent in 1944.

Figure 9 indicates that the in-migrants settled in all parts of the Hampton Roads area. Slightly more than half were in Norfolk City, Norfolk County, and South Norfolk. However, in proportion to prewar population, the in-migrants were more numerous in Warwick County where they comprised 44.7 per cent of the civilian resident population in 1944.

2. The special census taken in 1944 did not include the towns of Williamsburg and Suffolk and the counties of York, James City, Nansemond, and Isle of Wight.

3. U. S. Bureau of the Census, *Wartime Changes in Population and Family Characteristics, Hampton Roads Congested Production Area, May 1944,* Series CA-2, No. 7, p. 2.

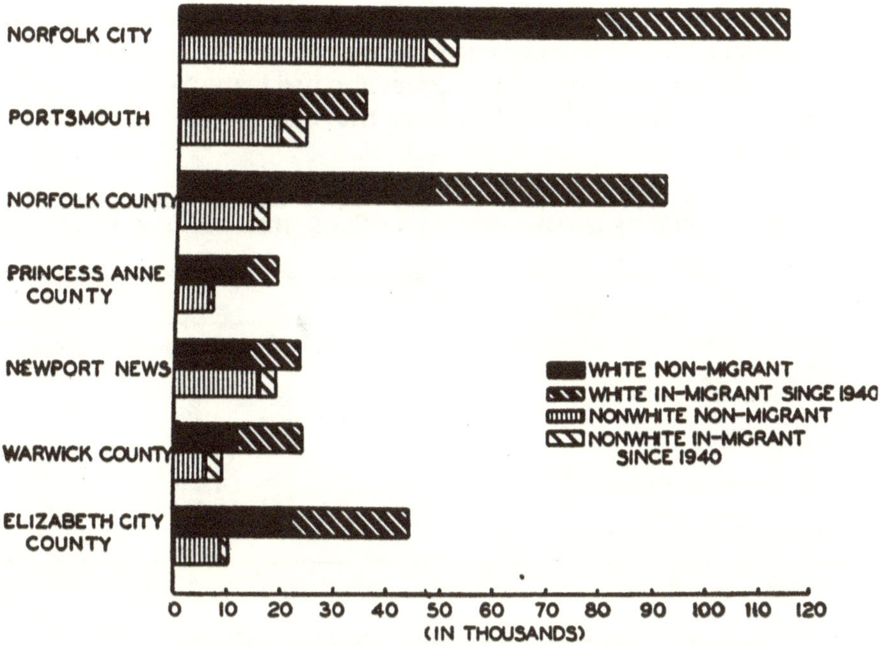

FIGURE 9. RESIDENT STATUS OF CIVILIAN POPULATION, HAMPTON ROADS AREA, 1944

Source: U. S. Census.

The largest percentage increases in civilian population occurred in the counties adjacent to the focal industrial centers. Space in the cities was virtually used up by already existing living quarters and business establishments. Thus it was necessary for in-migrants to locate in the outlying counties or find living quarters in the federal housing projects which were, in many instances, established just outside the major cities. Most of the in-migrants in Warwick County, for example, worked in Newport News but were forced to live in the county because of the lack of housing in the city. To meet housing needs a large federal housing project was erected. Located so that it extended into the two counties of Warwick and Elizabeth City, the Copeland-Newsome Park project reached a wartime population of 25,000. Although great numbers of persons lived in these two counties and others (Norfolk County in particular), in actuality they were a part of the city population in that they worked, found much of their recreation, and did most of their shopping in the cities. They lived in the adjacent counties more from necessity than by choice.

Most of the in-migrants came from elsewhere in Virginia or from neighboring states, especially from North Carolina. This was particularly true of the Negro newcomers, according to Table 20. A somewhat larger percentage of Negroes also had come to the Hampton Roads region from farms than was the case with the white in-migrants.[4]

TABLE 20. MIGRATION STATUS OF RESIDENT POPULATION AND 1940 FARM RESIDENCE OF IN-MIGRANTS, BY COLOR, HAMPTON ROADS AREA, 1944

	White		Nonwhite	
	Number	Per cent	Number	Per cent
All In-Migrants				
Total	143,570	100.0	22,190	100.0
On farm in 1940	20,524	14.3	6,650	30.0
From elsewhere in Virginia	28,098	19.6	4,228	19.1
South Atlantic states	63,938	44.5	14,560	65.6
All other states and abroad	51,534	35.9	3,402	15.3

Source: U.S. Census.

CHARACTERISTICS OF THE CIVILIAN POPULATION, 1944[5]

Differences between the characteristics of the in-migrants and those of the prewar inhabitants of the area led to some striking changes in the composition of the population. At the same time the operation of Selective Service was bringing about additional important shifts in population characteristics.

Age-Sex Composition

The great demand for new labor supply because of the increase in war production activities created an unprecedented demand for labor. The types of jobs available attracted a much younger population than had been in the area before the war. For example, only 10.6 per cent of the in-migrants to the area were forty-five years of age or more, while 25.5 per cent of the nonmigrant population was at this older age level. Ordinarily the population of the younger productive age group would have declined by virtue of the heavy induction of young males into the armed forces.

4. See also, Housing Authority, City of Norfolk, "Data on War Workers for Use in Planning Future Housing Program," July 31, 1944.

5. All figures in the remaining part of this section come from U. S. Census, *Characteristics of the Population, Labor Force, Families and Housing, Hampton Roads Congested Production Area, May 1944*, and apply to the Hampton Roads area proper.

The number of children in the area under five years of age also increased rapidly, as a result of both the in-migration of whole familes and the increasing birth rate. For the Hampton Roads area proper, the number of children under five years of age more than doubled from 1940 to 1944 and comprised 10.6 per cent of the population in 1944 as compared with only 7.3 per cent in 1940.

Other changes in the age-sex composition of the population are shown by Figure 10. The heaviest percentage losses occurred among

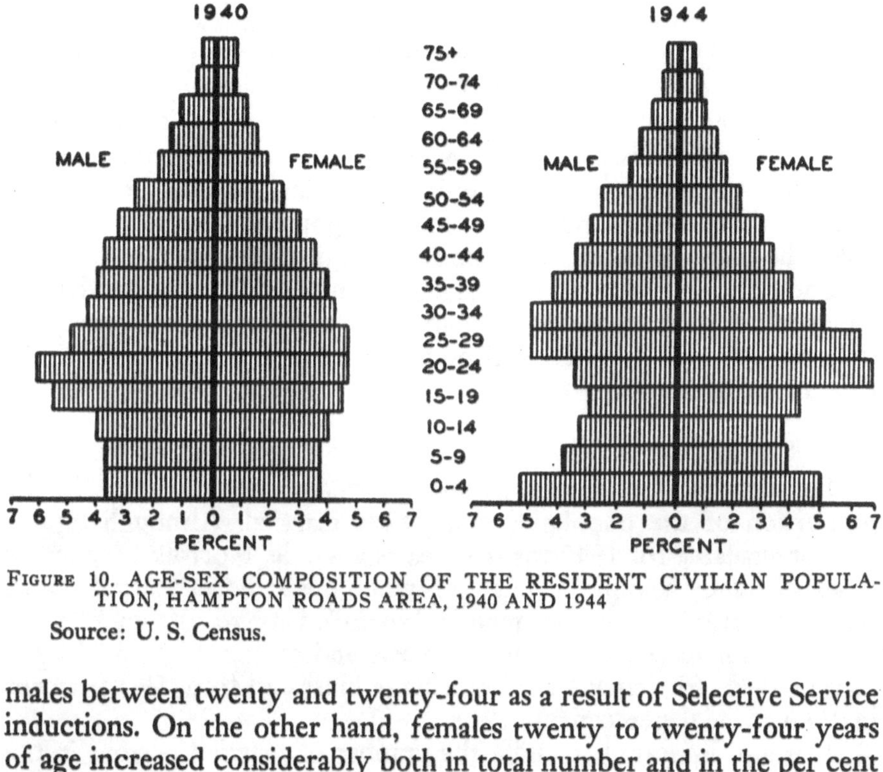

FIGURE 10. AGE-SEX COMPOSITION OF THE RESIDENT CIVILIAN POPULATION, HAMPTON ROADS AREA, 1940 AND 1944

Source: U. S. Census.

males between twenty and twenty-four as a result of Selective Service inductions. On the other hand, females twenty to twenty-four years of age increased considerably both in total number and in the per cent they comprised of the total female population. This was due to the heavy in-migration of females of industrially productive ages at the same time men of the same age were leaving the area for military service.

The per cent of the total population in the age groups twenty-five to thirty-nine also increased during the war years with heaviest gains occurring among females between twenty-five and twenty-nine. Although there were numerical increases among all age-sex groups of the population, the per cent that persons over forty years of age comprised of the total population generally declined. This may be explained by the comparatively heavier in-migration of persons in productive and younger age groups and by increasing birth rates rather than any out-migration or loss of population among older persons.

Sex Ratio

The number of males per 100 females dropped from 107 in 1940 to 91 in 1944, whereas before the war an excess of females existed only in the nonwhite population. For whites the sex ratio dropped from 114 males per 100 females in 1940 to 92 in 1944; for nonwhites it declined from 95 to 89. Much of the decrease in the sex ratio was caused by the heavier in-migration of female workers coupled with the departure of civilian males by induction into the armed forces. However, the deficit in male population was made up by the presence of some thousands of men in the military population stationed in the area who were not counted in the census figures of 1944.

Such drastic changes in the age-sex composition had considerable effect on various aspects of community life and was indirectly responsible for some of the increased number and intensity of social problems in the area during the war.

Marital Status

During the war there was an abnormally large increase in the proportion of the population who were married. Although figures are not available for 1940 for the area as a whole, Norfolk City serves as an adequate example of changes which occurred in marital status. The proportion of married men in Norfolk City rose from 57.3 per cent of the male population fifteen years and over in 1940 to 72.2 per cent in 1944; for females the percentage increased from 59.3 per cent in 1940 to 66.0 per cent in 1944.

It is also important to note the number of married persons in the area who were living apart from their spouses during this period. Out of a total of 268,000 married persons in the Hampton Roads area in 1944, 31,710 were living apart from their spouses. Of these, 20,468 were women, living away from their husbands, more than half of whom were under thirty years of age.

The in-migrant population accounted for a considerable proportion of these temporarily separated married people. All together, 13.4 per cent of the in-migrant married men and 13.2 per cent of the in-migrant married women were living apart from their spouses. The former were probably for the most part war workers who left their families at home for the time being when they moved to this region. Many of the in-migrant women were the wives of service men stationed in the Hampton Roads area who moved there to be near their husbands.

BIRTH RATES

While the war caused the birth rate to rise sharply throughout the country, the intensity of war activity in the Hampton Roads-Peninsula area, with the resultant population increase in the young age groups, brought considerably greater increase in the birth rate for this area than for the United States or for Virginia as a whole. The following tabulation shows the comparative birth rates for the war years:[6]

	Hampton Roads	*Virginia*	*United States*
1939	17.9	19.9	17.3
1940	20.2	20.5	17.9
1941	20.0	21.2	18.9
1942	26.7	23.1	20.9
1943	25.9	23.8	21.5
1944	25.7	23.4	20.2
1945	24.9	22.7	19.6

Birth rates in every city and county of the area were considerably higher than the national rate. Wartime increases did not follow any rural-urban pattern, but rather varied according to concentration of population. The highest birth rate in the area was reached in Warwick County in 1942, when there were 38.8 births per 1,000 population. The rate for whites that year was 47.6 compared to 15.6 for nonwhites. These figures reflect the concentration of a young white in-migrant population living in the county at that time.

Generally throughout the area the white birth rate exceeded the nonwhite during the war. (See Figure 11.) In the prewar years the nonwhite birth rate was the higher as was true for the state as a whole, reflecting the southern pattern. However, in 1944 and 1945 when so many white males were overseas and when jobs were most plentiful for Negroes, the nonwhite birth rate exceeded the white rate in the area under study.

The large cities of the area, namely, Norfolk, Newport News, and Portsmouth, served as focal centers where the majority of actual

6. Virginia Bureau of Vital Statistics and *Statistical Abstract 1947*.

births took place. That is, women living in the counties and smaller cities either by choice or necessity had to go to one of the major cities in the metropolitan area if they desired a hospital delivery. As

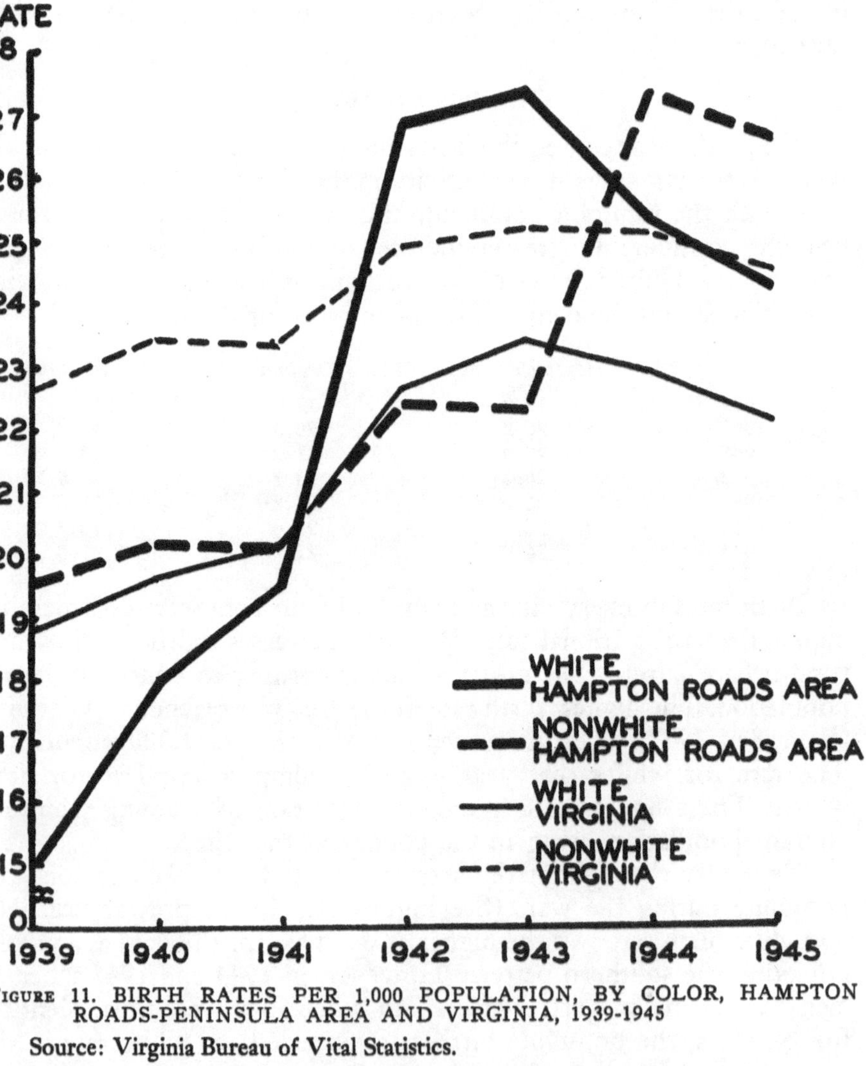

FIGURE 11. BIRTH RATES PER 1,000 POPULATION, BY COLOR, HAMPTON ROADS-PENINSULA AREA AND VIRGINIA, 1939-1945

Source: Virginia Bureau of Vital Statistics.

a result, the recorded birth rates for these centers increased phenomenally, while those for the outlying districts decreased. Newport News, which had a recorded birth rate of 23.7 in 1939, saw it rise to 58.3 in 1944. It is obvious that considerable strain was brought to bear on hospital facilities, doctors, and baby clinics in these cities during the war.

LABOR FORCE

In 1940 there were 153,881 persons in the labor force in the Hampton Roads area proper. This number increased 48.5 per cent between 1940 and 1944.

TABLE 21. POPULATION 14 AND OVER IN LABOR FORCE AND EMPLOYED WORKERS, BY SEX, HAMPTON ROADS AREA, 1940 AND 1944

	1940			1944		
	Total	Male	Female	Total	Male	Female
Population 14 and over	271,131	141,307	129,824	379,106	177,212	201,894
In Labor Force:						
Number	153,881	116,915	36,966	228,578	159,040	69,538
Per cent	56.8	82.7	28.5	60.3	89.7	34.4
Employed Workers:						
Number	140,287	107,901	32,386	225,890	158,214	67,676
Per cent	51.7	76.4	24.9	59.6	89.3	33.5

Source: U.S. Census.

As shown by Table 21 both sexes contributed to the increase in the labor force with the increase in females being higher than that for males. The increase of persons in the labor force was more rapid than the growth of the total population of working age. As a result of this the percentage of males in the labor force rose from 82.7 in 1940 to 89.7 in 1944. The female increase was even more pronounced, with the percentage rising from 28.5 to 34.4.

Four-fifths of the additional female workers were in-migrants. Out of the total of 71,498 in-migrant women fourteen years old and over, more than one-third were in the labor force. The remaining one-fifth of the increase was incurred by fuller employment of native women than before the war.

Since there was relatively little in-migration of nonwhites, the percentage that they comprised of the labor force declined from 34.3 in 1940 to 30.7 in 1944.

Practically all able-bodied civilian men between twenty and fifty-four were in the labor force both in 1940 and in 1944. During the war there were considerable increases in the proportions of workers from among youths of school age, among men over fifty-five, and among women of all age groups. In Norfolk City the proportion of workers among youths fourteen to seventeen years of age rose from 13.1 per cent in 1940 to 24.6 per cent in 1944. In the same period, the percentage for men fifty-five years old and over increased from 68.7 to 78.3. Among women eighteen to sixty-four years of age, the percentage of workers rose from 36.0 in 1940 to 42.8 in 1944.

POSTWAR POPULATION PICTURE[7]

Whereas after the First World War the Hampton Roads area experienced a rapid exit of a sizeable portion of its wartime population, five years after the cessation of hostilities of World War II found a population exceeding even that of the war period. The increase in the population of the Hampton Roads-Peninsula area between 1940 and 1950 was from 408,624 to 629,356. The peak population of the war, 567,075, was reached in 1943.

Compared with Virginia's increase of 22.1 per cent in the ten-year period from 1940 to 1950, the Hampton Roads-Peninsula area gained 54.0 per cent. While Virginia gained 591,013 people during this period, the Hampton Roads-Peninsula area gained 220,732, which comprised 37 per cent of the state's gain. In 1940 the Hampton Roads-Peninsula region comprised 15.3 per cent of the total population of the state. This percentage had risen to 19.3 by 1950.

All cities and counties of the region experienced some growth over the ten-year period, but greatest growth was concentrated in the counties around the principal cities (see Table 22). The largest increase in total numbers was in Norfolk County but in percentage increase Warwick County, with an increase of 324 per cent, was by far the highest.

The greatest increases in both numbers and per cent came in the counties of the area and in particular, Norfolk, Warwick, Princess Anne, and Elizabeth City counties. The cities of the area experienced an increase of 77,203 persons or 29.5 per cent whereas the counties gained 143,529 people or an increase of 97.5 per cent. This is significant in considering the future development of the area in terms of schools and governmental facilities. The cities have apparently realized

7. This section based on preliminary 1950 census estimates and on Lorin A. Thompson's "Population Change in Virginia," Bureau of Population and Economic Research, University of Virginia, July, 1947.

their optimum population in terms of available space for housing. Unless annexation or consolidation takes place it may be expected that the future growth will occur mainly in these surrounding counties which, with the cities, form a metropolitan district.

TABLE 22. POPULATION OF CITIES AND COUNTIES, HAMPTON ROADS-PENINSULA AREA, 1940 AND 1950 AND PERCENTAGE CHANGE

	Number		Per cent Change
	1940	1950	1940–1950
VIRGINIA	2,677,773	3,268,786	22.1
Entire Area	408,624	629,356	54.0
North Side	102,202	165,695	66.5
Newport News	37,067	41,571	12.2
Warwick Co.	9,248	39,177	323.6
Hampton	5,898	5,957	1.0
Elizabeth City Co.	32,283	54,369	68.4
Williamsburg	3,942	6,726	70.6
James City Co.	4,907	6,306	28.5
York Co.	8,857	11,589	30.8
South Side	306,422	463,661	51.3
Norfolk City	144,332	188,601	30.7
Portsmouth	50,745	70,376	38.7
South Norfolk	8,038	13,050	62.4
Norfolk Co.	35,828	99,350	177.3
Princess Anne Co.	19,984	39,892	99.6
Nansemond Co.	22,771	25,226	10.8
Suffolk	11,343	12,287	8.3
Isle of Wight Co.	13,381	14,879	11.2

Source: Preliminary 1950 census estimates published in *The Richmond News Leader*, June 23, 1950.

The 1950 preliminary census estimates do not break down the population by race, so in order to get a picture of the changes which occurred here comparison will be made between the 1940 census figures and the 1947 estimates made by Dr. Thompson.

The increase in white population between 1940 and 1947 was nearly three times that for nonwhites. The Hampton Roads-Peninsula area had an increase of 69 per cent in white population, whereas the increase in the nonwhite population was 23 per cent.

The proportionate increase in the Negro population was much greater on the north side of the area even though Hampton and York County had a loss in the Negro population. Warwick County, location of a large Negro housing project, had an increase of 343 per cent. This large increase caused the percentage increase on the north side to be 42.7 as compared with 17.8 on the south side. Of the localities on the south side, Portsmouth had the largest increase—36.8 per cent. Norfolk County, which gained 64,055 whites, added only 1,276 nonwhites.

Although the increase in the Negro population was much smaller in numbers and in proportion than in the white, the increase in the Hampton Roads-Peninsula area was greater than for the state as a whole. Virginia gained 31,538 nonwhites between 1940 and 1947 and the Hampton Roads area 34,261. This means that other parts of Virginia, especially rural areas, lost in nonwhite population as this segment of the population migrated to areas of industrial opportunity. The Hampton Roads region was one of these areas and attracted both Negro and white population from elsewhere in the state. Thus, while in 1940 this area had 22.1 per cent of Virginia's nonwhite population, in 1947 it had 26.0 per cent. Among whites the increase was from 13.0 to 18.7 per cent.

Although it may be expected that the population of the Hampton Roads area will continue to increase somewhat in terms of total numbers, the rapid rate of increase since 1940 cannot be expected to continue unless great industrial expansion of a peacetime nature takes place or the country is confronted with another war crisis which would demand a further increase in the production facilities of the area. Since the population of this region is so dependent upon shipbuilding and military operations no future population estimates should be made without first analyzing the economic and industrial future of the area. This will be done in later chapters of this volume.

CHAPTER VI

EFFECT OF THE WAR ON THE INCIDENCE OF MARRIAGE*

THE IMPINGEMENT during wartime of thousands of in-migrants of marriageable age upon the Hampton Roads-Peninsula area resulted in several measurable changes in the incidence of marriage. Marriage rates, the time within the year at which persons married, the percentage of marriages involving non-residents of the area, the age at marriage, proportion of marriages performed by the clergy, and the percentages of single, widowed, and divorced persons who married were all affected.[1] A presentation of the data on these items, analyzed in conjunction with the circumstances of the region under war conditions, reveals the most important of the changes in the incidence of marriage.

NUMBER OF MARRIAGES

The number of marriages taking place in the Hampton Roads-Peninsula area,[2] according to Table 23, increased from 3,932 in 1939 to a high of 8,801 in 1945, or 124 per cent. White marriages accounted

TABLE 23. NUMBER OF MARRIAGES, BY YEAR AND BY COLOR, HAMPTON ROADS-PENINSULA AREA, 1939–1945

Year	Total	White	Nonwhite
1939	3,932	2,381	1,551
1940	4,536	2,960	1,576
1941	5,158	3,413	1,745
1942	8,542	5,702	2,840
1943	8,697	5,813	2,884
1944	8,505	5,894	2,611
1945	8,801	6,418	2,383

Source: Virginia Bureau of Vital Statistics.

*By R. Wayne Kernodle, Associate Professor of Sociology, College of William and Mary.

1. All statistical data in this chapter, unless otherwise indicated, are based on figures furnished by Virginia Bureau of Vital Statistics.

2. This chapter excludes Nansemond and Isle of Wight counties and Suffolk since these periphery areas showed little effect of the war's impact on marriage data.

for most of this increase, as they rose 170 per cent as compared with only 54 per cent for nonwhites. This represents an increase much higher than the relative increase in population. While the peak number of total and white marriages did not come until 1945, it is interesting to note that the peak year for nonwhite marriages was 1943, which was the time of peak employment for this group.

MARRIAGE RATES

Table 24 compares the marriage rates for the United States, Virginia, and the Hampton Roads-Peninsula area for the years 1939-1945. It may be observed that annual differences in the marriage rates occurred in each of these three areas. The degree of change in the rates for the Hampton Roads area compared with the rates for the United States and Virginia, for each year, is quite noticeable. However, the general trend is fundamentally the same. Marriage rates, which had begun to increase generally in 1939 with the return of economic prosperity, rose perceptibly as war became more imminent in 1940 and hostilities actually began in 1941 and 1942. Thereafter the marriage rate declined until 1945 when the return of servicemen from overseas added thousands of potential marriage partners to the population.

TABLE 24. MARRIAGE RATES PER 1,000 POPULATION, BY YEARS, UNITED STATES, VIRGINIA, AND THE HAMPTON ROADS-PENINSULA AREA, 1939–1945

Year	United States	Virginia	Hampton Roads–Peninsula Area
1939	10.7	19.8	11.1
1940	12.1	19.6	12.7
1941	12.7	12.7	12.2
1942	13.2	14.4	18.6
1943	11.8	11.7	16.2
1944	11.0	10.8	16.4
1945	12.3	12.1	16.9

Sources: Virginia Bureau of Vital Statistics and *Statistical Abstract*, 1947.

The degree of change in the marriage rate from year to year in the Hampton Roads-Peninsula area, however, stands out in comparison to the United States and Virginia. The marriage rate in the Hampton Roads-Peninsula area reached a higher peak and at all times during the war years stayed above the rate for Virginia and the nation.

Perhaps the major cause for the greater increase in the Hampton Roads area was the heavy concentration of military personnel and both male and female civilian in-migrants who were of marriageable age. Other factors, such as increased economic well-being, imminence of war, the Selective Service Act, special war events, and certain psychological motivations indirectly related to the war, contributed to the increase in marriages. These factors, although operating in most American communities, were even more forceful in this region where

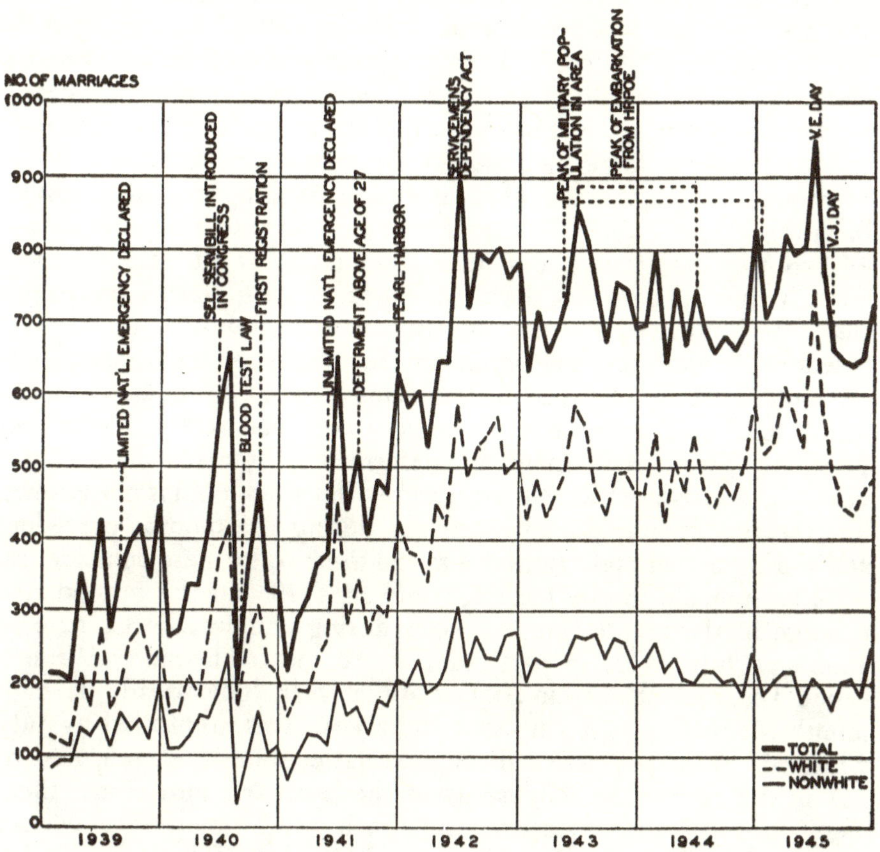

FIGURE 12. MARRIAGES, BY MONTH, HAMPTON ROADS-PENINSULA AREA, BY RACE, 1939-1945

practically everything was geared to war. Figure 12 points out the changes in the number of marriages by month as the war progressed and brings into sharp focus the increases against the chronology of important wartime events.

The early increase in the marriage rate in the Hampton Roads-Peninsula area from 11.1 in 1939 to 12.7 in 1940 reflected several events during this period which affected both the rate for the year and the time within the year at which people married. By 1940 considerable appropriations had been made to shipbuilding companies in the area for the expansion of their facilities. This expansion encouraged the in-migration of a young age group, thus increasing the number of potential brides and grooms. With this in-migration occurring at the same time that money was becoming more plentiful, the marriage rate was accelerated. Early in 1940 Congress began the serious discussion of peacetime conscription and on June 20, 1940, the Burke-Wadsworth Bill, providing for conscription of men into peacetime military service, was introduced.[3] The effects of this measure are reflected by the large increases in the number of marriages which came in succeeding months. If the marriage rate is figured on a monthly basis this is seen clearly. The marriage rate per 1,000 population was 14.1 in May, rising to 19.8 in June and a peak for the year of 22.8 in July. It thus appears that the time at which many persons were married was influenced by the passage and the later operation of the Selective Service Act. The administrators of the Selective Service Act recognized the importance of the family as the "foundation social institution" of the nation and that it was to be preserved wherever possible.[4] This meant, in effect, deferments for married men. Just how many marriages were contracted with this in mind is not known, but the perceptible rise in marriages during the months preceding and during actual conscription was too great to be mere coincidence.

The increase in the marriage rate in 1940 and the unpredicted upsurge in the number of marriages during certain months, namely June and July, were in part reactions to the forthcoming Virginia Blood Test Law enacted in August of that year. June, usually the high month for marriages during any single year, was supplanted by July when 657 persons married during the latter month as compared to 567 in the former. In August when the law went into effect, there were only 202 marriages even though by that time it was certain that the first draft call would come in October. The noticeable increase in the marriage rate which occurred substantiates the belief that the imminence of war was responsible for much of the increment in marriages at this time, and also indicates the effect of social and

3. *Selective Service in Peacetime*, Washington: G.P.O., 1942, p. 23.
4. *Ibid.*, p. 137.

legislative measures, such as the blood test law, in stimulating marriage.

A comparison of the white and nonwhite marriage rates and number of marriages per month reflects the variance in cultural expectations of these two color groups. It was well known throughout the country that local draft boards were not drafting Negro youth in any appreciable numbers, since there was at that time no definite policy concerning the assimilation of the Negro into the armed forces. Thus, the psychological reaction to the Selective Service was different for the Negro than for the white. The blood test law of August, 1940, however, was a greater deterrent to nonwhite marriages than to white. As shown in Figure 12 the number of white marriages increased in September and October as the draft went into effect, while nonwhite marriages did not begin to increase significantly until influenced by higher wages in the area. Thus nonwhite marriages apparently responded more to changes in economic opportunities and social legislation than to factors directly connected with the war, such as the Selective Service Act, Pearl Harbor, V-E Day, and other such war-connected events which greatly influenced the marriage rate among whites.

During 1941 the continued in-migration of workers and military personnel, the growing imminence of war, increased prosperity, and related factors affected the usual pattern of fluctuations in monthly marriages. The perennial decline which usually precedes the June rush to the altar did not occur in 1941. There was, rather, a steady rise in marriages each month from February through June, with small fluctuations in the months following until December, when the attack on Pearl Harbor and the declaration of war brought an upsurge in marriages in the area and established an unprecedented peak of 628 marriages. In contrast there were only 327 marriages in December 1940. After Pearl Harbor there were never less than 500 marriages in any single month throughout the entire period from 1942-1945. Thus the actual declaration and pursuit of war was reflected in the increased marriage rate as people were faced with swift adjustments to the exigencies of the time.

Other special events in 1942 related to the war affected both the time at which some persons married and the marriage rate. In February, 1942, an act to amend the National Service Life Insurance Act of 1942 increased the amount and extent to which the serviceman's life was insured. On June 23, 1942, the Servicemen's Dependents Allowance Act of 1942 increased the income of the serviceman considerably. These financial considerations were sufficient to cause a number of women to seek out servicemen as marriage partners and also supplied many servicemen with a financial base sufficient to contract marriage.

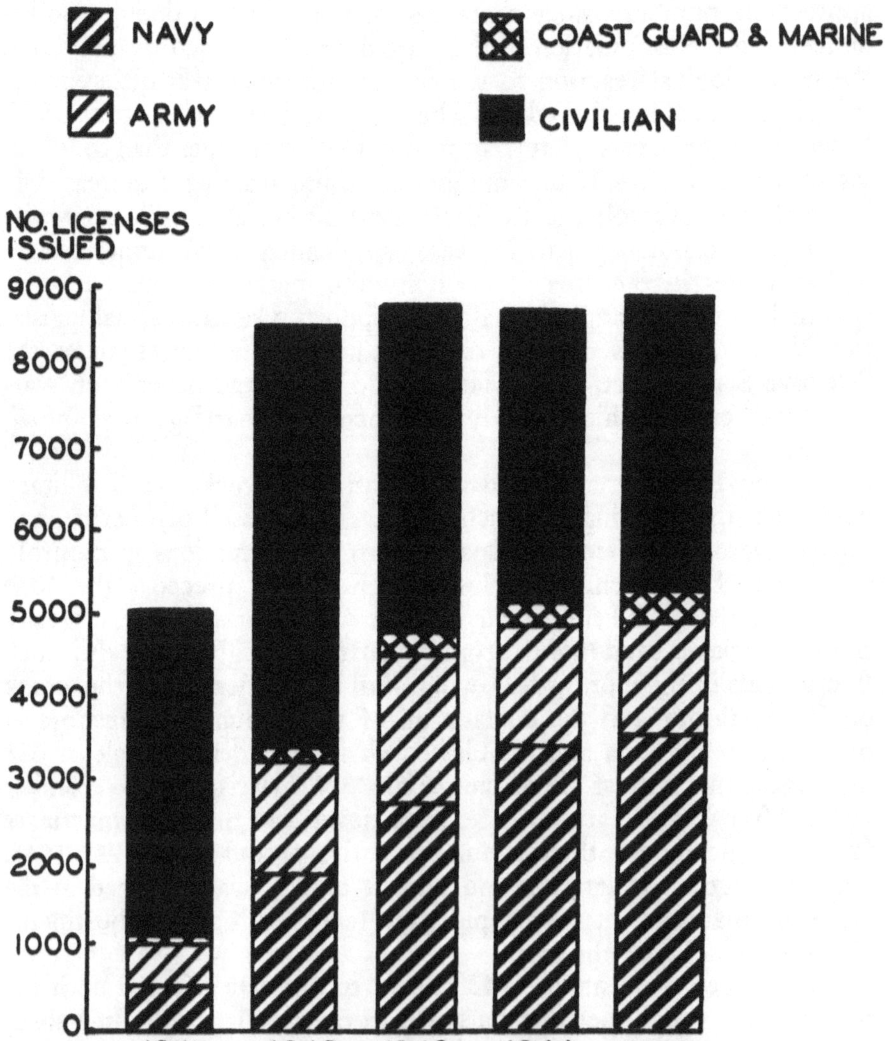

FIGURE 13. MARRIAGE LICENSES ISSUED, BY MILITARY OR CIVILIAN STATUS OF GROOM, HAMPTON ROADS-PENINSULA AREA, 1941-1945

Source: Compiled from marriage registers of the area.

During 1942 the civilian population of the area had risen to 459,538 with the largest gains being among white females twenty to twenty-nine years of age The military population had increased to more than 120,000, not counting the fleet or transient population. In response to these population increases and other war-connected factors, the rate in the Hampton Roads-Peninsula area rose to 18.6 marriages per 1,000 population, representing an increase of 65.6 per cent over the previous year. The marriage rate for the United States for the same year was 13.2. Increases in the marriage rate in the area were greatest at the focal centers of in-migration and location of military camps. In Norfolk City, for example, the marriage rate rose from 13.5 in 1941 to 22.9 in 1942.

That the marriage of servicemen in the area was responsible for much of the increase in the marriage rate, and also in leveling the fluctuations in marriages by month, is evidenced by the fact that out of 8,559 marriage licenses issued in 1942 in the area, 40.6 per cent were applications made by couples of which the groom was a member of the armed forces (see Figure 13).

During 1943 and 1944 increasing numbers of men were overseas, draft quotas were enlarged, and the potential marriage population decreased. The "shooting phase" of the war was reflected in the decreased marriage rate. These factors and the growing tensions developing out of the lengthening war served to eliminate almost all of the usual seasonal variations in the number of marriages. Three months in 1944 had more marriages than June, although there was little noticeable difference in the number of marriages which occurred during any months of the year. The former folkways concerning traditional months for marriage had apparently broken down completely as the war increased. Fewer people actually waited or were in a position to wait for the coming of June, October, or December to get married. The elimination of seasonal variations to this extent suggests that a large percentage of marriages during these two years were hasty, unplanned, or unexpected. Others represented immediate marriages of servicemen returning from overseas. Some were planned, while others were hysteria marriages. The time of marriage, at any rate, became of secondary importance.

It was also during this period that the marriage rate for nonwhites increased most. With the departure of white males from the civilian population, and the increased demand for production workers, Negroes were called upon to fill jobs formerly closed to them.

With the subsequent rise in wages and economic security, the non-white marriage rate increased more than did the white rate in certain parts of the area.

With the end of hostilities and the return of servicemen to the area in 1945 the marriage rate increased phenomenally in some localities. The marriage rate in Norfolk City for whites reached 28.2 in 1945 and 30.8 in Portsmouth. Figure 12 shows the correlation between these events and the increase in the number of marriages. Just after victory in Europe in June, 1945, there were 951 marriages in the Hampton Roads area, the highest marriage peak for any single month ever recorded in the area. Almost the entire increase over June, 1944, was due to white marriages.

With the general demobilization of armed forces and production workers, the number of marriages in the area began to decline temporarily.

The war, then, influenced certain changes in marriage rates and in the pattern of monthly variations or time of marriage. These influences operated in the nation as a whole but were even more influential in the Hampton Roads area.

MARRIAGE OF NON-RESIDENTS

Other aspects of marriage incidence, such as the percentage of total marriages occurring in the area which involved persons who were not residents of Virginia, were also affected by the war. Normally it is expected that the larger percentage of marriages in any area will unite persons who reside there. This is less true, however, as the area becomes increasingly urban and the number of transients increases.

The Hampton Roads area was already predominantly urban before the war and it was not unusual to have a high percentage of non-resident marriages occurring each year. The war however greatly increased both the number of non-residents who married in the area and the percentage they comprised of all persons marrying in the area.

It has been pointed out that in-migrants accounted for one third of the civilian population of the area in 1944. In addition there were almost 200,000 servicemen stationed near by and an unknown number of transients, both male and female. Under these characteristic wartime conditions it was to be expected that the percentage of non-resident marriages would increase. The extent to which this occurred is shown by the following tabulation showing the percentage of nonresident marriages to all marriages.

	1941	*1942*	*1943*	*1944*	*1945*
Total	21.1	32.9	41.4	45.2	46.0
White	30.2	47.0	56.3	59.5	57.9
Nonwhite	3.4	4.6	11.3	13.0	14.0

It may be seen that marriages of which one or both members of the couple were nonresident to Virginia constituted over 40 per cent of all marriages from 1943 through 1945 in the Hampton Roads area. In some cities and counties this figure exceeded 60 per cent. Marriages of this nonresident character comprised 56.3 per cent of all white marriages in the area during these years but less than 14.0 per cent of nonwhite marriages. The comparatively low frequency of nonresident marriages among nonwhites suggests considerably less mobility among that group and reflects the smaller number of Negroes in the military population of the area.

Increases in nonresident as compared to total marriages during the war years reflects the highly mobile and in-migrant nature of the white population generally. It further suggests the increased mating of couples with varying geographic and socio-economic backgrounds under the problematical circumstances of war and congested conditions.

AGE AT MARRIAGE

Apart from biological factors, the age at which people marry is largely determined by social customs, which change rather slowly within a given population group or area. During wartime, however, these customs were modified by new overpowering needs and circumstances and the "given population" was infused with new masses of people unfamiliar with and uninhibited by the traditional customs regarding age at marriage. At the same time the customs of all groups were subject to swift change under war conditions.

A study of the available data on age at marriage in the Hampton Roads-Peninsula area during the war reveals that changes were different among the various age groups, according to both sex and color.

Females

There was an increase in the number of marriages of females of all ages, both white and nonwhite, in 1942 over the preceding year.

This sudden spurt in marriages represents the greatest and most widespread increase of the war period. After 1942 the number of females in certain age groups who married continued to increase while others decreased. Figure 14 shows the percentage distribution of females who married each year, 1941-1945, according to age and color.

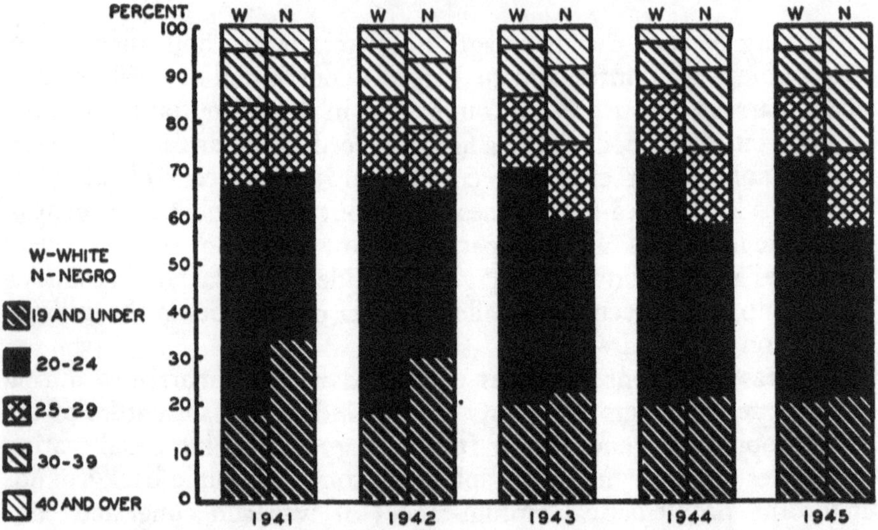

FIGURE 14. PERCENTAGE DISTRIBUTION OF AGE AT MARRIAGE OF BRIDES, BY COLOR, HAMPTON ROADS-PENINSULA AREA, 1941-1945

Source: Virginia Bureau of Vital Statistics.

There was a sudden increase in the number of both white and nonwhite brides under seventeen years of age who married in 1942. Prior to the war the large majority of brides under seventeen had been nonwhite. After 1942 the number of brides under seventeen decreased every year through 1945. Decreases in marriages were especially prominent among nonwhite females under twenty years of age after 1942. This suggests that once Negro girls were able to get jobs in the industries of the area, they chose to take such jobs instead of early marriage. For some, it was probably the first real opportunity to make such a choice. Another factor here was the shortage of young nonwhite males in the civilian and military population.

The marriage of white females from sixteen to nineteen, however, continued to increase as the war lengthened. There were, of course, large in-migrations of white females under twenty. It is apparent, however, that the war stimulated white females under twenty to marriage in greater proportions than nonwhite females of the same age.

The greatest numerical increases in the marriage of females during the war period occurred in the age group twenty to twenty-four, especially among whites. This reflects the steady in-migration of white females of this group into the area and the presence of the large military bases with predominantly young populations. The same factors stimulated numerical increases in the marriage of white females twenty-five years of age and above; however, proportionate increases were less as age increased and as the war lengthened.

Thus, although there were increases in the number of brides in most of the age groups, the greater proportionate increase of brides twenty-four and under caused the per cent they comprised of all females married each year to rise, while the per cent that brides twenty-five years of age and over comprised of the total decreased. The war, then, accelerated the trend toward earlier marriages among white females. Of the total white brides in 1941, 66.2 per cent were twenty-four years of age and under; in 1945 females in this same age group comprised 72.0 per cent of the white brides in the area.

Males

Prior to the war males generally married later than females in the Hampton Roads-Peninsula area. This is evident from the fact that only five grooms sixteen years of age and under married in 1941 as compared with 163 brides in this age category. Again, only 35 males under seventeen year of age married in the area during the entire period 1941-1945 whereas 1,338 females of this age were married during this period. Figure 15 shows the age distribution of grooms by color, 1941-1945.

There was, however, a great increase in the number of males who married in the area during the war at ages eighteen and nineteen. The number of eighteen-year-old grooms doubled between 1941 and 1942 and remained at this level through 1945, with gains being proportionately higher among whites. The number of white males in the area who married at nineteen years of age almost quadrupled between 1941 and 1945. Such increases reflect the changing age structure of both the military and civilian populations of the area as well as the various motivating influences toward earlier marriage. Conversely, the proportion of colored grooms nineteen and under decreased throughout the period.

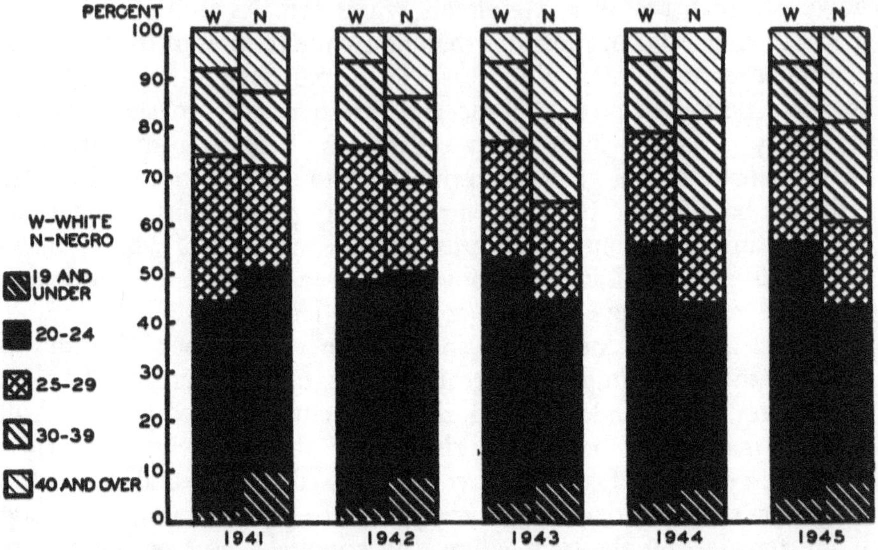

FIGURE 15. PERCENTAGE DISTRIBUTION OF AGE AT MARRIAGE OF GROOMS, BY COLOR, HAMPTON ROADS-PENINSULA AREA, 1941-1945

Source: Virginia Bureau of Vital Statistics.

Largest numerical increases occurred in the marriage of males at ages twenty to twenty-four. The large number of servicemen stationed in the area who were predominantly in this age group were responsible for most of this increase which, with the additional marriages of eighteen- and nineteen-year-old males, precipitated the general trend toward earlier marriage among the male population of the area. According to Figure 15, white grooms under twenty-five increased from 44.6 per cent of the total in 1941 to 56.4 per cent in 1945. On the other hand, the per cent distribution in all age groups twenty-five and over decreased.

On the other hand, increases among nonwhite grooms were proportionately greater after thirty years of age. The war thus reversed the prewar pattern at which time nonwhite males tended to marry considerably earlier than white males.

Summary

It may be concluded from the data available that the war brought together a young population into a series of new situations which decreased ordinary community controls and provided the momentum for widespread intensification of self-oriented behavior. In an attempt to adjust to these situations, to utilize the opportunities of increased individual freedom, and to satisfy personal wants and needs, many of these people entered into the marriage relationship earlier than they would have had they remained at home.

OFFICIANT

Marriage in the United States normally carries with it many religious connotations, and the minister as chief functionary at wedding ceremonies is a symbol of forgiveness for any errors of the past and protection of the new relationship. With urbanization, secularism, and changes in marriage patterns in the last few decades, many couples have transgressed these customary wedding folkways. Weddings performed by a minister take time, preparation, and often more capital outlay than the quick ceremony performed by a civil appointee.

The changes which occurred in the Hampton Roads area under wartime conditions increased the trend away from marriages performed by the clergy. The in-migration of civilian war workers, the presence of transients and a large military population contributed to the growing urbanity and heterogeneity of the area. The size and mobility of the population made it difficult for ministers to contact personally many of the in-migrants. Transients and in-migrants also had difficulty contacting busy ministers, even if they wished to do so. Many marriages were contracted in haste, often under circumstances which denied couples the opportunity of a church wedding even if they desired one.

In the prewar year 1939, the clergy officiated at 88.7 per cent of all marriages which were solemnized in the area. Generally ministers officiated at a larger proportion of marriages in rural communities than urban ceremonies before the war. Whereas in Norfolk City in 1939 the clergy officiated at only 85.7 per cent of all marriages, in rural Warwick and York counties the clergy performed all marriages in that year.

Beginning in 1942 there was a widespread decline in the percentages of marriages performed by the clergy throughout the area, both for whites and nonwhites. There were probably more new people in the area for the first time this year than any other single year of the war.

The trend away from marriages performed by clergymen became

greater as the length of the war increased, so that by 1945 ministers officiated at only 79.2 per cent of all marriages in the area that year. In certain communities the trend was even more pronounced. For example, in Norfolk City in 1945 only 76.5 per cent of white marriages and 61.7 per cent of nonwhite marriages were solemnized by clergymen. In Princess Anne County the data for 1944 show that clergymen officiated at 86.1 per cent of white marriages and at only 54.4 per cent of nonwhite marriages.

Generally, throughout the entire area during the war period this trend was more predominant among Negroes than whites. The greater availability of chaplains to white couples probably was influential in supporting the greater tendency of whites to call on clergy to perform the marriage ceremony.

This decrease in the percentage of marriages performed by clergy indicates that the church had less influence on marriage during the war and further challenged the concept that the marriage ceremony was a sacrament and the sole province of the church. The Hampton Roads-Peninsula area presented the situation under wartime conditions in which the folkways concerning the traditional marriage ceremony performed in the church or by a minister gave way to new conventions which enabled people to marry without the blessing of the church which often insisted on more time and ritual than the people wanted or could afford at the time.

PREVIOUS MARITAL STATUS

The great majority of marriages which occur in any one year are those which bring together men and women who are marrying for the first time. The rapidly increasing divorce rate in the United States, however, particularly in urban centers, and the subsequent decline in social criticism of divorced persons has tended to increase the percentage of divorced persons who remarry every year.

The remarriage of widowed persons, although not as frequent as that of divorced persons, has also tended to increase recently. During and after a major war when there are a large number of war widows, many of whom have spent little time with their husbands, there is an increase in the potential number who can remarry.

Grooms

Of the 5,158 males married in the Hampton Roads-Peninsula area in 1941, 87.1 per cent had never been married before. This percentage decreased steadily and by 1945 had dropped to 83.8 per cent of the 8,801 males who married that year.

During the war, the percentage of previously widowed white males to the total number of grooms declined from 6.0 in 1941 to 5.0 in 1945. The percentage of nonwhite grooms in this category, however, increased in the last two years of the war.

Remarriages of previously divorced grooms moved upward during the period. They increased every year during the war period, reaching 11.2 per cent of all grooms in 1945 as compared with 6.8 per cent in 1941. The largest gain came in 1945 when men were returning from overseas and remarrying in large numbers after being granted divorces from war marriages.

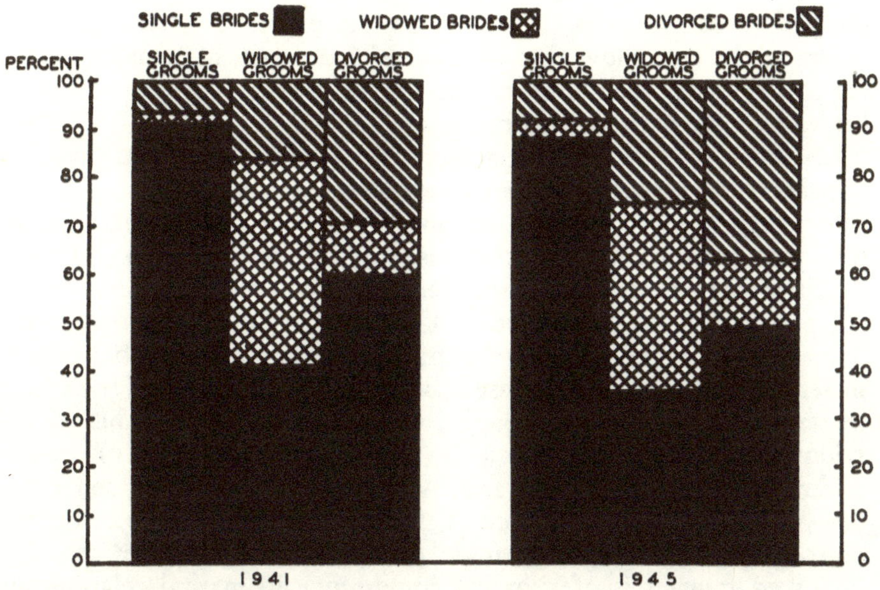

FIGURE 16. PERCENTAGE OF SINGLE, WIDOWED, AND DIVORCED GROOMS MARRYING SINGLE, WIDOWED, AND DIVORCED BRIDES, HAMPTON ROADS-PENINSULA AREA, 1941 AND 1945

Source: Virginia Bureau of Vital Statistics.

It is interesting to note in the further analysis of these data that the larger percentage of previously divorced men were remarrying either previously divorced or widowed women, while a decreasing percentage were marrying single women (See Figure 16).

The percentage of previously divorced nonwhite males to all nonwhite grooms increased from 4.5 per cent in 1941 to 10.5 per cent in 1945 with steady increments every year. By 1945 there were proportionately as many divorced Negro men remarrying as there were white men in this category. These increases indicate the influence of greater economic security on Negroes and further reflects the increasing divorce rate among this group in the area. According to several divorce court judges in the area, this new economic security gained through war jobs caused Negroes to seek legal divorces in an increasing number, whereas before the war they often listed themselves as single or widowed after separating themselves from a marriage.

Brides

The war also stimulated remarriage among widowed and previously divorced females. The data on the previous marital status of brides in the area show that whereas 85.7 per cent of females marrying in 1941 were marrying for the first time, only 81.8 per cent of all brides in 1945 were in this category.

Noticeable increases in the proportions of widowed and divorced females who remarried began to appear in 1943. These increases were sufficiently high to cause a decline in the percentage that females marrying for the first time comprised of all brides in 1944 and 1945.

Previously widowed white females who remarried constituted 4.4 per cent of all white brides in the area in 1941. This percentage decreased during the first two years of the war as the number of men in service and overseas increased. Beginning with 1944 and the return of servicemen to the area, coupled with the increasing number of war widows, the percentage of white brides who had been previously widowed began to increase and by the end of 1945 was well above prewar levels. The importance of this increasing postwar trend of the marriage or remarriage of single, widowed, and divorced males to widowed females is of growing importance in marital relationships generally. Some of these marriages doubtlessly linked single men with "war widows" who already had one or more children, or conceivably the remarriage of a divorced man with a widowed woman might involve children from both sides. These are not new situations, but denote an increased acceptance of such relationships within the cultural norm.

Conversely, the percentage that previously widowed females comprised of all nonwhite brides in the area increased as the war progressed and declined in 1945 at the close of hostilities. This difference in the racial pattern suggests that Negro women, left by their husbands who were finding better jobs during the war, created a larger than normal group of deserted Negro females who traditionally refer to themselves as "widows." As hostilities ceased and war jobs gave out, the percentage in this category decreased.

The remarriage of divorced females increased as the war progressed. Females in this category comprised 8.4 per cent of all brides in 1941. This percentage rose each year, except in 1942, reaching 12 per cent of the total in 1945. This was a slightly smaller change than for divorced males who remarried during the same period. Figure 16 shows the increasing trend in the choice of divorced females as marriage partners as the war ended. It shows that the war tended to increase the remarriage of widowed and divorced women to single men, of divorced women to widowed men, and of widowed and divorced women to divorced men.

Summary

For the Hampton Roads-Peninsula area, the war tended to increase the total number of men and women in all categories of previous marital status. However, in this area characterized by an unusually high civilian and military in-migration and one which focused the sharp changes of wartime, the tendency toward remarriage of widowed and divorced females to single, widowed, and divorced males increased even more in percentages they comprised of annual totals than marriages of single persons to each other. The increasing trend toward the marriage of divorcees by males of all previous marital statuses is evidence that former taboos on marrying divorced women are swiftly broken down and supplanted with new group ways which provide support for meeting needs in such situations.

CHAPTER VII

PREMARITAL, MARITAL, AND FAMILY RELATIONSHIPS*

THE PROCESSES OF SOCIAL CHANGE engendered by the war accelerated modifications in the social definitions of courtship, marriage, and family which were expressed in the changing behavior of the people in the Hampton Roads-Peninsula area, as elsewhere. Thousands of persons were uprooted from their primary groups and thrust into a new and coldly impersonal situation to which quick adjustments were necessary. Quite often the adjustments made under these circumstances were inadequate and led to a complex web of problems which became too complicated for individuals to solve alone.

The recent war set the stage for the continuation of many of the same forces that originally led to a redefinition of acceptable behavior in dating, courtship, marriage, and family relationships. Increased mobility in wartime, the anonymity of both sexes in congested areas such as Hampton Roads, and the general temper of the times hastened the secular trend toward increasing sexual freedom (both before and after marriage), individual choice of mates, and a further decline in the attention given prudential factors concerning the choice of life partners. The war also probably decreased the amount of time which elapsed between the time many couples first met and their subsequent marriage. There was less time available for initial adjustment of partners during the honeymoon and the first weeks of marriage. Others already married lived under abnormal conditions with accompanying changes in their behavior. Partial evidence of the impact of the war on the marriage and family institutions in the area was collected from the case studies of private and public welfare agencies, from interviews with individuals in the area, and from written records of the agencies.

TEMPER OF THE AREA DURING THE WAR

The civilian men in the area during the war were largely engaged in either war production or related activities. Those native to the area

*By R. Wayne Kernodle, Associate Professor of Sociology, College of William and Mary.

were able to remain by virtue of their status as workers essential to the war or because they did not fulfill qualifications for Selective Service. A considerable proportion of civilian males in the population were in-migrants who came to the area primarily to work in war industries. Servicemen comprised the other part of the wartime male population of the Hampton Roads area. These men usually were not in the area by choice. They were in the armed forces to do a specific job and place of residence was entirely secondary. It is thus obvious that for a large part of the male population, the Hampton Roads area had no personal attraction and community group ways were of much less importance than for long-time residents of the area.

The women in the Hampton Roads-Peninsula area during the war period may also be classified in two major categories: (1) the in-migrants, and (2) those native to the area. Female in-migrants manifested several characteristics. First, they were selected by their willingness to break away from home or their former location. For various reasons they had become dissatisfied with their own communities. Secondly, movement into the area was motivated by a desire for new experience. Such new experiences were easily gained in the Hampton Roads area through war jobs, marriage, or association with military personnel. The civilian male population was insufficient to maintain the necessary volume of wartime production and thus unusual opportunities for employment were offered female in-migrants. At the same time, however, the great concentration of young men in the various military establishments of the area was incentive enough to attract certain females into the area. In some areas of the nation the young male population was virtually depleted and women were left without the opportunity for male companionship. Many women migrated to such areas as Hampton Roads in order to be near the men.

Both of the above factors were partially generated by the dissatisfaction of some women with their status during the war. With the opportunity to contribute objectively to the war effort through working at war jobs and at the same time be near a concentrated number of young men, some of these women were able to make a more satisfactory adjustment. Once in the area and in constant association with both civilian and military men, their chances for marriage were enhanced under wartime conditions.

Females who were native to the area shared many of these feelings. In addition, some found it necessary to make adjustments in their day to day activity as husbands, fiances, and boy friends left the area for military service. Especially for girls and women of dating and marriageable age, the need to fill the gaps in their courtship activities often caused them to form hasty associations with the military and civilian in-migrants.

That thousands of men and women were brought together in the Hampton Roads-Peninsula area for various reasons related to the war is beyond question. Such a concentration of population, however, is not an unusual phenomenon in American society. To understand the behavior of these people it is necessary further to characterize the area as it might have appeared in the minds of these people at the time.

As was indicated in earlier chapters, the Hampton Roads region was one in which everything was geared to war. Thousands of men and women from different parts of the nation were thrown together in undefined situations to meet the needs of total war. Little concern was given their personal needs and only haphazard attempts were made to meet individual problems. The absence of parental and primary group control for many of these people left them to make decisions on their own. As long as they fulfilled the requirements of the job or of the army, few controls were exerted upon them in regard to their leisure time. Many were housed in overcrowded rooming houses and barracks where there was complete absence of primary controls and where the individual's behavior was the concern of no one but himself.

In such an area it might be expected that individuals would make their adjustments in various ways and that these adjustments would sometimes cause a change in their usual behavior pattern. The fact that quite a few men and women did exhibit unconventional types of behavior indicated a desire or willingness on their part to break away from the normative patterns of behavior.

In the Hampton Roads-Peninsula area where both men and women were living in nonfamily institutions and where community controls were relaxed, the sexual life flowed in unconventional channels. The wholesale lot of hasty marriages which took place and the increase in promiscuity and prostitution indicate such behavior.

PREMARITAL BEHAVIOR

Courtship etiquette involves a wide range of expected behavior on the part of young people in the premarital association such as the customs of initial contacts, courtship finances, the limits of petting and physical intimacy, and the severance of the relationship. Perhaps the most important aspect of courtship etiquette revolves around mores which deal with petting and other forms of premarital sex adjustment. There is constant change in the range of acceptable behavior in these relationships, and with the advent of war the rate of change was greatly accelerated. Many were unable to adjust to these changes and in the process made problems instead of solving them.

Thousands of unattached young men and women from different parts of the nation were thrown together in undefined situations in the area. The absence of parental and primary group control left young people to make decisions on their own. The shortness of time, the great mobility of the soldier, and the general uncertainty of wartime stimulated new behavior among all people and especially among unmarried youth. The coexistence of a large female population in juxtaposition with a concentration of military personnel in the area tended to create a period of experimentation with new customs and forms of dating, courtship, and the moral sex code in general.

The impact of the war on premarital behavior is exhibited in the increase of this type of case reported by Travelers' Aid-U.S.O. agencies in the area. Table 25 reveals the increase in such problems. It should be pointed out, however, that the figures in this table represent only those cases which were contacted by these two agencies alone.

TABLE 25. CASES NEEDING FURTHER SOCIAL SERVICES REPORTED BY TRAVELERS AID-U.S.O. AGENCIES IN NORFOLK, NEWPORT NEWS, AND PORTSMOUTH, ACCORDING TO SELECTED PROBLEMS, 1942–1945

Type of Problem	1942	1943	1944	1945
Under 16 Alone	39	100	112	88
Illegitimate Pregnancy	2	16	35	94
Runaway	43	156	168	176
Girls in Need of Social Protection	24	305	407	514

Source: Combined annual reports of the two agencies in the given cities.

Throughout the war period there was a definite increase in the number of girls picked up by police on morals charges. Many of these girls were not common prostitutes but were promiscuous with selected servicemen. They knew the region was a concentrated military area and that they could always pick up enough money from servicemen to supplement the wages they were making at their regular jobs.

The Travelers' Aid-U.S.O. in Norfolk reported the following case:

A nineteen year old girl was referred to the agency by her landlady who had rented a single room to the girl and a sailor who claimed to be her husband. After about three weeks the sailor left and did not return. The girl was unable to pay the rent, and finally admitted to the landlady that she was not married. She revealed further to the caseworker that she had been fairly promiscuous, but was not a prostitute. She had lived at Ocean View for some time before coming to Norfolk and had been supported by four different service men. When asked if she were not afraid of pregnancy she replied, "Oh, no, the men I sleep with are sterile." She indicated that she would like to have married before the war, but that she found this kind of life much more interesting since she has plenty of young men friends now, whereas she had not had many at home because she was too fat. She thought that maybe sometime she would get married but at present thought this a much better way to live.[1]

The Social Service Bureau in Norfolk also reported an increasing number of girls picked up on morals charges as the war period lengthened. Other premarital problems centered around the transient females in the area who had come to be near the men in service. All over the country agencies reported a noticeable amount of unrest and instability among adolescent girls and young women. Whereas plans for young men were provided in the armed forces, many young women found their plans for the immediate future uncertain. Volunteer services apparently did not completely satisfy the need for active participation in the war effort.[2] This is evidenced by the marked increase in promiscuity in the area. It was pronounced among unstable and unsupervised girls who sought the attention of servicemen who were out for a final fling prior to their embarkation. There were also cases of girls who thought they had become impregnated by the serviceman but were not sure. The soldier was aware of his departure and of the possibility of an early death. Many felt that life owed them at least this one pleasure before dying or facing death.

The director of the Florence Crittenton Home in Norfolk, a home for unmarried mothers, indicated that "generally speaking, about 90 per cent of the girls now in the Home (June, 1946) had come to their condition through the efforts of servicemen." It was stated further that crowded housing conditions, neglect of children by parents who had either gone to work or who had left the girls with relatives while they had taken jobs outside the area were also factors

1. Records of Travelers' Aid-U.S.O., Norfolk, 1946.

2. See Felix M. Gentile, "The Effects of the War Upon the Family and Its Members," *Psychiatry*, 6 (February, 1943), p. 43.

in causing the increase. Many girls, both below and above twenty years of age, became pregnant by servicemen whom they met in recreational centers sponsored by social agencies, churches, and other organized institutions. The records of the Florence Crittenton Home revealed that several girls in the home as of July, 1946, were former U.S.O. hostesses. This agency increased its intake from 34 cases in 1940 to over 75 during the war years although no additional space was made available. The number would have been much higher had there been sufficient staff and space to care for all the unmarried mothers who applied for assistance.

The Jewish Family Welfare Association of Norfolk also reported an increase in cases of premarital pregnancy. It was pointed out further that enough of these girls were from a high income group to reflect a pattern of breakdown in the sex mores among all the socio-economic groups. Both this agency and the United Seamen's Service Organization reported that one of the most confusing problems of the war period revolved about girl friends and fiancées who chose to live in the port cities of Norfolk, Newport News, and Portsmouth while their boy friends were overseas. Large fleets of men moved in and out of this area during the war. These men were from naval vessels, merchant ships, and troop transports from all over the world. Many of them had money to spend and free time. An untold number of fiancées, unattached girls, and even wives found themselves engaging in premarital and extramarital sex adventures promiscuously, and often for money, with the mobile and to some extent unresponsible population of men. Some entered these relationships out of sheer boredom, some for financial reasons, and others because they believed their fiancés or husbands unfaithful. Many women changed loyalties and accepted new relationships, not once, but many times during the course of the war.

Time and space does not allow the presentation of the many cases of this kind which reflect the impact of the war on the premarital behavior of youth. The foregoing remarks and data are sufficient testimony to reveal some of the premarital behavior in the area during war which affected the family institution as a whole.

MARRIAGE UNDER PRESSURE

While war changes the plans of many people, still it was to be expected that such changes would affect marriage plans which had been arranged prior to the war. It is thus obvious that many of the marriages which occurred in the Hampton Roads area during the war period were those which manifest the characteristics of the ideal type of marriage in normal times and which came as the culmination of ordinary courtship and engagement processes. The fact that the wartime population of the area was comprised predominantly of persons of marriageable age was a major factor in causing the marriage rate to rise far beyond the rate for the nation as a whole. The fact remains, however, that a sizeable proportion of these marriages were contracted in haste and many were motivated by factors closely associated with the war. In order to understand the large scale increase in the marriage rate in the Hampton Roads area at this time, it is therefore necessary to discuss briefly the various motivations to marriage which, if operating in other areas, were certainly less likely to be of as much importance as in Hampton Roads. In such an area, it was to be expected that individuals would make their adjustments in various ways and that their adjustments would sometimes cause a change in the usual behavior pattern. The shortness of time, the great mobility of the servicemen, and the general uncertainty of what separation, war, and international disturbance would bring often made it necessary for men and women who decided to marry to do so without the usual family approval, waiting period, honeymoon, concern over economics, future interpersonal adjustments, living conditions, childbearing, and many other ordinary components of the usual American marriage.

Under such circumstances marriage was often entered into as a means of achieving prestige status, as an escape from boredom, for security, and even with cool calculation of marriage as a means of financial support or escape from military service. Usually the motives to marriage were mixed and very often the individuals involved were not conscious that such motives affected their choice. Others openly admitted such reasons for marriage and choice of mates.

An illustration of marriage for prestige status was reflected in the statement of a young girl in the area who remarked that it was "better to marry a lieutenant than a private but better to marry a private than a civilian and better a civilian than not at all."[3]

Considerable evidence of hasty marriages during this period was found in the case records of social agencies in the area and through interviews with individuals who were in a position to observe them.

Hasty marriages occurred in wholesale lots among girls living in

3. Case Study, Travelers' Aid-U.S.O., Newport News, June, 1943.

the dormitories for unattached women employed at the Navy Yard in Portsmouth. According to a social worker who lived in one of the dormitories during this period "these girls often went, as many as four or five at a time, to South Mills, North Carolina, to get married over the weekend. They would get up a party on Friday night with a bunch of sailors or men working in the shipyards. All would pile into a taxi and drive off down to South Mills and be back Monday morning—married and a little less bored with life for the time being. This was not an unusual case—it happened every weekend."[4]

The haste with which some persons married and the time element involved often negated the possibility of getting a minister to perform the wedding ceremony. That marriages characterized by haste were more widely prevalent during the war was substantiated by a worker in the office of the clerk of court in Norfolk City who had been there since 1942. According to this person, "It was not unusual during 1942, '43, and '44 in Norfolk to see a dozen couples within a half hour get a marriage license from the clerk, walk across the street over there and be married by a notary public. At one point in 1944, it was no longer humorous to see couples turn in surprise when hearing their boy friend or girl friend answer questions regarding age, birthplace, religion or other such information required on marriage licenses. In a great many cases, couples were married within five minutes of the time they got their license."[5]

Cases of hasty marriages, both during and after the war were reported by local ministers, chaplains, and workers in social agencies. The following case illustrates one type of hasty marriage during this period:

This couple met for the first time when the boy, James C., came to Norfolk to join the merchant marine. The girl had been in Norfolk for almost a year and was employed in the shipyard there. They met casually at an afternoon movie when she discovered that she had forgotten her purse and could not purchase a ticket. He offered to take her to a movie and after a brief exchange of courtesies she finally consented to accept. After the movie they decided on eating a bite together. After a tornado courtship of five hours, a trip to South Mills, North Carolina was arranged and they were married that night. The wife was able to find an apartment and the couple lived together for a week, at which time the husband was called away on a voyage. The wife then brought an unmarried girl friend in to live with her. The trouble started with the husband's first leave and

4. Interview with case worker, Travelers' Aid-U.S.O., Portsmouth, August, 1946.

5. Interview with worker in the office of the Clerk of Court, Norfolk, June, 1946.

became progressively worse. He always came in drunk and riotous, and usually brought a bunch of seamen with him. On one of these occasions, in 1943, he came in and demanded the wife to give him back the wedding ring. He also demanded other jewelry and money to "lend a friend of his." He also beat her up rather badly several times and called her "vile names." The last episode occurred when the husband came in drunk and asked for $15 for a friend. When she would not comply with his wishes he called her a dirty rat and beat her. He left then and had not returned. The wife filed for a divorce on the grounds of desertion. The girl who had lived with her testified that the above statements were all true and that the wife had been faithful in every respect.[6]

The case records of the juvenile and domestic relations courts and other social agencies revealed a large number of marriages consciously planned by women whose major purpose was to achieve economic security or temporary financial support. A case in point is one obtained from the Domestic Relations Court in Newport News:

A great number of prostitutes came to Newport News because of the presence of large numbers of soldiers and sailors who were stationed there. Among them were many young girls who later married servicemen, either for presumed love or in order to get the allotment check. At the time the writer was interviewing the head of the domestic relations office, an old time prostitute, well known in the city, came into the office at the request of the probation officer. She had been jailed in Newport News several times and had been given the rapid treatment for syphilis during those periods. She had finally picked out a young sailor some 13 years younger than herself and had persisted in offering him comfort until the $50 a month arrangement had been consummated by marriage. The domestic relations officer was very annoyed with her because he felt that she had trapped the boy into a relationship which could only result in ruining his future life, if he should return to the States alive. The boy was from a rather good family in the rural Middle West, and the officer was certain that the prostitute would not fit into the family situation and that the whole affair would terminate in unhappiness for the boy. The woman was very frank in her explanation of the situation. "It is strictly a business proposition with me," she said. "He wants a little of what I can give him. In return I get the security of the allotment while he is overseas and his insurance if he gets killed." And she added, "If he gets back alive, you needn't worry about any problem with me—and he needn't worry either. If he does get back I'll be so far away that you nor he will ever see me again. If he don't, well then, I get the security as his widow."[7]

6. Chancery Court records, office of the Clerk of Court, Norfolk, 1945.
7. Interview with Probation Officer, Domestic Relations Court, July, 1946.

After she left, the officer went on to explain that this case could be multiplied several times in Newport News and that he was sure it must have occurred frequently throughout the area just before men went overseas when they were on liberty from their ship which was docked in the harbor. To them marriage was merely an easy and conventional way for unmolested sex relationships, and they held little regard for the future, since the future might be short. For the women, in such cases, marriage was merely a business proposition. Other cases could be cited where a girl was married to several servicemen at the same time and was receiving allotments from all of them.

No record is available as to the number of persons who married to escape induction into military service. However, it was well known during the initial phases of the Selective Service Act that married men were to be deferred. Marriages contracted specifically for this reason, of course, were not honored. The increase in the number and rate of marriages when the Selective Service law first went into effect indicated that many men attempted to avoid or delay induction by getting married. The Social Service Bureau in Norfolk, which was responsible, among other things, for the checking of persons who failed to appear for a draft call by reason of a recent marriage, judged that a "considerable number of them were marriages of convenience. Many others were thought to be so, but sufficient evidence was lacking to be conclusive."[8]

The effects of marriages contracted under the pressure of wartime on the family as a basic social unit cannot easily be determined. Some, of course, were doomed to fail from the start. Other couples married in haste and may well have profited from the venture. It is clear, however, that the folkways of courtship, choice of mates, and time of marriage were considerably altered at this time.

IMPACT OF WAR ON THE INITIAL PHASES OF MARRIAGE

Perhaps no other phase of marriage interaction is more important than the first few months when initial adjustments must be made. Such a period includes not only a honeymoon away from the usual associations and life routine, but also the general period of personal adjustments which necessarily occur during the early months of married life.

During wartime there often is too little time for either honeymoons

8. Interview with Mr. Frank Burleson, Director of Social Service Bureau, Norfolk, July, 1946.

or uninterrupted periods during which the young married couple can make these necessary adjustments to each other. Honeymoons in general were limited according to the time and money available. It was not unusual for couples to meet at some city between their respective residences where they would be married and spend a short time together before being separated. The difficulties of travel, hotel reservations, and procurement of adequate housing during the war period often negated much that was traditional behavior in this respect. Some couples were separated for the entire duration of the conflict after having been married only a few hours. Incidences of such separations were not unusual in case history files of the various social agencies in the Hampton Roads area.

An illustration of the adverse circumstances under which many couples began married life during this period was that of a young soldier who was seeking assistance in finding a place to live. He had married in California three months previously while stationed on the west coast. He had spent 12 hours with his wife after the wedding in a hotel room. They were unable to locate housing there, whereupon she returned home to her parents in Minnesota. Later he was transferred to an army base near Newport News and was eager to find living quarters where he and his wife could be together for the 60 days before he was shipped overseas. The only thing available at the time was a single room in a boarding house where several merchant seamen lived. He decided to take it since "this might be the only chance we'll ever have to live together."[9]

Other instances where initial adjustment among married couples was materially hampered by wartime circumstances were reported by the chaplain at Fort Monroe, Virginia. This chaplain indicated that many of the couples whom he married had little opportunity to adjust to each other before being separated by the war. He mentioned at least two cases, which had occurred within two weeks, of couples who had been together less than forty-eight hours before the husband was sent overseas. The more fortunate newlyweds who did have more time were usually forced to live in what the chaplain called "cracker-box houses which, for the most part, provided nothing but the most cramped living quarters. These couples, under the pressure of time, emotions, and inadequate living quarters had little or no opportunity to know each other under normal circumstances."[10]

9. Files of Travelers' Aid-U.S.O., Newport News, July, 1946.

10. Interview with Chaplain, U. S. Army Reserve, Fort Monroe, Virginia, August, 1946.

Several effects of the strain on early marriage relationships grew out of such situations. The attempts of young married couples in wartime to make adjustments to these circumstances caused several changes in marital behavior. To some extent the "dating" of married people, separated from their husbands or wives by the war, was condoned, if not approved by the family and other social groups. Examples of this type of behavior could be found in the increasing number of young married women who became hostesses at U.S.O. clubs, others who evinced no criticism from their own in-groups for dating other men while their husbands were overseas.

The growing number of young married women picked up on morals charges in Norfolk City as the war progressed indicates further the amount of difficulty experienced by these people.

The executive officer of the United Seamen's Service in Norfolk also considered the difficulty of initial marriage adjustment under wartime pressure as paramount among the problems handled by this agency. According to this worker:

> There was . . . an indication of much worry by young wives over periods of separation from their husbands in the merchant marine. They needed help especially in getting through the first periods of separation without turning to undesirable sources for entertainment. The problem was particularly noticeable among the women who had been recently married. Sometimes the wife began going with other men out of loneliness, while others became jealous of what they suspected their husbands were doing. Often they judged their men by the actions of the servicemen they came in contact with everyday. Such judgement was often unfounded. In Norfolk, and other port cities of the area, there were always plenty of uniformed men and civilian workers who were willing to help the young wife of a merchant seaman forget her loneliness.[11]

Initial adjustments of married couples were often hampered by the necessity of one or both members having to live with in-laws during the first few weeks or months of married life. This does not apply to all cases, of course, but where either member of the relationship objected to the arrangement, or was not accepted by the parents, it sometimes destroyed the possibility of successful adjustment.

While these few cases are not in themselves proof that problems of early marriage adjustment were greatly increased by the war alone, they do illustrate the difficulty encountered by thousands of young

11. Interview with Executive Director, United Seamen's Service, Norfolk, July, 1946.

men and women who chose to marry at this time. The continuing difficulties of problems generated under these circumstances need further intensive study. Sufficient data are not available at present to state that such conditions operating in the initial stages of marriage adjustment resulted in family disorganization in each instance. It is possible, however, to suggest that the existence of these circumstances during the war was sufficiently widespread to cause additional strains on certain marriages and was an inherent, if not the major, factor in their eventual dissolution.

LATER MARRIED LIFE

The war also had a disrupting influence upon many marriages of somewhat longer standing. Thousands of families were separated from each other for the first time. During wartime it was often necessary for entire families to suddenly change their habits and modes of living. Husbands and wives were separated and necessarily lived apart for long periods of time, often under great strain both economically and psychologically. In many cases there was the ever present possibility of death of the husband in combat.

In Norfolk the number of females in the resident population whose husbands were absent rose from 3,436 in 1940 to 6,986 in 1944. Of the 91,434 married persons in Norfolk City in 1944, a total of 10,542 were living apart from their husbands or wives.[12] Similar figures prevailed for the other communities in the area where population concentration was the heaviest.

This separation had a definite impact on marriage relations, creating tensions and frustrations. By way of illustration, there was, all during the war, evidence of extreme jealousy existing among men at the various military camps regarding their wives living or visiting in the city near by. Their being so close and yet so inaccessible seemed more aggravating than if the wives had been back home some hundreds of miles away. Boys in disciplinary barracks or in the rehabilitation area who knew that their wives were just a few miles away and possibly seeing other men, or at least being in close contact with them, often caused a great deal of friction. Such new situations in marital living arising out of wartime conditions are indicative of the havoc that war plays with family relationships. This and other factors are involved in the increase of married women picked up on morals charges

12. U. S. Bureau of the Census, *Wartime Changes in Population and Family Characteristics*, Series CA-2, No. 7, p. 7.

and is also evidence that while the soldier is away at war, his girl or wife is open to the advances of other men. The same might be said for civilian war workers who leave their wives behind to go and work in production areas somewhat removed from their local community.

Some men away from home tend to grow away from family relationships. In a congested production area such as Hampton Roads where there were literally thousands of in-migrants in addition to almost 200,000 servicemen, ordinary group controls break down. Many, if not most of these people, are emancipated from close family and community group surveillance and are free to behave in a manner which more or less strikes their fancy. Their patterns of behavior often tend to be quite different from those practiced within their normal primary group.

It has been pointed out that the number of women in the labor force doubled between 1940 and 1944. This meant that many women were out of the home for a great part of the day, thereby decreasing their functions as a homemaker. On the other hand, it increased their status as a wage earner and generally enhanced their opportunity to achieve equality with men in the economic order.

In not a few instances the war offered men and women the opportunity to break away from marriages already in the process of decline. The attainment of wartime jobs with higher wages made it possible for others to dissolve an unsatisfactory marriage whereas before the war they were unable to do so for lack of funds. In the case of some women such jobs often provided sufficient economic freedom to break away from a marriage of some years duration. Cases were not infrequent where married men and women in the area formed strong attachments with new sex partners in the absence of their spouses.

In all probability a large percentage of these long-time marriages which were either already broken or materially disorganized during the war were somewhat unstable in character before that time. The war period often was the excuse for breaking a relationship which actually no longer existed except in name. In other instances the swift separation, the opportunity for new and unfettered associations, and the general psychological temper of the times provided the impetus.

It should be pointed out, however, that separation under wartime conditions also served to strengthen the marriage association of couples who under ordinary circumstances may have dissolved their marriage. The memory of the family relationship in comparison with the somewhat routine aspects of military life or life in an impersonalized area often caused a man or woman to overidealize the past. Thus they often came to view their past married life more favorably in retrospect than they did while involved in the routine necessities of day to day adjustments.

The experiences of men in the actual fighting zones of the war brought significant pressures upon their marriage and family relationships. These difficulties were manifest in a wide array of adjustment problems exhibited by men returning from the overseas expeditions. While it cannot be demonstrated that these war experiences were the sole cause of family maladjustment in any number of cases, they were often the crisis experience which precipitated the final phase of disorganization. The following is one example of many such cases which appeared in the records of social agencies in the area:

> The wife of a young man discharged from the navy in 1945 came to the United Seamen's Service seeking aid in locating her husband. She thought he had joined the merchant marine and "shipped out" with a fruit company. He had left her no money and had made no provision for an allotment. According to the wife, "he stayed around home for a while after his discharge from the navy, but did not do anything much. He acted funny most of the time—sorta surly and not caring. His whole attitude toward me and the children has changed since his going into the navy. He doesn't even know if his last child is a boy or a girl—he never has seen it and doesn't seem to care to. Before the war he was always happy and interested in fixing up the house and playing with the children. You couldn't have asked for a better husband and father. The war just seemed to change his whole outlook. Finally, he just up and left without seeming to care what happened to me or the children. I only found out about his joining the merchant marines from a neighbor boy that he had spent most of his time with after getting out of the navy. Maybe he didn't even join the merchant marine." The agency was able to locate the husband on a merchant ship and encouraged him to provide his family with an allotment, but he would not do so saying that he had no interest in the past. This case was referred to the public welfare office in the county where the wife was a resident.[13]

The additional strains which were brought to bear on marriage and family associations which had been formed sometime before the war often were sufficiently great to cause the more loosely integrated families to break. Such strains also made necessary continuous

13. Records of the United Seamen's Service, Norfolk, 1946.

adjustment and modifications in the stronger families to keep them from dissolution. Basically, the war brought about new situations not ordinarily met by many families. The change in the folkways of marriage under wartime circumstances was often too swift for either one or both members of a marriage relationship.

DISORGANIZATION OF FAMILY RELATIONSHIPS

In cases where there were children in the home, the absence of both parents for most of the day very often led to a relaxation of behavior standards, the shifting of children for themselves, and a decrease in family interpersonal relationships. Evidence of the disorganizing effects of the war on the family were numerous in the social agency records in the area. In many instances mothers took jobs when they had never worked before. They could be bus drivers at $50 a week, taxi drivers at a higher rate, and in more instances workers in the shipyards.

This situation in Newport News has been summarized as follows:

> In April, 1943, approximately fourteen thousand children of eighteen years and under were living in the city of Newport News, of whom between two and three thousand came after the beginning of the war. Forty to fifty per cent of these children were not reached by any youth organization, church or other agency. In 1943, mothers of four hundred and fifty pre-school children were working. A large number of children of school age whose parents were at work remained unsupervised after school hours. There was evidence of family breakdown in an increase of domestic relations court cases.[14]

One index of the disorganizing effect of the war on the family is the number of cases heard by the Juvenile and Domestic Relations Court. The number of juvenile delinquents appearing before this court in Newport News rose from 383 in 1940 to 647 in 1942 and 919 in 1944. Similarly, in Norfolk City the number of cases heard rose from 710 in 1940 to 905 in 1942 and 1,018 in 1944.[15]

The war workers in the area had a great deal of money to spend. Wages were high, even for unskilled labor. Not a few in-migrant workers were making more money in one week during the war than they made in a month or two before that time. The responsibility of spending this increased amount of money was just as disorganizing

14. World War II History Commission, *Newport News during the Second World War*, p. 95.

15. Annual Reports of the Virginia Department of Public Welfare.

to some families as the lack of it had been to other families during the depression. This point is portrayed clearly by the case of an in-migrant family to the Hampton Roads-Peninsula area during the war period. It was not an isolated situation, since similar cases appeared constantly in the files of the various community social agencies in the area. One agency reported that the highest incidence of family problems in a particular community was the result of financial and budgeting difficulties among in-migrant families with incomes above the average. The following case illustrates the point:

This is the case of a couple, both 25 years of age, who had moved into a federal housing project unit from the rural southeast with the early in-migration. There were already two small children in the family and two more had been added since the parents' arrival in the area. The husband worked in the shipyard, and the wife drove a taxi during her spare time. The average weekly income was sufficient for a decent level of living (approximately $130 a week). However, the couple was unable to meet basic financial obligations, such as a $30 a month rental on their housing unit.

The house was always very dirty and flies swarmed over everything. Most of the money was spent on trips to the beach, on movies, and on lavish clothing for the children. Although there was regular bus service at 15 minute intervals to the community store and to the city, the mother insisted on "taking a cab" each day to and from town at the cost of $1.80 round trip, to buy a small supply of groceries. Bus fare could be had at four rides for 25 cents, or cheaper at commuter's rates. The food diet was meagre and insufficient for health. The diet suffered partly because of the mother's inability to understand purchasing techniques in the city and partly because too much money was spent on beach trips, movies and especially on clothing. For example, the mother paid $19.45 for a pongee dress for the eighteen month old baby. At the time the author visited this family, the baby was crawling through a puddle of water on the floor (which it had made) while clad resplendently in pongee. The mother was not at home at the time. One of the small sons said she had gone up town to the store. Fifteen minutes later she came riding home in a taxi with a loaf of bread, a five pound box of chocolate candy, and a hair-net. Several attempts had already been made to get the couple to use a budget. They were unable to follow instructions, and, once when supervision was relaxed they went on a spree to the beach and spent $350 in two days. They would try out the budget for a couple of days after such "sprees" and then get bored with it. "Ain't worth it," they said.[16]

16. Case study made by author in Copeland-Newsome Park federal housing project, July, 1946. Preliminary case work done by Family Counseling Service of Copeland-Newsome Park.

The vast exodus of young men from their homes to the armed forces, the increasing demand for women in essential industries, and the resultant separations of family members from each other had serious repercussions upon the behavior of children. This was particularly true in the Hampton Roads area where every available person was utilized in producing the tools and supplies of war or in training the men for military service. As a consequence many children made their initial life adjustments in home situations either completely devoid of parental care or where contact with parents was at a minimum. Many communities attempted to meet the problems of child care and development during the war through the establishment of day nurseries and other such efforts. In many communities of the area, however, there were neither sufficient trained personnel nor space in which to operate adequate facilities for the growing child population of the area. Further, many of the families that migrated into the area during the time were unable to make optimum use of existent facilities because of their lack of experience in utilizing community resources. This was particularly true of those families who migrated from rural areas of the South into the metropolitan sections of wartime Hampton Roads.

The data on rising juvenile delinquency and parent-child problems suggest the increasing intensity of this type of family disorganization. The reproduction of a few specific cases here provides the reader with a closer view of some of the problems with which children and parents were confronted in the area at the time.

Neighbors reported to the housing officer of a large federal housing unit that a ten year old boy in their section was staying away from school to care for his four smaller brothers and sisters who ranged in age from 16 months to 7 years. The mother worked in the navy shipyard nearby. The father was away in military service. A social worker investigated and found that a Negro woman helped out occasionally, but did not come every day. Conditions in the home were very unsanitary. All of the children looked neglected. When the mother was contacted she became very angry, saying that she paid that "nigger" enough to take care of the children and would have to fire her and get another one.[17]

A number of cases were reported where children of all ages were left at home alone while the mother and father were both at work. There were many instances of preschool age children being left in the

17. Family Counseling Agency, Newport News, June, 1943.

care of neighbors or part-time workers while both parents worked. Other parents arranged work schedules so that one parent was at home while the other worked.

An example of family life under such circumstances was that of a couple in the area who had two children under five years of age. The mother worked the night shift in a restaurant which kept her away from home from 6 P.M. to 4 A.M. The father worked the day shift at the shipyards. According to neighbors who also worked nights and frequented the restaurant, the mother had "taken up" with a married man and frequently went home with him after work. His wife had gone to her daytime job. "Sometimes," the neighbors reported, "the children were left locked in the house all day without anybody there to look out for them." The older boy climbed out the bathroom window one day without any clothes on and woke up the neighborhood screaming. Another day when the children were left alone the older boy broke out four windows with a hammer.[18]

Similar occurrences were reported in many of the crowded housing areas of the region and suggest a part of the repercussions of wartime living on child behavior at that time.

Many children of school age were also left to fend for themselves between the close of school each day and the arrival of parents from work. In one district of a large housing area in Hampton Roads a gang of boys ranging from eight to eleven years of age were reported to be accosting little girls and using "filthy language." In other instances they threw rocks at the girls and generally destroyed neighborhood property. Investigation showed that in all but one case both parents were either working or else the mother worked outside the home and the father was in the service elsewhere.

There were further strains between parents and children in the area when older (high school age) children took war jobs. Often the young people were able to make higher wages than their parents. The sudden acquisition of monetary income among these youths sometimes encouraged them to break away from the family. Others demanded greater freedom from parental control. In many poorly integrated families this sudden rise in economic prestige was actually a crisis situation which they were emotionally and intellectually unprepared to meet. Varying degrees of family maladjustment resulted and personal antagonisms arose as family members became confused as to just what statuses and roles they had in relation to each other.

18. *Ibid.*

CHAPTER VIII

THE WAR AND THE COMMUNITY*

WAR BRINGS PRESSURE upon institutions and causes swift changes in the habits of people. Most of the societal changes during the recent war period grew out of the great movement of population to areas where tools of war were being produced. The population data, given in Chapter V, indicate the great movement of population into the Hampton Roads-Peninsula area which was one of the largest shipbuilding and repair bases in the United States. From 1940 to 1943 the population of the Hampton Roads area increased about 40 per cent in civilian resident population alone. In certain of the communities the increase was much greater, being 152 per cent in one county and 267 per cent in another. In these same two communities in-migrants in 1944 made up close to 50 per cent of the population. In an area of such great population shifts pressure is bound to be brought upon the institutions of the community.

HOUSING

Under such heavy population movements housing shortages became almost fantastic. Families were forced to live in rooming houses, in single rooms, or to crowd up in close quarters in apartment houses or trailer camps in and surrounding the cities. As late as 1945 the author counted 17 Negro men coming out of one trailer early in the morning. Upon investigation he was told by one of the occupants that all seventeen of the men slept there every night and then added, "You shoulda seen it a year or two ago. It were worse'n this."

Housing conditions were already strained in 1940. Of 86,103 dwelling units in the area in April, 1940, only 3.2 per cent were vacant. This was lower than the 4.7 per cent vacancies for 140 metropolitan districts in the United States and below the 5 per cent held by some authorities as necessary to give tenants freedom of choice. For Newport News the vacancy rate was only 2.6 per cent. In 1940, 6.2 per cent of the dwelling units were overcrowded in the urban areas with more than 1.51 persons per room. Rural dwellings were even

*By R. Wayne Kernodle, Associate Professor of Sociology, College of William and Mary.

more overcrowded. In addition nearly one-fourth of the houses were in need of major repairs.[1]

By 1944 there were 132,496 resident-occupied dwelling units in the area or an increase of 54.2 per cent. Of these 4,032 were one room units in hotels and dormitories where twenty-five or more lodgers lived under one roof. In Norfolk in 1944 the gross vacancy rate was 1.3 per cent for whites and 0.7 per cent for Negroes; in Portsmouth it was 1.1 per cent for whites and 0.3 per cent for Negroes. Likewise in Newport News, a November, 1941, Works Progress Administration survey showed a gross vacancy rate of 1.1 and a net habitable vacancy rate of 0.5 per cent. For Negroes the net habitable vacancy rate was 0.1 per cent. These rates were even below the 2 per cent "critical" standard. In the area as a whole 7.2 per cent of the dwelling units in 1944 were overcrowded (more than 1.51 persons per room) and among nonwhites 12.5 per cent were overcrowded.[2]

As a result of this critical situation in housing the defense and war industries in the area had difficulty in securing and keeping employees. The Newport News Shipbuilding and Drydock company reported particular difficulty in keeping Negro employees at full-time work because they were unable to bring their families into the area because of lack of housing. The Norfolk Navy Yard in September, 1941, had 6,284 employees (2,076 Negro) in need of housing. It reported a loss of about 100 employees each month, often because of unsatisfactory housing.

That housing projects for in-migrant workers could not be erected fast enough to keep up with the need for them in 1940 and 1941 was evidenced by the fact that the U. S. Housing Authority late in 1941 had 1,651 applications for the 500 U.S.H.A. defense dwelling units in Newport News and 1,031 applications for the 252 nondefense dwelling units. On the south side of Hampton Roads the U.S.H.A. had 2,937 applications for the 1,010 defense dwelling units constructed there.[3]

Most of the housing projects constructed had to be placed in the near-by counties as most of the land in the cities was already occupied by business establishments and permanent residences. An example of this was the Copeland-Newsome Park federal housing project located

1. U. S. Bureau of Labor Statistics, *The Impact of War on the Hampton Roads Area*, Industrial Study No. 23, December, 1944, pp. 46-48.

2. U. S. Bureau of the Census, *Wartime Changes in Population and Family Characteristics: Hampton Roads Congested Production Area, May 1944*, p. 27.

3. Office of Defense, Health and Welfare Services, Washington, December, 1941.

in Warwick and Elizabeth City counties. At the time of its erection it was the largest single federal housing project in the United States. It covered an area of 1,184 acres and contained 5,200 units. At the peak of the war this project had a combined white and Negro population of some 25,000 persons.

Table 26 presents further evidence of the fact that the bulk of these units was not ready for occupancy until the war had been underway for several years, with the result that the early years of the war were ones of acute congestion. The table also shows that rela-

TABLE 26. WARTIME HOUSING DEVELOPMENTS IN THE HAMPTON ROADS–PENINSULA AREA

	White	Negro
NORFOLK-PORTSMOUTH-NORFOLK COUNTY		
Public Housing		
Number projects	12	5
Number units occupied	9,882	2,219
Men's dormitories	1,219	427
Women's dormitories	496	0
Trailers	1,445	376
Apartments	2,323	666
Houses	4,399	750
Constructed:		
1941 or before	360	0
1942	2,561	179
1943 or later	7,065	2,170
Private Housing		
Number projects	24	4
Number units programmed	3,369	483
Constructed:		
1941 or before	1,371	188
1942	270	0
1943 or later	1,728	295
LOWER PENINSULA		
Public Housing		
Number projects	8	6
Number dwelling units	6,249	2,502
Number beds (in dormitories)	1,098	242
Private Housing		
Number units	2,956	111

Sources: Housing Authority of the City of Portsmouth, "Housing Study," January, 1945; Lower Peninsula Planning Commission, "Survey Study and Recommendations on Housing for the Lower Peninsula of Virginia," March, 1946.

tively little was done in the way of housing for Negroes thus making the shortage even more acute among this part of the population.

THE MAN-WOMAN RATIO

Another important change in the normal pattern of the community under in-migration was in the man-woman ratio. In the civilian resident population there was a surplus of females in the productive age groups, while in near-by military camps there were almost 200,000 males who ordinarily did not belong in the community.[4] Chapter V points out that during the war the number of civilian males per 100 females dropped greatly.

This reduction of the sex ratio had several important effects. First of all it put a social premium on the males in the resident population and also on service personnel when they were on leave. The large-scale increase in female population also suggests the important gains of women with regard to industrial jobs. In 1940 there were 33,480 women between the ages of eighteen and sixty-four in the labor force in the Norfolk-Portsmouth-Newport News Metropolitan District. In 1944 this figure had reached 66,876 or almost double the 1940 figure.[5] In this respect the war period reversed the usual pattern of predominance of males in heavy industrial areas. Other changes growing out of the unbalanced sex ratio were the rise in birth rates; the increase in prostitution, promiscuity, and illegitimate pregnancy as indicated by the increased number of girls taken into the Florence Crittenton Home; and the changing economic status of women.

COMMUNITY SERVICES

During the war period it was extremely difficult to make the ordinary community services available to these dislocated populations. First of all, in-migrants to the area were unaware, to a large extent, of the nature and availability of community aid organizations. Secondly, the agencies in the various communities had neither the funds nor the trained staff needed to handle effectively the problems of the prewar resident population. With the imminence of war a number of community leaders were called to administrative jobs in Washington and elsewhere or to serve in the armed forces. Still others found it necessary to give full time to their expanding businesses. Community

4. Figure 10 shows the change in age-sex composition of the population, 1940 to 1944. Also see Figure 8 for military population.

5. Compiled from U. S. Bureau of the Census, *op. cit.*, p. 7.

agencies thus were unable to make their services available to large groups of in-migrants. A third factor was that these local community agencies were not familiar with the new wartime problems which descended upon them. A detailed account of this may be found in an unpublished paper by the author[6] and in Robert F. Nelson's *Family and Child Welfare Survey*.[7]

Illustrations of the unpreparedness for handling wartime problems by social agencies in the area are numerous. In Newport News "there was no private family agency organized to provide all-around casework services for the community."[8] The job of administering to family and child problems in the city was handled by several different public agencies with little or no coordination of effort. Specialized child-welfare workers were either nonexistent or too busy with other tasks of their agency to give special attention to any particular work. As late as July, 1943, "efforts to obtain at least one child-welfare worker had been unsuccessful. (Other) public and private agencies (were) organized for limited functions and, in most instances, with limited resources. There was little provision for coordination. The Council of Social Agencies was a discussion group without a staff."[9]

In Norfolk, as pointed out by the Nelson Survey, the approach of most family welfare agencies showed little vision as to the needs of families over and above those being met by categorical agencies. "They had little idea of how to reach the group of families needing their services."[10] The Family Welfare Association had neither the respect of, nor cooperative relationships with, other agencies and individuals in Norfolk that would make effective meeting of community needs possible. For instance, the Juvenile Court referred only one case to this agency in 1944, although the court had over 1,000 unofficial cases in the same period, many of which ordinarily should have been handled by the family welfare organization. Referrals were not made because the Juvenile Court believed that the Family Welfare Association could not or would not give adequate service. The crux of the prob-

6. R. Wayne Kernodle, Community Efforts to Deal With Marriage and Family Problems During World War II, Hampton Roads Peninsula Area, 1946, in files of Hampton Roads Studies Committee, College of William and Mary.

7. Robert F. Nelson, *A Survey of Family and Child Welfare Agencies*, Norfolk, Virginia, 1945.

8. U. S. Department of Labor, *Organizing a Community for the Treatment and Prevention of Juvenile Delinquency in Wartime*, Progress Report No. 1 (July, 1943), p. 3.

9. *Ibid.*, p. 4.

10. Robert F. Nelson, *op. cit.*, p. 9.

lem consisted primarily of lack of qualified workers, insufficient resources, and the use of outmoded techniques. The report points out in some detail the inadequacy of all the agencies to handle the increased problems of wartime in the area.

One illustration of the problems created in supplying community services to in-migrant workers is provided by a 1943 estimate that nursery care was needed for 2,760 children, while Norfolk's three day nurseries could accommodate only 150 children.[11]

Community recreational facilities were unable to meet wartime needs. At the beginning of the war and even during the first years of the war, the recreational facilities of the Hampton Roads area, which were scarcely sufficient to care for the normal population, were wholly inadequate to care for the increased number of civilian workers and military personnel. Servicemen, of course, fared better than civilians as war emphasized recreation for servicemen as a function of government.

Appropriations for recreation in the various cities and counties of the area prior to the war were meagre. In 1938, Newport News carried nothing in its budget for recreation. The Norfolk city council appropriated for 1940 only $8,446 to be used for a population of more than 140,000 people. According to the city manager in Newport News there was practically no recreation for war workers. Most of the noncommercial facilities had been erected by the federal government, specifically for servicemen. No existing structures could be found which were usable for recreational purposes to meet civilian needs. There was actually no club or facility where the war worker or his family could go for recreation.

Virtually every foot of space which might have been used for playgrounds, ball fields, and other recreational facilities had been requisitioned by the army to meet its own needs. There were no swimming pools in the community and pollution prohibited swimming in the tidal waters. Near-by beaches and fishing spots were restricted by the Coast Guard. In short, the civilian population had to depend entirely upon the city's commercial recreational facilities which did not begin to meet the needs.[12]

Much the same conditions prevailed throughout the area. Admiral Manly H. Simons, Commandant of the Fifth Naval District, de-

11. Norfolk Housing Authority, *This Is It*, p. 8.

12. *Hearings*, Hampton Roads Naval Affairs Sub-Committee Investigating Congested Areas, p. 24.

scribed the recreational facilities in the Norfolk area as being utterly inadequate, with attempts at alleviation being made only by "religious and charitable organizations, by the United Service Organizations, and by questionable operatives of 'hot spots.'"[13] Most of the work done by the religious and charitable organizations was restricted to uniformed personnel. The few places civilian workers had found recreation before the war became inaccessible through overcrowding by servicemen and the resulting pyramiding of prices. The few attempts at providing recreational facilities for civilian workers and their families during the early part of the war were seriously lacking in coordinated effort.

Thus the war brought recreational needs into sharp focus and spotlighted the paucity of facilities to meet these needs. The efforts of the federal government through the Lanham Act were instrumental in initiating and coordinating recreational programs in the area. The communities themselves eventually came to take over the burden of their own needs in this respect, although it was not until the war was almost over that they really came to grips with this problem.

EDUCATION

The children of the war workers who migrated into the area with their parents put a strain on educational facilities and personnel. Schools were already overtaxed in terms of teacher-pupil loads, classroom facilities, and money spent for educational purposes. In 1939-1940, expenditures per pupil in the area were below the average for the United States. In the same year the average value of school property per pupil enrolled was $227 for the Hampton Roads area, or considerably below the average of $300 for the United States.[14]

The total school population in the area rose from 79,293 in 1940 to 97,520 in 1945. Many of these were children of war workers who had jobs in near-by Norfolk, Portsmouth, or Newport News, but it fell to the lot of the counties where they lived to provide schooling for them. The problems growing out of this situation were immense. The following figures of school population for selected localities in the area in 1940 and 1945 show this clearly:[15]

13. *Ibid.*, p. 24.
14. U. S. Bureau of Labor Statistics, *op. cit.*, pp. 40-41.
15. A. J. Mapp, Impact of World War II Upon School Population, Enrollment, and Attendance in the Hampton Roads Area, (Master's Thesis, Department of Education, College of William and Mary, 1946), p. 18.

	1940	1945
Norfolk City	25,550	23,342
Portsmouth	9,252	9,543
Norfolk County	10,407	23,893
Newport News	7,246	7,797
Warwick County	2,350	5,805
Elizabeth City County	6,542	8,500

Actual school enrollment also increased during the war period with total enrollment rising from 74,302 in 1939-1940 to 93,512 in 1944-1945. Largest increases occurred in the white enrollment because of the heavier in-migration of whites to the area. The increase in enrollment was so great that it was necessary to call on the federal government for aid in building new schools and enlarging existing buildings. In some cases it was necessary to operate on two shifts to take care of the enrollment until facilities could be enlarged.

In addition to increased enrollments there was a vast turnover in student personnel. There was much shifting within the area and it was not unusual for a child to be enrolled in several schools within the Hampton Roads-Peninsula area during the same school year.[16]

The problems of increased enrollments were further complicated by the fact that fewer qualified teachers and school administrators were available. During the crisis period the schools lost many of their most capable teachers, principals, and athletic directors to the armed services, to government jobs, and to war industries which paid considerably higher salaries than the public schools. At the same time the increase in enrollment in some localities made it imperative to secure even more teachers than the school system employed in the prewar years. For example, the number of white teachers in Norfolk County increased from 151 in 1939-1940 to 284 in 1942-1943 and to 497 in 1945-1946. Other counties which had large housing developments experienced similar though somewhat smaller increases in number of teachers required by their school systems. This meant that unqualified teachers often had to be employed. In Norfolk City 35 per cent of the teachers in 1945 held only emergency certificates. In the counties this percentage was higher. The school system suffered some disintegration from this situation, coupled with the overcrowding and lack of adequate facilities, and there was a consequent rise in youth problems. It is not implied here that the school was responsible for all the juvenile delinquency and other youth problems which occurred in

16. *Ibid.*, p. 23.

the area. Rather it is implied that overtaxing the schools resulted in certain youth problems which might not otherwise have occurred.

RELIGION

Churches had difficulty reaching war workers and thus often lost the resulting opportunity to serve them. In-migrants to the area had no attachment to any particular local church and were not as likely to affiliate with one for the relatively short duration of their stay in a community. They were not under the pressures of the normal neighborhood and congregational mores. Pastors, even though they desired, did not have the time to have personal contact with the thousands of new persons who came into the area. Too, the wartime recreational program of the church was aimed at entertaining and serving the service personnel stationed in the area, and thus lost another possible point of contact with the civilian in-migrants.

Most denominations made attempts to increase their facilities to meet the larger population. Chapels were erected in or near the larger housing projects; trained workers were brought into the area. Annual records, however, giving figures on membership of two of the leading Protestant denominations in the South—Presbyterian and Baptist—indicate that between 1940 and 1943 membership in the area increased 11.3 and 18.2 per cent, respectively, as compared with an increase of 50 per cent in the civilian population. Since a complete religious census has not been taken since 1936, it is not possible to compare the prewar religious structure of the area with that of the war and early postwar years. Since the majority of in-migrants to the area however came from the southern states which are traditionally Protestant in religion, it is quite probable that there has been no material change in the religious structure of the region since the 1936 religious census.

ECONOMIC ORGANIZATION

The effects of the drastic economic changes were felt in all institutions of the community. The increased military and civilian demands for goods and services at a time when millions of men were in military service drew large numbers of women and children into industry. The results in terms of the changing status of women and children as wage earners brought about new habits in the normal pattern of family life. The wife worked on an equal wage base with her husband or with other men. She was released from certain household duties or attempted to carry the full domestic load as well as the industrial job.

Working outside the home during wartime also increased the contacts of women, making them more susceptible to extra-familial relationships. According to Judge H. G. Smith of the Superior Court in Newport News, "The new location, the increase in wages because of war work, and the possibility of meeting a new person potential of becoming a marriage or sex partner, were the major factors in many divorces and other family problems."[17] He also pointed out the loss of interest in child bearing and child care on the part of the working woman and increase in the desire of women for property in their own name.

Children of school age were also affected by this upsurge in economic activity. The movement of high school youths into war production industries and other jobs gave them the sense of contributing to the war effort before they were old enough to be in active military service. In Norfolk in May, 1944, 33.1 per cent of the males and 16.5 per cent of the females from fourteen through eighteen years old were in the labor force.[18] The percentage of school withdrawals to total school enrollment rose from 11.7 for whites in 1939-1940 to 19.9 in 1941-1942 (which was the highest year). For Negroes the percentage rose from 9.7 to 14.5 for this period. In Newport News, by the end of the 1942-1943 school year, about 400 of the 600 to 700 employable high school boys and girls (sixteen years and over) were employed. Similar figures were reached in other communities of the area.[19]

The relatively high wages paid to these boys and girls, often considerably higher than salaries made by their parents, helped to produce a feeling of economic independence from the family and tended to break down certain controls on the behavior of young people formerly exerted by the parents.

EVIDENCES OF PERSONAL AND SOCIAL DISORGANIZATION

Wartime increases in divorce and crime rates evidenced growing personal and social disorganization.

Divorce

The divorce rate in the Hampton Roads-Peninsula area, which in 1940 was already higher than that for the nation or the state, continued to stay well above the rate for the United States or Virginia

17. Personal interview, July, 1946.
18. U. S. Bureau of the Census, *op. cit.*, p. 14.
19. A. J. Mapp, *op. cit.*, Table 20.

during the war years and showed a definite increase in the first postwar year. Table 27 shows that during the entire war period the cities in the area exhibited a much higher rate than that of the nation or the state. As was already true in 1940 this relatively high rate reflected the urban and generally heterogeneous character of this particular section of the area.

An interesting phenomenon which began shortly after the beginning of the war and increased as the war lengthened was that of the high divorce rate among nonwhites. Whereas in 1940 the divorce rate per 1,000 white population in the Hampton Roads-Peninsula area was 4.5 and 2.9 among the nonwhites, by 1942 the nonwhite rate surpassed that of the whites and continued so into the postwar period. This probably does not reflect increased family disorganization among the Negroes as much as increased awareness of legal rights and greater economic well-being during the prosperous war years. For many it was the first time that a divorce was financially possible.

TABLE 27. NUMBER OF DIVORCES PER 1,000 POPULATION, BY COLOR, UNITED STATES, VIRGINIA, AND HAMPTON ROADS-PENINSULA AREA, 1940–1946

Place	Color*	1940	1942	1944	1946
United States	T	2.0	2.4	2.9	4.4
	W				
	C				
Virginia	T	1.9	1.8	2.3	3.0
	W	2.1	1.7	2.0	2.8
	C	1.4	2.2	3.0	3.8
Hampton Roads Area	T	3.9	3.4	3.8	4.7
	W	4.5	3.3	3.1	4.0
	C	2.9	4.3	5.4	6.2
Norfolk	T	5.3	5.2	5.6	5.7
	W	6.4	4.9	4.9	5.1
	C	3.0	5.7	7.0	6.9
Portsmouth	T	4.4	5.4	6.0	8.0
	W	5.1	4.5	5.0	6.2
	C	3.3	6.9	7.4	10.5
Newport News	T	4.8	3.5	6.0	6.9
	W	4.2	2.4	4.9	6.3
	C	5.7	5.0	7.4	7.7

*T–total; W–white; C–colored

Sources: United States rates from *Statistical Abstract;* Virginia and Hampton Roads rates from Virginia Bureau of Vital Statistics.

It is probably significant to note that the increase in the divorce rate in the Hampton Roads area from 1940 to 1942 was due entirely to the increase in divorces among the nonwhites. The divorce rate among whites of the area actually decreased during the war and even in the postwar year of 1946 was below the rate for 1940.

Crime

Using the same index to measure this phenomena as was used in Chapter II, that of the number of offenses known to the police as reported in the *Uniform Crime Reports*, it is seen that the war had a startling effect on personal and social disorganization in the Hampton Roads communities. Figure 17 compares the rate for 1940, 1943, and 1945 for various classes of crimes for the three major cities of the area as compared with other cities in the nation of similar size. This chart shows that the rates for most crimes in the Hampton Roads cities doubled and some tripled during the war. In most classes of crimes, Newport News was the "most criminal" of the Hampton Roads cities during the war and its rates were three to five times greater than those for cities of similar size in the United States.

Since the rates are based on 1940 population, this picture may be slightly distorted because of the great population increases in the Hampton Roads cities. Even if the rates are adjusted on the basis of the estimated actual population in 1943 and 1945 the rates for the Hampton Roads cities remain much higher than those for the rest of the nation.

In comparing crime rates of various cities in the United States,[20] it was found that Norfolk was one of the "most criminal" of the major cities in the nation. An index number was obtained for each city based on the number of offenses known to the police per 100,000 population for the various classes of crimes. The index numbers for Norfolk are as follows:

	Norfolk		
	1940	*1946*	*All Cities*
Murder	119	278	100
Robbery	150	286	100
Aggravated Assault	100	198	100
Burglary	144	163	100
Larceny	130	158	100
Auto Theft	172	191	100
Composite Index	136	212	100

20. Austin L. Porterfield and Robert H. Talbert, *Crime, Suicide and Social Well-Being* (Fort Worth, Texas: Texas Christian University, 1948).

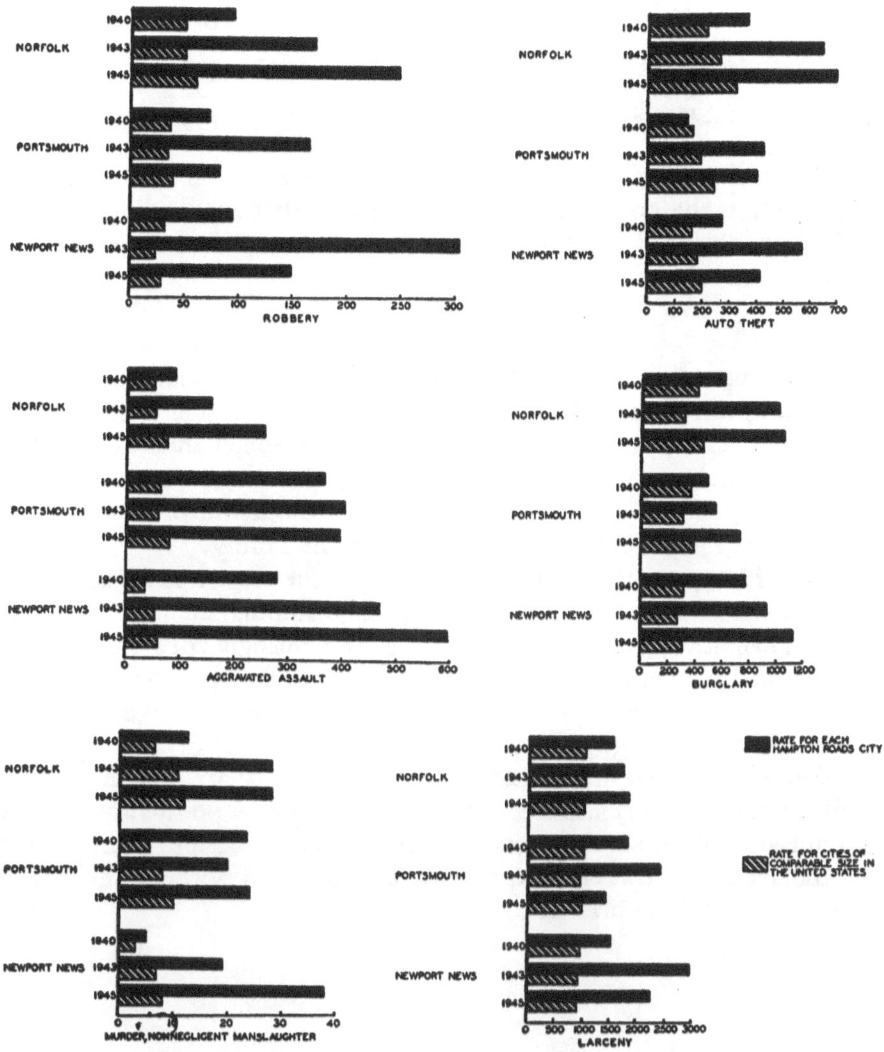

FIGURE 17. NUMBER OF OFFENSES KNOWN TO THE POLICE PER 100,000 INHABITANTS, HAMPTON ROADS CITIES COMPARED WITH CITIES OF COMPARABLE SIZE, BY CLASSIFICATION OF OFFENSE, 1940, 1943, AND 1945

Source: Uniform Crime Reports, 1940, 1943, and 1945.

In 1946 Norfolk ranked second only to Greensboro, North Carolina, among 86 major cities in the composite index. In an aggregate crime index for 402 cities in the United States in 1946 the Hampton Roads cities were as follows:

402 cities	100
Newport News	272
Norfolk	235
Portsmouth	159

Thus, if crime is to be used as an index of personal and social disorganization the conclusion must be reached that the war period saw a definite increase in such disorganization in the cities of the Hampton Roads area.

SUMMARY

The impact of the Second World War on the social structure of the Hampton Roads area is readily seen in this analysis of war-influenced changes in the vital statistics, the social institutions, and the social behavior of the people during this time. Many of these changes are brought into sharper focus through the presentation of their impact upon the basic institution of the family.

The Hampton Roads area, even before the war, was an area with a somewhat unstable social structure. The impingement of wartime conditions, including heavy increases in heterogeneous population, widespread inadequacy of social agencies, and changing behavior patterns, made the area even more unstable in this respect. In a sense, the glue of the society gave way.

Since all the major institutions within a society are interdependent and interacting, it is apparent that such changes as pointed out above would also place severe pressures on the economic and political life of the area. It is therefore appropriate to proceed with an analysis of the nature of these pressures.

III

IMPACT OF THE WAR UPON THE ECONOMIC STRUCTURE

Newport News Shipbuilding and Dry Dock Company

"To many residents of the Hampton Roads communities, especially Newport News and Portsmouth, the 'impact of the war' means just one thing—shipbuilding."

CHAPTER IX

THE VOLUME AND STRUCTURE OF ECONOMIC ACTIVITY*

ANALYSIS of the war's impact is complicated by several factors. First, some of the channels through which the war's influence was felt were themselves passive elements which experienced the war's effects as well as active carriers of the impact. A second complication grows out of the fact that census reports comparable to those drawn upon in sketching the 1940 economy will not be available, except for a few items, until after the Census of 1950 has been tabulated. To the extent that the long-run effects of the war upon the region's economy may be clearer by 1950 than during and immediately after the war, this delay might be advantageous. On the other hand, the immediate and contemporaneous changes of 1939-1945 were of such magnitude and necessitated such drastic adjustments throughout the Hampton Roads economy as to warrant careful study of what statistics are available if the full impact of war upon this and other strategic areas is to be understood. It is recognized, of course, that war influences did not disappear immediately after V-J Day. Accordingly, considerable attention will be given in the concluding chapter of this volume to the postwar economic developments in the Hampton Roads region with primary emphasis here upon what happened to the region's economy from 1939 to 1945.

WARTIME CHANGES IN VOLUME OF ECONOMIC ACTIVITY

A logical first step in analyzing the impact of World War II upon the Hampton Roads-Peninsula region is the measurement of the changes in volume of economic activity during the war years. While shipbuilding has been the leading activity, the great volume of trades and services needed by the swollen population prevents manufacturing employment or any other single index from giving the full picture of wartime economic changes. Three approaches to the problem of measuring the magnitude of economic change during 1939-1945 are

*By Charles F. Marsh, Professor of Economics and Business Administration, College of William and Mary.

suggested. One is a comparison of fluctuations in shipyards employment and military population, the two major channels through which the war came to Hampton Roads, with changes in the volume of economic activity as measured by a composite index. A second consists of a comparison of the behavior of the individual series making up the composite index. The third is an analysis of changes in the size of the labor force and its employment.

Changes in Shipyards Employment, Military Population, and Volume of Business

Monthly indexes of shipyards employment, military population, and the volume of business, with 1939 as a base, are portrayed in

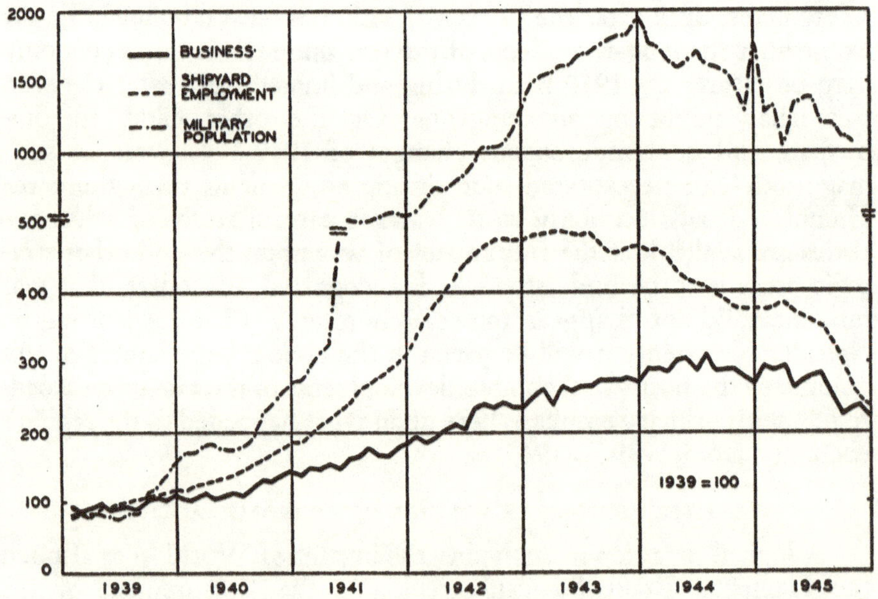

FIGURE 18. INDEX OF BUSINESS VOLUME, SHIPYARD EMPLOYMENT, AND MILITARY POPULATION, HAMPTON ROADS-PENINSULA AREA, 1939-1945

Figure 18. The first two indexes are derived from data presented in Chapters IV and V. (See Figures 5 and 8). The composite index of business activity requires some explanation.[1] It is a rather unorthodox

1. This index was developed by Mary Hudson Robinson from data compiled by her and by the author. All of these data and Mrs. Robinson's explanation of procedures used are in the files of the Hampton Roads-Peninsula War Studies Committee at the College of William and Mary.

index combining several traditional measures of economic change with sales data for particular business firms derived from field studies made by the author. In includes the following series:

1. Kilowatt hours of electricity delivered
2. Dollars of postal receipts
3. Gallons of water pumped
4. Bank debits to individual accounts
5. Dollar sales, retail chain grocery company
6. Dollar sales, wholesale drug company
7. Dollar sales, wholesale plumbing and heating company
8. Tons sold, retail coal merchant
9. Dollar sales, large department store
10. Dollar sales, small department store in Negro trading center
11. Dollar sales, large retailer of women's clothing

All except the last four of the above series, which relate to representative Norfolk or Newport News firms, cover Norfolk, Portsmouth, Newport News, and environs. Bank debits cover only these three central cities and tributary banking territory. Figures for electricity and postal receipts include Hampton and Williamsburg in addition. Water pumpage includes Hampton, Suffolk, and Virginia Beach but not Williamsburg. The two wholesalers' figures represented sales throughout the entire Hampton-Roads-Peninsula area and adjacent localities outside the area. In general, it does provide fair coverage of the region. Monthly figures for each of the above series were adjusted for seasonal variation and relatives, with the monthly average for 1939 as a base, computed. The composite index for each month, 1939-1945, inclusive, is the unweighted geometric mean of these relatives. While the eleven groups of data vary considerably in importance, no sound basis exists for assigning weights to such a diverse set of data. The unweighted geometric mean has been used, accordingly, as the best available alternative to a system of weighting.

It is obvious from Figure 18 that increases in the Hampton Roads military population and shipyards employment, as would be expected, were accompanied by increases in the volume of general business activity. Two other conditions shown by the chart are not so obvious and warrant special consideration. One is that business increased to a much smaller degree than either the number of soldiers and sailors stationed in the region or the number of shipbuilding employees. Business activity experienced about a three-fold increase during the war years whereas military population rose to almost twenty times the 1939 average and shipbuilding employment to almost five times the prewar level. In the second place, there was a definite time lag of the business index behind the two indexes of war activity. While shipbuilding reached its peak in April, 1943, and the highest military population was reached in December, 1943, the peak index for economic activity was attained in July, 1944. Similarly, the business downturn in 1944 and 1945 lagged behind the decline of the two indexes of war activity. By November, 1945, indeed, the indexes for business volume and for shipyards employment had become virtually identical.

It appears from the above comparisons that wartime changes in the volume of economic activity in a given area tend to be more closely associated with changes in employment in such a war industry as shipbuilding than with changes in military population. Can it be reasoned further that communities have more to gain economically from expansion of war industries employing civilians than from increased military population? One reason for answering this question affirmatively is the tendency for most soldiers and sailors to live on the posts and to buy much of their goods and services at ship service stores, post exchanges, and commissaries. Some idea of the extent to which the

TABLE 28. SALES BY VARIOUS TYPES OF SHIP SERVICE STORES, FIFTH NAVAL DISTRICT, JANUARY–JUNE, 1944

Type of Facility	Number of Sales Outlets	Sales (in thousands of dollars)
Stores	100	9,803
Restaurant	4	110
Soda Fountain	23	1,194
Laundry	21	808
Barber Shop	42	176
Cobbler	15	117
Presser	21	203
Photographer	5	111
Gasoline Station	7	63
Garage	2	79
Beauty Shop	6	28
Vending Machine	30	255
Special Services	17	117
Miscellaneous	21	145
All Facilities	314	13,209

Source: Monthly financial reports of Ship Service Stores filed at Fifth Naval District Headquarters, Norfolk, Virginia.

purchasing power of sailors failed to reach civilian businesses of various types adjacent to naval establishments is provided by Table 28. Incidentally, the figures shown in the table understate the volume done by service enterprises which might have swelled the coffers of civilian businesses, since prices of goods and services in navy stores were usually below those of private firms.

Changes in Volume of Particular Economic Activities Included in the General Index

Analysis of the behavior of the individual series included in the composite index of business activity shown in Figure 18 provides an even sharper picture of the impact of the war upon the volume of economic activity in the Hampton Roads area. It also provides a check on the validity of the composite index. The magnitude of the wartime growth in each type of activity and the month in which the peak was reached, as compared with the composite index, is shown below:

	Maximum Wartime Volume	
	Index (1939 ave.–100)	*Month*
Wholesale plumbing and heating	758	December, 1941
Small department store, Negro center	323	February, 1943
Bank debits	303	September, 1943
Chain grocery	321	December, 1943
Retail coal	343	July, 1944
Large department store	346	September, 1944
Postal receipts	314	October, 1944
Wholesale drug	359	November, 1944
Electricity delivered	253	January, 1945
Women's clothing	411	March, 1945
Water consumption	268	April, 1945
Composite index of general economic activity	310	July, 1944

It will be noted that nine of the eleven series showed wartime maxima ranging within 20 per cent of the maximum of 310 for the composite index. Only wholesale plumbing and heating and sales of women's clothing showed considerable deviations from this average. A similar tendency for the individual indexes to cluster fairly closely around the composite index is shown by the annual averages for the eleven types of activity and for the composite index presented in Table 29. Only wholesale plumbing and heating departed widely from the annual composite index in each of the war years. Sales of women's clothing deviated from the general index by more than 20 per cent only in 1945, the year in which its peak monthly sales occurred. Consistently high sales to government and private agencies for war-related housing and other construction accounts for the great increases in plumbing and heating sales. The relatively high 1945 sales of women's clothing reflected both higher prices for luxury items and the fact that many women, both white and colored, for the first time in their lives enjoyed sufficiently high incomes to buy high-priced lines.

TABLE 29. ANNUAL CHANGES IN VOLUME OF SELECTED ECONOMIC ACTIVITIES, HAMPTON ROADS-PENINSULA AREA, 1940–1945 (1939 = 100)

Selected Economic Activities	1940	1941	1942	1943	1944	1945
Kilowatt hours	115.5	144.6	185.0	222.1	233.8	234.9
Postal receipts	113.0	145.4	183.8	234.9	292.1	278.1
Water consumption . .	112.0	135.5	164.8	215.2	249.5	256.5
Bank debits	116.7	154.7	223.2	239.2	252.0	253.2
Retail grocery	116.0	154.5	223.3	264.9	290.3	269.7
Wholesale drug	118.4	177.5	255.3	300.7	323.5	309.7
Wholesale plumbing and heating	166.6	329.9	392.4	394.7	517.0	326.7
Retail coal	122.4	139.3	188.3	251.7	257.8	201.6
Department store (large)	119.3	161.3	223.3	260.2	284.2	277.7
Department store (small)	119.2	153.9	223.6	266.1	265.8	222.5
Retail women's clothing	121.6	172.8	235.7	302.9	342.5	353.8
Composite Index	119.4	163.1	219.1	264.9	291.8	264.7

Source: Data furnished by the various agencies and firms to the Hampton Roads-Peninsula War Studies Committee, College of William and Mary.

The months in which the maximum volume of each activity was reached tell an interesting story. The boom in sales of plumbing and heating supplies shortly after Pearl Harbor was apparently caused both by panic buying by local contractors stocking up with essentials before government controls should set in and by increased war construction. The early 1943 peak in department store sales in the Negro trading center coincided with the peak employment in shipbuilding and several military construction projects in the region which brought many Negro in-migrants into this store, according to the store's owner, to buy work clothes. The late 1943 and 1944 maxima for bank debits, postal receipts, retail coal and department store sales, and wholesale drug business reflected the continued rise in population and purchasing power, shipping of Christmas packages to overseas service men and women, and, to a moderate degree, price increases. Price increases no doubt played a somewhat greater part in swelling department store and wholesale drug sales than other types of activity because of the many luxury items sold which were subject neither to price control nor to rationing. The fact that electricity and water consumption lagged both in amount and time behind the other series is attributable to shortages of material and labor which prevented plants from being expanded rapidly enough to meet wartime demands as well as to the fact that volume is expressed in kilowatt hours and gallons, respectively, and thus is completely free from the influence of price increases.

For the most part, the highest annual indexes for each series were reached in the year in which the monthly peaks occurred. The year 1944 showed the peak annual figure of 291.8 for the composite index as compared with the monthly maximum of 310 in July, 1944. Only plumbing and heating, bank debits, and chain grocery sales showed annual maxima in years other than those in which the monthly peaks occurred. The December, 1941, peak sales for the plumbing and heating wholesaler was a "sport," statistically speaking, as sales in the rest of 1941 as well as in 1942 and 1943 were far below those of that first war month and the largest annual sales were not realized until 1944. The fact that annual bank debits were highest in 1945 and chain grocery sales in 1944, in contrast to 1943 monthly peaks for those two series, indicates merely that declines from these earlier monthly maxima during later months were gradual.

It appears from the above analysis of the behavior of the individual series included in the composite index of general economic volume that this index, unorthodox though its inclusion of sales of particular firms and government activities along with such traditional business index components as bank debits and electricity consumption may be, does provide a reasonably accurate picture of the war-related economic changes in the Hampton Roads-Peninsula area. It may also make some contribution to the broader problem of developing helpful indexes of business activity for regions generally.

Changes in Labor Force and Employment

The changes in the Hampton Roads labor force between 1940 and 1944 and the degree to which it was employed in each year, as mirrored in the 1944 special report of the Bureau of the Census,[2] provides

2. The 1944 Census of Congested Areas figures are comparable with those of 1940 except that the 1940 Census included the relatively small number of members of the armed forces living in the area and students away at resident colleges. It covered only the cities of Norfolk, Portsmouth, South Norfolk, Hampton, and Newport News and the counties of Norfolk, Princess Anne, Warwick, and Elizabeth City.

further information on changes in the volume of economic activity during the war. The total labor force for the area covered in this special census rose from 153,881 to 228,578, or almost 50 per cent, as compared with an increase of only 40 per cent in the total population fourteen years of age and over. (See Table 21.) In other words, the proportion of the population in the labor force increased through the entry of housewives, children, and old people.

Still further evidence of the increased economic tempo during the war years in the Hampton Roads area is provided by the increase in employment from 91 to 99 per cent of the labor force. Unemployment had virtually disappeared by 1944 not only among white male workers but also among women and Negroes, groups in which employed workers had comprised in 1940 a somewhat smaller proportion of the labor force than was the case with white male workers. Moreover, at the time of the 1944 Census, more than 70 per cent of all employed workers in the region were putting in forty-eight or more hours per week, with 10 per cent working in excess of sixty hours. With the war's end, however, unemployment grew. By December 1, 1945, 4.75 per cent of the non-agricultural labor force of the entire Hampton Roads-Peninsula area was unemployed.[3] That this was largely the result of layoffs of shipyards workers is indicated by the fact that 16.6 per cent of Newport News' labor force of 22,700 workers were unemployed. The tendency, however, for many of these workers to leave for their homes in North Carolina or elsewhere almost immediately prevented this unemployment from being a serious problem for the Newport News community.

It is clear that the quantitative pressure of wartime economic activity upon the labor resources of the area was overwhelming and that this pressure could be met only through migration from other areas, entry into the labor force of groups traditionally outside this force, and more intensive and more efficient utilization of employed workers by management.

CHANGES IN ECONOMIC STRUCTURE

Changes in the structure or organization of the economic life of the Hampton Roads-Peninsula area can be indicated by studying changes in the number and size of business firms, the relative importance of the various types of economic activity, and in the internal structure of each of the leading classes of activity.

3. Files of the Richmond office, U. S. Employment Service.

Changes in the Number of Business Firms

Dun and Bradstreet reference books provide the best information as to changes in the number of firms in the Hampton Roads communities during the war years, though some firms are too small or too recently established to be included in these listings. In spite of such discouraging factors as shortage of manpower, managerial as well as rank and file, shortage of materials and equipment, and government restrictions, the total number of firms in the area increased from 5,322 in September, 1939, to 5,759 in July, 1945, or 8.21 per cent.[4] Most of this increase took place during the last year of the war, however, as only 5,440 firms, representing a mere 2.2 per cent increase, were listed in July, 1944.

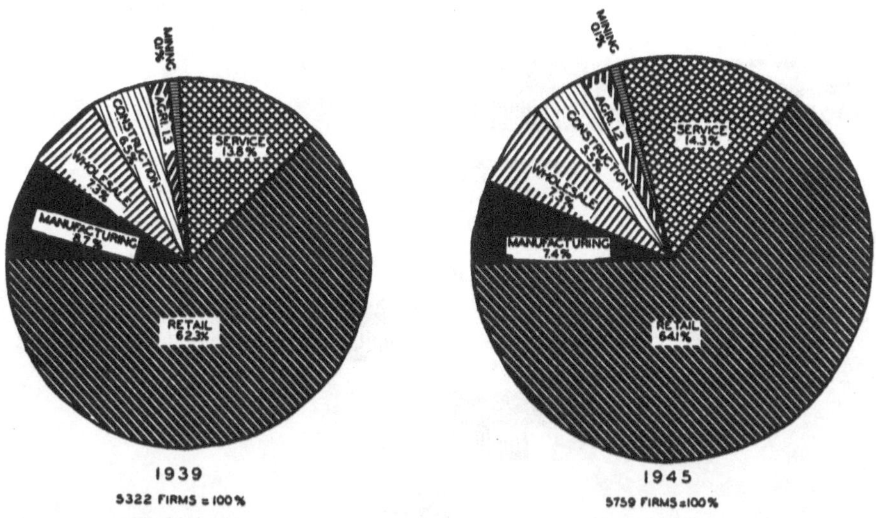

FIGURE 19. BUSINESS STRUCTURE, HAMPTON ROADS-PENINSULA AREA, 1939 AND 1945

Source: Dun and Bradstreet Reference Book, September, 1939 and July, 1945.

Surprisingly little change occurred during the war years in the relative importance of the major types of business, as measured by the number of firms. (See Figure 19.) Retailing establishments continued to predominate and increased from 62.3 per cent of the total number of firms in 1939 to 64.1 per cent in 1945. Service trades also

4. The Marketing and Research Division of Dun and Bradstreet prepared special compilations for the Hampton Roads-Peninsula War Studies Committee from which these figures were derived.

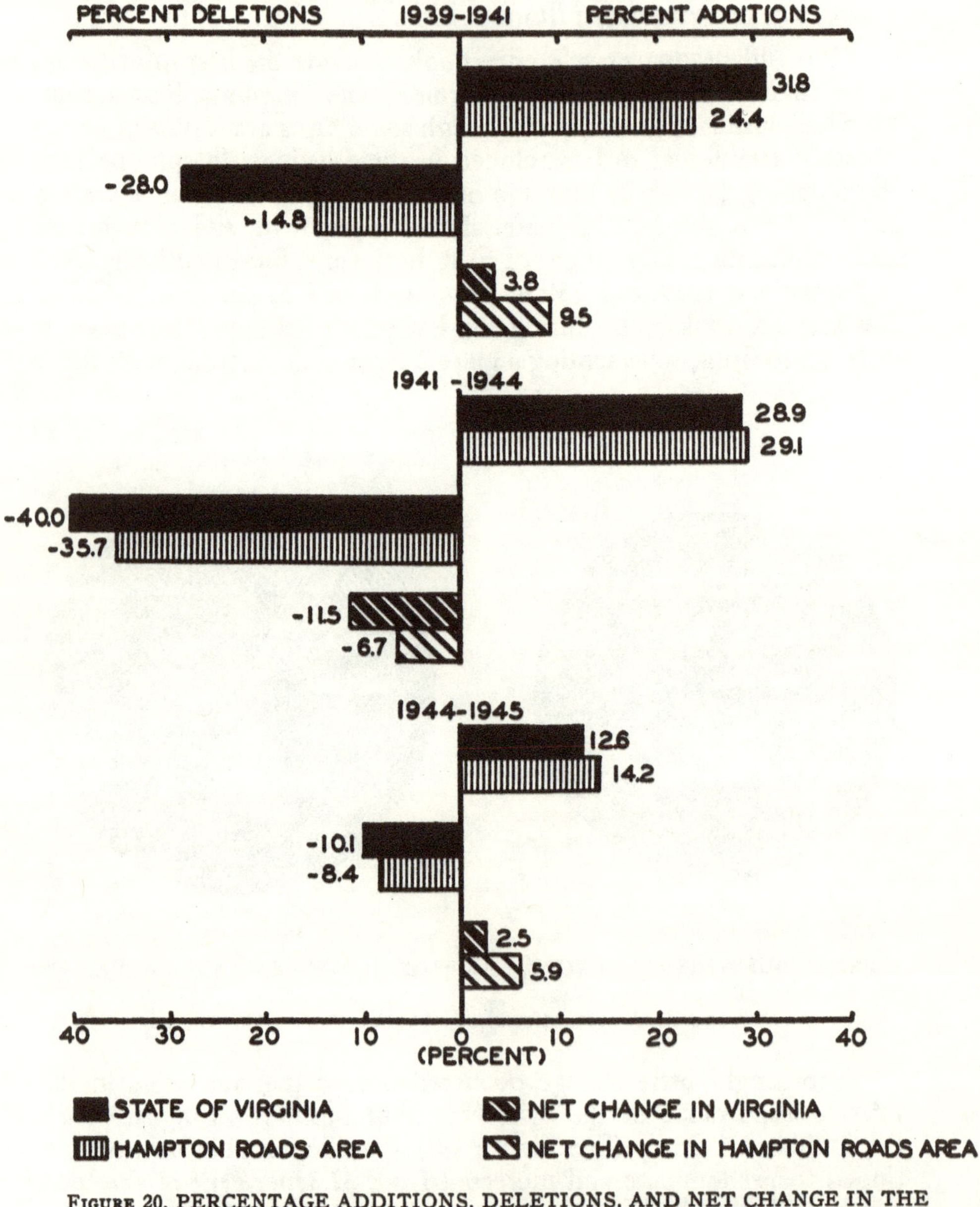

FIGURE 20. PERCENTAGE ADDITIONS, DELETIONS, AND NET CHANGE IN THE NUMBER OF BUSINESS ESTABLISHMENTS IN THE HAMPTON ROADS-PENINSULA AREA AS COMPARED WITH VIRGINIA, 1939-1941, 1941-1944, AND 1944-1945

Source: Dun and Bradstreet Reference Books.

increased slightly. The relative numerical importance of manufacturing and construction firms, on the other hand, declined. Other classes showed little change.

Figure 20 compares the turnover of business firms in the Hampton Roads communities with that for Virginia as a whole during the war. For each of the three periods shown on the chart, the Hampton Roads area showed a smaller percentage of deletions of firm names from the Dun and Bradstreet reference book than did the state in general. Except for 1939-1941, the Hampton Roads percentage of additions of firm names to the total number of names listed exceeded that for the state. For each of the three periods, the net change was in favor of Hampton Roads, though during the 1941-1944 period the deletions exceeded additions for both Virginia and Hampton Roads. It is evident that war activities in the Norfolk-Portsmouth-Newport News region stimulated the establishment of new businesses and kept old businesses alive to a greater degree than in the rest of the state, which, with a few exceptions, received much smaller war stimuli.

Changes in Size of Business Firms

The size of business firms is customarily measured in terms of value of product, value added by manufacture, amount of invested capital, and number of employees. Of these indices, only the latter is available for the entire Hampton Roads-Peninsula area during the war years, though certain data concerning the value of product of a group of Norfolk manufacturing firms will be considered later in this chapter. The fact that all firms covered by unemployment insurance which employ eight or more persons and some smaller firms make quarterly reports to the Virginia Unemployment Compensation Commission as to the number of workers employed during each month of the preceding quarter makes it possible to construct from the U.C.C. cards a rough picture of changes in the size of firms during the period 1939-1945. The total number of firms reporting and the number of firms in each size group increased from 1939 to 1944. From 1944 to 1945, however, while the total and the number of firms in the three smaller groups continued to grow, the three larger groups—those employing more than fifty persons—showed a decline though still in excess of 1939. Percentagewise, the end of the war found employers of twenty-five or fewer to be relatively more important in the total picture and those employing between 26 and 100 workers to have declined in relation to the total group. The two largest groups of employers—

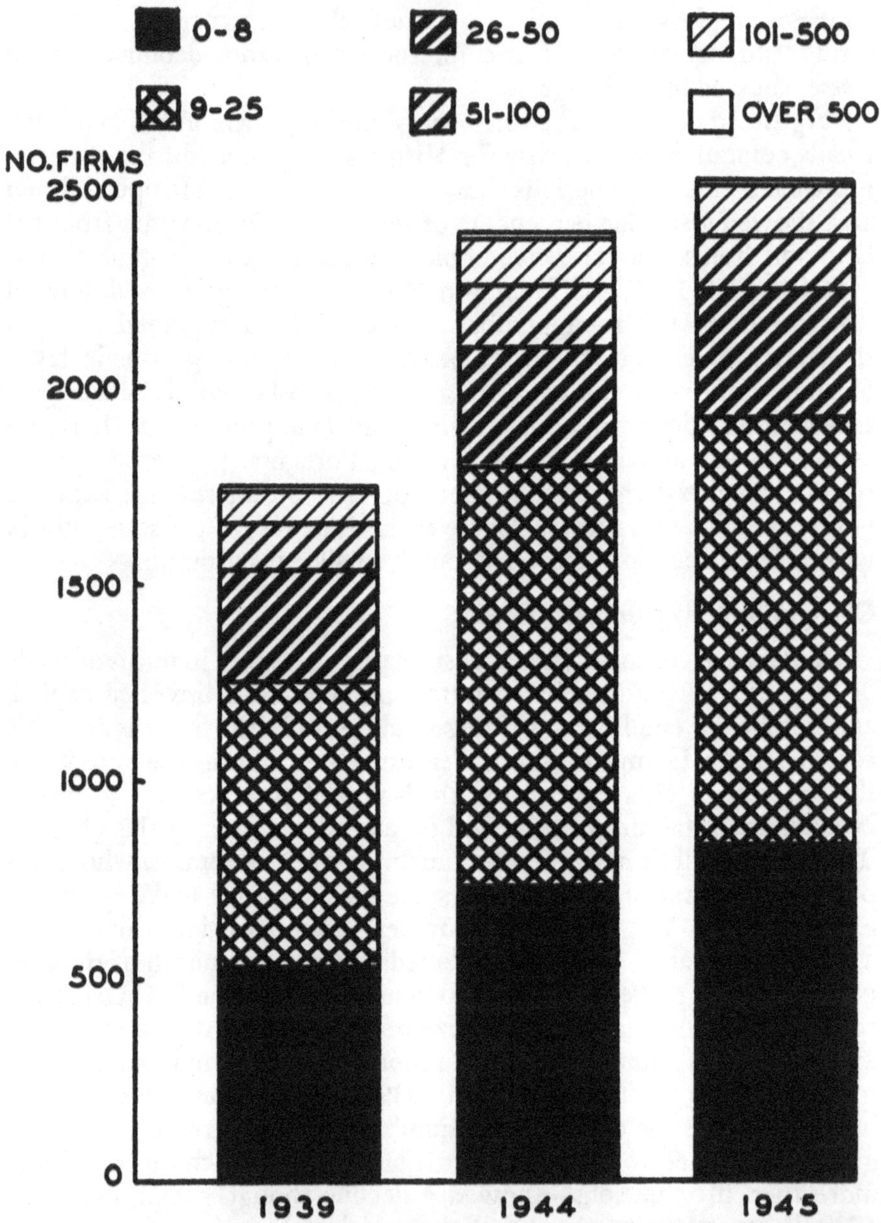

FIGURE 21. NUMBER OF FIRMS REPORTING TO VIRGINIA UNEMPLOYMENT COMPENSATION COMMISSION, BY NUMBER OF EMPLOYEES, HAMPTON ROADS-PENINSULA AREA, 1939, 1944, 1945 (THIRD QUARTER)

Source: Virginia U. C. C. files.

101 to 500 workers and more than 500 workers—had about the same relative position in 1945 as in 1939. (See Figure 21.)

It appears from these figures that in spite of the constant wartime pressure for employees of ordinary firms in the area to go into the armed services or the employ of the shipyards or other government establishments, there was a steady tendency for firms which before the war had fewer than eight employees and thus were not required to report to the U.C.C. to move into the reporting group and even into the group employing up to twenty-five persons or for new firms to begin operations. On the other hand, the establishment of new firms with forces of twenty-five or more workers or the expansion of existing firms to such a degree as to bring them into the larger size groups was relatively less frequent.

One further source of information is available as to size of firms in the Hampton Roads region during the postwar period. An analysis of the firms reporting under the Federal Old-Age and Survivors Insurance Program for the first quarter, 1947,[5] indicates a somewhat greater preponderance of small firms in Hampton Roads than in the rest of Virginia. Those employing seven or fewer persons comprised 76.4 per cent of all firms reporting in the Hampton Roads-Peninsula region as compared with 74.8 per cent for the state as a whole. Similarly, only 3.4 of Hampton Roads firms reported average work forces in excess of 100 as compared with 3.8 per cent in the entire state. Unfortunately, no comparable analysis has been made for 1940.

Types of Economic Activity

The Old-Age and Survivors Insurance data referred to above also provides information as to the relative importance of the various types of economic activity covered by the Federal program in 1947, though the fact that it does not cover government employment, ordinary farming, domestic service, and self-employed persons prevents these data from being directly comparable with the 1940 Census data used in sketching the prewar economic structure in Chapter III.

The general pattern of 1947 employment in the Hampton Roads communities as compared to Virginia, however, as indicated in Table 30, appears to be somewhat similar to that existing in 1940. (See Figure 3 and Table 6.) While manufacturing was the largest single source

5. U. S. Department of Commerce, *Business Establishments, Employment and Taxable Payrolls, under Old-Age and Survivors Insurance Program, First Quarter 1947, by Industry Groups and by Counties,* Part II, Virginia.

of employment in Hampton Roads, it was relatively less important than in the state as a whole. Retail and wholesale trade, the service trades, and transportation, communication, and utilities continued in 1947 as in 1940 to be relatively more important, as to per cent of total employees, than in the rest of Virginia. These characteristics were particularly marked in Norfolk and other south side localities. The north side district, through the influence of the Newport News Shipbuilding and Drydock Company, on the other hand, showed relatively greater manufacturing employment and proportionately smaller employment in other lines. In general, it appears that little change occurred in the relative importance of the various classes of employers between 1940 and 1947, though by the latter year, of course, the extreme expansion of certain types of war employment, especially government, had lessened somewhat.

The following analysis of the impact of the war upon manufacturing, trades and services, transportation and shipping, agriculture, and other extractive industries sheds further light on changes in the relative importance of these major types of economic activity in the economic structure of the Hampton Roads area.

Manufacturing. The dominance of the Newport News Shipbuilding and Drydock Company and the government-owned Norfolk Navy Yard at Portsmouth in the total manufacturing picture of the Hampton Roads-Peninsula area has been emphasized throughout this report. Even in the peacetime year of 1939, these two plants employed approximately half of the area's manufacturing workers. Shipyards employment was doubled under the pressure of World War I while the number of workers in other types of manufacturing showed little change. The Second World War brought a more than four-fold expansion in the work force of these two major shipyards but other types of manufacturing showed comparatively small increases or actual declines.

While shipbuilding was one of the major channels through which World War II came to the Hampton Roads region, the two large yards themselves experienced the impact of other war activities. Officials of the Newport News Shipbuilding and Drydock Company have been emphatic in believing that the loss of shipyards workers, directly to the Hampton Roads Port of Embarkation following its establishment in 1942 and indirectly because of the increased pressure upon housing facilities in Newport News as the port personnel expanded, delayed the construction of aircraft carriers and other needed ships

TABLE 30. EMPLOYMENT, FIRST QUARTER 1947, VIRGINIA AND HAMPTON ROADS AREA

	Total	Extractive	Construction	Manufacturing	Transportation, Communications, Utilities	Retail Trade	Wholesale Trade	Finance, Insurance, Real Estate	Services	Not Reported
VIRGINIA										
Number	554,251	23,723	41,138	209,684	41,934	110,598	46,291	22,825	54,225	3,833
Per cent	100.0	4.3	7.4	37.8	7.6	20.0	8.3	4.1	9.8	0.7
ENTIRE AREA										
Number	105,789	687	8,149	32,087	10,690	25,076	9,988	4,513	13,917	682
Per cent	100.0	0.6	7.7	30.3	10.1	23.7	9.4	4.4	13.2	0.6
South Side										
Number	74,691	490	6,170	18,052	8,618	19,293	8,131	3,496	9,898	543
Per cent	100.0	0.6	8.3	24.2	11.5	25.8	10.9	4.7	13.3	0.7
North Side										
Number	31,098	197	1,979	14,035	2,072	5,783	1,857	1,017	4,019	139
Per cent	100.0	0.6	6.4	45.1	6.7	18.6	6.0	3.3	12.9	0.4

Source: U.S. Department of Commerce, *Business Establishments, Employment and Taxable Payrolls, Old-Age and Survivors Insurance Program, First Quarter 1947, Virginia.*

and perhaps even prevented an earlier end of hostilities, particularly in the Pacific.[6] They feel strongly that it would have been better national strategy to have permitted Hampton Roads to specialize in shipbuilding and naval training and to use other Atlantic ports for the embarkation and debarkation of troops and matériel. Additional impacts on the yards came through terminating deferments of key workers in the younger age groups as the tempo of overseas action stepped up in 1943 and 1944 and through shortages of steel and other materials.

In the absence of detailed information for the war years comparable to that provided by the Census of Manufactures in 1939, the best picture of the impact of the war upon the smaller shipyards and other types of manufacturing is provided by annual reports made by a varying number of manufacturing concerns in the Norfolk-Portsmouth area to the Norfolk Industrial Commission, a private agency interested in the industrial development of that locality. One phase of the war's impact upon these manufacturing concerns is indicated in Table 31. It appears that the size of manufacturing concerns in and

TABLE 31. CHANGES IN SIZE OF MANUFACTURING* ESTABLISHMENTS REPORTING TO NORFOLK INDUSTRIAL COMMISSION, 1939–1946

	Employees		Value of Product	
Year	Number of Firms Reporting	Average Number of Employees Per Firm	Number of Firms Reporting	Average Value of Product per Firm (000)
1939	271	65.2	176	$307
1940	266	82.0	178	408
1941	264	77.0	169	588
1942	267	84.5	174	554
1943	270	82.4	205	784
1944	262	80.8	196	840
1945	257	69.5	199	706
1946	288	80.9	201	813

*Includes electric light and power, gas, street railway, steam railway repair, and oil distributors as well as those activities which are more commonly classed as manufacturing.

Source: Files of the Norfolk Industrial Commission.

around Norfolk, as measured by product value, grew steadily during the war years until an average of approximately $840,000, more than twice the average value reported for 1939, was reached in 1944. A sharp decline in 1945, as labor and material scarcities became acute,

6. Personal interviews with President Homer J. Ferguson, September 11, 1945, and Assistant Personnel Manager A. Albert Giese, September 17, 1945.

was followed by an increase almost to the 1944 level in the first full postwar year, 1946. Higher price levels were responsible, of course, for a part of this increase in value of product, especially after OPA controls were removed in 1946. Expansion in shipbuilding and repair by the small Norfolk yards was also a major factor, as the average value of product for these firms skyrocketed from $124,000 in 1939 to more than $3,000,000 in 1943 and 1944. No other industrial group approached this rate of increase. Similarly, the big drop in average value of product for shipbuilding and repairs in 1945 was the prime factor in the downward trend in the average of all manufacturers reporting to the Industrial Commission.

The relatively small size of manufacturing establishments in Norfolk and Portsmouth is also evidenced by Table 31. At no time during World War II did the average number of employees per firm exceed 84.5. It may be noted also that only three of the 271 firms reporting number of employees in 1939 had more than 500 persons on their payrolls. The doubling of the value of product during the war years with only a relatively small increase in the average work force indicated that businessmen learned how to get more work done with fewer employees. This labor shortage and the necessary adjustments in business practices to meet it called for all of the ingenuity and down-to-earth thinking that harassed businessmen could muster. How some of them met this managerial problem and others resulting from war conditions is described in the following chapter.

The Norfolk Industrial Commission reports from individual manufacturers provides some evidence, also, of wartime changes in the structure of manufacturing in the Norfolk-Portsmouth area. This information, as summarized in Table 32, indicates that manufacturers of food and kindred products, chemicals (chiefly fertilizer), and furniture and finished lumber accounted for almost half of the total workers reported for 1939. Transportation equipment (chiefly railway repair shops), lumber and timber products, and automobile manufacturing employed almost an additional one-fourth of the total. The three 1944 leaders, on the other hand, which were shipbuilding and repair, food and kindred products, and railway repair shops and other transportation equipment, in that order, comprised almost three-fifths of the total. Automobile manufacturing had dropped by the wayside early in the war when the Ford plant was taken over by the navy. The "nonessential" status of fertilizer kept the chemical group from maintaining its prewar share of the total work force of manufacturing companies. Such consumer goods industries as textiles, apparel, and furniture and finished lumber, while holding up fairly well during the early war years, lost ground as employers after 1942. The essential

TABLE 32. PERCENTAGE DISTRIBUTION OF MANUFACTURING EMPLOYEES BY INDUSTRY GROUPS, NORFOLK AND PORTSMOUTH, 1939–1945

Industry Groups	1939	1940	1941	1942	1943	1944	1945
All manufacturing	100.0	100.0	100.0	100.0	100.0	100.0	100.0
Food and kindred products	20.0	19.8	22.7	22.7	21.3	21.2	20.4
Textile mill products	3.4	2.6	2.8	2.9	1.8	1.6	1.2
Apparel and other finished products	5.5	5.2	5.5	6.3	4.7	3.3	4.4
Lumber and timber products	7.4	8.8	6.4	3.6	3.7	3.5	4.7
Furniture and finished lumber products	12.3	10.3	10.8	9.2	8.1	7.6	8.5
Paper and allied products	0.6	—	0.1	0.1	0.1	0.1	0.1
Printing and publishing	3.5	2.9	2.9	2.9	3.0	2.7	2.9
Chemicals and allied products	14.0	10.6	10.0	11.4	10.3	9.3	10.4
Products of petroleum and coal	4.8	3.9	4.1	3.5	3.5	3.6	3.1
Stone, clay, and glass products	3.5	5.2	6.7	6.2	4.6	3.7	2.7
Iron and steel and their products	3.3	2.7	3.6	5.0	4.8	5.4	4.8
Nonferrous metals and their products	0.8	0.7	1.1	0.8	0.4	0.4	*
Electrical machinery	*	0.1	0.1	*	0.9	1.1	0.9
Machinery, except electric	0.3	0.3	0.2	0.2	0.3	0.3	0.3
Automobiles and automobile equipment	7.0	7.6	0.4	0.1	0.1	*	*
Shipbuilding and ship repair	4.6	6.3	9.9	12.5	22.3	24.2	16.5
Transportation equipment, n.e.c. (largely railroad and bus repair)	9.0	13.0	12.7	12.6	10.1	12.0	19.0

*Less than 0.1 percent

Source: Norfolk Industrial Commission.

nature of food manufacturing, on the other hand, is suggested by its ability to employ a larger portion of the total group of workers during the war years than in 1939 and 1940. Similarly, printing and publishing (largely newspapers) was able to employ an almost constant percentage of the entire group from 1940 through 1945. The effect of the early war construction boom is clearly reflected in the relative expansion of employment in lumber and timber products, stone, clay, and glass through 1941 and the steady decline thereafter. Finally, the close relation of shipbuilding and railroad and bus transportation to the war effort was evidenced by the substantial increase in the relative number of workers in these fields.

In general, it appears that the pattern of the war's impact upon manufacturing in the Hampton Roads area in World War II was somewhat similar to that of the First World War, with shipbuilding and related war industries expanding to an even greater degree in the recent struggle than in 1917-1919 and other manufacturing, except food, railroad and bus repair, and other direct auxiliaries of the war effort, scarcely holding their own. The surprising feature, however, of the impact of World War II upon manufacturing in the Hampton Roads communities is that the anticipated postwar slump was far smaller or at least was slower in materializing than had been anticipated. Preliminary 1947 Census of Manufactures[7] statistics show this to be true. In Newport News, 28 establishments in 1947, approximately two years after the end of hostilities, employed an average of 390.2 workers per plant as compared with 23 plants with 343.7 employees per plant in 1939. Similarly, 273 Norfolk-Portsmouth-Norfolk County plants in 1947 had an average of 48.6 workers per establishment while in 1939, 244 plants employed only 26.4 workers, on the average. The large employment per plant in Newport News reflects, of course, the dominant position of the Newport News Shipbuilding and Drydock Company. The employment per plant in the Norfolk-Portsmouth area would have been considerably larger, similarly, if the Census of Manufactures included the government-owned Norfolk Naval Shipyard. Value added by manufacture in the southside plants, both total and per plant, in 1947 was almost three times as large as in 1939. The large value added by manufacturing in Newport News in 1947 ($1,719,964 per plant) indicates the continued high rate of activity in the shipyard in the postwar period, though no comparable figure was reported for 1939.

Shipyards employment, though curtailed after V-J Day, was maintained at a much higher relative level than after World War I and higher than in 1939. Civic and industrial leaders on both the north and south sides of Hampton Roads have shown considerable resourcefulness, intelligence, and energy in attracting new industries to the region. Further attention will be given to these postwar developments and their implications for the future in the final chapter of this report.

Trades and Services. The role of retail, wholesale, and service trades in the Hampton Roads-Peninsula economy, already large before World War II, appears to have been enhanced by wartime de-

7. U. S. Bureau of the Census, *Census of Manufacturer: 1947, Summary Statistics for Selected Local Areas of Virginia,* Preliminary Report, June 22, 1949.

velopments. More than 46 per cent of Hampton Roads workers covered by the Federal Old-Age and Survivors Insurance Program early in 1947 were employed in these trades, as compared with only 38 per cent of all covered workers in Virginia. (See Table 30.) According to the census data summarized in Table 6, workers in these fields in 1940 comprised 29 per cent of all employed workers in the Hampton Roads region and 24 per cent of the total for the state. While the Old-Age and Survivors data do not cover government employees, the bulk of farm workers, domestic servants, and self-employed persons and are thus not directly comparable with the 1940 Census figures, it is apparent that the proportion of all employed workers in the Hampton Roads communities engaged in trades and services increased during the war period.

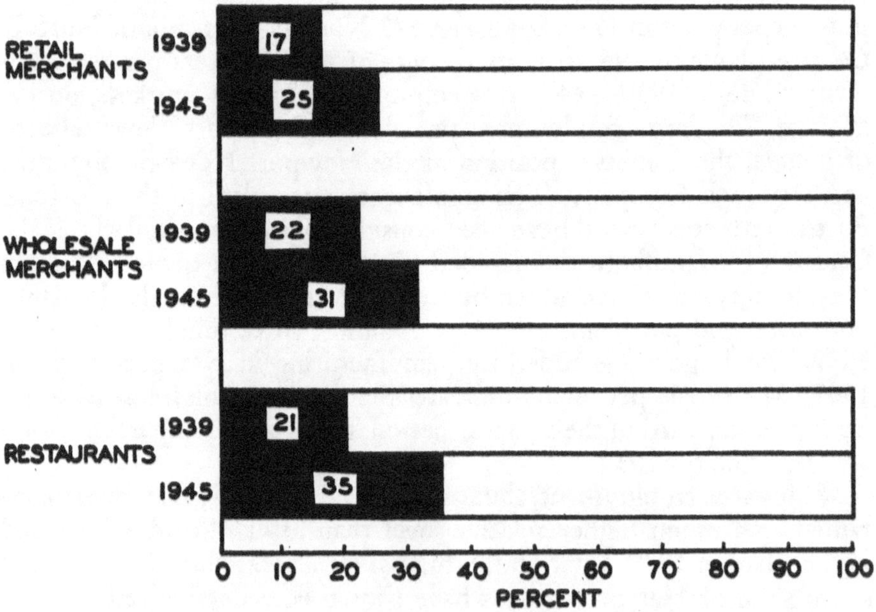

FIGURE 22. PERCENTAGE OF TOTAL STATE LICENSE TAXES ON VIRGINIA RETAIL-WHOLESALE MERCHANTS AND RESTAURANTS PAID BY HAMPTON ROADS-PENINSULA FIRMS, 1939 AND 1945

Source: State Department of Taxation.

Additional evidence of the growth of trades and services under the impact of the Second World War is provided by Table 33, which summarizes wartime changes in the number of, and taxes paid by, retail and wholesale merchants and restaurants paying state license taxes. Since these taxes are based upon gross receipts of retailers and restaurants and gross purchases of wholesalers for the year before the tax payment, they afford a rough measure of changes in the volume of business done by these trades. It is recognized that changes in the number of firms and amount of taxes paid may reflect changing efficiency of tax administrators as well as changes in the volume of business. Such administrative variations, however, were probably not sufficient during the war years to invalidate the data as indexes of business volume, though it is likely that shortages of qualified administrative personnel, together with the high rate of change in number of firms and volume of business, caused the figures on amounts of license taxes paid to understate the actual volume of business.

One conclusion to be drawn from the table is that the war brought a much greater expansion of retailing, wholesaling, and restaurant operation in the Hampton Roads communities than in the state as a whole. Figure 22 presents graphic evidence of this tendency.

TABLE 33. CHANGES IN NUMBER OF FIRMS PAYING STATE LICENSE TAXES AND IN AMOUNT OF TAXES PAID, RETAIL AND WHOLESALE MERCHANTS AND RESTAURANTS, HAMPTON ROADS-PENINSULA AREA AND VIRGINIA, SELECTED YEARS, 1939–1946 (1939 = 100)

	1942		1944		1945		1946	
	No. of Firms	Taxes Paid	No. of Firms	Taxes Paid	No. of Firms	Taxes Paid	No. of Firms	Taxes Paid
Retail Merchants								
Virginia	104.5	130.6	92.8	151.2	97.5	164.8	113.9	184.7
Entire Area	113.1	164.0	114.2	229.9	123.9	247.8	142.7	254.1
Norfolk	112.0	159.1	111.6	221.4	115.3	234.4	124.8	240.4
Portsmouth	111.0	176.5	112.9	249.3	122.2	268.2	140.4	272.4
Newport News	112.9	190.3	116.9	261.8	128.6	282.7	130.6	261.0
Wholesale Merchants								
Virginia	110.1	149.0	112.5	186.6	117.4	202.7	134.4	229.3
Entire Area	128.8	186.0	134.8	257.3	145.6	281.5	167.1	299.1
Norfolk	123.2	185.3	132.9	258.7	141.6	288.7	154.8	302.6
Portsmouth	150.0	178.4	155.0	244.4	160.0	249.2	165.0	243.6
Newport News	136.4	202.5	129.5	307.2	147.7	324.4	186.4	359.8
Restaurants								
Virginia	105.7	150.1	91.6	201.4	95.2	211.5	109.7	228.7
Entire Area	126.9	210.0	133.5	382.0	129.3	362.5	158.6	400.9
Norfolk	122.3	198.6	129.7	390.3	130.2	416.2	135.9	403.5
Portsmouth	111.4	179.4	130.9	358.1	163.1	394.0	173.2	400.8
Newport News	140.9	251.0	161.7	500.0	163.1	998.3	184.6	430.5

Source: Derived from data furnished by the State Department of Taxation.

A second aspect of the wartime growth of these three major types of trade, as revealed by Table 33, is the smaller rate of growth, both in terms of number of firms and amount of taxes paid, of retailing as compared with restaurants and wholesaling. Taxes paid in 1946, based on volume of business done in 1945, were only two and one-half times those paid in 1939 for retailers in the Hampton Roads localities as compared with three and four times, respectively, for wholesalers and restaurants. In view of the large transient population during the war years, it is not surprising that the volume of business done by restaurants increased more than either class of merchants. The reasons for the relatively greater growth in the volume of wholesale trade than in the volume of retail trade and the reasons for the number of wholesalers increasing throughout the war years at a greater rate than either retailers or restaurants are not as clear. It is possible, of course, that their larger size made it easier for tax officials to collect the full amount of taxes due. A larger proportion of retailers and restaurants were small, fly-by-night firms which were able to get by with paying taxes on only a portion of their receipts or which went out of business before they paid any state license at all. Similarly, the fact that the number of wholesalers was less than one-tenth the number of retailers and one-third the number of restaurants made small numerical increases loom large percentagewise. After making allowances for these miscellaneous factors, however, the fact remains that the impact of the war upon wholesale trade in the Hampton Roads region was surprisingly heavy. This suggests the possibility that wholesaling is somewhat more sensitive to sharp changes in the volume of economic activity, whether from war or other causes, in any locality than retailing and that this sensitivity is evidenced by changes in the number of firms as well as in the total volume of business.

Perhaps the most interesting conclusion suggested by Table 33, is that Newport News, the smallest of the three cities, experienced a greater rate of growth throughout most of the war period in all three lines of trade than either Norfolk or Portsmouth, although the latter showed slightly higher indexes for retail trade in 1946 and for the number of wholesalers in each year shown in the table. While the fact that Norfolk accounted for approximately half of the volume of retail and restaurant trade and three-fourths of wholesale trade of the entire Hampton Roads-Peninsula area before the war has helped to keep its indexes of wartime change below those of Newport News, the consistently larger rate of increase for the trade of the latter city during the war years seems to support the view expressed earlier in this chapter that local businesses in war-swollen communities are stimulated to a somewhat greater degree by the expansion of war industries employing civilians than by increases in the number of military personnel stationed at near-by camps. The dominant position of shipbuilding in the Newport News economy caused manufacturing to loom much larger in the wartime economy of Newport News than either Norfolk or Portsmouth, particularly the former, where trades and services have depended to a much greater degree upon members of the armed forces and their families.

Transportation and Shipping. Hampton Roads transportation and shipping activity received the impact of World War II in two distinct installments. The first consisted of the shift from peacetime shipping, predominantly outbound coastwise shipments of coal, to the embarkation and debarkation of troops and the handling of military cargoes exceeded in volume only by the ports of New York and San Francisco.[8] Evidence of the extent to which railroads serving Hampton Roads ports were taxed by exports of war materials is provided by the following summary of the number of cars, exclusive of coal, delivered by the Chesapeake and Ohio Railway at the Newport News piers through 1944:[9]

Year	*Number of Cars*
1941	9,023
1942	9,260
1943	29,382
1944	44,620

In addition, the C. & O. embarked from September, 1942, through September, 1945, 625,000 soldiers, debarked troops totalling 272,000, handled 134,000 prisoners of war, and brought more than 20 million tons of coal to the port for trans-shipment. Coal shipments, however, dropped off during the wars years as colliers were diverted to other services and all-rail routes, free from the submarine menace, were substituted for the traditional Hampton Roads to New England water routes. The railroads serving Norfolk and Portsmouth, while less directly related to the main activities of the Hampton Roads Port of Embarkation, also experienced great increases in traffic other than coal.

8. Hampton Roads Maritime Exchange, *The Ports of Greater Hampton Roads Annual, 1947*, p. 13.

9. Newport News *Daily Press,* December 21, 1945.

The second installment of change administered to Hampton Roads shipping by the war was the export during the postwar years of vast quantities of coal, foodstuffs, livestock, and other commodities needed in the rehabilitation of war-torn Europe. So great was this traffic that an embargo on rail shipments into Hampton Roads and other Atlantic ports was imposed in July, 1946, through the Association of American Railroads on authority of the Office of Defense Transportation because rail freight had been routed into these ports faster than the ships could be provided to take care of it.[10] A few months later, thirty ships from the idle fleet in the James River and elsewhere were temporarily brought back into service to haul coal and grain to Europe.[11]

Figure 23 portrays the general effect of these war and postwar developments upon the volume and structure of Hampton Roads shipping. While the statistics upon which this chart is based probably understate somewhat the total volume of war shipping and, of course, do not include the carrying of troops and prisoners of war, the decline in peacetime shipping was apparently greater than the increase in military cargoes handled. This was largely the result of the sharp decline in coastwise shipments of coal noted above. Hampton Roads coal dumpings in 1943 were less than half the 1941 total. The revival in waterborne commerce in 1945 and 1946, moreover, was largely in foreign trade as coastwise and other domestic commerce failed to come back. Foreign commerce of the Hampton Roads ports actually increased 108 per cent between 1939 and 1946 but domestic commerce fell off 29 per cent.[12]

The increase in foreign trade was even greater in 1947, when it reached 20 million long tons as compared with only 4 million in 1940. While exports accounted for most of this increase, rising from 3 to 18 million tons, imports of less than one million long tons in 1940 had almost doubled by 1947. For the first time in its history, Hampton Roads in 1947 led all Atlantic coast ports, even New York, in the movement of outbound cargoes. It cleared one-third of the total export tonnage of the principal Atlantic ports and its percentage of total foreign waterborne commerce of these ports rose from 12 per cent in 1946 to 24 per cent in 1947, while Baltimore's share of this

10. *Norfolk Virginian-Pilot*, July 13, 1946.

11. *Ibid.*, January 9, 1947.

12. See Federal Reserve Bank of Richmond, *Monthly Review*, March 31, 1949, for comparison of the commerce of Hampton Roads with that of Baltimore, Wilmington, and Charleston in 1939 and 1946.

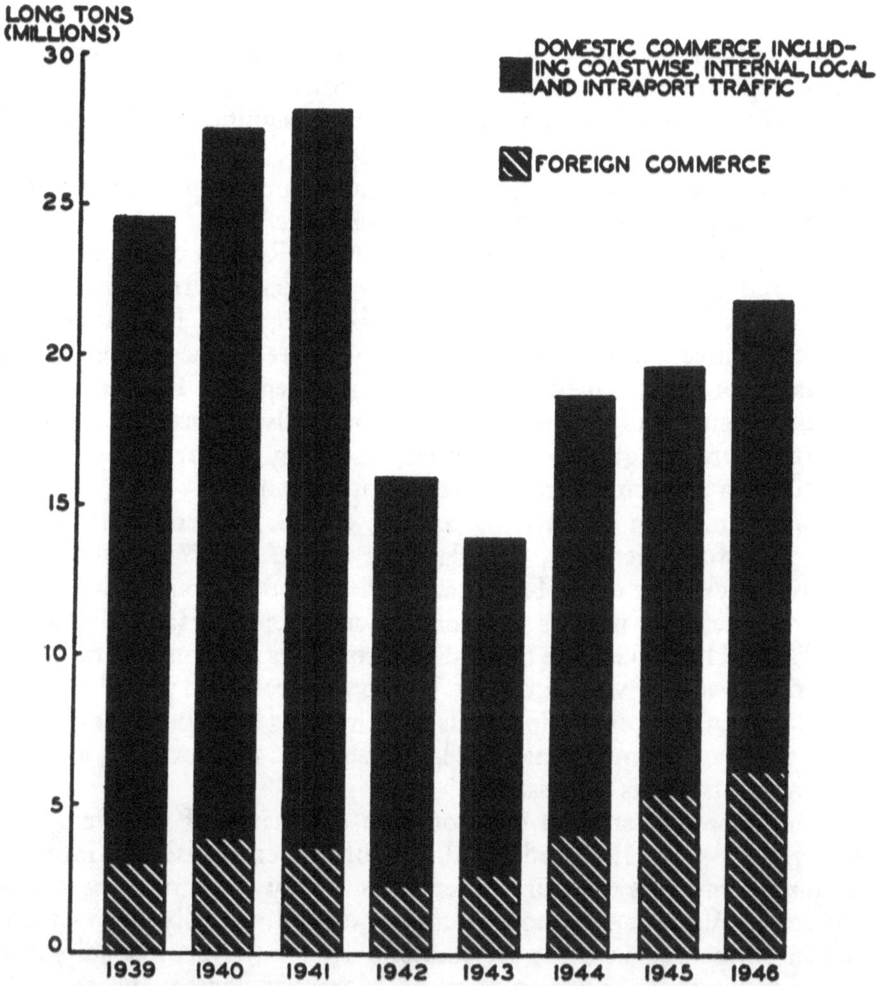

FIGURE 23. WATERBORNE COMMERCE OF THE HAMPTON ROADS PORTS, 1939-1946

Sources: Hampton Roads Maritime Commission, *The Ports of Greater Hampton Roads,* 1947, p. 13; *Annual Report of the Chief of Army Engineers,* 1940 and 1947, Part 2, Table 4.

total remained constant and other ports showed a relative decline. The great needs of Europe's slowly recovering economy for American coal was the prime factor in this increase, as 95 per cent of Hampton Roads exports consisted of coal. Grains and tobacco were the next largest group, followed by chemicals and related products and a varied list of other commodities. Imports were so far below those of New

York and Baltimore that both of these ports surpassed Hampton Roads in total foreign commerce in 1947 in spite of the latter's large exports. The combined population of Hampton Roads cities and of its hinterland has not been large enough to make it significant as a general import center. Residual fuel oil accounted for 70 per cent of all 1947 imports through these ports, with manganese ore, gypsum, fertilizers and products, and newsprint following in order.[13]

Europe received 82 per cent of Hampton Roads exports in 1947, with Latin American countries getting 9 per cent, Africa 6 per cent, Canada 2 per cent, and Asia and Oceania 1 per cent. This represents an increase over prewar years in Europe's share of these exports and decreases for Latin America and Far Eastern regions. The temporary distress shipments of coal to Europe undoubtedly distorts this regional export picture as a guide to the future, since they will probably fall off as European coal mines are restored to operation.

Latin American countries accounted for 73 per cent of 1947 imports, Asia for 9 per cent, Canada 8 per cent, Africa 7 per cent, and Europe only 3 per cent. This again, reflects a temporary situation as it is probable that Europe's share of total imports into Hampton Roads will rise and its percentage of total exports fall as its economy recovers from the ravages of war. Similarly, Hampton Roads will probably get a somewhat smaller proportion of its total imports from countries to the south and send them a somewhat larger share of total exports, as wartime maladjustments are lessened.

The depressed state of the domestic commerce of the Hampton Roads ports since 1945 reflects the failure of coastwise and internal shipping companies to resume operations on anywhere near their prewar scale. Wartime ship construction included virtually none of the smaller ships used in these services and use of the prewar ships for war purposes wore out most of them. Moreover, increased speed and availability of truck and rail facilities and high labor and other operating costs in the coastwise services placed the latter at a competitive disadvantage following the war. Such operators as the Eastern Steamship Company and the Merchants and Miners Transportation Company between Norfolk and other Atlantic ports found the resumption of operations to be uneconomic. The latter company, indeed, had only two vessels with a combined tonnage of 8,000 available for service

13. The facts on exports and imports in 1947 have been compiled from Hampton Roads Maritime Exchange, *The Ports of Greater Hampton Roads Annual, 1949*, pp. 25-32.

in September, 1946, as compared with its prewar fleet of 22 vessels totalling 86,000 gross tons.[14]

Strenuous efforts on the part of Hampton Roads shipping interests to obtain federal aid in the form of underwriting part of operating costs and assisting in procuring vessels for the coastwise trade were unsuccessful. Intercoastal shipping, never more than a small part of the total shipping of the port, revived shortly after V-J Day as the five lines connecting Hampton Roads with the west coast ports before the war were able to obtain under favorable terms fast Victory-type freighters. These lines, like the coastal services, however, were beset with high operating costs and truck and rail competition and have had difficulty keeping their heads above water.[15]

Two other features of the war's impact upon the shipping of the Hampton Roads ports of somewhat less significance should be noted. One is that the relative importance of Newport News as compared with its sister port of Norfolk increased somewhat during the war period. While Norfolk's total waterborne commerce decreased 20 per cent between 1939 and 1946, Newport News showed an increase of 14 per cent. This reduced Norfolk's share of total Hampton Roads commerce from 72.5 per cent in 1939 to 64.9 in 1946 while Newport News' percentage of the total grew from 27.5 to 35.1.[16] Whether this was merely a temporary change in the relative importance of the two ports reflecting the increase in exports of coal to Europe remains to be seen.

Another impact of World War II upon the Hampton Roads ports was the great expansion during and immediately after the war of physical facilities under governmental pressure to meet military needs and to ship needed supplies to postwar Europe.[17] Railroads serving the port have, in addition, on their own initiative, constructed new facilities which should do much to enlarge the volume of Hampton Roads shipping. Of particular note is the Norfolk & Western's new $6,000,000 merchandise pier facility which can accommodate four of the largest ocean-going steamers at the same time and the new Chesapeake & Ohio coal piers.[18] In spite of these increased physical facilities,

14. *Norfolk Virginian-Pilot*, September 1, 1946, and January 23, 1947; *Richmond Times-Dispatch*, April 20 and December 11, 1946.

15. *Norfolk Virginia-Pilot*, October 9, 1945; March 13, 1946.

16. Federal Reserve Bank of Richmond, *op. cit.*

17. *Ibid.*

18. See Hampton Roads Maritime Exchange, *op. cit.*, pp. 33-64 for description of these and other facilities.

however, and the fact that under war pressure Hampton Roads became a full-cargo port for shipments other than coal for the first time in its history, the war was unable to bring about a permanent change in its traditional role as a secondary port. As before the war, virtually all of the steamship companies engaged in overseas shipping are owned by outside interests and the volume of local export-import business, other than coal, has been insufficient to give it any permanent prospect of becoming a full-cargo port. Boats still pick up part of their cargoes in northern ports and finish them off with Hampton Roads shipments.

Agriculture. The flooding of the Hampton Roads-Peninsula area with a host of soldiers, sailors, and civilian war workers and their families and followers brought a sharp increase in the demand for agricultural products, particularly meat, poultry, dairy products, and vegetables. In spite of a constant drain of farm laborers to construction crews, shipyards, and civilian employment at military establishments, as well as to the armed forces, agricultural operations expanded to meet these needs and most farmers in the area prospered mightily.

This wartime expansion, however, brought little change in the prewar agricultural structure of the Hampton Roads region, as outlined in Tables 9 and 10. Table 34 shows that small farms with relatively high values operated largely by owners rather than tenants were still the rule in 1945. The proportion of tenancy dropped from 12.1 to 2.6 in Warwick County between 1940 and 1945. Nansemond County showed a slight increase from 45.3 to 47.2. The booming market, however, brought an increase in the proportion of total acreage devoted to farming and in the average size of farms in most of the Hampton Roads counties. York County, in which thousands of acres of farm land were converted into naval establishments, was the chief exception with per cent of total acreage in farms decreasing from 31.5 in 1940 to 22.0 in 1945 and average size of farm decreasing from 58.9 to 36 acres. The profitability of agricultural operations throughout the area is suggested, not only by the sharp increase in value of farm products, but also by the increased value of land and buildings per farm and the greatly decreased rate of farm tenancy in most counties. While the decline in number of farms from 1940 to 1945 may also be evidence of increased prosperity to the degree that this was the result of the more successful farmers buying the farms of their less efficient neighbors and of those who moved into the armed forces or war jobs,[19] this

19. This consolidation tendency was particularly marked in Princess Anne County, according to information received in a personal interview with Mr. Grayson Whitehurst, July 25, 1947.

may also be the result of the expansion of urban population into farm territory as urban centers became saturated.

The influence of the proximity to the shipyards and other war

TABLE 34. AGRICULTURAL STRUCTURE, UNITED STATES, VIRGINIA, HAMPTON ROADS-PENINSULA AREA, 1940 AND 1945

	United States		Virginia		Hampton Roads-Peninsula Area	
	1940	1945	1940	1945	1940	1945
Number of farms	6,096,799	5,858,889	174,885	173,051	6,224	5,894
Per cent of total acreage in farms	55.9	30.8	64.4	64.1	49.0	48.5
Average size of farm (acres)	174.0	196.1	94.0	94.5	88.4	92.3
Average value of land and buildings per farm	$5,518	8,100	3,860	5,021	4,759	6,871
Average value of products per farm	$1,309	3,148	878	1,845	1,621	3,270
Proportion of farm tenancy	38.7	31.7	26.9	20.3	31.5	26.5
Number of family and/or hired workers	9,694,000	8,373,239	269,227	209,559	15,595	7,228

Source: U.S. Bureau of the Census, *Census of Agriculture 1945*, Vol. 1, Part 15.

TABLE 35. SOURCE OF AGRICULTURAL INCOME, IN PER CENTS OF TOTAL, UNITED STATES, VIRGINIA, AND HAMPTON ROADS-PENINSULA COUNTIES, 1945

	United States		Virginia		Hampton Roads-Peninsula Area	
Product	1940	1945	1940	1945	1940	1945
Total	100.0	100.0	100.0	100.0	100.0	100.0
Livestock sold or traded	24.0	25.1	15.2	14.5	8.3	11.5
Dairy products sold or traded	14.3	13.9	9.4	9.7	15.6	14.8
Vegetables harvested for sale	2.6	3.4	3.2	3.4	12.1	11.2
Products used by farm households	14.5	10.4	28.2	21.1	12.1	9.5
Horticultural specialties	1.6	1.2	1.1	1.1	5.2	6.4
Poultry products	7.1	8.7	10.3	13.3	5.6	7.0
Field crops sold or traded	31.6	30.8	28.8	28.8	37.9	37.2
All other sources	4.3	6.5	3.8	8.1	3.2	2.4

Source: U.S. Bureau of the Census, *Census of Agriculture 1945*, Vol. 1, Part 15.

activities upon Hampton Roads farm labor is indicated sharply by the drop in the total number of farm workers, including operators and family workers, in the eight counties from 15,595 in 1940 to 7,228 in 1945, or 53.7 per cent as compared with a decline of only 22.2 per cent for Virginia as a whole and only 13.6 per cent for the entire United States. The paradox of departing farm workers and increased agricultural production was resolved through increased use of tractors and other mechanical devices and the assignment of German prisoners of war and casual workers brought in from the West Indies. The POW's were stationed at various camps on both sides of Hampton Roads and proved to be an excellent source of labor for the farmers of the region.

While dairying, as shown in Table 35, continued to yield in 1945 a larger share of total farm income in the Hampton Roads-Peninsula counties than in the entire state and nation, its relative importance declined somewhat during the war years. Livestock and products, poultry, and vegetables accounted for relatively larger shares of the total value of farm products in most of the counties in 1945 than in 1940 in response to swollen populations, high wages, and rising standards of living. Similarly, as sales of cut flowers for the wives and girl friends of service men and other transients boomed and as landscaping was provided for new housing projects, "horticultural specialties" became more important. They took over the top place in terms of value of farm products in Norfolk County and became one of the three leading sources of farm income in Elizabeth City County. Products used by farm households declined in relative importance as the cash market improved and the households gave up some of their members to the armed forces and urban war centers. Field crops provided a smaller share in 1945 of the total value of farm products in the Hampton Roads region than they did before the war; inflated demand for, and prices of, fresh vegetables and small fruits in the crowded cities caused many prewar general farmers to shift to truck farming. This was particularly the case in Princess Anne[20] and York counties.

Fishing. Hampton Roads fishermen, like the farmers of the region, experienced a tremendous increase in the demand for their products during the war years. As the thousands of newcomers to the Hampton Roads communities, as well as people in other parts of the country, found it increasingly difficult to buy meat, they turned to seafood. Prices soared and after a period of greatly reduced catches because of

20. *Ibid.*

the diversion of fishermen to the armed forces and war industries, restriction of fishing because of war activities in waters of the area, and natural causes, the eight Hampton Roads counties were able by 1945 to almost double their prewar catch and to sell it for almost seven times the prewar value. The general pattern of the impact of World War II upon Hampton Roads fishing is indicated by the following summary of statistical surveys by the U. S. Fish and Wildlife Service of the size and value of the catch of fish in these counties:

	Thousands of pounds	*Thousands of dollars*
1939	40,561	$1,277
1940	41,644	1,378
1941	33,399	1,483
1942	30,594	2,035
1944*	43,204	3,840
1945	76,865	8,745
1946	61,778	6,011

*No survey made in 1943

Fin fish accounted for most of the increased catch in the later war years. Almost two and one-half times as many pounds of this type of seafood were caught by Hampton Roads fishermen in 1945 as in 1939.[21] The oyster catch was only 64 per cent of that for 1939, however, and crabs and other shellfish amounted to only 81 per cent of the harvest for the prewar year. Fin fish comprised almost nine-tenths of the total 1945 catch as compared with only two-thirds of the total pounds of seafood caught in Hampton Roads waters in 1939. Oysters accounted for only 5 per cent and crabs and other shellfish approximately 6 per cent of the 1945 catch. That this decline in the relative importance of shellfish as compared with fin fish was due more to supply factors than to decreased demand is indicated by the fact that the value per pound of the two shellfish groups increased between 1939 and 1945 almost as much as did that of fin fish. The values per pound of seafood caught in these two years for the three classes, as derived from U. S. Fish and Wildlife Service statistics for the Hampton Roads counties, were as follows:

	1939	*1945*
Fin fish	2.2 cents	10.0 cents
Oysters	8.4 cents	38.0 cents
Crabs, etc.	2.3 cents	8.3 cents

21. Data used in this section are derived from "Annual Surveys on Catch, by Counties," Fish and Wildlife Service (Statistical Section), U. S. Department of Interior.

While the factors responsible for the decreased supply of oysters and crabs are a complex of such things as water and climatic conditions, diseases and parasites, and harvesting methods, which are beyond the scope of this paper,[22] it is possible that it also reflected the manpower shortage. The harvesting of oysters and crabs requires somewhat more labor in relation to the size of the catch than the emptying of fish nets.

As in 1939 (see Table 11), Elizabeth City, Norfolk, and York counties continued during the war years to account for upwards of nine-tenths of the total catch of the eight Hampton Roads counties. In every year except 1945, when Norfolk County took over the top spot, Elizabeth City County was the leader, though Norfolk County was relatively more important during each of these years than before the war.

Changes in Income

Changes in incomes received by Hampton Roads-Peninsula residents should provide the most significant measure of the impact of World War II upon the area's economy. Only rough estimates of income changes, however, are available. The best of these estimates, as summarized and compared with similar estimates for Virginia as a unit in Table 36, indicate that the great wartime expansion in economic activity described in the foregoing pages was accompanied by substantial increases in both aggregate and per capita income.

Aggregate income payments and gross buying income for 1945, as estimated by the University of Virginia's Bureau of Population and Economic Research and the magazine *Sales Management*, respectively, rose 153 and 171 per cent over 1940 as compared with only 130 and 163 per cent for the entire state. That the increase in *aggregate* income of the Hampton Roads communities was greater than that of Virginia as a whole and reflected population growth to a greater degree than the improved economic status of individual residents is suggested by the somewhat smaller increases in per capita incomes in the Hampton Roads region than in the entire state from 1940 to 1945. While this region's share of Virginia's total population increased from 15.3 per cent in 1940 to 20.6 per cent in 1945, its proportion of total income payments rose only from 21.3 to 23.3 per cent and it accounted for only 22.8 per cent of Virginia's gross buying income in 1945, only

22. The Virginia Fisheries Laboratory and research agencies in other states are engaged in continuing studies of such factors.

TABLE 36. INCOME ESTIMATES, 1945, AND PER CENT INCREASE 1940–1945 VIRGINIA AND HAMPTON ROADS-PENINSULA AREA

	Bureau of Population and Economic Research[a]		Gross Buying Income Sales Management[b]		Income Values, Va. State Income Tax[c]	
	Dollars	Per cent Increase	Dollars	Per cent Increase	Dollars	Per cent Increase
Virginia						
Aggregate (millions)	2,902	130.4	2,798	163.2	494	237.2
Per capita	972	110.6	1,010	153.1	1,665[d]	56.5
Hampton Roads–Peninsula Area						
Aggregate (millions)	676	152.7	637	171.1	132	345.4
Per Capita	1,100	67.9	1,181	102.9	1,820[d]	89.0

a. Derived from U.S. Department of Commerce estimates of total income payments in Virginia. Estimates for cities and counties of the Hampton Roads-Peninsula and other regions of the state were based on a formula devised by the bureau, including (1) the pattern of employment, (2) the number of dependents per worker, and (3) the per cent of rural and/or Negro population. Later estimates for 1945 based upon federal and state income tax returns, which the bureau considers to be more accurate, are not used here because they are not comparable with the bureau's estimates of 1940 income. See Lorin A. Thompson, "Income Payments by Cities and Counties of Virginia, 1947 and 1945," *The Virginia Economic Review*, July, 1949, p. 3.

b. Sales Management, May 10, 1941, and May 10, 1946.

c. Virginia Department of Taxation, *Annual Reports*.

d. Average income value per return.

slightly above the 22.1 per cent realized by the Hampton Roads communities in 1940. Could it be that the folks back home in other parts of Virginia realized greater increases in individual incomes than those who rushed to the crowded Hampton Roads communities to take advantage of the "golden streets" flowing with the "milk and honey" of inflated wages in war activities? It would seem so, from the above analysis.

At first sight, figures on income values reported on state income tax returns, as shown in the last two columns of Table 36, seem to present a somewhat different picture. Not only did aggregate income values reported by Hampton Roads taxpayers increase much more from 1940 to 1945 than those for the whole state, but average incomes per return also grew at a greater rate. Moreover, the Hampton Roads share of total income values reported by all Virginians went up from 20.3 per cent in the prewar year to 26.7 per cent in 1945 while the share of the total number of state tax returns rose from 22.4 to 24.6 per cent. The conflict between the picture presented by these figures on income values and tax returns, however, and that provided by the other income estimates in Table 36 is more apparent than real. Average income values per tax return obviously do not reflect incomes received by the larger number of Hampton Roads residents who either received too small an amount to be subject to the state income tax or who, as transients or persons who had never previously earned enough to be liable for the tax, escaped or evaded the tax administrators. Per capita income figures would, of course, include most of such persons. The fact that the average income value per return for Hampton Roads residents increased during the war years more than for Virginians as a whole while per capita income payments and buying income showed a somewhat smaller percentage increase than in the rest of the state would appear to indicate that the war brought greater improvement in the economic well-being of the more stable, permanent residents of the Hampton Roads-Peninsula region and of persons living in other parts of Virginia than of the more transient Hampton Roads residents who did not report their incomes for state tax purposes. It should be emphasized, of course, that these conclusions can only be suggestive since the income figures upon which they are based are only rough estimates.

Further evidence of the impact of the war upon the income structure of the Hampton Roads-Peninsula area is provided by Table 37.[23] As in the prewar years, a slightly larger proportion of all Hampton Roads residents reporting 1945 income to the Virginia Department of Taxation had taxable incomes of $3,000 and under than of Virginians generally. Both groups in this lowest taxable income bracket, however, were smaller in 1945 than before the war. The $3,000 or less group declined from 90.2 per cent of those reporting taxable income in the Hampton Roads-Peninsula area for 1939 to 87 per cent in 1945; in the entire state, the percentage dropped from 89.0 to 86.1. Similarly, the number of persons reporting taxable incomes of $3,000 to $5,000 and those with incomes above $5,000 increased both for Hampton Roads and Virginia, with the latter continuing to show higher percentages in each of these upper income brackets.

These wartime developments reflect, on the one hand, the substantially higher individual incomes throughout the Hampton Roads region and Virginia and, on the other, the continuance of the prewar tendency for per capita incomes in localities with relatively large industrial populations to be somewhat lower than in centers where

23. The data in this table should be compared with that in Table 14.

TABLE 37. INCOME VALUES AND RETURNS, VIRGINIA STATE INCOME TAX, INDIVIDUALS AND FIDUCIARIES, BY INCOME GROUPS, HAMPTON ROADS-PENINSULA REGION AND VIRGINIA, 1947 (INCOME YEAR 1945)

Place	Number Reporting Income							Average Value Per Return
		$3,000 or under		$3,000–$5,000		Over $5,000		
	Total	Number	Per cent	Number	Per cent	Number	Per cent	
VIRGINIA	239,152	205,879	86.1	17,116	7.1	16,157	6.8	1,665
HAMPTON ROADS–PENINSULA AREA .	62,789	54,622	87.0	4,177	6.6	3,990	6.4	1,820
Norfolk City . . .	21,138	17,214	81.4	1,789	8.5	2,135	10.1	2,368
Portsmouth . . .	9,068	8,323	91.8	432	4.8	313	3.4	1,381
South Norfolk . .	1,282	1,218	95.0	42	3.3	22	1.7	1,224
Norfolk Co. . . .	8,491	7,904	93.1	401	4.7	186	2.2	1,379
Princess Anne Co.	1,399	1,040	74.3	154	11.0	205	14.7	2,813
Nansemond Co. .	552	497	90.0	22	4.0	33	6.0	1,785
Suffolk	1,540	1,258	81.7	99	6.4	183	11.9	2,387
Isle of Wight Co. .	668	592	88.6	31	4.7	45	6.7	1,059
Newport News . .	6,340	5,682	89.6	378	6.0	280	4.4	1,506
Warwick Co. . . .	3,923	3,421	87.2	315	8.0	187	4.8	1,687
Elizabeth City Co.	5,673	5,082	89.6	358	6.3	233	4.1	1,587
Hampton	836	709	84.8	53	6.3	74	8.9	1,869
York Co.	1,070	990	92.5	39	3.6	41	3.8	1,307
James City Co. . .	298	274	91.9	10	3.4	14	4.7	1,120
Williamsburg . . .	511	418	81.8	54	10.6	39	7.6	1,904

Source: Annual Report of the Virginia Department of Taxation, Table 13.

workers in trades, services, and professions were more numerous. This is borne out by the figures in Table 37 for particular Hampton Roads localities. South Norfolk, Portsmouth, Norfolk County, and Newport News, with their relatively large industrial populations, continued in 1945 as before the war to show larger percentages of state tax returns with values of $3,000 and under and lower average income values per return than Norfolk, Suffolk, Williamsburg, Hampton, and Princess Anne County (including the town of Virginia Beach), where trade, services, and the professions provided much larger shares of the total employment.

SUMMARY

It is evident from the materials presented in this chapter that World War II brought a tremendous expansion in the volume of almost all types of economic activity carried on in the Hampton Roads-Peninsula region. Local business, however, tended to lag somewhat behind the rate of increase in shipbuilding employment and military population. There is some evidence, also, to support the conclusion that local business expansion tended to be more closely related to changes in shipbuilding employment than to changes in military population.

The pressure for goods and services was so great during the war years that, in spite of shortages of manpower, stocks of goods, and business equipment and buildings, the number of business firms in the Hampton Roads area increased. Old firms stuck it out and new firms were established to a greater degree than in the rest of Virginia. The effect of the war upon the size of firms is not altogether clear, though there is some evidence that employers with 8 or less workers and more than 100 workers tended to expand their work forces, with prewar firms of intermediate size declining in size under war pressures.

To an even greater degree than in World War I, shipbuilding dominated the manufacturing structure of the Hampton Roads-Peninsula area during the Second World War. Other forms of manufacturing, except food, car and bus repair, and other direct auxiliaries to the war effort, scarcely held their own. The greatly feared postwar industrial slump was far smaller and slower in developing than had been expected. Both Newport News and the Norfolk-Portsmouth district were successful in attracting new manufacturing enterprises in the immediate postwar years and shipyards employment held up remarkably well during 1946, 1947, and 1948.

The role of retail, wholesale, and service trades in the Hampton Roads economy, already large before World War II, became even more important during the war years. Expansion in these lines was considerably greater than in the rest of Virginia. It was particularly great in wholesaling and the restaurant business. The fact that Newport News, whose economy was dominated by a private shipyard, showed a greater wartime rate of growth in trades and services than either Norfolk or Portsmouth, supports the conclusion that the expansion of war industries such as shipbuilding tends to have a more direct influence upon the volume of local trade than the coming to a community of large numbers of sailors and soldiers.

The Hampton Roads ports were drafted into hauling troops and military cargoes abroad at the expense of their large prewar coastwise traffic in coal and other commodities. While the war's end brought partial resumption of coastwise coal shipments, other coastwise traffic was a dead duck. On the other hand, exports of coal and, to a smaller degree, other goods to war-torn Europe pushed Hampton Roads for the first time in its history to top place among all Atlantic ports in export tonnage. Even imports from abroad increased. The fact remains, however, that the war destroyed much of the coastwise and intercoastal trade of the Hampton Roads ports and substituted a temporary expansion of foreign shipping, which European recovery should materially shrink, without remedying the fundamental factors which have kept these ports in a secondary status for many years. Such factors include insufficient population to support large import traffic, absence of locally owned steamship lines, and the failure of shipping companies to treat Hampton Roads as a full cargo port, except for coal. Wartime and postwar expansion of physical facilities has been on a large scale but what effect these new facilities will have upon the future growth of the ports remains to be seen.

Agriculture, particularly the production of such commodities as livestock, poultry, dairy products, vegetables, and cut flowers, for which the demand increased sharply as military and civilian transients poured into the Hampton Roads communities, was in a boom condition during most of the war. While the proportion of total acreage devoted to farming increased, with a consequent increase in the average size of the farms as the total number of farms in the area declined, little change occurred in the general prewar agricultural structure. Small farms of relatively high value operated largely by owners rather than tenants continued to be the rule. Seafood, like farm products, was in great demand as the population of the area grew and meat became scarce not only locally but throughout the country. In spite of a shortage of fishermen, sharp increases in prices obtainable for all classes of fish, after an initial decline in pounds of fish caught during the early war years, brought forth by 1945 a catch which was almost double the 1939 catch in pounds and seven-fold larger in value. Most of the increase, however, was in fin fish rather than oysters, crabs, and other shellfish.

What was the effect of all of this expanded economic activity upon the income of the people in the Hampton Roads-Peninsula communities? The rough estimates which are available indicate that both aggregate and per capita incomes increased substantially but that per capita income rose less in the Hampton Roads region than in Virginia as a whole. In other words, even though expanded population brought the Hampton Roads area a larger share of total state income in 1945 than before the war, Hampton Roads residents, from the standpoint of average incomes to individuals, lost ground in relation to the rest of the state during the war. The fact that average income values per state income tax return reported by Hampton Roads people increased to a greater degree than those reported by other Virginians, however, suggests that prewar residents of the area and the more stable of the newcomers experienced increases in their personal incomes but that many of the transient members of these communities realized smaller increases in incomes than residents of sections of Virginia not as directly related to war activities.

CHAPTER X

BUSINESS PROBLEMS AND PRACTICES*

UNDERSTANDING of the economic impact of war comes, not only through analysis of such generalized information as that presented in Chapter IX, but also through study of the problems war presents to particular business firms. Accordingly, case studies of a representative group of forty-five companies comprise an inherent part of this attempt to discover the economic impact of World War II upon the Hampton Roads-Peninsula area. The types and location of these businesses are indicated in Table 38. Every locality in the area is represented either by a firm operating exclusively therein or by multi-community firms, and most major types of business are covered. Owners or executives of each of these enterprises were interviewed[1] at their respective places of business as to the effect of the war upon: (a) lines of products or services offered; (b) types of customers; (c) financial structure, scope of operations, and physical facilities; (d) personnel problems and adjustments; (e) governmental requirements and adjustments; and (f) managerial personnel and structure. As might be expected, the response was somewhat uneven. Remarkably complete stories of wartime experiences were given by some firms while others offered only fragmentary information. Yet the composite picture as presented in the following pages, derived largely from these case studies, presents a reasonably accurate and representative account of the manner in which particular businesses not only in the Hampton Roads-Peninsula area but probably in many other American communities met the challenge of war activities in their midst.

*By Charles F. Marsh, Professor of Economics and Business Administration, College of William and Mary.

1. Since most of the information obtained in these interviews was obtained with the understanding that it would not be identified with the names of the particular firms from which it was obtained, very few footnote references are given in this chapter. It should be emphasized, however, that typewritten summaries of these interviews are in the files of the Hampton Roads-Peninsula War Studies Committee, College of William and Mary.

TABLE 38. BUSINESS FIRMS INCLUDED IN CASE STUDIES, BY TYPE OF BUSINESS AND LOCATION

Type of Business	Norfolk	Newport News	Virginia Beach & Princess Anne Co.	Williamsburg	Hampton	Two—Not All	All
Retail Trade (12)							
Coal and Oil . . .	X						
Grocery:							
Independent (2)	X	X					
Chain							X
Department stores (4)	X	XX		X			
Ladies ready-to-wear	X						
Auto sales & service	X			X			
Hardware & bldg. supplies . . .			X				
Wholesale Trade (4)							
Grocery	X						
Drugs	X						
Plumbing & heating						X	
Ship chandler . .						X	
Personal & Other Services (9)							
Laundry and cleaning	X						
Newspaper . . .		X					
Motion picture theatres (2) .				X		X	
Hotel			X				
Restaurants (4) .	XXX		X				
Finance, Insurance and Real Estate (4)							
Banking (3) . . .	X	X		X			
Real estate . . .						X	
Manufacturing (8)							
Shipbuilding . . .		X					
Marine engineering	X						
Men's clothing . .	X						
Truck bodies . . .		X					
Fertilizer (2) . . .	XX						
Coffee roasting . .	X						
Seafood					X		
Transportation, Communication & Other Public Utilities (6)							
Telephone							X
Local transportation						X	
Foreign freight forwarder . . .	X						
Stevedoring . . .	X						
Radio broadcasting	X						
Elec. light & power						X	
Other (2)							
General construction		X					
Commercial farming			X				
Total	20	8	4	4	1	5	3

LINES OF PRODUCTS OR SERVICES OFFERED

In addition to the introduction of "ersatz" or substitute products into the merchandise stocks of practically all retail and wholesale firms in the Hampton Roads communities as well as throughout the country, the Second World War brought many other changes in product lines and services offered. The dropping of "hard goods" like household appliances, other metal goods, and some lines of furniture and the expansion of "soft goods" lines was a common experience of most department stores. The influx of service people and war workers with relatively high incomes boomed sales of these ersatz and soft goods, especially work clothes and uniforms, to such a degree that in spite of the disappearance of many traditional lines, total sales of typical department stores almost tripled during the war years.

Automobile dealers, after an early war boom in sales of new cars in 1940 and 1941, found, much to their surprise, that it was possible to stay in business even after new car sales were virtually wiped out and gasoline and tires were rationed. War workers and military personnel with "B" and "C" ration cards made even the rationed gas and tire business fairly good in the Hampton Roads communities, and the used car and service departments came into their own as essential businesses which not only paid for themselves but also covered overhead expenses, in many cases, formerly borne by new car sales. An additional means by which at least one dealer attempted to take up the slack was the addition of a line of household supplies and toys.

Substantial profits were realized by timely wartime modifications in product lines. A retail coal dealer, for example, dropped its oil business because of threatened scarcity, strong competition, and the probability of strict government regulations, concentrated on sales of automatic stokers and stoker coal, expanded greatly a profitable distilled water business, and added packaged coal and a furnace and boiler-cleaning service to its offerings. A Norfolk restaurant, similarly, branched out late in the war with a profitable sideline consisting of the sale, on a fifty-fifty division of gross receipts basis, of "personalized music" delivered through semi-private outlets in forty odd eating places and beer parlors for five cents a "dose" via telephone wires from a central record-player.

Hampton Roads businesses modified services to customers in various ways to meet such wartime developments as more transient and less established customers, government restrictions, irregular working hours, and the overflow of city population into the outlying areas. The large number of strange customers combined with government regulations of credit and transportation to greatly curtail credit and delivery service of many stores. Department stores quite generally experienced a drop in credit sales from approximately 60 per cent before the war to about 30 per cent during the war years. Some grocery stores shifted completely to a cash and carry basis. A large retailer of ladies clothing saw its actual annual deliveries dwindle from about 40,000 packages in 1941 to less than 400 in 1944. One open-air market on one of Norfolk's through streets found it highly profitable to remain open twenty-four hours per day because of the large numbers of workers passing by at all hours of the night. The growth of the all-year population of Virginia Beach as transients stationed or employed in the Norfolk-Portsmouth area occupied every available building, summer or year-round in design, caused one Virginia Beach restaurant to provide all-year service. Before 1942, the owner had operated the beach establishment only between Easter and October and a Norfolk eating place the rest of the year.

One of the most significant changes in services offered to customers was a shift by a real-estate firm from the traditional rental business to the formation of real-estate syndicates concerned with planning, constructing, financing, and managing apartment and housing developments. Originally these syndicates were financed largely through New York City capital. In 1944 and 1945, however, as these projects passed out of the construction into the management state, the local real-estate firm assisted in the sale of the New York holdings to Newport News and Norfolk investors and became actively engaged in the management of these properties. Since the war, it has tended to get back into the rental business to some degree but it is probable that the war has put the company permanently into the management of these properties.

TYPES OF CUSTOMERS

Such businesses as construction, plumbing and heating, manufacturing of truck bodies and, of course, shipbuilding and ship repair found that World War II simplified their problems by substituting one customer—the federal government[2]—for a variety of private and

2. While the federal government purchased through several distinct procurement agencies, each of which used somewhat different procurement techniques, there was enough similarity in their procurement practices to make it comparatively easy for private firms to sell to first one and then another of these agencies.

governmental customers. One local construction company which had previously carried on as little as 5 per cent of its business in the Newport News-Norfolk area was able to concentrate practically all of its business in this center of naval and military construction during the war years, with consequent savings in cost and increased managerial efficiency, in spite of the many-fold increase in its volume of business. While it is not anticipated that this situation will continue for long after the war, the per cent of local work may remain higher than the prewar level.

A plumbing and heating wholesaler found that the substitution of large shipments by rail of standarized products to government establishments for small, miscellaneous deliveries by truck to scattered local contractors was a godsend during days of gasoline and tire rationing and labor shortage as well as a source of considerable savings in distribution costs. A manufacturer of truck bodies, unable because of concentration on government contracts to supply civilian customers during the war, was able to build up a backlog of deferred demand for truck bodies which has kept it busy during the postwar years.

Grocery stores, moving picture theaters, restaurants, and other retail and service trades experienced a less pleasing change in types of customers. The hordes of in-migrant war workers and military personnel and their families created serious managerial problems. While they were free spenders who enriched local tradesmen, many of them were inclined toward pilfering of merchandise, aggressive rudeness, and extreme disorderliness while in the various places of business. The problem of keeping movie theaters and stores clean, especially in view of the shortage of unskilled labor, created serious difficulties and sometimes extreme distaste on the part of businessmen and their employees for their daily work. The head of one system of movie theaters complained that even an increase in admission charges and the spreading of the patrons over six instead of five shows per day in the downtown theaters of Portsmouth, Norfolk, and Newport News were of little effect in keeping the crowds down to a manageable size. A by-product of the disreputable condition of the downtown theaters was a growth in the patronage at neighborhood theaters, which could be kept in somewhat better condition. The war probably accentuated this trend toward the neighborhood theater.

Many of the firms included in this study felt the impact of the sharp wartime increases in the incomes of such proverbially low income groups as Negroes and manual laborers generally. Department stores and specialty stores selling quality ladies clothing which had seldom been patronized by these people experienced a considerable influx of them as wartime employment opportunities and high wages swelled their purchasing power. Grocers and a dealer in hardware and building supplies observed a similar tendency for many of these formerly less privileged classes to shift from "bargain basement" buying attitudes to demanding quality merchandise. While a portion of the demand for quality goods by these new high-income groups probably represented temporary, irrational buying attitudes comparable to the silk-shirt orgies of World War I, many of these people experienced a rise in standards of living and appreciation of quality merchandise along with the rise in income which may have long-run significance in evaluating the markets available for businessmen of the Hampton Roads and other Southern communities, with their large population of Negroes and other persons with traditionally low prewar living standards.

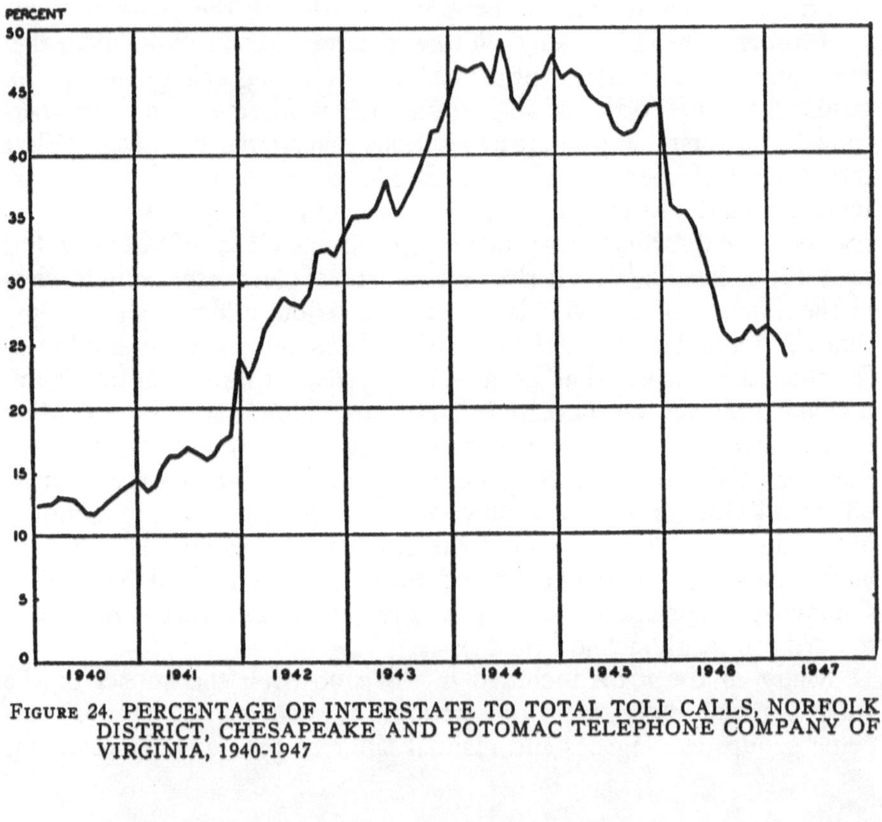

FIGURE 24. PERCENTAGE OF INTERSTATE TO TOTAL TOLL CALLS, NORFOLK DISTRICT, CHESAPEAKE AND POTOMAC TELEPHONE COMPANY OF VIRGINIA, 1940-1947

The impact of mass migration of people from other parts of the country into the Hampton Roads region upon the types of customers served by businesses in the area is graphically shown by Figure 24, which charts the changing percentages during the war years of interstate to total toll calls handled by the Norfolk District of the Chesapeake & Potomac Telephone Company of Virginia. As the 1940 trickle of civilian and military in-migrants, who kept in touch with their distant home folks by telephone, swelled to a mighty flood in 1943 and 1944 and slacked off thereafter, so the percentage of interstate to total long distance calls rose from less than 12 per cent in July, 1940, to 47.9 per cent in December, 1944, and declined to 24 per cent by February, 1947.

Somewhat similar evidence of the effect upon customers of war migration into and out of the Hampton Roads-Peninsula area was observed by a grocery chain serving all of the communities in this area and various North Carolina communities from which many shipyards and war construction workers came. Monthly sales in one of its large Greensboro, North Carolina, stores, for example, fell off from 1940 to early 1943 in almost inverse proportion to the increase in sales in a store of comparable size in Newport News as North Carolinians flocked to the construction and shipyards jobs open in the latter city. Conversely, as shipyards employment tapered off after the spring of 1943, monthly sales of the Greensboro store picked up almost in proportion to the decline in the sales of the Newport News store. While these relationships may be accidental in part and other factors may be involved, they do appear to indicate the great extent to which Hampton Roads war industries, and the Newport News Shipbuilding and Drydock Company in particular, provided customers for local retailers; the high mobility of in-migrant workers and their consequent lack of dependability as customers; and, finally, the reciprocal relationship between employment opportunities in Virginia's Hampton Roads area and the reserve of labor in Greensboro and other North Carolina communities.

Financial Structure, Scope of Operations, and Physical Facilities

Profitable business operations during the early war years gave various Hampton Roads firms opportunities to set their financial houses in order, realize long-standing desires to change their scope of operations, and provide needed physical facilities.

A retail coal and oil firm, which, since its organization on a shoestring basis by two young veterans of World War I in the early twenties, had waged an almost constant uphill struggle against inadequate capital, heavy indebtedness, and intense competition, was able to pay off all of its debts during the war years, take on various profitable sidelines, and build up by 1946, out of reinvested earnings, a $70,000 plant. Similarly, early war profits gave a young farmer his chance to buy or lease a sufficient number of small farms to make possible large-scale production and marketing of such truck crops as spinach, snap beans, potatoes, strawberries, and collards. Not only did he acquire his own warehouse, railroad siding, and fleet of trucks, but he also established his own repair shop to prevent breakdowns of trucks, tractors, and other machinery from obstructing the flow of vegetables to the lush markets.

A relatively small prewar fuel and feed dealer found himself at the end of the war with an enlarged and modernized warehouse, a new retail store, and a thriving building supplies, paint, and hardware business. While it continued to sell coal and oil, it had almost withdrawn from the feed business because of the greater profits in construction materials and hardware.

The proprietor of a successful twenty-year-old general grocery business in downtown Norfolk, which provided sales clerks, credit, and delivery service, bought the controlling interest in 1940 in an open-air curb market and grocery store, located on a through street travelled day and night by war workers. In spite of poor management by the associate on the ground, lack of records, thieving employees, and pilferage by customers, the volume of business was so large that the market yielded sufficient profits to give the downtown groceryman his chance to do what he had always wanted to do—shift from the general service grocery business, with all of its wastes and headaches, to a cash-and-carry, self-service business. When his lease expired on the downtown store in 1943, he closed it, combined the two businesses, and took over personally the active management of the curb market. The latter was converted into an all-year building, expanded considerably and run on a self-service basis.

A Virginia Beach restaurant's early war profits made it possible for it to meet the shortage of food and personnel through the installation of larger refrigeration boxes, various types of kitchen machinery, and a more efficient kitchen layout. The tendency for Virginia Beach to become a year-round business center because of the large number of in-migrants living there during the war years and the profits made by many businesses led to a veritable face-lifting for the entire business section of the town. In spite of the shortage and high costs of building materials, new stores and office buildings, a new theater, and a large new hotel were constructed near the end of the war. While some Virginia Beach businessmen believe that facilities and businesses have been overexpanded, the only adverse effects at the time of writing had been to place at a competitive disadvantage some of the older, poorly equipped firms in this resort community. The transient war population has long since departed but the continued shortage of adequate housing facilities in the Norfolk-Portsmouth district and the many attractive features of Virginia Beach have caused many people working in the cities to take up year-round residence in Virginia Beach and thus provide a foundation for a larger amount of permanent business activity than the prewar resort was able to do.

In spite of high priorities which made it possible for the various utility companies to expand greatly their physical facilities, the pressures upon them were so great that long waiting lists of applicants for telephone, electric, and gas service had to be established, and street car and bus riders had to be content with standing room and not much of that. Thanks to its foresight in expanding its Norfolk plant in 1938 and 1939, the telephone utility had probably the most nearly adequate facilities during the war period. Vast new construction was necessary, however, to provide adequate service at the various army and navy establishments and to keep essential communications intact. While electric light, power, and gas service were maintained on an amazingly high plane, the fact that power facilities in Newport News, Hampton, and vicinity were owned and operated by the Virginia Public Service Corporation, an orphan after the breakup of the Insull holding company empire in the early thirties until its merger in 1944 with the Virginia Electric and Power Company, which furnished electricity to all other Hampton Roads-Peninsula communities, prevented the unified handling of power problems in the area and may have retarded the provision of adequate facilities. The provision of adequate car and bus service in Norfolk and Portsmouth was also retarded by uncertainty as to the future ownership and management of the transit lines. The Virginia Electric and Power Company, knowing that there was a good possibility that its transit properties must be sold in the near future to an independent company, in accordance with Securities and Exchange Commission action under the Public

Utilities Holding Company Act of 1935, bought very few new cars or busses after 1939. Unfortunately for all parties, especially the passengers, the sale of the properties to the Virginia Transit Company did not occur until 1945 and the war had to be fought on the transit lines with inadequate equipment and under managers whose primary interest was in the electric light and power business and who expected to be relieved from their unwelcome and exceedingly trying task momentarily. In spite of these obstacles, the officers and employees of the transit lines, as the following figures[3] indicate, did an almost superhuman job of transporting civilians, sailors, and soldiers to and from their wartime assignments:

Year	Number of Local Railway and Bus Revenue Passengers	
	Norfolk	Portsmouth
	(in thousands)	
1939	28,505	5,706
1940	32,615	6,919
1941	41,629	10,775
1942	64,015	19,045
1943	72,158	21,042
1944	73,557	21,494
1945	69,313	20,029
1946	61,843	17,275

PERSONNEL PROBLEMS AND ADJUSTMENTS

The most serious problems presented to Hampton Roads businessmen by the Second World War concerned personnel. Expanded business volume created the need for additional workers. Yet war employment in the armed forces and a variety of civilian occupations in government agencies, shipyards, and other plants created a type of competition that made life miserable for ordinary employers. Labor turnover was almost unbelievably high. One bank, for example, which employed 50 persons in 1939 and 91 late in 1945, hired a total of 224 persons during the intervening years and recorded 183 terminations. A department store with an average work force of 300 during the war years had to employ from 600 to 1,000 individuals per year to maintain this force. Only one of 40 women employed by a coffee roasting firm before the war was still on the job in the spring of 1946. Many other employers could duplicate these experiences, though few of them had enough clerical workers to keep sufficiently accurate

3. These figures and the accompanying information were obtained from W. R. Triplett, Assistant to the Manager, Virginia Transit Company, in a personal interview March 24, 1947.

records during the years of peak war activity to know what their labor turnover was! A few employers, however, enjoyed remarkably stable work forces. One fertilizer manufacturer, a non-essential employer by government manpower standards, had virtually no labor turnover. Most of its employees were Negroes who had been with the company for some years, were over the draft age, and were paid high enough wages under a union contract to make them disinterested in the high wages paid by war agencies. A small department store was also able to maintain a stable work force because its employees were largely older women and men over the draft age. These were exceptions, however, to the general situation.

How did businessmen meet this condition of labor scarcity and high turnover? Ingenious recruiting methods, employment of women, more formalized personnel, training and upgrading programs, and a variety of labor saving procedures were used by different employers.

Recruiting Methods

The Newport News Shipbuilding and Drydock Company found the "transfer community" idea an advantageous recruiting device.[4] Good workers from certain North Carolina communities were encouraged to persuade their relatives and neighbors to join them at the shipyards and the company cooperated in finding housing so that the entire group could live close together. This not only provided a good source of labor supply but also reduced the feeling of loneliness and strangeness which so often causes workers to quit and go home. In effect, these workers brought the human phases of their home environment with them. As the war drew to a close, these communities ordinarily returned to their North Carolina habitat, though some have chosen to remain in Virginia.

Other employers, aided by the War Manpower Commission, recruited workers in the rural and non-war centers of Virginia and North Carolina. One automobile dealer, however, rather ruefully stated that he finally got tired of recruiting men and women from outside Hampton Roads and training them in his service department only to see them leave as soon as they learned anything about repairing automobiles for the higher wages paid mechanics at the various naval establishments. He depended thereafter on his core of older, experienced mechanics who worked long hours at overtime rates of pay.

Both the telephone and power companies recruited volunteers

4. Personal interview with President Homer J. Ferguson, September 12, 1945.

from company employees in communities not engaged in war activity to come as a war service to the Hampton Roads area. The telephone company, in particular, needed workers in this area so desperately that it paid traveling expenses to and from Norfolk and room and board during the emergency period. The method was effective though expensive.

The College of William and Mary, through its "Work-Study Plan" brought in each year from 1942 through 1945 approximately 200 sixteen- and seventeen-year-olds fresh from Virginia and other high schools to work in the stores, hotels, and offices of Williamsburg on a part-time basis while attending college. These boys contributed greatly to the solution of this community's personnel problems and, at the same time, through an accelerated program of study, completed two or more academic years before going into the armed forces.

Employment of Women

The local transportation companies, like many other employers, turned to the employment of women as a solution. By October, 1944, when the total number of car and bus operators south of Hampton Roads had risen from 279 late in 1939 to 461, women numbered 81. In general, they worked out well as they were treated exactly like men except that a "sponsor" or "dean of women" was employed to advise with them and lodgings were provided at the car barns for some. Marriages, divorces, and other problems growing out of the entrance of women into what had been an exclusively male environment made company officials wonder at times whether they were running a business or a sociological experiment, but the problems gradually worked themselves out. Some difficulties were encountered at the end of the war in laying off women operators, all of whom were union members, to make room for men returning from the armed forces. By March, 1947, however, their numbers had shrunk to only 20 and this group were accepted by the men without complaint. Some of them, indeed, were wives of male operators and the company customarily gave them similar shifts so that they could come to work and go home together.

The Negro women car cleaners constituted a more serious problem. Under union rules, the 30 or 40 women so employed—out of a total of roughly 200 car cleaners—were paid as high as 90 cents per hour, considerably above the wages paid in comparable employment. Company officials felt that about ten first class Negro men could do more work than the entire group of women, but the latter showed little disposition to leave their high-paid jobs at the war's end and union rules made it difficult for the company to lay them off.

Probably the major source of labor for the war-pressed stores and offices of the Hampton Roads communities was the wives of servicemen stationed at near-by posts. While many of this group showed little sense of responsibility or loyalty to their employers and often left without notice, either for better jobs or to accompany their husbands when they received orders to move, businesses of the area could scarcely have kept open without them. Some of these women, indeed, had such excellent capabilities and past business experience that they were veritable bonanzas to the harassed employers. A building supplies and hardware dealer avowed that the service wife who walked into his store one morning to apply for a job and who had managed a large hardware store in her home town was the best thing that had ever hit his establishment. A Williamsburg bank was similarly blessed for more than a year with the services of an army officer's wife, who had been head bookkeeper in a large Pittsburgh bank, at the very time that it was reeling from a horde of new depositors and a manyfold increase in its volume of business.

Formalized Personnel Programs

One department store met the problem of labor scarcity and turnover by adopting early in the war a rather complete personnel program. It employed for the first time a qualified full-time personnel manager and established training, pension, and group insurance plans. Wage rates were increased during the early war years and just before the wage "freezes" under the national wage stabilization program it instituted a system of bonuses and commissions which gave the employees a share in the increased sales. In addition, store officials studied possible changes in merchandising practices which would require less labor and adopted such devices as glass display cases in the aisles and the elimination of phonograph records and other merchandise which required considerable attention from salespeople. Two other large retailers included in this study also hired their first personnel managers as a means of meeting wartime labor troubles.

A wholesale dealer in plumbing and heating equipment found that its warborne, intensive, six months' training program, through which experienced employees given special teacher training taught new recruits, was just as effective as the prewar "absorption" method under which approximately four years were needed to develop greenhorns into good employees.

Labor-Saving Procedures

Through substituting a system of cost analysis of only a restricted sample of its invoices for its prewar analysis of every bill of goods shipped, a plumbing and heating wholesaler decreased the number of skilled clerical workers on this job from twenty-five to ten. Moreover, much to its surprise, the sampling basis provided just as accurate cost analyses as the universe system used before the war. The pressure to save labor during the war years thus forced the company more or less accidentally into a costing practice which it will probably continue to use indefinitely even after labor becomes plentiful.

Two independent food stores instituted the self-service plan, a chain grocery system closed groups of near-by, small service stores and opened one large supermarket in their place, and a restaurant shifted to the cafeteria system in the attempt to curtail personnel requirements. None of the grocery stores have considered shifting back to the prewar service store basis as the self-service system has been generally satisfactory. The restaurant, however, found that its sales declined because of the preference of customers in the Hampton Roads area for table service and abandoned the cafeteria system as soon as waitresses became available.

The electric power company economized on labor through the discontinuance of various home services and reading meters and billing customers every two months instead of on the customary monthly basis. The transit lines in Norfolk and Portsmouth decreased the frequency of periodic overhauls of street cars and busses, the standard mileage between such checkovers increasing from 5,000 to 10,000 miles for street cars and 1,000 to 5,000 for busses. The inevitable increase in break-downs and accompanying traffic tie-ups were simply written off as one of the costs of war. The substitution by the Virginia Transit Company in 1945 of a replacement schedule for individual parts, such as carburetors, starters, etc., for the periodic tying up of the entire vehicle proved to be a very successful way of meeting this problem.

GOVERNMENT REQUIREMENTS AND ADJUSTMENTS MADE

Businessmen in the Hampton Roads-Peninsula region, like those in other parts of the country, were enthusiastic in damning wartime government restrictions and red tape and in looking forward to their release from such shackles. Yet many of them reaped great benefits from their relations with government agencies. These experiences can be evaluated most effectively by considering the impact of government requirements upon: (1) businesses selling little or nothing to government agencies, and (2) firms which worked under government contracts.

Ordinary Civilian Businesses

O.P.A. and W.P.B. requirements made life miserable for many Hampton Roads firms, as well as those in other parts of the United States. Two large independent grocers in the Norfolk-Newport News area experienced considerable difficulty with the O.P.A. regulation, which classified them with chain stores, on ceiling prices merely because their sales volume exceeded a certain minimum which was far below the sales volume of the typical chain system. They felt it necessary to charge somewhat higher prices than the chains because of their inability to enjoy such chain store economies as centralized purchasing and warehousing and to benefit from the advice of merchandising and storekeeping specialists employed by the chains. One of these independents—an open-air market—deliberately shortened its store hours from twenty-four to twelve, in spite of the continued demand for the continuous service from war workers, in order to bring its sales volume below the minimum for the chain-store classification and thus be permitted to have higher ceiling prices. The chain grocery included in this study, on the other hand, cited evidence to show that O.P.A. investigators were particularly tough on chain stores for innocent and almost unavoidable departures from price and rationing regulations and inclined to be more lenient with the independents.

Local newspapers, faced with the dilemma of rapidly rising circulation and W.P.B. restrictions on newsprint and type metal, had to resort to rationing news space through curtailing the length of important news stories, eliminating some stories entirely, and cutting down the size of the papers. WTAR, the Norfolk radio station, in the face of a great increase in the demand for time by commercial advertisers and a shortage of technical personnel, was faced with an overwhelming demand for war effort and public service announcements and programs. Through December, 1945, this station contributed to the war effort 4,401 announcements, 574 programs, and 291 hours of broadcast time. While the Treasury Department's bond drives accounted for approximately a third of the announcements and a fifth of the programs, more than 120 other agencies required war effort broadcasts. In addition, WTAR contributed in the "general public service" 1,793 announcements, 1,758 programs, and 385 hours of broadcast time sponsored by approximately 190 different non-governmental organizations.[5]

Fertilizer manufacturing provides an excellent example of a predominantly civilian business struggling to keep going in a war environment. Aside from the sale of insignificant amounts of sulfuric acid to the federal government for munitions purposes, the Hampton Roads companies had no war contracts. Indeed, the basic impact of wartime government action on these firms was the vastly increased demand by government and private munitions makers for the basic chemicals used in the manufacture of fertilizer. The companies were forced to cut down the plant food content of their products thus impairing their effectiveness to farmers. This shortage of basic ingredients continued into the postwar period, as government policy apparently favored the assignment of materials freed from munitions production to the Tennessee Valley Authority and other government agencies preparing semi-processed fertilizer or basic materials for shipment to foreign countries to aid in agricultural recovery.

In other respects, however, government action was beneficial to the fertilizer producers. Orders of the War Food Administration and the War Production Administration reduced the number of fertilizer grades from the fifty to sixty shipped from Norfolk in 1939 to only twenty-one in 1946. This action cut production costs, reduced inventory investments and losses, and simplified distribution to the farmer. So advantageous was this wartime simplification of fertilizer grades that the industry was successful in getting the Virginia legislature to enact a 1946 law providing that not less than fifteen nor more than twenty-five grades might be sold in Virginia plants.[6] Most beneficial of all government action affecting the Hampton Roads fertilizer producers was the favorable wartime price treatment accorded farm products and the accompanying prosperity of farmers. As agricultural demand, prices, and incomes soared, the demand for fertilizer kept pace. While shortage of materials kept shipments from the Norfolk-Portsmouth plants down to a modest wartime gain of 20 to 30

5. H. C. Whitehead, *WTAR Public Service and War Effort*, 1945 (mimeographed).

6. *1948 Cumulative Supplement to the Virginia Code of 1942*, Sect. 1115.

per cent, the intensity of the farmers' demand made them willing to take fertilizer when they could get it rather than just before planting. At least one Norfolk company was thereby able by 1944 to spread the major portion of its shipments over the six months from November through April in contrast to the prewar concentration of shipments and production in the late winter. While the company planned to make every effort to maintain this improved situation, it was not too optimistic about its ability to sell the farmers on its desirability once wartime abnormalities in adjustments of demand and supply disappeared.

Another Hampton Roads business which labored under the disadvantage of being a non-essential industry in a war environment was a maker of men's suits. Its attempts to obtain contracts to manufacture military uniforms failed because of the policy of the federal government to assign all available labor in the Hampton Roads region to shipbuilding and navy and army activities and to place war clothing contracts with plants in other sections of the country. The Norfolk clothing company was thus unable to obtain any priorities whatsoever for materials or labor and its production dropped during the war to approximately half its prewar volume. Material shortages became so acute at the end of the war that the plant was closed down completely during September and October, 1945. As wool and other materials became more plentiful early in 1946, however, production boomed to more than its prewar level with the plant operating three shifts per day and seven days per week to satisfy deferred demands and to clothe the returning veterans.

Government Contractors

Contractual arrangements between Hampton Roads businesses and government representatives ranged all the way from forced "quartering of troops" at hotels in the area, with fair compensation, of course, to those resulting from the vigorous solicitation of government purchases.

Most of the luxury hotels at Virginia Beach and elsewhere in the area and several of the Norfolk commercial hotels were taken over for the duration or for brief periods to provide housing for navy and army officers and their families. While some of the larger hotels welcomed this arrangement in view of their probable inability to maintain full houses at their customary high rates, others found it a heavy burden. One Virginia Beach hotel which was able to operate at capacity with its old clientele during the war years was seriously embarrassed by the forced quartering of forty to fifty naval air officers from near-by Oceana Air Base for three periods in 1944 of three months each. While the management was glad to assist with the war effort, it felt that the arrogance and lack of consideration shown by the naval representatives who negotiated these seizures contributed little to the winning of the war and trampled unnecessarily on private rights. These people customarily telephoned the hotel manager one or two days before the detachment of officers was due to arrive. When the manager demurred that his house was filled with private guests, the naval representative threatened to take over the hotel entirely unless the private patrons were ejected to make room for the naval officers. A Norfolk hotel had a similar unpleasant and very unprofitable experience when arrogant representatives of the United States Merchant Marine, in order to provide housing for men of the Merchant Marine early in the war, broke the lease of the hotel operator at just the time when it appeared that it would be possible for him to make reasonable profits after years of barely breaking even.

Some Hampton Roads firms, on the other hand, were firm in the belief that the difficulties incident to wartime contracting, shortages of merchandise, and the whole family of government controls were more than offset by the advantages of selling to the government. In addition to the local shipyards, construction companies, and the large plumbing and heating wholesaler previously mentioned in this chapter, almost 100 per cent of whose sales were to the federal government during the early forties, certain smaller concerns did business advantageously through government contracts. The war strengthened the opinion of a wholesale food merchant, for example, that government business is, as he put it, "clean business." Deliveries are in large units, bookkeeping is simplified, accounts are paid properly, and haggling over prices is at a minimum. This wholesaler proudly lists himself as a "government contractor" and plans increasingly to concentrate on selling to government agencies—municipal and state as well as federal. A wholesale drug company similarly found government business extremely beneficial. Early in the war, local procurement officers for the ships stores and post exchanges bought large quantities of goods from this firm and other local wholesalers on a piece-meal basis, and supply officers of naval vessels docking in Hampton Roads depended on this company for guidance in replenishing their stocks of first-aid equipment and drug sundries. After a few years, the wastefulness of this decentralized purchasing, without the economies possible through large-scale centralized buying, eventually came to the attention of naval authorities and was largely discontinued. While it lasted, however, it was an exceedingly profitable source of business for the local drug firm.

A somewhat more lasting type of benefit growing out of contractual relations with the government were various business practices required of some local contractors as a condition of selling to government agencies. For example, a marine engineering company repairing anything connected with a ship but the ship itself worked almost exclusively for the War Shipping Administration during the war, as that agency took over all merchant shipping. The reports required in connection with every repair job aroused the ire of the rather conservative officials of this company. Yet they finally admitted to the writer that much of what was included in these reports provided so much valuable cost data which had never previously been available that these reports, in modified form, would probably be continued voluntarily as a matter of internal control after W.S.A. turned the ships back to their private owners. Similarly, a manufacturer of truck bodies was amazed to find that the Philadelphia Ordnance Depot required a cost analysis from its suppliers which contributed so greatly to the efficiency of doing business that he wished he had known about it years before the war. This company also planned to continue this cost analysis work as a matter of good business practice.

Two auxiliaries of the shipping industry which remained in private hands while shipping itself was taken over by the government—stevedoring and foreign freight forwarding—felt the impact of the war in entirely opposite ways.[7] Stevedoring, or the loading and unloading of cargo onto and off of the ships, boomed. From June 15, 1942, when the Hampton Roads Port of Embarkation was activated, to May, 1945, the number of stevedores or longshoremen rose from less than 500 working in about 20 gangs to more than 3,000 grouped in 150 gangs. Between V-E Day and V-J Day, the number dropped to about 1,500 men. The additional longshoremen, all of whom were Negro members of the International Longshoremen Association, an A.F. of L. union, were recruited from among former employees who had gone to the shipyards early in the war, farmers and small town

7. This information was derived from a personal interview with Mr. J. H. Devereux, the active head of both Norton & Ellis, Inc., a freight forwarder, and the Southern Stevedore Company, August 22, 1945.

laborers, and railroad car unloaders. The high wage scale of the longshoremen of $1.25 per hour basic, $2.50 per hour for handling munitions, and $3.75 per hour for overtime munitions loading, of which there was a large amount, created a serious scarcity among the railroad car unloaders, whose base pay was only sixty-four cents per hour. In fact, much of the unloading of cars had to be done at night when the overtime rate of ninety-two cents per hour could be paid. The end of the war brought a rather confusing period of reconversion to the stevedoring industry as the government agencies withdrew and stevedoring contracts had to be negotiated anew with private steamship companies. The period of reconversion, however, could be scarcely more confusing than the war period which, in spite of the profitability of dealing with W.S.A., the army, the navy, and the British Government, brought almost unbearable tension because of the recruiting and supervising of inexperienced workers who showed an understandable tendency toward absenteeism because of long hours and high wage rates.

The eight prewar foreign freight forwarders at the Hampton Roads ports, whose business was to provide ship space, insurance, properly made out shipping papers, and other essentials for inland exporters, saw the bottom drop out of their business as the four government agencies made all but a small part of their services unnecessary. Only their unification, under a 1942 bill (H.R. 6291) introduced into Congress by Representative Bland of Newport News, into the Hampton Roads Freight Forwarders, Inc. and the payment of what in effect were subsidies kept these businesses going during the war. This union was dissolved in 1945 with some misgivings as to their ability to survive free competition during the new postwar shipping era.

MANAGERIAL PERSONNEL AND STRUCTURE

The great increase in business volume and the necessity of facing complex new business problems created severe strains upon Hampton Roads managers as human beings and upon managerial structures. Several deaths and physical breakdowns of responsible officials of businesses covered by this study were directly attributable to these stresses. Some individuals in the middle or lower levels of management grew restive as employees and pulled out to establish their own businesses. The men's wear buyer of one department store resigned to establish his own men's clothing store. Successive heads of the bakery department of a large independent food store opened up bake shops of their own, with most of them seeking their old jobs after a few discouraging months with rationing of ingredients, price control, and other difficulties. The armed services claimed some of the ablest and most vigorous of the managerial group. One department store lost every executive under forty to the armed forces. Small wonder that ill health forced the partial retirement of the president of this company in 1945! Both the president and secretary-treasurer of a large laundry and cleaning firm went into the services. The plumbing and heating wholesaler discovered that the young men it had been grooming as executives since its establishment in the late 1920's were just ripe for the draft. The telephone and radio broadcasting companies found that their technical leaders and their most promising understudies were fair game for the Army Signal Corps and, in spite of their essential classification, found it difficult to retain sufficient specialists to carry on.

Various modifications in management structure were made to meet these conditions. The laundry and cleaning firm attempted to substitute committee management by department heads for the leadership formerly provided by the president and secretary-treasurer who had gone off to war. Everything that the textbooks on management say concerning the weaknesses of plural management was experienced by this company. After a year or so in which only the company's great volume of business and an occasional bit of direction by the president who was stationed near-by kept it from falling apart at the seams, a temporary manager was picked up from among medical dischargees from the armed forces. The two top officials, fortunately, were released from military duties in time to prevent too serious a breakdown. Formalized upgrading and training of experienced workers and of newly recruited employees with executive capacities was useful to the plumbing and heating company. A ladies ready-to-wear store, early in the war years, assigned a number of key salesladies to responsibilities as section chiefs and raised their salaries substantially in return for their promise to stay with the store rather than follow the siren call of war jobs. Most of them kept their promise and provided the company with a solid core of supervisory help.

Several concerns which experienced considerable increases in volume of business and number of employees made fundamental changes in their entire managerial structure. Departmentalization and functionalization developed as a substitute for the informal, personal, and centralized management which had been adequate in prewar days. The establishment of personnel departments by some firms in response to acute personnel difficulties has been noted earlier in this chapter. One of the first acts of the Virginia Transit Company after it assumed control of the Norfolk-Portsmouth transit properties in 1945 was to establish a traffic department whose function was to make periodic studies of demand and supply relationships at particular points on the system in order to provide a factual basis for modifying the service at these points. A local construction company, whose business pyramided to fantastic heights, increased its permanent supervisory personnel from about 50 to 150 individuals. Vice-presidents in charge of various types of construction activities, a central purchasing agent, and other functional officials were provided for in a thorough reorganization of its managerial system. A biscuit manufacturer which before the war had serviced Hampton Roads retailers out of its Richmond branch office met the increased sales volume in this area, travel restrictions, and related war problems by opening a Norfolk branch. The owner of one of the rapidly growing independent food stores had the good sense to create departments within the store and to delegate authority as well as responsibility to the new heads of these departments.

In spite of these and similar definite attempts to grapple with managerial problems, the majority of the heads of Hampton Roads business firms probably made little or no change in managerial organization but attempted to solve the problems through working longer hours themselves or frankly letting some of them go unsolved. From the standpoint of sound business principles, this "muddling through" approach is vulnerable to criticism. There is another approach, however, which is illustrated by the attitude of one store owner who stated quite frankly that he was more interested in developing himself as a human being and as a community servant than in continually working to make his business more successful. He took the position that his parents had built up a good business and that he saw no necessity of doing more than keeping it in reasonably good shape and taking care of the needs of those customers who depended upon it. He commented, somewhat ruefully, that he guessed he took what he learned in college too seriously to be a top-notch business man. In a somewhat similar vein, the young owner of a successful independent food store, who rose during the war years from truck driver, clerk, assistant manager, and manager, sold the business in 1946 and, like the brilliant David Ricardo who retired while still in his twenties from a successful banking business to study and write, this young man retired to do what he had always wanted to do. He moved with his family to a Florida orange grove purchased out of his war profits and now devotes his time to painting.

CONCLUSIONS

Several summary comments on this study of the impact of the war upon business problems and practices are appropriate. Only two out of forty-seven businessmen refused to cooperate in the study. They were forthright in stating that they could not see how such cooperation would benefit them, that they were not interested in the impact of the war upon the region's economy as long as they were making money, and that they were not impressed with the relationship of their own businesses to the economic and social structure of the entire region. It is significant, however, that representatives of forty-five businesses were sufficiently interested in a broad study of the war's impact upon the Hampton Roads-Peninsula region to give generously of their time and thought and to furnish confidential information to a project which might or might not be of any benefit to them as individual businessmen.

It is apparent from this sample of managerial attitudes in the region that Hampton Roads businessmen are conscious of the close relationship of their businesses to the general economic and social structure of the community of which they are a part. It is probable, also, that their war experiences played a large part in developing this sense of oneness with other elements of the community.

It is even possible that many businessmen in the area have gone too far in their belief in the dependence of their own businesses upon general community forces. The outside observer senses a certain paralyzing fatalism in the belief of some Norfolk businessmen that their fortunes rise and fall with the number of naval personnel assigned to the community, and in the feeling of some Portsmouth and Newport News enterprises that employment at the two shipyards is more important than their own business efficiency in determining their success. There is probably somewhat less of this feeling in Newport News than in the southside cities because the dominant economic force in the former city is provided by an alert private enterprise, and slow-moving government establishments set the pace in the latter.

While the postwar activities of the Norfolk Industrial Commission, the Peninsula Industrial Committee at Newport News, the Portsmouth Chamber of Commerce, and other groups active in developing the private industry of the area have been moderately successful, the development of vigorous business management which will take pride in its own accomplishments rather than passively accept the role of adjusting its business practices to changing governmental policies, particularly as to naval warfare, will require constant vigilance and great energy.

CHAPTER XI

LABOR RELATIONS*

In General, the effects of World War II on labor relations in the Hampton Roads-Peninsula area were similar to those felt in war areas throughout the nation. It is probable, also, that while employer-employee relations during and after the war varied from employer to employer in the Hampton Roads region, a reasonably accurate picture of the war's impact upon the general pattern of labor relations in the region is provided by the experiences of the Newport News Shipbuilding and Drydock Company, the largest private employer on either side of Hampton Roads. It is appropriate, accordingly, to consider in this chapter: (1) certain general effects of the Second World War upon labor relations throughout the country; (2) the prewar, war, and postwar changes in the relations of the Newport News Company and its workers; and (3) the extent to which the war's impact upon the Newport News Shipbuilding and Drydock Company was typical of the experiences of Hampton Roads employers.

WARTIME LABOR RELATIONS IN THE NATION

Paramount in importance were the numerous no-strike, no-lockout pledges. Labor and management gave up the use of their coercive weapons in order that war production could go forward without serious interruptions. In return for foregoing its right to strike, labor, in some instances, was granted by employers, union shop or closed shop conditions which probably would not have been granted if labor had not given up temporarily the strike weapon. In addition, the War Labor Board felt it necessary to call for the inclusion of "maintenance of membership" clauses in some contracts signed during the war period.

A second effect was observed when many employers saw that in order to meet production requirements of the armed forces it was necessary to make use of a relatively new technique, union-management cooperation. Though some notable examples of union-manage-

*By John A. McGuire, Assistant Professor of Economics and Business Administration, College of William and Mary.

ment cooperation existed before World War II, the practice did not become widespread until management recognized that such a technique would give workers a genuine feeling that wartime production was their job as well as management's.

The fact that the war on the home front was directed to a considerable extent by civilian agencies of the federal government pointed up two further effects of the war upon labor relations. The first of these had to do with government regulation and stabilization of wages. The second concerned government authorized adjustments in wage rates to offset cost-of-living increases. The former effect came about in order to prevent employers from "pirating" scarce labor from other defense plants through use of higher wage payments. The War Labor Board and the Wage Stabilization Board (covering the construction industry) tried to prevent this practice by requiring prior approval of all wage increases proposed by employers. This meant, in effect, that the bargaining process was often subordinated to federal compulsory arbitration.

Throughout the war period, many industries found that wage adjustments had to be given from time to time in order to compensate for advances in the cost of living. The cost-of-living index began rising as early as 1940 with the result that wage increases to offset this advance had to be granted even before our actual entry into the war. Not long after Pearl Harbor, Congress passed the Emergency Price Control Act (February, 1942). Federal wage controls came via an executive order in November, 1942. Though price lids were held on tightly well into 1943, certain changes in O.P.A. policy permitted some price increases and "controlled inflation" became the order of the day. With such a policy in effect, the government had no choice but to grant wage increases where cost of living increases justified them.

A final effect of the war was the increased use of up-grading. As millions of men were drafted into the armed forces, most war plants were confronted with the problem of how to hold on to the all too short supplies of workers. Hemmed in by governmental wage regulations, many employers turned to the technique of up-grading workers in order to give them the higher wages required to induce them not to quit and take jobs in other plants. Thus, up-grading was used to insure higher wages regardless of whether the worker's added or improved skill justified such a promotion in grade.

LABOR RELATIONS OF THE NEWPORT NEWS SHIPBUILDING AND DRYDOCK COMPANY

The important role played by the Newport News Shipbuilding and Drydock Company in the economy of the Hampton Roads area, as well as in the affairs of the nation, has already been indicated. From the early nineties through 1946, it constructed a total of 114 vessels for the United States Navy, 49 of which were built during World War II, and many private ships. In addition during the recent war the yard repaired, converted, and reconditioned over 700 ships. At one time there were 17 ships under construction. Peak employment of the Newport News Company was reached in early 1943 when the total number of workers exceeded 30,000. The yard was able to carry out its tremendous wartime building program despite the fact that from 1939 to 1943 it experienced a 100 per cent turnover in personnel. In addition, during the entire war period, a total of over 40,000 workers were trained for all types of jobs, 13,000 being trained in the welding school alone. Small wonder that the manner in which the Newport News Company has handled its relations with its workers has influenced considerably the general pattern of employer-employee relationships in the Hampton Roads communities! An understanding of wartime developments in this company's labor relations requires careful consideration, not only of its relations with the Peninsula Shipbuilders Association, the agency through which workers and management bargained during and after World War II, but also of certain earlier conditions which led to the formation of this association.

Individual Bargaining and Employee Representation Plans

In the years before 1927 these relations were conducted on an individual bargaining basis. Presumably the arrangement was one of an open shop, for it is claimed by company representatives that the company never discriminated in hiring, firing, or as to seniority on the basis of union membership or lack of it. By 1927, however, the company felt that the time was right for the initiation of some formalized labor relations plan where terms of employment could be discussed on a collective rather than on an individual basis. The company probably was influenced in this choice by the wave of "American Plans" in vogue in the twenties. Mr. Albert A. Giese, Assistant Personnel Manager of the yard, states that the so-called "employee representation" plan submitted to the employees at that time for approval was almost completely fashioned after the "Bethlehem Plan" then in effect in the plants of the Bethlehem Steel Company.[1]

Original Employee Representation Plan—1927. The company put into effect in 1927, with the cooperation of its employees,[2] a plan known as the Representation of Employees. The purposes of the plan were set forth in its preamble, as follows:

> In order to give the employees of the company a voice in regard to the conditions under which they labor, and to provide an orderly and expeditious procedure for the prevention and adjustment of any future differences, and to anticipate the problem of continuous employment, a method of representation of employees is to be established.[3]

The original plan called for the annual election of twenty-eight employee representatives (to be known as the Employees Representative Committee) each of whom was to be paid $100 per year by the company and whose function was to bring up workers' grievances to be settled. Workers in supervisory positions were not eligible to vote or to serve as representatives. Administration of the plan was vested in four joint committees, each made up of five elected representatives and not more than an equal number chosen from among the employees by the management. In addition, provision was made for a Management's Representative whose function it was "to keep the management in touch with the representatives and represent the management in negotiations with their officers and committees."

Another provision called for arbitration of differences between employees and the company, if the president of the company concurred. The plan could be amended by an affirmative vote of the full membership of one of the joint committees or by a majority of all the employees' representatives and representatives of management at an annual conference. Independence of action of elected representatives was "guaranteed" by permitting them to take questions of discrimination "to any of the Superior Officers, to the Joint Committee and to the President of the Company." It is significant that the original plan contained no provision for the payment of dues by the workers, thus by-passing one of the basic rules of a *bona fide* trade union.

1. Most of the expressions of company opinion cited herein and factual information concerning company practices are based, unless noted otherwise, on personal interviews with Mr. Giese during the spring and summer of 1948.

2. Who by a vote of 2430 to 204 approved the plan as submitted by the company.

3. The author has relied upon *Decisions and Orders of the National Labor Relations Board,* Vol. VIII, pp. 870-73, for information concerning the plan.

Revision of the Plan—1931. The original representation plan was revised in 1929, 1931, 1934, 1936, and 1937. The 1931 revision, which was the most far-reaching and remained in effect without significant change until 1937, brought about several significant changes. (1) Two representatives were elected by employees for each department and division, and the company appointed a number of management representatives equal to the total elected by the employees. (2) Annual pay given by the company to elected representatives was reduced to $60 from $100. (3) In place of the four governing joint committees, a General Joint Committee was set up to administer the plan. This new committee was composed of all elected representatives and all management representatives, and it was to take action upon matters presented by any of its members with final action dependent upon the approval of the president of the company. (4) An Executive Committee was formed consisting of five elected employee representatives and five management representatives. (5) Election arrangements were made by the management representatives but in the words of the revised plan, elections were to be "insofar as possible conducted by the employees themselves." (6) The plan could be amended by a two-thirds vote of the General Joint Committee, but an amendment became effective only "when approved by the president of the company."

Final Revision of the Plan—1937. The plan's final revision came in May, 1937, after the Supreme Court of the United States had upheld the constitutionality of the National Labor Relations Act in a series of important cases. The secretary of the General Joint Committee stated that this revision was undertaken in order to bring the plan "within the letter as well as within the spirit of the Wagner Act." Company officials took an active part in bringing about the revision and it was only after the Management's Representatives had announced that the revision was acceptable to the company that the General Joint Committee adopted the new plan.

The two principal changes brought about by this revision were the elimination of compensation paid by the company to elected representatives in an attempt to make it conform with the National Labor Relations Act, and the substitution of an Employees' Representative Committee for the General Joint Committee and the Executive Committee. This new committee was to be composed *solely* of representatives elected by the employees. The proviso was made, however, that any action of the E.R.C. was to become finally effective *only upon agreement by the company* (Article VI). Furthermore, any article in the plan could be amended by a two-thirds vote of the full membership of the E.R.C. with the stipulation, however, that a proposed amendment was to become effective on the date specified by the E.R.C. unless *specifically disapproved by the company within 15 days of the date of passage* (Article IX). Further, a new procedure for the handling of grievances was outlined. If the grievance could not be settled by the E.R.C. it was sent for decision to either the company's personnel manager or its general manager.

When the 1937 revised plan went into operation on June 30, it was printed in booklet form at company expense and distributed by departmental supervisors. Two weeks previous to this on June 15, employees elected the first slate of representatives to the E.R.C. Out of 6,300 eligible voters present for work that day, 5,718 elected 43 members to the new E.R.C.

For a period of about twelve years, the company's labor relations policy was carried out through the mechanism of the 1927 employee representation plan as amended from time to time. During the twelve years of the plan's existence, the company noted that grievances were settled amicably and pointed out that no serious labor dispute or strike occurred while the plan was in operation. It also stated that the plan was revised from time to time in the interests of workability, and in order that it might cope with changing conditions of labor relations.

The Challenge of the National Labor Relations Act

Before the 1937 revision of the Employee Representation Plan went into effect, the plan was bombed with a complaint issued by the National Labor Relations Board against the company to the effect that it was guilty of certain unfair labor practices under the Wagner Act in connection with the operation of the plan. So far-reaching were the effects of this litigation upon the company's later labor relations that the handling of the case by the N.L.R.B. and the subsequent decision by the Supreme Court merit special consideration.

Action by the National Labor Relations Board. On June 18, 1937, as a result of charges filed by the Industrial Union of Marine and Shipbuilding Workers of America (C.I.O.), the National Labor Relations Board issued a complaint against the company alleging that it had engaged in certain unfair labor practices affecting interstate commerce. These charges were that the company had: (1) discharged an employee because he had attempted to form an industrial union

(I.U.M.S.W.A.) among employees of the company; (2) discharged four other employees because they had joined and assisted the industrial union in question; and (3) dominated, supported, and interfered with the formation and administration of the Representation of Employees or the Employees Representative Committee as it was known after June 30, 1937. The company filed an answer to the complaint, in which it objected to the Board's jurisdiction, and in addition denied the allegations. The E.R.C. also answered the complaint denying the charges and filed a motion for leave to intervene. This motion was granted by the regional director.

On March 9, 1938, the N.L.R.B. Trial Examiner, after a hearing, reported that the company had engaged in, and was engaging in, unfair labor practices. He recommended that the company: (1) cease and desist from the unfair labor practices with which it was charged; (2) disestablish and withdraw recognition from the E.R.C. as the collective bargaining agent of its employees; and (3) reinstate the four employees who joined the union to their former jobs with back pay. He also recommended that the complaint against the company be dismissed insofar as it alleged the discriminatory discharge of the other employee in question.

After a hearing and full consideration of exceptions to this report by both the company and the E.R.C., the full board found no merit in them.

On June 7, 1938, a referendum was held at the yard in order to determine whether the employee representation plan should be continued. Seventy-five per cent of the employees present at work that day participated in the referendum and voted to continue the plan by a vote of 3,455 to 562.

On August 9, 1938, the board handed down its final decision and order in the case. Speaking first of the domination of the E.R.C. by the company, the board pointed out that from the plan's inception in 1927 until its final revision in 1937, the company had "dominated, assisted, and interfered with the administration of the labor organization . . . in its revised as well as its original form."[4] Commenting on the company's contention that the final revision in 1937 was made in order to bring the plan "within the letter as well as within the spirit of the Wagner Act," the board pointed out that the provisions of the final revised plan, no less than the method of revision, indicated that

4. *Decisions and Orders of the National Labor Relations Board*, July 1, 1938 to September 30, 1938, Vol. VIII, p. 872.

it was still the creature of the company. It noted two specific points here. First, though the new E.R.C. was composed solely of employee representatives elected by the employees, any action which it took became final and effective only when the company agreed to the action. Secondly, the plan could be amended by the E.R.C. only if the company did not disapprove within fifteen days of the passage of the amendment.[5]

On the other hand, the board found that the evidence did not support the original complaint that the one employee in question had been discharged for attempting to form a union. As to the four employees who had joined and assisted the union, the board found that the evidence did not support the contention of the original complaint that they had been discriminatorily discharged.

With these findings of fact as a basis the board ordered the company and its officers and agents to:

1. Cease and desist from:
   (a) Dominating or interfering with the administration of, or contributing support to the E.R.C.; or dominating or interfering with the formation or administration of, or contributing support to, any other labor organization of its employees.
   (b) Interfering with, restraining, or coercing its employees in the exercise of the right to self-organization, to form, join, or assist labor organizations, and to bargain collectively through representatives of their own choosing as guaranteed in Section 7 of the N.L.R.A.

2. Take the following affirmative action which would effectuate the policies of the N.L.R.A.:
   (a) Withdraw all recognition from the E.R.C. as the representative of any of its employees for the purpose of dealing with the company concerning grievances and conditions of employment, and completely disestablish the E.R.C. as such representative.
   (b) Post immediately in conspicuous places throughout the plant copies of the order.
   (c) Maintain posted notices of the order for a period of at least 30 consecutive days from the date of posting.
   (d) Notify the regional director of the Fifth Region in writing within ten days from the date of the order as to what steps were being taken to comply therewith.

5. *Ibid.*

Finally, the board ordered that the complaint of the Trial Examiner, insofar as it alleged that the company had discriminated in regard to the tenure of employment of the five men in question, should be and was dismissed.

The Supreme Court Decision. After the N.L.R.B. order had been issued, the company petitioned the United States Circuit Court of Appeals, Fourth Circuit, for a review of the order. This court modified the order to the extent of eliminating Section 2(a) which had required the withdrawal of recognition of the E.R.C. and its disestablishment as a representative of the company's employees. The board appealed this decision to the U. S. Supreme Court which agreed to pass judgment because of asserted conflict with previous decisions of the highest court (particularly N.L.R.B. *v.* Pennsylvania Greyhound Lines).[6]

In its opinion handed down December 4, 1939,[7] the court made clear that the sole issue in the eyes of the court concerned that portion of the board's order (2a) which ordered the company to withdraw recognition of the E.R.C. and to disestablish it as the bargaining representative of the employees.

The court in arriving at its decision made the following findings:

1. An employee representation plan which could not be amended if the employer disapproved such an amendment meant that such control of the form and structure of the E.R.C. by the company deprived employees of the complete freedom of action guaranteed to them by the N.L.R.A. Such control justified an order of the N.L.R.B. requiring the company to disestablish the E.R.C.
2. The Circuit Court of Appeals erred in considering facts brought to its attention in a brief presented after the hearing in that court advising the court that the plan had been amended by striking out provisions requiring the agreement of the company for effectiveness of action of the E.R.C. In other words, the case had to be heard on the record as certified by the Board.
3. The N.L.R.B. was not in error in maintaining that when an employees' representative organization had existed for as long as ten years with joint control only, the effects of such long practice could not be eliminated and the employees left entirely free to act upon

6. N. L. R. B. *v.* Pennsylvania Greyhound Lines 303 U. S. 261, 82 L. ed. 831, 58 S. Ct. 571, 115 A. L. R. 307 (1938).

7. N. L. R. B. *v.* Newport News Shipbuilding and Drydock Company, 308 U. S. 241, 84 L. ed. 219, 60 S. Ct. 203 (1939).

their own initiative without the complete disestablishment of the plan.

4. The right of employees to form a labor organization of their own choosing might be obstructed by the existence of, and recognition by management of an old plan, the original structure or operation of which was not in accordance with the provisions of the law. The action of the Board in ordering the company to take affirmative action was to effectuate one of the policies of the N.L.R.A.: namely, that employees shall be free to choose their own form of organization. As was pointed out in the Pennsylvania Greyhound Lines case, disestablishment of a bargaining unit previously dominated by the employer might be the only effective way of wiping the slate clean, thus affording employees a chance to begin afresh in organizing for the adjustment of their relations with the employer.

5. The N.L.R.B. was correct in its conclusion that the purpose of the N.L.R.A. could not be attained without complete disestablishment of an existing employer-dominated and controlled employees' representation organization, even though the organization had operated to the apparent satisfaction of employees, even though serious labor disputes had not occurred during its existence, and despite the fact that employees at an election (held on June 7, 1938, before the N.L.R.B. order) had signified their desire for the continuance of the organization. The Board did not err therefore, in this contention, in view of a provision of the N.L.R.A. (Section 8[2]) that a labor organization shall be free from interference or domination by the employer.

6. In applying the statutory test of independence of an employee representative plan, it was immaterial that the plan had not engendered or had obviated serious labor disputes in the past, or that any company interference in administration of the plan had been incidental rather than fundamental. This was immaterial since it was for Congress to determine whether as a matter of policy, such a plan should be permitted to continue in force, and the N.L.R.A. plainly evinced a contrary purpose.[8]

On the basis of these findings, the court ruled that the decree of the U. S. Circuit Court of Appeals should be reversed and the order of the N.L.R.B. carried out. In compliance with this decision, the company abolished the E.R.C. on January 10, 1940, thus leaving the yard with no collective bargaining agent for its employees.

8. The above material was taken from *Supreme Court Reporter*, West Publishing Company, St. Paul, Minn., 1940, Vol. 60, pp. 203-8.

The Peninsula Shipbuilders Association—1940 to Present

For a period of five months following the Supreme Court decision the company resorted to the pre-1927 method of individual bargaining. Apparently it was not ready to take another step in the direction of collective labor relations until a *bona fide* labor organization made the first move.

In June, 1940, an independent local industrial union called the Peninsula Shipbuilders Association made such a move. This union, which had developed between January and June, in a letter dated June 7, requested that the company recognize it as the bargaining agent for its own members only. In a letter dated June 17 the company granted this request. From that date forward the company and the P.S.A. bargained collectively as to hours, wages, and conditions of employment, and settled grievances for all employees who were dues-paying members of the union at the time of the bargaining.

Constitution and By-laws. The Peninsula Shipbuilders Association whose nucleus consisted of about 125 shipyard workers, lost little time in organizing after the Supreme Court decision calling for the dissolution of the E.R.C. Its original constitution with by-laws was adopted on January 11, 1940, just one day after the company had formally disestablished the Employee Representatives Committee. According to the constitution, the purposes of the union were: (1) to secure to its members the right to self-organization and the right to bargain collectively through delegates of their own choosing; (2) to select delegates who were to be the bargaining agents of the employees of the company; (3) to negotiate contracts and enter into collective agreements with the company concerning grievances, wages, rates of pay, and hours and conditions of employment.

Article I of the by-laws provided that any employee of the company not representing management was eligible for membership in the union upon the payment of a nominal initiation fee and upon the further condition that dues were to be paid in advance. In this connection Article IX pointed out that there was to be no discrimination against any member (or presumably any prospective member) because of race, sex, political or religious affiliations, or membership in any other organization. Non-payment of dues for a period of sixty days was a ground for suspension from membership in the union.

Rules governing membership approval of actions taken by the union were described in Article VIII. First of all, any agreements between the management and the union concerning wages, hours, and working conditions could be terminated only by a majority of the entire membership. Secondly, affiliation with any other organization (A.F. of L., C.I.O., etc.) or termination of the union itself, could be accomplished only after an affirmative vote of two-thirds of the membership. In the third place, no strike could be called except upon a two-thirds vote.

First Written Agreement with the Company. On November 5, 1941, after the P.S.A. had furnished the company with satisfactory evidence that it had been designated by a substantial majority of all employees (eligible for membership in the P.S.A.) as their bargaining agent, the company and the union entered into their first written agreement. The contract was to run from November 6, 1941, until June 2, 1943, and thereafter from year to year.[9] The agreement was thus to be continued indefinitely until either party notified the other in writing, at least thirty days before the expiration of the term, of its desire to change or terminate the agreement. If such a notice was given, both sides agreed to meet within ten days to negotiate with respect to the proposed change or termination.

In Article I of this original agreement, the company recognized the association as the *sole* collective bargaining agent of *all* the employees, including apprentices, who were eligible for membership in the union, with the exception of patternmakers.[10] Not eligible for membership in the union, among others, were the following types of employees: company officers, superintendents, foremen, other supervisory employees, apprentice instructors, time study, employment office, and medical department employees, and office workers in supervisory positions.

Article IV, dealing with "Rates of Pay," indicated that labor relations in the yard were beginning to experience the impact of the war effort. First, because of the preponderance of Navy and Maritime Commission shipbuilding contracts, all basic wage rates set forth in the agreement were those prescribed by the Navy Department and the Maritime Commission as governing on war contracts. The minimum rate was set at fifty cents per hour. Rates ranged upwards to a basic rate of $1.12 per hour for first-class skilled mechanics. Both sides

9. *Agreement between Peninsula Shipbuilders' Association and Newport News Shipbuilding and Drydock Company*, Nov. 5, 1941, Article II, pp. 2-3.

10. These employees belonged and still belong to a local of the Patternmakers League, an A. F. of L. affiliate. The company bargains with this union as to conditions of employment, etc., for patternmakers only.

agreed that there was nothing to preclude the company from making individual wage increases on the basis of improved skill and ability. Here was a foreshadowing of a second impact of the war in the form of upgrading through the use of individually increased pay rates in order to attract workers with skills short in supply. During the war years this practice became almost a necessity to such an extent that the usual company balance among skilled, semi-skilled, and unskilled workers (normally a ratio of 4:3:3) was completely upset. As recently as 1948 the company had not been able to reclassify completely its working force on the basis of actual skills so that its prewar balance could again be attained.

The remainder of this wage rates phase of the agreement gave a further indication of how the impact of the war was being felt. Both union and company were apparently becoming aware of the fact that prices had already begun to rise because of the pressure of increased demand on an ever-shortening supply of consumer goods. They both agreed that adjustments in wage scales were to be made in accordance with changes in the cost of living. All calculations involving changes in wage scales were to be made from a cost of living "base level." This level was described as the average cost of living in the United States on December 15, 1941, as shown by the U. S. Bureau of Labor Statistics index of the cost of goods purchased by wage earners in large cities. If the cost of living six months beyond this date had increased over the "base level" index by 5 per cent or more, a corresponding percentage wage adjustment would be made. After the first adjustment in the wage scale, further increases, if warranted by advances in the cost of living, were to become effective only at the end of six month periods.

Turning next to the important subject of hours of work and overtime pay, the agreement stated that the work week was to be forty hours (eight hours per day, five days per week), "unless otherwise provided by Congress, or directed by the President or some other governmental authority."[11] Here again the two parties foresaw the possibility of an impending pressure of the war effort in the not too far future. With war contracts piling up there was always the chance that the federal government might have to increase the length of the work week in defense industries in order to keep abreast of the production of war matériel. As did many other agreements throughout

11. *Agreement between Peninsula Shipbuilders' Association and Newport News Shipbuilding and Drydock Company,* Nov. 5, 1941, Article V, Section 1, p. 7.

the nation, this one made provision for the payment of time and a half overtime pay for all work in excess of eight hours per day and forty hours per week, and for all work on Saturday. Sunday and holiday work was to be paid for at a double rate, and evening and early morning shift workers were to receive a 7 per cent premium on top of base rates.

Working up to the subject of grievances and their disposal, the agreement guaranteed that during its life there would be neither strikes nor lockouts nor a limit on, or curtailment of, production. Here was an attempt on the part of both parties to make sure that defense production would not be impaired because of the use of peacetime coercive weapons. The union and the company agreed to arbitrate all grievances which could not be settled by the usual methods of conference between employee and supervisor, direct appeal to the personnel manager, or conference between the general manager and officials of the union.

Amendment to the Original Agreement: July 13, 1942. Some eight months after the original master agreement had been in effect, the company and the union agreed, in view of the national emergency and the government's attempt to stem the rising tide of prices, that amendments to the November, 1941, agreement would have to be made. The preamble to the amendments of July, 1942, stated that their purpose was "to conform to the national program to control the cost of living and thereby curb inflation."[12]

Amendment I rescinded Article IV, "Rates of Pay," of the original agreement and made effective retroactive to June 22, 1942 (unless and until the Navy Department and the U. S. Maritime Commission prescribed otherwise) a new scale of wage rates. The rate for first-class skilled mechanics was raised to $1.20 per hour and various semi-skilled and unskilled rates were raised ten, twelve, or fourteen cents per hour. The rate for specialists was raised to $1.40 per hour and the new minimum wage for the yard became sixty-four cents per hour. The weekly minimum rate therefore became $25.60 and all weekly rates above this minimum were increased by the amount of $3.20.

The second amendment made significant changes in Article V, "Hours of Employment, Shift Premiums and Overtime Pay." In view of the need for overlapping shifts in order to step up production, the regular work week was no longer to be defined as Monday through

12. *Agreement between Peninsula Shipbuilders' Association and Newport News Shipbuilding and Drydock Company*, as amended July 13, 1942.

Friday. Saturdays and Sundays were also to be considered regular work days and work performed on these days was to be paid for at straight time rates, with the proviso that a sixth regular shift worked would be paid for at the rate of time and a half, and a seventh regular shift worked would receive double time pay.

The mounting pressure of the need for more and more hours of defense production was acknowledged by a third amendment. Here the parties agreed that when the services of a given worker entitled to a paid vacation were required in order to maintain production, the worker in question would be allowed to waive his vacation rights. In return for this waiver, the company agreed to pay the worker his vacation pay in addition to such wages as he might receive for work actually performed during the vacation period.

Supplemental Agreement: June 1, 1943. On June 1, 1943, the union and the company signed what was called a "supplemental" agreement which like the original agreement as amended was to run for a year and then from year to year unless either party desired to make a change. Basically this contract was the same as the original one as amended with few exceptions. The first significant change concerned rates of pay. With the approval of federal wage stabilization regulations, the following new changes in wage rates were put into effect: first class specialists were increased from $1.40 to $1.48 per hour, and the minimum hiring rate of sixty-four cents per hour for unskilled workers was to go to sixty-eight cents per hour after a three month period. In addition, acknowledgment was made of a new effect of war-time production on wage rates. Section 3 of Article IV, "Rates of Pay," pointed out that there was no obligation on the part of the company to make any wage increase if it was not entitled to receive reimbursement from the federal government for such an increase. Here was the first intimation of war contracts containing "escalator" clauses to cover any legalized wage increases granted during the life of such contracts. Furthermore, this section of the agreement noted still further the impact of the war effort in this connection, when it stated that "any general increase in shipbuilding wages . . . authorized by the "federal government for the Atlantic Coast Zone will be made effective . . . if authorized prior to the expiration date of this agreement."[13] In effect, the company was serving notice here that it would maintain wage rates on a par with competitive shipyards in order to hold on to workers whose supply was short.

13. *Op. cit., Supplemental Agreement,* June 1, 1943, Section 3, p. 6.

The next important change in this supplemental agreement concerned shift premiums. Section 3 of the article (V) covering this topic made provision for a 7 per cent premium payment (on the sum of base pay plus piecework earnings) for all employees working on the second and third shifts. Once again the influence of the war effort was felt when a note to this section reminded the two parties that such an arrangement would become effective only *after* the approval of federal wage stabilization authorities, request for which was then (June 1, 1943) pending. As was the case in other war plants, an attempt was being made here to assure continuous twenty-four hour production by making financially more attractive work on the late evening and early morning shifts. It should be noted that governmental approval of such a procedure was required in order that rival plants could not attempt to outbid each other for scarce labor on the sole basis of financial ability to hire such labor.

The final change (Article XV) noted that the company would make payroll deductions for union dues ($1.00 quarterly) for employees who gave individual written and voluntary authorization for such a procedure. Here was a four-year anticipation of a significant section of the Taft-Hartley amendment to the Wagner Act. (See Sec. 302[c][4] of the Taft-Hartley Act.)

The Challenge of the C.I.O. The first serious opposition to the P.S.A., as exclusive bargaining agent for the yard's employees came in 1944, when another attempt was made by the Industrial Union of Marine and Shipbuilding Workers of America (C.I.O.) to organize workers in the yard.[14] The P.S.A. had never seen fit to affiliate with the C.I.O., preferring rather to remain an independent local industrial union. The I.U.M.S.W. carried on its organizing drive to such an extent in 1944 that it soon became convinced of its ability to seriously challenge the right of the P.S.A. to continue to be the bargaining agent for all the employees in the yard. So confident was the C.I.O. union of its strength that midway in 1944 it petitioned the National Labor Relations Board for an election to determine whether the workers in the bargaining unit wanted the P.S.A. or the I.U.M. S.W. to represent them for bargaining purposes. The P.S.A. and the company had no objections to the petition and the N.L.R.B. agreed to hold a consent election.

The board examined the company's lists of workers and decided

14. It will be remembered that this was the same union which brought charges against the company in 1938 in connection with its organizing activities at that time.

that of the 19,887 employees, 15,947 would be eligible to vote and thus constitute the appropriate unit for bargaining purposes. The board decided further that the eligible voters would be given the choice of voting either for the P.S.A., or the I.U.M.S.W., or for no union. As was the case in all bargaining elections held by the board under the National Labor Relations Act, no participant could be declared the winner in the election unless it received a *majority* of the eligible votes *actually cast.*

On September 1 the board held the election for all shifts in the company's yard and plant. Out of 15,947 eligible voters, 13,710 or 85.9 per cent actually cast their ballots on election day. Of the 13,710 votes counted, 82 or 0.6 per cent were declared void, and 189 or 1.4 per cent were challenged by one or more of the participants. No union was desired by 341 or 2.5 per cent of the total. The I.U.M.S.W. received 3,858 or 28.1 per cent and the P.S.A., 9,240 votes or 67.4 per cent of all votes cast.

The board, accordingly, declared that the P.S.A. was to remain as the exclusive bargaining agent of the company's employees. While the size of the vote received by the C.I.O. union was larger than had been expected, the P.S.A. discounted the significance of this vote when, in a throw-around bulletin issued the next day (September 2), it boasted of having beaten the C.I.O. by a margin of "3 to 1."

Supplemental Agreements: 1945-1949. After the C.I.O. threat of 1944 had been dispelled, the P.S.A. turned once more to its role of bargaining for the employees of the company. During 1944 neither the company nor the union desired to modify the supplemental agreement of 1943, so that contract was allowed to run through June 1, 1945. Supplemental agreements, however, were signed on June 2, 1945, 1946, and 1947. The latter agreement was amended on December 9, 1947, and reprinted in June, 1948, and at the time of writing was still in force.

For the most part, the supplemental agreements signed since June 1, 1943, do not differ radically from the basic one signed at that time. In the 1946 contract, a new section 4, concerning the union shop, was added to Article I (Recognition). Previous to the signing of this agreement, the P.S.A. had requested a union shop and the company had refused to grant such an arrangement. In place of the union shop the company agreed in 1946 to present to each newly hired employee (eligible for union membership) *before* beginning work a copy of the union-management agreement, a union membership application, a voluntary dues deduction order form, and a letter from the company advising that the P.S.A. was the accredited bargaining agency and stating that membership in the union, though not required, would not be discouraged by the company.

Article IV dealing with "Rates of Pay" took note of the fact that government regulation of wages had disappeared since the 1945 agreement. No longer were pay rates prefixed or suffixed with such words as "unless and until a duly constituted and authorized governmental agency otherwise prescribes" or "subject to government wage stabilization regulations." Here was an impact of the war effort in reverse. The wage lid was off and the new wage rates in the agreement reflected the popular 18 cents per hour wage increase pattern then current throughout the country. All classes of specialists and mechanics were raised 18 cents per hour. Piecework rates were increased by 15 per cent and helper rates were upped an average of 13 cents per hour.[15]

Article X, "Seniority and Preferences," took further note of the impact of V-J Day and the rapid rate at which men were being discharged from the armed forces. When employees were drafted (or had enlisted) in World War II, they had been assured by Congress that they would be entitled to their former jobs after being discharged. Numerous court decisions after V-J Day indicated that time lost in the service should count toward seniority in the event the worker discharged from the armed forces returned to his former job. Section 4 of Article X reflected this attitude, saying in part, that an employee absent, because of military service, would have his length of service (in the company) calculated as though he had been continuously employed by the company.

While the June 2, 1947, agreement made no changes of any import in wage rates, it did make provision for the reopening of the contract after January 1, 1948, so that wage rates could be discussed further. In December, 1947, however, both parties waived the January 1, 1948, stipulation and reopened the contract for this purpose. By an amendment to the June agreement, the union won a "second round" of 18 cent per hour increases. By this time all effective federal price controls had gone by the board and with the price lid off, unions throughout the country were pressing for a second 18

15. All of these increases had been made effective March 4, 1946, by a special supplemental agreement dated March 19. They were incorporated in this June 2 agreement and were to remain in effect until June 2, 1947.

cent increase in wages. This again was a national "pattern" and again the union demanded that the pattern be followed in the shipyard. This demand was partially met with 18 cent increases being granted to first and second class specialists, bringing these rates from $1.66 to $1.84 per hour and $1.58 to $1.76 per hour respectively. Third class specialists and first class mechanics were raised 16 cents per hour from $1.50 and $1.38 to $1.66 and $1.54. Second class mechanics went from $1.32 to $1.46; third class mechanics from $1.22 to $1.32; first and second class handymen from $1.04 to $1.14. All helpers were raised 10 cents per hour, and all laborers 8 cents. Piecework rates were upped 8 per cent, and all workers on weekly salaries were granted increases running from $3.20 to $6.40 per week.

In return for receiving these increases (effective December 22) the union agreed not to reopen the contract again for this reason until the agreement ran out in June, 1948. Further, the union and the company recognized that the limited postwar demand for new ship construction alone did not permit the working force to be kept at the wartime level. Thus, in view of the wage increases granted and the lack of new contracts, the company had to cut its force to about half of the wartime peak. The company agreed that it would reduce all unnecessary costs and, where possible, increase productivity in order to continue the employment of as many workers as possible. In return for the new high level of wages and salaries, the union agreed to cooperate fully in reducing all unnecessary expenses and in increasing productivity of workers.

The 1947 agreement, as amended, continued in force into 1948 and was still in force at the time of writing. In August of 1948 the union requested that the contract be reopened in order that further wage increases could be discussed. Still following the nation-wide pattern, the union was striving for a third postwar round of wage increases in order to compensate for further increases in the cost of living. The first reaction of the company to the reopening request was one of indifference. It maintained that it was not in a position financially to grant wage increases, and it indicated that it was somewhat reluctant to reopen the contract, although it did not close the door to such a possibility. The union then formally requested the reopening in a letter written to the personnel manager of the company. A few days later the company agreed to reopen the contract in order to discuss possible wage increases. The first union-management conference on the question was set for the last week in August. The company maintained that wage increases granted since 1939 had more than equalled increases in the cost of living, and thus no further wage increases were needed. The union's contention was that a third round of increases was needed to keep pace with an advancing cost of living. Conferences on the wage proposal were held from time to time in September, October, and November. In December the company offered to grant a seven-cent across-the-board increase. This was agreed to by the P.S.A. and the new wage rates were incorporated into the agreement by an amendment dated December 9, 1948.

The 1947 agreement and the 1948 agreement as amended were extended by a supplemental agreement dated June 1, 1949. The current agreement makes provision for a reopening for wage rate discussions after January 1, 1950. Finally, one further recent move of the company concerning wage payments should be noted. In late July, 1949, the company announced that it would drop the use of war-born "service bonuses." These bonuses had been paid during the war to hourly paid workers to parallel incentive payments then being earned by piece rate workers. The company's decision to do away with this practice is an indication of a wartime impact in reverse. The union has protested this proposed move and as yet the bonuses have not been dropped. At the time of writing both sides were discussing the issue in a series of conferences.

Summary and Conclusions

The Newport News Shipbuilding and Drydock Company is proud of the fact that in the sixty-year span of its existence, it has never had a serious labor dispute nor a strike of its working force. It attributes this to healthy labor-management relations and there can be little doubt that it gives credit for such a condition to the employee representation plan which was initiated in 1927. By 1927 the company had experienced a relatively long period of individual bargaining; from 1927 to 1940 it looked to employee representation for the solution to labor relations problems, and since 1940 it has turned to collective bargaining.

It is probably natural that labor relations in this company have gone through these phases. An examination of the history of labor relations in large numbers of American businesses over roughly the same period (1888-1949) would reveal about the same pattern. The last twenty years of the nineteenth century and the first thirty of the twentieth century comprised for the most part an era of *laissez faire* in labor relations as far as most American employers were concerned. It was only natural, until 1920 at least, that most businessmen relied upon individual bargaining and the open shop to set the tone of their labor relations policies. In this respect, the company studied here merely followed the pattern of labor relations used in the nation as a whole.

During World War I, aided by government guaranteed collective bargaining, union membership grew by leaps and bounds. After the war, with this guarantee removed, but with the trade union movement stronger than it had ever been, many employers saw an opportunity to kill, or at least weaken, unionism. Some unions aided the employers' cause by losing some important strikes with the result that membership figures began to decline rapidly. Industry observed these weaknesses and used the opening to initiate the "American Way" of labor relations, a somewhat thinly disguised name for company sponsored and dominated unions. The period of the twenties saw the mushroom-like growth of this philosophy of labor relations in American industry. The Newport News Shipbuilding and Drydock Company, again following the national pattern, installed its employee representation plan which had been used with success by the Bethlehem Steel Company. Here, the company followed the national development in labor relations by substituting collective bargaining of a sort for individual bargaining.

The company stayed with the plan throughout the thirties and revised it in a major way in 1937 in an attempt to bring it in line with the National Labor Relations Act. Like many other large employers it threw the plan overboard only after it had been required to do so by the National Labor Relations Board and the Supreme Court. It is perhaps coincidental that the date of this move (1940) came at almost the same time as the opening of the defense and war boom in the shipbuilding industry. Faced with a rapid growth in its defense orders and the size of its labor force, the company was fortunate to be able to help formulate, with the Peninsula Shipbuilders Association, a collective bargaining plan which provided a convenient vehicle for systematizing a rather complicated group of labor relations problems growing out of the war.

The written agreements which the company and the P.S.A. signed handled these problems in a very satisfactory manner and, equally significant, demonstrated conclusively to the company as well as to the workers the value of collective bargaining. Thus, for example, in the original agreement with the union, the company agreed to set *all* basic wage rates in accordance with those prescribed by the Navy Department for war contracts. Furthermore, both sides agreed that the company could make individual wage increases on the basis of improved skill and ability. Here provision was being made for the common wartime practice of upgrading. Again in the same agreement, cognizance was taken of a wartime rise in prices when the company and the union agreed that adjustments in wage scales for all workers were to be made in proportion to changes in the cost of living. Equally significant was the guarantee in the original agreement that during its life there would be neither strikes nor lockouts nor a limit on production. Finally, it is important to note the extent to which the company was willing to go concerning the request of the P.S.A. for a union shop. In the 1946 contract the company came a long way in this direction when it agreed to present to each newly hired employee a statement to the effect that the P.S.A. was the accredited bargaining agency and that membership in this union, though not required, would not be discouraged by the company.

These are some of the results of the company's first effort in bargaining collectively with a *bona fide* labor union. It is significant that the company voluntarily recognized the P.S.A. for bargaining purposes, especially in view of the fact that for a period of twelve years labor relations had been company dominated. The company does not appear to regret this decision. The National Labor Relations Act brought in its wake a new era of labor relations which involved a revamping of the attitudes of employers toward *bona fide* labor unions. The methods used in the twenties were out if they involved company domination or control of any labor relations plan or of any union. Though individual bargaining and the open shop still persist in some areas of American business, most labor relations policies today are built around the principle of collective bargaining. In this latter respect, the Newport News Shipbuilding and Drydock Company has been following the trend of current labor relations policy prevalent throughout the nation. The company has probably discovered that bargaining collectively with a genuine labor union makes for more businesslike labor relations than was the case when individual bargaining or employee representation was in vogue.

LABOR RELATIONS OF OTHER HAMPTON ROADS EMPLOYERS

Finally, it is essential to consider the extent to which the war's impact upon the Newport News Shipbuilding and Drydock Company was typical of the experiences of Hampton Roads employers.

In this connection the following pertinent points may be made:

1. Most of the wholesale, retail, and service trades tended to continue the use of individual bargaining because of small size and non-union labor traditions in these fields.

2. The railroads and maritime trades continued bargaining during the war, as before the war, with established national unions.

3. The building trades unions handled the problem of absorbing thousands of untrained recruits employed in the construction of armed forces training facilities by charging weekly permit fees and by the use of other similar devices. This procedure enriched union treasuries and maintained a measure of union control over jobs.

4. Unionization during the war of local transit systems, ferry companies, telephone workers, and electric light and power workers went forward at a rapid pace. In these fields the trend had been in this direction before the war, but the wartime shortage of labor and the strategic collective bargaining status of unions probably hastened the process. Though few of these companies had the background in employee representation to lay the groundwork for independent local unions, comparable to the Peninsula Shipbuilders Association of the Newport News Shipbuilding and Drydock Company, they experienced, in common with this company, the coming of vigorous collective bargaining.

5. Strikes were virtually nonexistent during and after the war except for post V-J day strikes in the transit industry, on ferry lines, among dock workers and seamen, and in the electric and power industry. These strikes were of relatively short duration except for that affecting the Chesapeake Ferry Company. In this instance the company was taken over by the state and the ferries were incorporated into the state highway system.

In conclusion, it appears that the significant effect of World War II in the field of labor relations in the Hampton Roads area was to accelerate the development of collective bargaining in a region which had been predominantly an open shop or individual bargaining area. This, in harmony with developments throughout the nation, will probably be a permanent effect rather than a transitory impact of war conditions upon the Hampton Roads economy.

IV

IMPACT OF THE WAR UPON GOVERNMENTAL STRUCTURE AND SERVICES

Photo Craftsmen Company

"Stuart Gardens, a war housing project constructed by the Defense Homes Corporation, is a permanent and well-planned neighborhood located on the north side of Hampton Roads."

CHAPTER XII

STRUCTURE AND MANAGEMENT OF LOCAL GOVERNMENT*

SEVENTEEN MUNICIPAL CORPORATIONS are located in the historic Hampton Roads-Peninsula area of Virginia. Seven of these are independent cities, eight are counties, and two are towns. This section of the study is concerned with the core localities, including the south side cities of Norfolk, Portsmouth, and South Norfolk, the counties of Norfolk and Princess Anne, and the town of Virginia Beach; and the north side cities of Newport News and Hampton, the counties of Warwick, Elizabeth City, and York, and the town of Phoebus.[1]

The predominant type of government in the cities and towns of the region is the council-manager system. Portsmouth was the first to adopt the plan in 1916. The latest adoptions were by the city of South Norfolk and the town of Virginia Beach. It is possible that the increased population recorded by the 1950 Census may stimulate the town of Virginia Beach, with its lucrative resort business, to become an independent city and therefore to enjoy greater independence from the tightly knit county political organization which has its seat in the rural community of Princess Anne. The town of Phoebus, in Elizabeth City County, has the mayor-council form of government. Its 1947 charter provides for election of the town council on a general ticket at large and election of a town treasurer. A town clerk, attorney, and sergeant are elected by the council. Both towns, as is customary in Virginia, are in the counties and share certain officers with the county. The cities are independent of the counties. The county administrative offices may be located in the city, as is true of the counties of Norfolk and Elizabeth City, but their jurisdiction is outside the city limits. This separation of local governmental areas and functions has its advantages.

*By James E. Pate, Professor of Political Science, College of William and Mary.

1. The outlying cities of Suffolk and Williamsburg and the counties of Nansemond, Isle of Wight, and James City are not included in this section since governmental changes incident to the war were not as significant as in the core communities listed. The end papers of the book show the geographic location of these localities.

While all cities in the area have the council-manager government, none of them integrate all administrative agencies and officers under the manager's control. Such so-called constitutional officers as the treasurer, commissioner of the revenue, commonwealth's attorney, and clerk of the court are elected by the voters. The city auditor is appointed by the council. The key finance officers are therefore outside the manager's control. An exception is found in the county of Warwick, with its county-manager system, which is allowed by state law to have a more integrated finance department. In Hampton, the city manager's supervision extends only over the departments of streets and police and over fiscal planning.

Manager government has shown the greatest stability in the city of Newport News. Since 1920 this city has had only two managers. The present incumbent has served since 1925. The average term of Norfolk's city manager before the appointment of the present incumbent was 5.5 years. Portsmouth has had the greatest turnover, with ten managers since 1916, and an average tenure of three years.

The Hampton Roads counties represent all types of county government permitted under Virginia laws. During the war, both the county of Warwick and the county of Elizabeth City adopted improved types of government, the county-manager and the county-board, respectively. Norfolk County has the county board of supervisors with a purchasing agent. Both York and Princess Anne have the traditional county board of supervisors with several elective officers but no executive.

Several of the local governments felt the war's impact on their structure, and all experienced great pressure on governmental services. The change to a more responsible government in both Warwick and Elizabeth City counties was directly related to the extraordinary wartime population increase. These new residents put pressure on local governmental services which required stronger organization and better management. Annexation proceedings successfully brought by Portsmouth and South Norfolk against Norfolk County, proceedings considered by Newport News against Elizabeth City and Warwick counties, and proceedings considered by the city of Norfolk against Norfolk and Princess Anne counties have resulted from urban growth around the cities. The study initiated in 1946 by the Lower Peninsula Planning Commission of consolidation of the local governments of Newport News, Hampton, Phoebus, and of Elizabeth City and Warwick counties and the vigorous though unsuccessful campaign early in 1950 to bring about such a union was the outcome of the physical, economic, and governmental interrelations of these communities, which war pressures tended to make more intense.

CHANGES IN COUNTY GOVERNMENT

An important force behind the changes in governmental structure in the county of Warwick was the demand of the population for improved public services. Another factor was the dissatisfaction with the school board which by Virginia's traditional system of selection was out of touch with the school patrons. The board was selected by the school trustee electoral board appointed by the judge of the circuit court who in turn was elected by the state legislature. A third cause of discontent among Warwick County's urban population was that so few people had anything to do with the government. The county offices were controlled by two families.[2]

These were some of the factors that stirred the revolt which in September, 1944, by a vote of 1,386 to 909, brought in the county-manager form of government. A clean sweep was made. A new board of supervisors was elected, a new school board selected, and a county manager appointed. While this was a satisfactory experience for the 80 per cent of the population who live in the 20 per cent of the county's area nearest to Newport News, the people in the upper rural part of the county were not happy. There were grounds for belief at that time that they would be relieved to get rid of the urban part of the county by its annexation to Newport News. Only in this way could the former rulers hope to get back in control of the county's affairs.

Warwick County has the best integrated government of any in the Hampton Roads area. All county line and staff functions are departmentalized under directors who are responsible to the county manager. The new county manager has introduced progressive management methods such as budgeting, purchasing, store keeping and inventory controls, maintenance of county equipment, central filing, and activities for promoting personnel welfare.

The most important structural change in the government was the creation of an integrated department of finance. All fiscal officers and transactions are centralized in this office. The county treasurer and commissioner of the revenue, formerly elected, are now appointed officers in the department of finance under a full-time director who

2. See Report, Secretary of the Commonwealth, 1938.

assists the manager in the preparation of the county budget, controls all disbursement, and supervises purchasing, assessments, and the collection and custody of public funds.

Complete integration, however, was prevented by the state enabling act which requires the election of the sheriff, county clerk, and commonwealth's attorney. There is some overlapping in the sheriff's office and the county police. This could be relieved by combining the offices of sheriff and chief of county police as in Elizabeth City County or by confining the sheriff's duties to that of an officer of the court. An obvious attempt in 1946 to combine the two offices by trying to get the chief of police elected as sheriff failed when the incumbent sheriff was re-elected. Outwardly the two offices have been working harmoniously, but there has been a natural tendency for supporters of the sheriff, successful in the election, to feel that he should be head of the county police force.

Division between the state and county governments of supervision of the departments of health and public welfare, especially the former, have created problems. Some of these are suggested in the following statement by County Manager Morris:

> We feel that where the State participates in the function of the county departments that the personnel should meet our minimum requirements in regard to office hours, days of employment and vacation, and that the county minimum should be complied with. . . . My observation has proven that in many instances these cooperative agencies who feel they are responsible to the State more so than to the county have been far less efficient in their functions than those directly responsible to the county.[3]

Elizabeth City County, one of Virginia's original shires, moved a step toward progressive government in 1943 when it adopted the county-board form of government, under which the county board of supervisors controls policy but selects a county executive who is responsible to the board for the administration of all county affairs. While the county manager of Warwick County is responsible to the board of supervisors, there is no doubt of his being the county's chief executive officer. On the other hand, the executive secretary of Elizabeth City County has limited powers. He shares, for example, the appointment of police officers and firemen with the judge of the circuit court and the county board of supervisors. His control of public works emphasizes this phase of his work more than any other.

3. Letter to the author dated January 29, 1947.

The first executive secretary remained a year and a half. His place was filled temporarily by the deputy clerk of the court who also continued his political activities as chairman of the local executive committee of the Democratic Party, a combination of administrative and political duties somewhat inconsistent with the charter principles of managerial government. This situation was changed in 1948 when the director of public works was made full-time county executive.

Elizabeth City County's wartime progress in governmental structure is also seen in the enactment of a comprehensive zoning ordinance, and the appointment of a zoning administrator. A complete reassessment of property, with the aid of outside professional appraisers, in 1945 set an example in progressive methods of locating, recording the facts, and assessing real estate.

An important movement related to the population pressures and to the social, economic, and governmental problems of the Second World War consisted of proposals for changing the boundaries of the local political units, either by annexation, consolidation of functions, or by outright consolidation of governments.

The cities proposed annexation. The counties fought back. The county of Norfolk carried its annexation fight against the city of Portsmouth to the Supreme Court of Appeals which upheld the city and supplemented the county's defeat by the dictum that "urban areas should be under urban government and rural areas under county government."[4] On the north side of Hampton Roads, the small counties won a temporary respite by the Massenburg Anti-Annexation act passed by the General Assembly in 1947, which prevents any annexation proceedings brought by a city against a county of sixty square miles or less. This act, as long as it stands, protects all of Elizabeth City County against Newport News' annexation design and most of Warwick County.

In the meantime, the Lower Peninsula Planning Commission initiated a study of consolidation. As a basis for consolidation proposals, a detailed study was made by two of the authors of the present study of the existing local government structure and services. It was found that substantial progress had been made in consolidating such functions as planning, water supply, sewage disposal, and airport. Such further extensions of functional consolidation that involved no structural changes in the existing governments as a regional jail farm, a personnel board and administrator to serve all the Lower Peninsula

4. County of Norfolk *v.* City of Portsmouth, 187, Va. 1947.

governments, a joint school board, a public welfare department, and a health center for the entire region were proposed.

Several plans for more comprehensive consolidation involving structural changes were analyzed. The committee's research staff recommmended, as a long range approach to the problem, a consolidation whereby the urban areas would be put in a city with the council-manager government; the remaining rural areas would be consolidated into a large county, either with a county-manager or a county-executive government; and a joint board would be set up to coordinate problems of region-wide significance. The committee itself, however, recommended consolidation of all five local governments into one city. This proposal was submitted to the voters March 21, 1950, after a hectic campaign. While Newport News and Warwick County voted in favor of the plan, it was defeated in the other three localities.

MUNICIPAL STRUCTURE AND MANAGEMENT

Norfolk's city government entered the war with several organizational defects that greatly overtaxed the manager's span of control. He was director of the departments of safety and of finance, which meant that each chief officer in these departments had direct call upon the manager's time. At the same time, the manager attempted to follow the "open-door" policy of meeting the public. As seen in Figure 25, the manager's span of control was overtaxed by increased pressure on a wartime government. The war's impact increased the number of direct managerial contacts. Numerous special war agencies and activities engaged his attention. He acted as director of civilian defense, as temporary chairman of the war price and rationing board, and as chairman of the Hampton Roads Sanitation Commission. In addition to this assortment of chairmanships and directorships of war agencies, there were numerous contacts with Washington civilian war agencies and with navy personnel in the Hampton Roads area.

War activities absorbed so much of the manager's time that some other essential municipal activities for which he was accountable were bound to suffer from neglect. The war disturbed the routine of some management methods. Collective conferences with department directors were discontinued. Departmental reports, in some instances, were curtailed. During the war, the city manager employed an executive secretary to handle some of the public relations and to adjust as many departmental situations as possible. Many of the difficulties, however, were caused by war conditions and were beyond any immediate

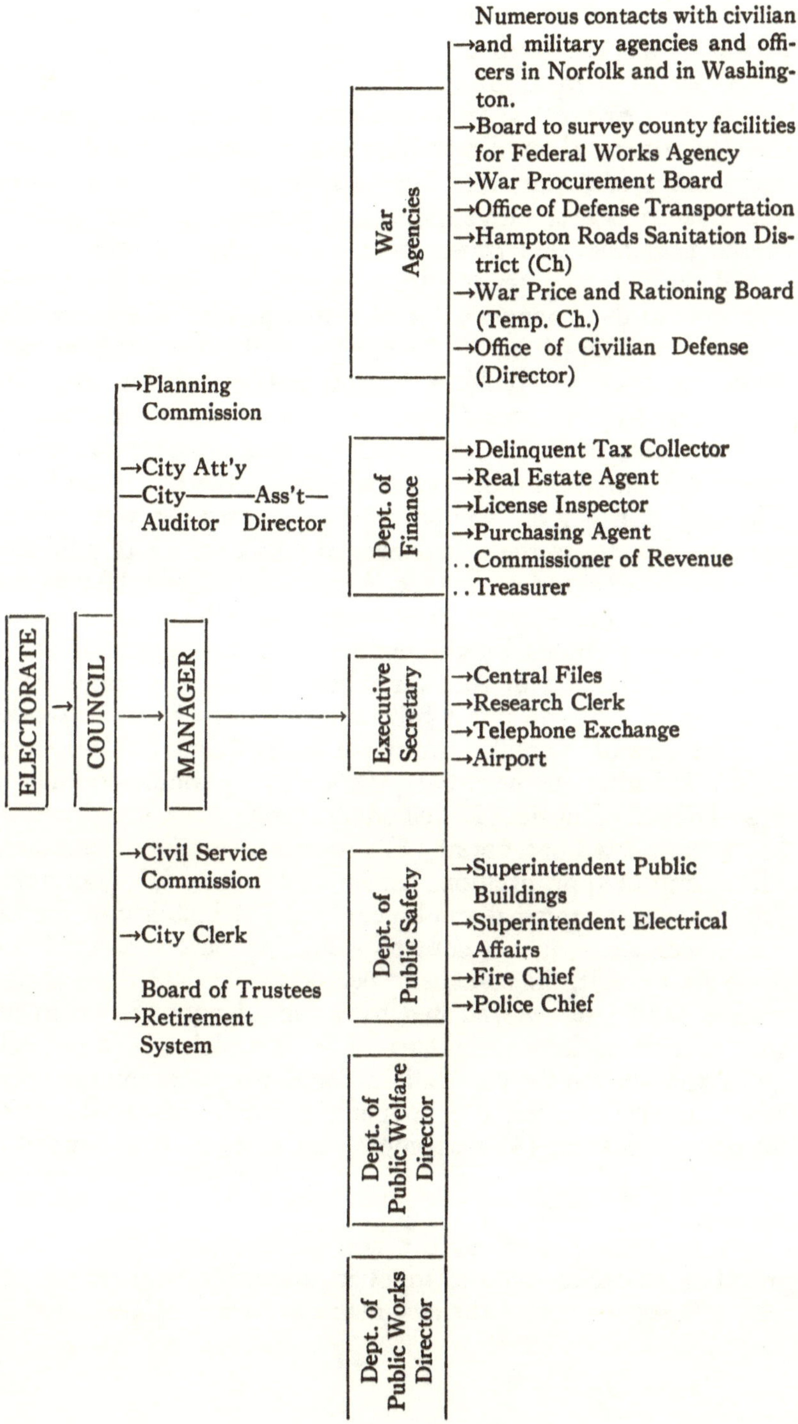

FIGURE 25. MANAGER'S SPAN OF CONTROL (1940–45) CITY OF NORFOLK

remedy. During the war, for instance, the turnover in the city's personnel was extraordinary.

A partial reorganization of government in the city of Norfolk during the first postwar year separated the public health services from the department of public welfare and put them in a department of equal status with the other line departments. A full-time director of public safety was employed. A complete reorganization and expansion of the personnel department was made. Another important change pulled the planning agency from out of the council's direct control and set it in the manager's line of responsibility. These organizational changes were expedited by the burden of the war and postwar conditions put upon the welfare, health, police and fire, and personnel services, and by the need for postwar planning at the managerial level.

The story of the war's impact on municipal structure and management is similar in other political units of the Hampton Roads area. The city manager of Newport News entered the war period as the personal director of the department of public safety, of public welfare, of public works, and of finance. As a matter of fact, he was the director of all the city departments except law, which was headed by the city attorney chosen by the council. No organizational change was made until the end of the war when the manager employed an administrative assistant and a full-time director of public works.

The city of Norfolk's principal governmental changes came just before and after the war. One of the city's periodic council-manager upsets occurred in the 1938 elections. Grievances, imaginary and real, had accumulated because of (1) favored treatment of certain sections of the city in appropriations for improvements, (2) discrimination in salary among municipal employees, and (3) inability of the rank and file of citizens to get a courteous hearing before council and manager. As a result, the so-called "people's ticket" of three antiadministration candidates was elected by a record vote of two to one over the "administration" candidates. The "people's platform" called for (1) administering the city's affairs for all the people and in accordance with the city charter, (2) cooperation with and equal treatment of all city employees, (3) stopping of the delegation of council's duties, and (4) adopting a general policy for courteous reception and interviewing of citizens.

A majority "bloc" of the council interpreted the election as a mandate to make some changes in administrative personnel. Three city officials, including the city manager, were replaced. The councilmanic "bloc" soon disintegrated. Only two members of the council served continuously during the war period.

The city's wartime manager, Colonel C. B. Borland, appointed as a result of the councilmanic changes of 1938, had come up through the municipal ranks from chief of police and director of the department of public safety. From almost the beginning of Colonel Borland's term, there were indications that council-manager relations were not going smoothly. Comments in the press showed that the city manager opposed election of certain persons to the council. There were indications of bad feeling on both sides, of temperamental difficulties, and of mutual encroachment on each other's jurisdiction. The council, for example, went over the manager's budget recommendation and increased the salaries of policemen and firemen. The explosion came at the end of the war, December, 1945, when Colonel Borland resigned.

The wartime council came to an end a few months after Mr. Borland resigned. A group of businessmen were stirred into action, and at a meeting at the Monticello Hotel they launched a so-called "people's ticket," which was called everything else by the opposition. The grievances aired in the postwar councilmanic election of 1946 were similar in many respects to those of the prewar election of 1938, which resulted in a turn over in the office of city manager. Charges were made of violation of the charter provision on council-manager relations and of failure of the council to give courteous attention to citizens.

The people's ticket won by a large majority, as in 1938. Commenting on the results, the Norfolk *Ledger Dispatch* had this to say:

> The voters have done so in such circumstances and with such emphasis as to leave no doubt that they expressed a deep-seated and manysided dissatisfaction with the city in its first postwar year and with the government which has been struggling amidst unusual difficulties with its affairs.
>
> This is a call for a change in the clearest possible tones. It is a demand for improvement all along the line of government and city leadership—for stricter regard to charter-decreed relationships inside the City Hall, for co-operation and harmonious spirit among officials, for the businesslike conduct of affairs, and for bold and resolute tackling of the long list of complaints which had swelled up during the war, and of the many problems demanding opportunity for Norfolk people to turn from the national problems which had demanded their attention and to look inward to the city as it has survived the extraordinary demands of the war and the enforced postponement of many developments and improvements.[5]

5. Norfolk *Ledger-Dispatch,* June 12, 1946.

The new council reached the conclusion that in filling the position of city manager it should look for a man "who was free from local political entanglements and whose ability and integrity had been demonstrated by his previous recorded experience as a city manager." On October 10, the council announced the appointment of C. A. Harrell, city manager of Schenectady, New York, who was installed November 6 as Norfolk's sixth city manager.

The war stimulated planning in the Hampton Roads area, especially in the field of planning for future development. The cities of Norfolk, South Norfolk, and Portsmouth and the county of Warwick have planning commissions. Portsmouth's commission was appointed in 1945, and in 1947 the city had Harland Bartholomew and Associates draw up a comprehensive city plan. South Norfolk's commission was selected in 1948. In that same year, Elizabeth City County appointed a one-man planning commissioner and also a zoning administrator. There has been some departmental planning largely by the public works department. The Lower Peninsula Planning Commission, established in 1944, operated on the north side of Hampton Roads as an overall planning agency for the Lower Peninsula area. This agency has done good work. Special mention should be made of the Peninsula airport, the projected Grand View Park, a housing survey, the proposed tuberculosis hospital at Camp Patrick Henry, and the consolidation study. Failure of several localities to continue financial support of this commission resulted in its dissolution early in 1950.

Planning in the fields of public works, health and welfare, and safety, in cooperation with federal war agencies, produced some important results which will be discussed in the appropriate sections of this report. Under the Lanham Act, as we shall see, the Hampton Roads area profited by public works sponsored by the federal government because of conditions created by the war emergency. A notable contribution in the field of recreational planning in the city of Norfolk was the Batchelor report. The Taber debt reorganization plan went into effect in 1940 before the United States entry into the war, but during the time when Norfolk was becoming a focal point of defense activities. This plan resulted in adopting a partial cash budget and a leveling off of the debt service by refunding certain term bonds.

In the city of Norfolk, planning for the postwar period resulted in a proposed three-year program for capital expenditures covering improvements and extensions for such things as streets, bridges, water mains and sewer system, parks and playgrounds, school facilities, public welfare, and health centers. This program called for an expenditure of about $6,000,000. In presenting the program, the city manager said:

> We are in a period of great uncertainty. Materials are scarce, labor is scarce and wages are high. Contractors, in self-defense, are bidding high—higher than even the scarcity of labor and materials warrant. As long as this condition exists, we should go slow with our improvement program, because we are paying too much for what we buy. For these reasons the proposed three-year program is set up for a total expenditure of $6,292,000 only.[6]

In commenting editorially on this program, the *Norfolk Virginian-Pilot* stated:

> In its totality the three year public works schedule measures roughly the capital improvement deficit that the City of Norfolk has accumulated during the past years—particularly during the war years when, save for Federally-aided public works (some of them of great importance), the physical plant of the city was largely neglected.[7]

The uncertain and inflationary postwar tendencies made it necessary for the planning agency to select those improvements that could not very well be put off until conditions were better adjusted. The planning authority recognized that a postwar boom was a poor time to start public improvements that could wait for a possible settling down of the economic spiral.

FINANCE

The war had little effect on fiscal management, except in Warwick County where an integrated department of finance was established as part of the county-manager government adopted in 1944. Traditional fiscal practices were disturbed very little. The routine of budget planning was changed somewhat by priorities that the war put on strategic materials, as replacements requiring such materials had to be postponed until after the war. The assessed valuation of real estate and personal property increased only slightly during the war period, chiefly from new construction rather than revaluation of old properties. Tax collections during the war were good. There was less tax delinquency and the collection of past delinquent taxes improved as incomes of property owners rose. Costs of supplies increased but dis-

6. *Norfolk Virginian-Pilot*, January 3, 1946.
7. *Ibid.*

counts decreased. Sales of surplus property and junk were greater.

Wartime changes in municipal revenues and expenditures in the Hampton Roads area indicate the war's impact, not only upon municipal finance, but also upon governmental functions and the manner in which they were performed.

Changes in Total Revenues and Expenditures

The great increases in total revenues and expenditures of the local governments in the core communities of the Hampton Roads region are shown in Table 39.

While all governments experienced sharp increases in both revenues and expenditures during the war years, the counties, as noted elsewhere in this report, felt the sharpest growing pains. This was particularly true of Warwick and Norfolk counties, whose revenues increased 385 per cent and 259 per cent, respectively, and whose operating expenditures rose by 291 and 404 per cent during the years 1938-1946. The cities as a whole showed a 70 per cent increase in revenues as compared with a 224 per cent increase for the counties. Expenditures were pushed up during these years approximately 71 per cent in the five cities listed in Table 39 as compared with 282 per cent in the counties.

That local governments of the Hampton Roads area were on the average able to keep their financial houses in order is evidenced by the fact that the 1938-1946 increase in expenditures was only slightly in excess of the gain in revenues. This was somewhat more true of the cities, however, than the counties. The financial solvency of these local government units becomes even more evident when it is realized that the excess of expenditures over revenues in 1946 was more than offset by the surpluses which piled up during the war years, when revenues continued to grow but shortages of labor and materials prevented cities from making many needed expenditures. That this favorable financial condition was somewhat misleading, however, is indicated by the fact that the trend toward spending more than revenues received, which began in 1946, has continued during the postwar years as deferred maintenance, the pressure of increased population upon government services, and rising price levels have forced expenditures upward. In other words, while the immediate effects of the war upon local government finance were favorable, the combined effect of the war and postwar years has been to create recurring financial crises for local governments in the Hampton Roads region which have necessitated careful reappraisal of their tax systems and, in most instances, have resulted in higher tax rates and assessments.

TABLE 39. TRENDS IN TOTAL REVENUES AND EXPENDITURES,* HAMPTON ROADS CITIES AND COUNTIES, 1938–1946**

	1938	1942	1946	Per cent Increase 1938–1946
	(thousands of dollars)			
TOTAL REVENUES				
Cities				
Newport News	1,301	2,022	2,316	78.0
Hampton	195	280	371	90.3
Norfolk	6,424	8,380	10,904	69.7
Portsmouth	1,310	1,834	2,183	66.6
South Norfolk	266	307	390	46.6
Total	9,496	12,823	16,164	70.2
Counties				
Warwick	181	388	878	385.1
Elizabeth City	342	586	1,006	194.2
York	94	128	199	111.7
Norfolk	744	1,254	2,672	259.1
Princess Anne	296	402	612	106.8
Total	1,657	2,758	5,367	223.9
Total Cities and Counties	11,153	15,581	21,531	93.1
*TOTAL EXPENDITURES**				
Cities				
Newport News	945	1,310	1,947	106.0
Hampton	175	246	289	65.1
Norfolk	6,613	8,039	10,665	61.3
Portsmouth	1,188	1,518	2,318	95.1
South Norfolk	159	210	303	90.6
Total	9,080	11,323	15,522	70.9
Counties				
Warwick	163	269	637	290.8
Elizabeth City	228	375	760	233.3
York	84	104	159	89.3
Norfolk	431	673	2,173	404.2
Princess Anne	190	289	462	143.2
Total	1,096	1,710	4,191	282.4
Total Cities and Counties	10,176	13,033	19,713	93.7

*Exclusive of capital outlays and debt service.

**The fact that all of the cities except Hampton have fiscal years ending December 31, and Hampton and all of the counties end their fiscal years on June 30, limits the comparability of the figures for any given year.

Source: Annual Audits of counties and cities included in table.

Changes in Revenue and Expenditure Patterns

Chief among the changes in revenue structures of local governments in the Hampton Roads area was the tendency for local property taxes to become somewhat less dominant as a source of revenue. In the cities, the slack was taken up (1) by such local sources as license taxes based upon the swollen gross receipts of merchants, increased fines and penalties, presumably upon transients, and greatly increased profits from waterworks and ferries; and (2) by state and federal payments. Most of the state payments came from Alcoholic Beverage Control Board profits from liquor sales to the many military and civilian in-migrants in the Hampton Roads-Peninsula communities. Federal subventions consisted chiefly of public housing authority payments in lieu of taxes, public assistance grants, and grants under the Lanham Act for expanding municipal services for war-inflated populations in the region. The city of Norfolk provides a good example of these changes. The contribution of local property taxes to total revenues dropped from 63 per cent in 1938 to 44 per cent in 1946, though they increased in absolute amount approximately 23 per cent during the period. Licenses, on the other hand, increased more than 80 per cent; all other revenues, including state and federal payments, rose 164 per cent; and state payments alone increased 334 per cent. Revenues of Portsmouth and Newport News were effected somewhat similarly by war conditions. Special mention should be made of the more than three-fold increase in the yield to the city of Portsmouth from the municipally owned ferries connecting Norfolk and Portsmouth as war workers and service men and women almost swamped these key transportation agencies.[8]

The counties had to depend largely on state and federal payments to take up the slack resulting from the rather sluggish response of local property taxes to the need for increased revenue during the war period. Only cities and towns are permitted under Virginia laws (*Tax Code of Virginia*, Chap. 20, sec. 296) to impose license taxes. Most of the Hampton Roads counties, in addition, have had little opportunity to reap large profits from municipal services. While conditions varied among the counties of the region, the experience of Norfolk County is indicative of the Second World War's effects upon county revenue structures in the area.[9] Local sources, chiefly

8. Annual Audits, cities of Norfolk, Portsmouth and South Norfolk, 1938-1946.

9. See *Comparative Cost of Local Government in Virginia*, Auditor of Public Accounts, Commonwealth of Virginia, 1938-1946, inclusive, for details as to revenues of the various counties.

the property tax, yielded 83 per cent of that county's revenues in 1938 but less than 50 per cent in 1946. The state's contribution increased from 17 per cent in the prewar year to 29 per cent in 1946 and the federal share grew from zero in 1938 to 22 per cent in the first post-war year. The peculiar impact of the war upon York County revenues merits special mention. Whereas most of the local governments in the area received substantial federal payments, York County, from which the federal government took more real estate from the tax base of the county for military purposes than in any other governmental unit of the area, received only 4.5 per cent of its total 1946 revenues from the federal government. It was unfortunate in having its land taken for military purposes, upon which the federal government was able to pay nothing to the county government, rather than for housing for which the government made payments in lieu of taxes in other parts of the Hampton Roads region. The large military population at Camp Peary, Cheatham Annex, the Naval Mine Depot, and the Naval Mine Warfare School, however, swelled ABC sales in the area and helped to account for the fact that state contributions to York County revenues increased from 39 per cent in 1938 to almost 50 per cent in 1946.

The war's effect upon the pattern of government expenditures in each of the cities and in the metropolitan counties of Norfolk, Warwick, and Elizabeth City was similar. In each of these localities, schools accounted for much the largest share of total expenditures throughout the 1938-1946 period but their share declined steadily throughout the period in spite of absolute increases in amount of expenditures. In Newport News, for example, school expenditures declined from 42 per cent of the total in the prewar year to 33.5 per cent in 1946. Similarly, the increase in school expenditures during this period was only 55 per cent as compared with increases of 119 per cent, 174 per cent and 359 per cent, respectively, for public safety, public works, and public welfare. Recreation, street repairs, and garbage collection were the specific Newport News activities where costs showed the greatest relative increase. Warwick County, with its rapid rate of wartime population growth, found it necessary to increase school expenditures 240 per cent, but increases of 1,535 per cent, 1,072 per cent, and 2,045 per cent, respectively, were registered for crime prevention and detection, fire prevention and extinction, and public works. It is apparent from these examples and from similar trends in the other urban portions of the Hampton Roads-Peninsula area that, in spite of wartime pressures upon school facilities, the most critical impact of war activities upon the local governments were upon such functions as police and fire protection and public works. Experience since 1946, however, indicates that school expenditures tend to become the leader again in rate of increase, as community life becomes stabilized during the postwar period and emergency needs in other areas of government service are met. Even during the war years, school expenditures continued to increase more rapidly than any others in the less urbanized counties such as Princess Anne and York, where other types of municipal service make relatively smaller claims against public funds.[10]

MUNICIPAL EMPLOYMENT

The pressure on municipal employment came from competition with wages paid in private industry as well as the selective service drafts. Municipal management was hard pressed to hold sufficient police, fire, and public works employees to meet the emergency.

North of Hampton Roads, Newport News was losing police officers as fast as they were employed. The city council, in an attempt to meet this loss, increased salaries four times for a total increase of 25 per cent over the prewar base pay—an increase that brought the pay of patrolmen from a minimum of $130 per month in 1938 to a minimum of $175.50 in 1945, which is about the median entrance salary paid patrolmen in cities of this class. The maximum salary moved from $145 in 1938 to $202 in 1945—an increase that approximated the median maximum salary of $2,160 paid by cities in the same class.[11]

During the war, the city of Norfolk encountered the worst personnel problem in its history. In 1944, 1,229 employees left the city's service, and 1,343 left in 1945. In 1944, the turnover among municipal employees was 75.5 per cent; and in 1945, it reached the all-time high of 81.8 per cent.

Some of the effects of this unstable personnel condition, as pointed out in the city manager's 1945 summary, are as follows:

> The acute shortage of personnel made it necessary to divert the efforts of the employees remaining on the city's payroll to the most essential functions of the government. Suffering heavily were the Divisions of Police and Street Cleaning. In the latter division, the lack of personnel required the assignment of available men to the collection of garbage and refuse for

10. See Annual Audits of the cities and counties listed in this chapter.
11. International City Managers Association, *The Municipal Year-Book 1945*, p. 429.

the protection of public health, with the result that the cleaning of streets had to be neglected. To offset the loss of personnel, a number of mechanical sweepers were pressed into service, but the problem of the parked automobile rendered this method less effective than hand sweeping. Furthermore, the employment of women for the cleaning of streets was unsatisfactory. At one time in 1945, the employee strength of the Division of Street Cleaning dropped as low as 152, to serve a population of 200,000 or more scattered over the city's area of thirty-eight square miles. Only by working employees on holidays and Sundays was it possible to maintain a two-day-a-week collection schedule of garbage and refuse.[12]

An analysis of the annual reports of the Norfolk Civil Service Commission shows that the war disrupted the competitive system. In 1939, two years before the United States entered the war, 72.3 per cent of the total of 977 municipal employees were in the classified service. During that year, 25 competitive examinations were held; 745 applicants filed, of which 391 passed and 354 failed, and 46 appointments were made. Competition was continued in 1940. There were 348 applicants examined competitively of which 188 passed and 160 failed. Competitive examinations were held in 1941, but the secretary reported that the city received no response to newspaper advertisements of vacancies which were then filled as provisional appointments. The physical requirements for police and fire forces were reduced, and the requirement of five years residence was waived.

Civil service activities for the war years, 1942-1945, are summarized in the following tabulation:[13]

	1942	1943	1944	1945
Competitive				
Examinations given	14	2	6	3
Applicants	397	6	109	*
Number Passed	188	5	55	
Non-Competitive Examinations Given				
Applicants	104	303	355	409
Number Passed	79	148	155	
Appointments	230	138	93	162
Promotions	65	28	19	33
Reinstatements	7	7	4	33
Transfers	8	3		3
Total Certified	310	176	116	231

*Competition resumed in police and fire divisions. There were 258 applicants interviewed, 81 examined competitively, and 36 certified for appointment.

12. *Norfolk Virginian-Pilot*, January 2, 1945.
13. Annual Reports of the Norfolk Civil Service Commission.

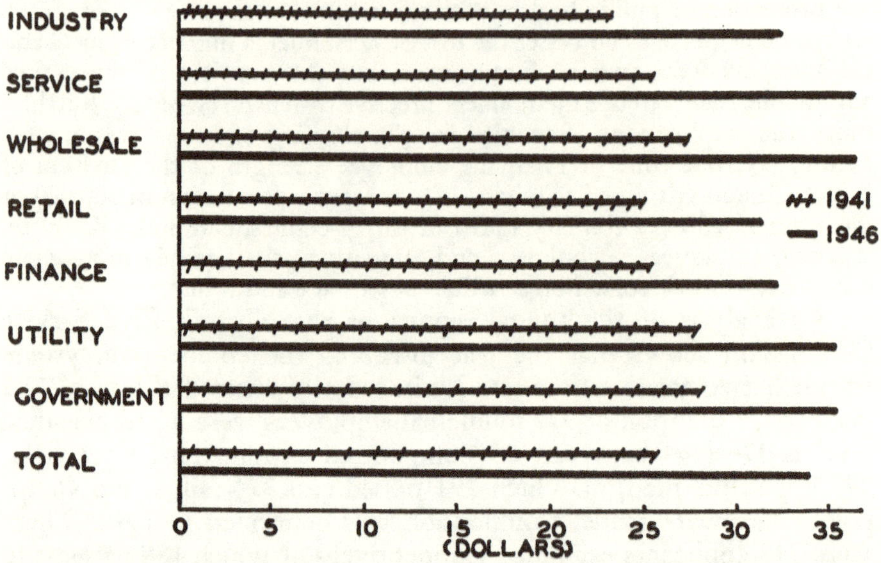

FIGURE 26. AVERAGE WEEKLY SALARY OF STENOGRAPHERS IN THE HAMPTON ROADS AREA, 1941 AND 1946

Source: Hampton Roads Association of Cost Accountants, Report on Confidential Salary and Wage Survey of the Hampton Roads, Virginia Area.

Salary schedules were badly disrupted. In many instances, those employed during the war were paid higher salaries for the same work than employees who had been in the service for several years. This, quite naturally, had a bad effect upon morale. A survey by the Hampton Roads Chapter of the National Association of Cost Accountants compares 1941 and 1946 salaries and wages paid by public and private employers in the following categories of employment: stenographers; secretaries; typists; bookkeepers; junior, intermediate, and senior clerks; calculating and accounting machine operators; chauffeurs; truck drivers; and unskilled labor. Public employers reporting included the cities of Norfolk, Portsmouth, and Newport News and the school boards of these cities and South Norfolk.

Government made the greatest wage increase in the unskilled trades and pulled its position from the bottom to next to the last place among the reporting employers (see Figure 27). The seventy-six employers reported an average hourly wage for unskilled workers of forty-two cents in January, 1941, and sixty-three cents an hour in January, 1946, an increase of 51 per cent. The increase for government

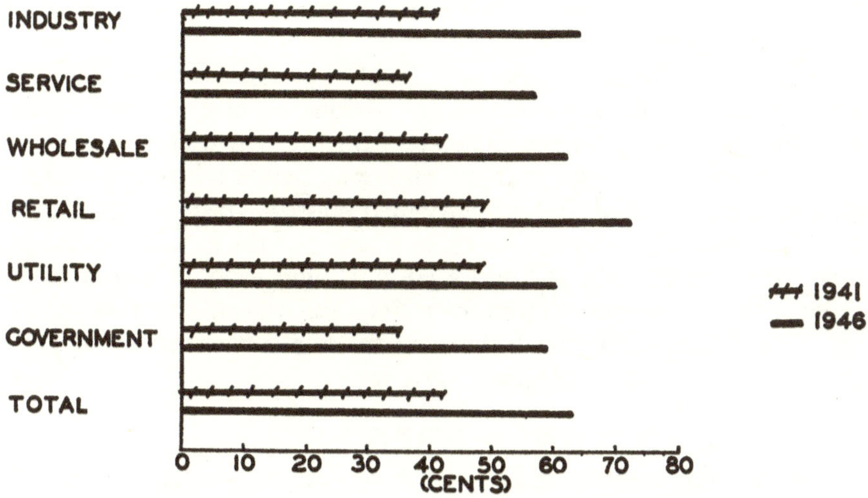

FIGURE 27. AVERAGE HOURLY WAGE OF UNSKILLED LABOR IN THE HAMPTON ROADS AREA, 1941 AND 1946

Source: Hampton Roads Association of Cost Accountants, Report on Confidential Salary and Wage Survey of the Hampton Roads, Virginia Area.

unskilled workers of 67 per cent brought the average rate from thirty-five cents per hour in 1941 to fifty-nine cents in 1946. As to stenographers, government was listed as the second highest employer in 1946, as the result of an increase of 26.5 per cent in weekly salary over that of 1941 (see Figure 26).

The war affected wages of other categories in public as compared with private employment, in varying ways. An increase of 41 per cent, for example, put the pay of government secretaries second from the top among the seven groups of reporting employers. Government typists moved up to third rank in pay as a result of an increase of 22 per cent. Government gave bookkeepers the second highest percentage increase but its rank in average weekly wage in 1946 was next to the last among reporting employers. Government had to give the fourth highest percentage increase for junior clerical employees to gain sixth place among the seven employer groups reporting. Government's position as to wages paid intermediate and senior clerks in 1946 was fifth and sixth, respectively, among reporting employer groups, which represented weekly salary increases of 27 per cent and 24 per cent respectively. In wages paid chauffeurs and truck drivers, public employers made the highest hourly increase of 72 per cent but this was insufficient to move them out of the lowest rank among the seven groups of employers.

The city of Norfolk is the only local government in the Hampton Roads area that has anything like an adequate personnel system and an actuarially sound retirement system for municipal employees. The latter, adopted before the war and almost suspended during that emergency, was expanded and strengthened shortly after the end of the war. The city of Newport News, as a result of the increase in municipal personnel, salaries, and wage costs is giving some thought to improvements in personnel administration. In 1947 the city employed the Public Administration Service to make a survey as the basis for adoption of a sound retirement system.

SUPPLIES AND EQUIPMENT

Besides the difficulties in recruiting personnel adequate to meet increased wartime demands for municipal services, there was the problem of getting the materials and equipment necessary to maintain these services. As the Newport News city manager stated, "One of the principal problems with which this city is confronted in its relation to the Federal government is the matter of obtaining priority ratings with which to secure necessary materials and equipment for essential municipal purposes."[14] The city manager of Portsmouth, similarly, complained of the interminable delay and red tape that it took to get municipal equipment through the War Production Board.[15] The pressure of war priorities on materials and equipment for performance of municipal service is reflected in the city budgets. Appropriations for material, equipment, and supplies and for replacements and repairs, held in abeyance during the war years, were increased in the first two postwar years.

IMPACT OF WAR ON MUNICIPAL POLICY

A review of the city of Norfolk's council minutes of 1942 to 1945 shows numerous contacts with the federal government which indicate that something out of the ordinary was going on. These federal-local contacts, as reflected in councilmanic ordinances, were concerned largely with such routine matters as "blackouts"; leasing municipal property for federal-military hospitals and for recreational uses; and contracts, fortified with federal grants, for enlarging the

14. Committee on Naval Affairs, Hampton Roads Hearings, p. 252.
15. *Ibid.*, pp. 309-327.

water supply and for extending civilian hospital and school facilities.

The war's impact on municipal management and policy in such matters as welfare, safety, and public works was considerable and will be discussed in some detail in subsequent chapters of this report. While the war's effect on municipal management and municipal policy is measurable in amount of work done, in money spent, and in results achieved, it is impossible to measure what was probably the war's greatest impact, which was on the minds and the spirit of the people in each locality, especially in bringing them together in a common effort.

CHAPTER XIII

PUBLIC SAFETY*

PUBLIC SAFETY in the Hampton Roads area, as elsewhere, includes police protection, fire prevention and protection, and traffic control.

IMPACT OF WAR ON CRIME

The pressure of increased population in congested war areas upon housing and recreational and police services was a major cause of the increase in crime measured in Figure 28 by the number of arrests in the two principal cities of the Hampton Roads area.

Arrests made by the Newport News police increased from 6,353 in 1939 to 38,377 in the mid-war year of 1942, or more than 500 per cent. The greatest increase in arrests were for such offenses as drunkenness, disorderly conduct, reckless driving and speeding, vagrancy, housebreaking, robbery from person, grand larceny, assault, felonious assault, prostitution, and being fugitives from justice. These are the kinds of offenses that tend to be characteristic of a transient, unstable population.

In the city of Norfolk arrests also reached their peak in 1942, subsided in 1943, and rose again in 1944. The last year of the war (1945) showed the smallest number of arrests of the four year war period. Jail commitments, however, increased in 1945 but showed a decline in 1946. This is probably accounted for by the more serious nature of the offenses in 1945.

In the city of Portsmouth total arrests, as reported by the chief of police, increased from 5,647 in 1940 to 24,858 for the mid-war year of 1943. Police problems in order of frequency of arrests were: drunkenness, assault, larceny, and prostitution. In answer to a question by a member of the Izac Committee as to what had been done to remedy the situation, the chief of police listed the following measures:

*By James E. Pate, Professor of Political Science, College of William and Mary.

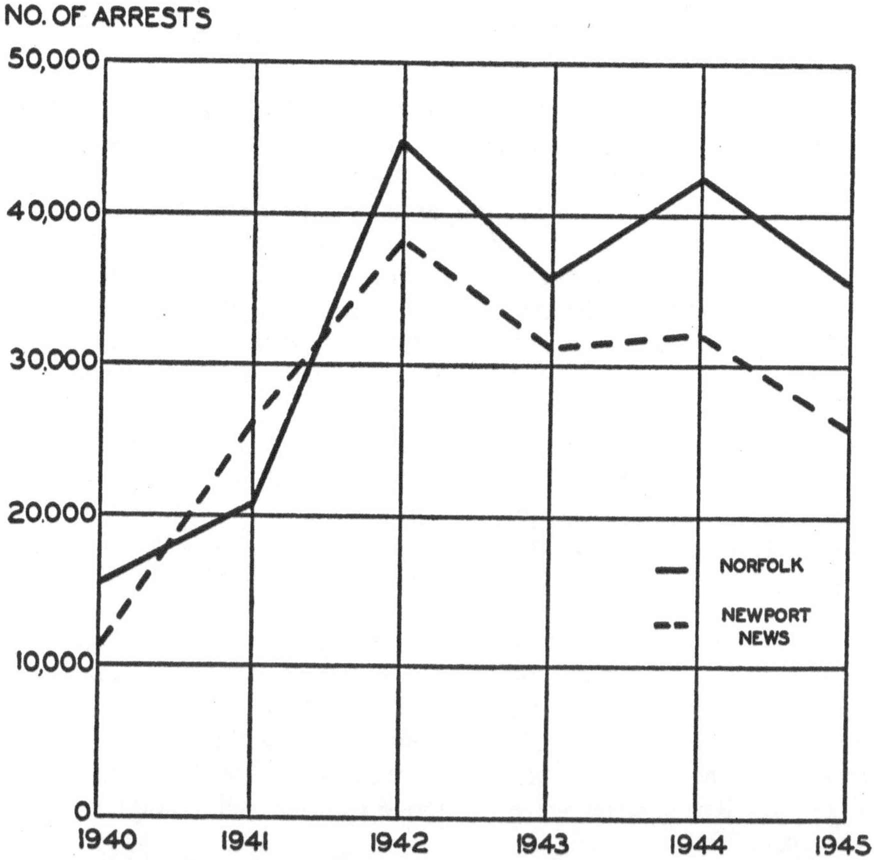

FIGURE 28. NUMBER OF ARRESTS, NORFOLK AND NEWPORT NEWS, 1940-1945
Source: Annual Police Reports.

(1) Increased the number of personnel in detective bureau, vice squad, traffic department, and the police department as a whole.
(2) Beats made smaller with the increased personnel.
(3) Furnished to officers new equipment such as revolvers, machine guns, and gas equipment.
(4) Installed parking meters to eliminate certain parking conditions.
(5) Established a permanent shore patrol.
(6) Appointed a woman special officer, in an effort to curtail prostitution.

(7) Established additional precinct at High and Effingham Streets for police and shore patrol.[1]

Arrests for ordinance violations by Hampton's police department during the war years increased tremendously. The percentage of increases for the years 1942 and 1943 over the prewar year 1938 were 324 and 277 respectively. As compared with 1938, the postwar year of 1947 registered an increase of 168 per cent. Hampton's nearness to important military reservations and role as the recreation center for the urban parts of Elizabeth City County accounts in part for its large police department and the volume of police activities.

The United States Department of Justice's Uniform Crime Reports measure crime by the number of offenses known to the police. A comparison of the principal cities in the Hampton Roads area with each other and with comparable cities in Virginia and other parts of the country sheds some light on the relation of crime to the conditions created by the war emergency. As indicated in Table 4, and by Figure 17, which compared the years 1940, 1943, and 1945, the Hampton Roads cities had more crime than cities in non-congested areas. Adjustment made for population increase in 1945 would of course reduce somewhat this high rating. In 1940, Portsmouth was the most violent city in the area, measured by number of murders and aggravated assault. In 1945, Newport News showed the largest rate of these violent offenses followed closely by Portsmouth. The Hampton Roads cities were far above the national average for both the years 1940 and 1945.

The State Department of Corrections classifies offenses into nine groups: offenses against decency and good order, government, person, property, public health, public justice, public peace, and public policy, and offenses involving currency and forgery. The department lists more than fifty offenses against decency and good order. One among these, however, overshadows all the others and constituted 36 and 47 per cent of the total jail commitments for the years 1944 and 1946 respectively—that was drunkenness and being drunk and disorderly.[2] During the war more than 60 per cent of the offenses against public health were violations of venereal disease laws; the leading offense against property was larceny; assault constituted

1. *Hearings*, Hampton Roads Naval Affairs Sub-Committee, Investigating Congested Areas, 1943, p. 316.

2. Reports on Commitments to the County and City Jails, June 30, 1946, State Board of Corrections.

most of the offenses against persons; being a fugitive and contempt of court were the principal offenses against public justice; violation of motor vehicle laws constituted about 90 per cent of the offenses against public peace; violation of alcoholic beverage control laws was the principal offense against public policy; the chief offenses against government during the war were being A.W.O.L., deserting the service, violating the U. S. Selective Service Act, and violating the U. S. Internal Revenue Act.

It was therefore quite natural for offenses against the government to show the greatest decrease during the first postwar year. Nearly every offense listed against persons showed a postwar increase; especially marked increases occurred in assault, homicide, rape, and robbery. Offenses against property showed a slight increase; offenses against public justice increased 15 per cent; offenses against public peace increased 40 per cent; offenses against public policy decreased; and offenses against public health declined 30 per cent during the first postwar year.

Among the factors responsible for the high incidence of crime during the war years were the following: depletion of manpower for police work as a result of the draft and higher pay in war industries; large increase of civilian population, especially transients; increased military personnel stationed or on leave in the area; and lack of adequate housing and recreation facilities.[3]

Prostitution was the offense most affected by conditions created by defense and war activities, and it was the most difficult to handle. One of the serious problems in controlling this offense in the first years of the war was inadequate facilities. No detention quarters existed in Norfolk and Portsmouth. As stated in the report of John J. Hurley, Field Representative of the Social Protection Service of the Office of Defense Health and Welfare Service:

> Police activities in the Hampton Roads area created serious problems concerning detention, with the result that a survey was made of all jail and detention facilities throughout the State. This revealed that of the 124 local jails there were only two with adequate facilities for housing women. Further exploration revealed that the State reformatory for women at Goochland was also crowded and could offer little hope for use as an active facility.
>
> Without suitable places for detention and correction, the activity of the police is practically nullified as there is little point in making an arrest

3. *Hearings, op. cit.*, p. 346.

if there is no place to lodge the prisoner. Moreover, even calloused policemen object to the incarceration of women in overcrowded unsanitary jails.[4]

The work of contacting the persons, tracing the source of infection, and treatment of venereal disease was one requiring the cooperation of both the medical and law enforcement authorities. The principal places of contact were tourist cabins, hotels, and taxicabs. When brought under control in one spot, it would break out in another—especially in the counties. Numerous "for hire" cars based in the near-by counties carried enlisted men and others to resorts outside the city limits.

A study of several hundred cases by the venereal disease control officer of the Navy Medical Corps early in the war indicates that the professional prostitute had been relegated to a minor position in the problem, and that the friend (20.8 per cent), the pick-up (65.6 per cent) or the young girl out for a good time had become the principal source of infection. Payment was reported in less than 30 per cent of the cases. This and similar reports from other sources testify to the suppression of the brothel, but indicate that new sources of infection had appeared and that new methods of treatment had become necessary. Many of these girls were in their teens, had recently come to town, and were not the type to be dealt with by the police as criminals.[5]

"In many cases," as Mr. Hurley told the Izac Committee, "the controlling factor is economic. A bed or a good meal. As a result of a study made last year it was discovered that girls in restaurants, beer parlors and the average drug store such as People's Drug Store, received an average salary of $10 to $12 a week. No transient girl can live on that."[6]

Shore Patrol

Indispensable assistance in handling military personnel was given by the permanent shore patrol established October 1, 1942. This organization's principal function was to handle the service personnel on leave. While its jurisdiction, as a rule, was limited to the service personnel, an understanding was reached with the local civilian authorities as to the relation between the naval and municipal police in

4. *Ibid.*, p. 248.
5. *Ibid.*, p. 306.
6. *Ibid.*, p. 225.

the inevitable jurisdictional conflicts. In 1943, the shore patrol had a complement of 300 men, including 15 Negroes. As stated by the shore patrol's commanding officer:

> This Negro unit has rendered valuable service and has done much to improve the racial difficulties that formerly existed. The ever increasing demands made upon the patrol, due to the expansion of the war effort cannot receive proper attention unless an increase is granted this organization; a conservative estimate at the present time is that patrol should be increased by 250 men, of which 50 should be Negroes.[7]

Police Irregularities

A charge was made during the war of certain irregularities in the city of Norfolk police department. One specific charge was that "the city manager and the chief of police have full knowledge of open operation of speakeasies, nip joints, gambling joints, and number writers." A grand jury investigation found that intoxicating beverages were illegally dispersed in state chartered clubs. Evidence also showed gambling, race-horse betting, and numbers writing were prevalent, but the jury did not find enough specific testimony to return an indictment.

The grand jury's report, dated August 5, 1944, condoned the complaints, as follows:

> In fairness, the members of the jury recognize that the police department is handicapped at the present time in the prevention and reducing of these infractions of the law by a totally inadequate police force due to the heavy drafts of war on the city's police department. The jury believes that the conditions complained of are in a large measure attributable to the unprecedented increase of population. The war has superimposed on the normal policing work of the city government a burden of great magnitude.[8]

The grand jury held that there was no connivance between the city manager and the police chief in such operations as charged, that the manager and chief were using all means to enforce the law, and were to be commended for the "excellence of their performance of duty under the difficult conditions of war."

Metropolitan Cooperation

Another problem in law enforcement which was accentuated during the war was that of contiguous city and county boundaries

7. *Ibid.*, pp. 57-58.
8. *Grand Jury Report*, August 5, 1944.

that delimit the overall use of police personnel and fire equipment, as well as the effective operation of other local functions. In some instances, probably in most, there was intercommunity cooperation. As Portsmouth's city manager said:

> The city of Portsmouth is most grateful for the splendid spirit of the Norfolk police department in assisting us in deterring crime and also their cooperative spirit in allowing the city of Portsmouth to use their radio broadcasting equipment, which is tied in with our receiver.[9]

On the other hand, a somewhat less favorable picture is presented by the following testimony of the chief of the city of Norfolk's police department at the Izac Committee's hearings:

Mr. Izac. What kind of cooperation have you received from the sheriffs adjoining the city of Norfolk?

Mr. Woods. From the standpoint of criminal practice, investigation of criminal cases, very very good, that is, if of a major nature. From the standpoint of repression of prostitution and vice, I would have to say "no."[10]

For the more effective handling of law enforcement and other problems in a region divided into several competing cities, counties, and towns, something more than cooperation is needed, especially during an emergency. Perhaps the answer is consolidation. This is what the Commandant of the Fifth Naval District had in mind when he said:

> . . . the conditions here would be much easier and more efficiently administered were a metropolitan area established in the Hampton Roads district. This would allow for an over-all planning to eliminate distressing conditions.[11]

THE JAIL SYSTEM

Except for the periodic inspections by the State Board of Corrections and the Federal Bureau of Prisons, which have some persuasive value in keeping up jail standards in regard to sanitation and safety, there is no outside supervision over these local institutions. They are controlled by locally elected sheriffs or sergeants and their jailors. The city government has no control over the jail, although the city pays half its running costs. Reports, such as are required, are made to the State Board of Corrections.

9. *Hearings, op. cit.*, p. 325.
10. *Ibid.*, p. 162.
11. *Ibid.*, p. 27.

JAIL CONDITIONS

The immediate vicinity of Hampton Roads is served by eight jails and two jail farms. The condition of the jail building in Newport News, and of both the building and the operation of the jail in Norfolk County, was such that during the war they were closed by the State Department of Corrections. Norfolk County used the Portsmouth jail, and Newport News used the city jail farm and the Elizabeth City county jail. Newport News, as a result of substantial federal aid, got a new public safety and jail building. The jail occupies the third and fourth floors of the building, and it is one of the best equipped in the Commonwealth with its cafeteria, laundry, provision for segregation of minors, and a recreation room.

The Norfolk County jail was closed because of bad operation in addition to the fact that it was a poor building. The records in the State Department of Corrections show that "of all the jails and lock-ups in the state of Virginia, the Norfolk County jail is the dirtiest;" that in at least one case a person was held for fifteen months without trial; that money taken from prisoners was not returned; and that some members of the Norfolk County police quite often held all night orgies with the prostitutes confined in the jail.[12]

The Portsmouth "bull pen" deserves to be mentioned in this report of the war's impact on municipal services. The "bull pen" was a place of confinement for persons waiting trial. It was a barred enclosure with a row of five cells, each with two bunks. Into this pen was thrown all types of offenders without any sort of segregation, except by sex. The pen's average daily population during most of the war period was more than fifty. It was badly crowded, with no place to sit except on the floor, badly ventilated, and unsanitary. Prisoners' hours in the pen varied from a few minutes to forty hours.

Jail Population[13]

The war's impact enlarged the jail population, as measured by the number of commitments; these increased 36.7 per cent and 56.3 per cent for the years 1944 and 1945 as compared with the year 1938.

One of the more striking facts disclosed by a study of jail popu-

12. See State Board of Corrections, Norfolk County Jail file, 1942-1945, Richmond, Virginia.

13. All statistics used in this section are from the annual reports of the State Department of Public Welfare, 1939 and 1941; and the State Board of Corrections, *Jail Commitments*, 1944, 1945, and 1946.

lation is that during the fiscal year ending June 30, 1944, the Norfolk city jail's population represented 33 per cent of all commitments to all city jails and 16 per cent of all the commitments to all the jails and jail farms in the commonwealth. Three times as many persons were committed to the Norfolk city jail during that year as were sent to the jail in the city of Richmond, a city that does not have an enviable crime record. Elizabeth City County jail, during the mid-war years of 1943-1944, had more commitments than any other county jail in the state, but this is partly accounted for by its getting some of those who would have been sent to the Newport News city jail had it been open. The large population of the Portsmouth jail was also partly the result of the closing of the Norfolk county jail. Among the five city jail farms in the state, those at Norfolk and Newport News got 3,972 and 2,328 respectively of a total of 7,280 commitments to all five farms. Many of those sent to the Newport News farm ordinarily would have been in the jail if it had been open.

Total jail commitments in the commonwealth for the fiscal year 1943-1944 were 33 per cent less than for the previous year. Major factors accounting for this decline were the large number in the armed forces of the age group who usually expand the jail population, opportunities for employment, ability to pay fines, and a better probation system. While several of these factors were present in the Hampton Roads area, they were offset by congested population and inadequate housing and recreational facilities for the civilian population. Classification by employment of those committed to jail for the years 1943-1944 reveals in order of number three groups: unskilled workers; domestic servants; and soldiers, sailors, and marines. All jail commitments in the commonwealth for the fiscal year ending June 30, 1945, were 10.89 per cent greater than for the year 1943-1944. This increase was almost entirely from those thirty or more years of age. Commitments for all jails in the commonwealth for the year ending June 30, 1946, were 11.27 per cent greater than for the previous year. The age groups twenty to twenty-four and twenty-five to twenty-nine showed the greatest increase of 48 and 40 per cent, respectively, over the previous year.

As reported by the State Board of Corrections: "The increase in jail commitments . . . is very alarming, particularly since there has been a conspicuous increase of commitments on charges of *offenses against persons*, many of which are of a very serious nature." Several factors account for the expansion of the postwar jail population.

These are, as defined by the State Department of Corrections:

> State and law enforcement agencies have been strengthened through increased and more efficient personnel; a very great number of men of the age groups that predominate in jail commitments have been released from military service during the year; this year has been a period of adjustment and idleness for a great many persons, not only for those who have been in the service but those who had been engaged in war-related activities and industries. . . . Many individuals who are not adequately stable or well adjusted were taught as a part of their military training to attain their ends through force and violence.[14]

IMPACT OF WAR ON JUVENILE DELINQUENCY

Juvenile delinquency increased greatly because in many cases both parents were at work and children were left without any organized outlet for their energies. There were more children, and as stated by a probation officer, many of these were accustomed to the freedom of open spaces and were not "house broken." As the superintendent of the Norfolk County Department of Public Welfare described the situation:

> The housing projects are made up of people from nearly every walk of life and nearly every state in the Union. Some have a rural background and some urban. The adults and children alike, have left their friends and communities and have moved into a large project consisting of strangers to the community. Their incomes in most cases are higher than previously, so they immediately seek recreation and diversion. Since the normal recreational facilities are inadequate and the means of travel are limited by lack of facilities and rationing, many of them are spending their money for pleasures which are morally and physically unhealthy. This and the fact that many mothers are working has resulted in domestic troubles and many neglected and delinquent children.[15]

The juvenile division of the Newport News police department received 484 complaints in 1938 as compared with 2,043 in 1942, or an increase of 322 per cent. In the city of Norfolk, the greatest increase in total number of juvenile cases handled was in 1944, although an increase in the fourteen-year-old to sixteen-year-old age group was seen in 1945. A noticeable increase occurred in 1943 in the early age groups, that is, children up to twelve years of age. For those seventeen years of age and over, the greatest increase of cases handled came in 1944.

14. State Board of Corrections, *Annual Report*, 1946, p. 4.
15. *Hearings, op. cit.*, p. 339.

The principal types of juvenile offenses, as covered by the war years, were larceny, sex offenses, being incorrigible or "ungovernable," and vandalism. In 1945, the last war year, the greatest increase was seen in drunkenness, sex offenses, assault, robbery, and store breaking. Disorderly conduct and petty larceny rose sharply in 1943. The greatest number of total problems presented was in 1944, with a slight decline in 1945.

A statistical study, by the director of the children's bureau of the State Department of Public Welfare, on juvenile delinquency in the Hampton Roads area during the years of war is summarized in Table 40. His conclusions point to the need for more expert administration of juvenile probation. He suggests that the problem of juvenile delinquency and probation could be handled much more expertly and sympathetically upon a region-wide basis with probation officers appointed by the judge from lists of eligible persons as

TABLE 40. JUVENILE CASES IN COURT, HAMPTON ROADS AREA*

	Total cases in court	Total cases committed	Total cases not committed	Total industrial school parolees	Total all possible cases for supervision
Elizabeth City Co.	44	11	33	3	36
Norfolk Co.	177	13	164	1	165
Princess Anne Co.	30	6	34	2	26
Nansemond Co.	30	2	28	1	29
Warwick Co.		3		2	2
York Co.		1		1	1
Hampton	12	4	8	2	10
Newport News	739	22	717	9	726
Norfolk	1,143	58	1,085	37	1,122
Portsmouth	496	32	464	15	479
South Norfolk	58	1	57		57
	2,729	153	2,590	73	2,653

*Figures represent annual average for four year period July 1, 1942, to June 30, 1946.

Source: Paul W. Keve, A Proposal System of Juvenile Probation for Virginia, (Master's Thesis, Richmond Professional Institute, 1947).

determined by the State Department of Public Welfare. The local probation officer would handle cases assigned by the judge of the juvenile court, but as to methods and technique, he would work under the State Department's supervision.[16]

16. Paul W. Keve, A Proposed System of Juvenile Probation for Virginia, (Master's Thesis, Richmond Professional Institute, 1947).

In connection with child welfare, mention should be made in this report of the joint project of the Children's Bureau of the United States Labor Department and the Bureau of Public Assistance of the Social Security Bureau in cooperation with the State Department of Public Welfare, which was started in 1942 in the city of Newport News as a wartime experiment to mobilize community resources and to handle the problem of juvenile delinquency with respect to its prevention as well as its control.[17] In a way, this was an experiment in intergovernmental relations to find ways by which all levels of government, federal, state, and local, could work together to solve a given problem. While the experiment was sponsored and financed by the federal government, it was carried on by local leadership and citizen participation which was enlisted through a broadly representative committee.

A trained social worker was placed in the field. He was paid by the federal agencies but was made responsible to the city manager. A full-time executive secretary was employed who provided technical service and advice, arranged the scheduling of committee meetings, and helped to find and develop community leaders. Important factual surveys included: a study of juvenile delinquency over a seven year period; a study of intake or rate of applications of welfare agencies in Newport News and Warwick County, which resulted in a report showing need of a clearance facility in a social exchange; and a block by block survey of day-care needs of families, which resulted in the establishment of day nurseries to meet the need where both parents were working.

As to the general results of this joint undertaking, the superintendent of the Newport News social service bureau says:

> This project developed a lot of important information and statistics for the social agencies which they had not had access to before and stimulated the process of closer coordination and cooperation between the social agencies and the City. It brought together a group of representative and substantial citizens who received a good grounding in the principles of community organization and social welfare, and became much better informed than they had ever been before on these subjects. It also started a number of worthwhile movements in the City for new facilities in the general welfare field and gave backing and support to various movements already underway. It would be very difficult indeed to say exactly how much of the progress in these various lines made during the time of the

17. See Report, U. S. Children's Bureau, "A Community Plans for Its Children," 1947.

operation of the project was directly caused by the project itself, and how much was only aided and expedited by the project. The operation of the project and the educational process to which the Child Welfare Committee members were exposed is probably having a continuing effect and will be felt for a long time in this community.[18]

FIRE PROTECTION AND CONTROL

Fire losses in 1941 in the city of Norfolk were more than 100 per cent higher than in the preceding year. Losses by fire receded again in 1944. There were 3,000 alarms in that year, but seven fires accounted for 51.5 per cent of the total loss. In 1945, ten fires resulted in 53.7 per cent of the total losses. The high loss rate during the war years was caused by concentration of war supplies in large buildings, manpower shortage, careless smoking, and let-down in inspection. Fire boats, operated by the Coast Guard, were effective in keeping the fire losses down around the dock area.

Fire losses in the city of Newport News increased greatly during the two mid-war years, 1943 and 1944. The high loss in 1944 occurred when the Chesapeake and Ohio railway pier was destroyed by fire, carrying with it war materials which were to be shipped to the war zones.

In 1938 the county of Warwick had one paid fireman and a volunteer fire force. War conditions created a necessity for a larger fire service. In 1942 a full-time fire chief and a staff of paid firemen were employed. The county now operates three fire stations. Improved equipment and personnel and available fire hydrants have resulted in a better rating which has reduced costs of fire insurance.

Fire losses in Hampton increased considerably during the period of this survey. The fire department personnel is largely volunteer with several paid members. It is outside the city manager's control. A contractual arrangement has been made between the city and Elizabeth City County for use of the city fire equipment in adjacent sections of the county.

TRAFFIC AND TRANSPORTATION PROBLEMS

Some idea of the problems confronting traffic officials because of the war can be seen in the fact that the Virginia Electric and Power Company in Norfolk in 1938 operated 80 street cars and 98 buses which

18. Correspondence, Mr. Herbert G. Ross, Superintendent of Social Service Bureau, Newport News, Virginia, July 26, 1948.

handled 15.5 million and 17 million passengers, respectively, while, in 1942, 120 street cars and 131 buses carried 41 million and 33.7 million people, respectively. In Portsmouth, VEPCO had 45 buses in 1938, which handled about 6.25 million passengers, as compared with 102 buses in 1942 which carried 21.5 million passengers. The Virginia Public Service Company operated the public transportation system on the north side of Hampton Roads before 1945. In that area the traffic increased 185 per cent in 1942 over that of 1940, but the situation was not as serious as that on the south side, which Admiral Taussig described as follows:

> . . . the population of this city which has doubled required at least double the transportation facilities which existed when the expansion began. However, one Federal agency puts a restriction on new buses and steetcars, another Federal agency puts a restriction on tires which can be obtained and another Federal agency drafts the motormen and operators of the transportation system; another agency by gasoline restrictions reduced the normal number of private automobiles in use; each agency acting for itself without regard to the effect on the total war effort caused by depriving the community of the means of sufficient transportation to carry on the war work; and there certainly is a lack of sufficient transportation.[19]

The Congressional Committee, appointed to investigate congested war areas, found that transportation and traffic constituted a serious war problem in the Norfolk area and recommended that the Office of Defense Transportation send a traffic expert to study the difficulties and work out remedies. The survey was made and a corrective transportation schedule instituted that pulled some of the buses from outlying districts and put them in the congested areas, cut off parallel street car and bus lines, and reduced the number of stops. While most of the people accepted these inconveniences, there was some rather strong criticism, especially at what some regarded as the O.D.T. traffic expert's arbitrary way of instituting transportation changes.

Another serious problem was the impact of the unusually heavy traffic on the street pavement. It was worn out faster than the city could get materials and labor to repair it. The situation in Portsmouth was typical of the congested area. The city manager described it as follows:

19. *Hearings, op. cit.*, pp. 184-91.

The streets of this city were laid for light traffic and the continual use of them by heavy trucks of the Navy, Coast Guard and many contractors has caused the city considerable damage. We are unable to secure sufficient asphalt to repair our streets, and the holes and breakage continue with great rapidity. The damage already done is estimated by our engineering department to be nearly one-half million dollars up to the present time.[20]

20. *Ibid.*, p. 310.

CHAPTER XIV

PUBLIC WELFARE*

As a General Term, public welfare has no sharply delimited boundaries. Its meaning conforms with the practice of particular governmental units. The communities of the Hampton Roads area include under public welfare such local functions as social services, recreation, health, and sanitation. Public housing, although administered by separate housing authorities, is so closely related to human welfare that to place it under the welfare roof is no violation of the meaning of the term.

SOCIAL SERVICES

Social services include the categories of old-age assistance, aid to dependent children, aid to dependent blind, general relief, and regular foster care. A comprehensive social service program and a good staff go beyond the mere financial and mechanical methods of interviewing clients and calculating public assistance budgets. It will provide such counseling as a trained worker can give families in these circumstances.

One of the significant results of the war on social service work in the Hampton Roads area was to emphasize this sort of counseling service.

In Newport News, for example, the war, in addition to decreasing case loads and applications, and increasing grants to recipients, enhanced the value of the Social Service Bureau as a community agency offering needed services to many individuals and families. The traditional value of such an agency in lending assistance in solving the human problems which grow out of financial needs was highlighted by the impact of wartime conditions, which brought to the Social Service Bureau a heavy flow of requests for services from people caught in the whirl of wartime events.[1]

Table 41 summarizes the war's effect on public assistance in the

*By James E. Pate, Professor of Political Science, College of William and Mary.

1. Unpublished report by George T. Kalif, on the impact of the war on public welfare departments in the Hampton Roads Area, September, 1947, in the files of the Hampton Roads-Peninsula War Studies Committee, Williamsburg.

Hampton Roads area. The case load in all categories of public assistance except aid to dependent children dropped. In this group, the case load almost tripled between the normal prewar year of 1939 and 1945. The rise in child dependency during the war period is partly accountable to the fact that it was not until late 1942 that the Servicemen's Dependent Allowance Act was passed by Congress. The case load decrease, according to the superintendent of the Norfolk City Bureau of Public Assistance, was due to "increase in income through employment, renting rooms, government allotments, and assistance from relatives who were more fully employed. These causes affected those families who had some resource, someone who could work, a room to rent, someone subject to draft. As these were dropped, the remaining families represented those with lesser resources. As the num-

TABLE 41. PUBLIC ASSISTANCE STATISTICS, HAMPTON ROADS–PENINSULA AREA, 1939–1947

	1939	1941	1943	1945	1947
Old-Age Assistance					
Number of cases	1,380	2,071	1,690	1,319	1,663
Average grant (dollars)	9.48	11.43	12.87	17.01	20.88
Total expenditures (000s dollars)	76	286	290	291	353
Aid to Dependent Children					
Number of cases	124	487	462	471	850
Average grant (dollars)	23.31	23.93	27.41	38.12	45.93
Total expenditures (000s dollars)	20	134	176	207	396
General Relief					
Number of cases	3,433	705	351	401	552
Average grant (dollars)	8.49	10.62	13.11	19.20	23.17
Total expenditures (000s dollars)	122	116	90	93	181
Aid to Blind Expenditures (000s dollars)	11	27	25	28	39
Regular Foster Care Expenditures (000s dollars)	*	*	*	26	60
Administration Expenditures (000s dollars)	75	121	124	154	214
Total Expenditures for Public Assistance (000s dollars)	304	684	705	799	1,243

*Started in 1945

Source: Annual Reports, Virginia Department of Public Welfare.

ber who could help themselves to some degree decreased, the ratio of those who could not help themselves increased, and the average of income per family dropped as also did the per cent of this income to the average budget."[2]

Total expenditures increased for all categories of assistance except general relief. The almost 100 per cent increase in this latter group in 1947 as compared with the last war year, 1945, is indicative of postwar employment conditions. The fact that total expenditures increased while case loads were decreasing is attributed by the Norfolk Superintendent partially to "increasing the budgetary standard in the attempt to more nearly meet the needs of the people" and partly "to the attempt to offset the effect of war employment on the remaining case load."[3]

RECREATION

The war emphasized recreation as a function of government. Well organized and supervised recreational activities are now considered as a necessary public function because of the relation these have to morale, delinquency, and health conditions.

In 1938 the city of Newport News carried nothing in its budget for recreation. In 1945 and 1946 the city council appropriated $38,809 and $48,441 respectively for this purpose. The recreation bureau which began a feeble existence in 1933 has developed into one of the important organizations in the city government. The city of Portsmouth established a recreation bureau in 1942. The city of Norfolk began in 1940 to consider this function. The appropriation for recreation by the city council in that year, however, was the meager sum of $8,446. This was increased in 1944, 1945, and 1946 to approximately $46,000, $90,000, and $114,000, respectively. The larger appropriations for the years 1945 and 1946 were to replace the federal support for this activity which was stopped in 1945.

During the first year or two of the war, community recreational facilities of the Hampton Roads area, which were scarcely sufficient to care for the normal population, were wholly inadequate to care for the increased number of civilian workers and military personnel. The servicemen fared better than the civilian. The Commandant of the Fifth Naval District, describes the paucity of recreational facilities on the south side of Hampton Roads as follows:

2. F. E. Burleson, *1946-47 Budgetary Status, Social Service Bureau, Norfolk, Virginia.*

3. *Ibid.*

Such recreation facilities as theaters, public parks, beach resorts, beer gardens and dance halls as existed here with the small population have proved utterly inadequate for the tremendous increase in population. The only attempts to alleviate this situation have been made by religious and charitable organizations, by the U.S.O., and by illicit or questionable operatives of "hot spots." The recreation facilities provided by the churches and charitable organizations have mostly been confined to uniformed personnel. Little, if anything, has been done for civilian war workers. The taking of recreational beaches and parks by the armed services for use as schools and training stations has still further increased the poverty of these welfare and recreation centers.[4]

Newport News, Portsmouth, and Norfolk County experienced difficulties because of the shortage of recreational facilities.[5]

The chairman of the recreational committee of the city of Norfolk, in his testimony before the Izac Committee, was sharply critical of the lack of coordinated recreational effort. He believed that more local direction would work better and that there was need for a recreation middle ground between "dives and divinity." More sailors, he said, patronized the beer joints in Norfolk than the U.S.O.[6]

The biggest recreational problem in the early part of the war, as stated before, was lack of coordination of effort and pitifully inadequate facilities for thousands of civilian workers and their families that had come into this congested area of war activities. Something, however, was done. Federal assistance from the Lanham Act and the spur of the Committee on Congested Production Areas began to bear fruit in 1943. Buildings were renovated; beach extensions made; golf courses made available; and new U.S.O. buildings opened where athletic events, dances, and shows were scheduled and sandwiches were sold. Local recreation bureaus in cooperation with community organizations and the churches conducted a large number of parties, dances, band concerts, and childrens' playground programs. These events were well patronized both by civilians and service men and their families.

PUBLIC HEALTH AND SANITATION

Conditions in the Hampton Roads area caused by war-related activities greatly intensified the work of the public health staff. In

4. *Hearings*, Hampton Roads Naval Affairs Sub-Committee Investigating Congested Areas, U. S. Congress, p. 24.
5. *Ibid.*, p. 174.
6. *Ibid.*, p. 193.

Portsmouth the principal public health services were communicable disease control, classes for nurses, laboratory service, inspection of food handling places, and a milk sanitation program. The city of Norfolk expanded its activities to include control of venereal disease, typhus control, general sanitation, and protection of the milk and food supply.

During the war, the food problem in Norfolk was of concern to the army and navy as well as the civilian population. The problem concerned distribution as well as sanitary inspection. A cooperative city and navy inspection program was operated. The city had the principal responsibility for sanitary conditions in public eating places. The United States Public Health Service code on food establishments was used as a group study text for providing inspectors with in-service training. The civilian population found it difficult to get adequate food because of two factors. One was that the distribution quota was based on the 1940 population which was considerably below the actual population of this congested area. Another was the natural inclination of the servicemen, when on liberty, to take their meals at restaurants. A Congressional investigating committee made the following recommendations for improving conditions:

> To alleviate this intolerable condition, the subcommittee recommends that immediate provision be made by the Federal Food Administrator to insure adequate food distribution in the Hampton Roads area. The allotments should take into consideration the present greatly increased civilian population and the servicemen from outside, and eliminate the practice of regulating food requirements on the basis of 1941 population figures.... The Navy also should take steps to establish and operate naval mess facilities in downtown areas of Norfolk and Portsmouth as a means of relieving the drain on civilian stocks of food and of clearing up congestion in public eating places patronized by civilian war workers. Servicemen on liberty should be required to take their meals in these proposed Navy mess halls.[7]

Control of venereal disease was a special problem of the city, the state, and the United States Public Health Service. At the very beginning of defense activities (1940), the Hampton Roads region was declared an emergency area for venereal disease control and a case

7. Report on Hampton Roads Area of the Subcommittee Appointed to Investigate Vice Conditions in the Vicinity of Naval Establishments, House of Representatives, 1943, p. 646.

finding and treatment program was instituted.[8] By the end of 1942 the venereal disease rate was halved. The problem, however, was not easy to solve. As the source of infection in the Norfolk area declined, the rate rose elsewhere, which indicated that local control could do only part of the job.

Mosquito control has been a perennial Hampton Roads problem. During the war it also became a concern of the United States Public Health Service. "The enormous construction programs in the Norfolk area," writes the superintendent of the bureau of mosquito control, "created many mosquito problems. Careful and systematic ground drainage is one of the most useful means of preventing mosquito breeding in a low and flat country such as this. But the war development was too rapid and too important to allow questions of drainage to interfere with its accomplishment, and as a result, new breeding hazards have been created."[9]

Intergovernmental relations in the field of mosquito control apparently were not as satisfactory as in other areas of the public health services. The superintendent of Norfolk's mosquito control describes his wartime problems, as follows:

> A substantial part of the United States Public Health Service's Virginia anti-malaria unit was assigned to the Hampton Roads area. It was hoped that this federal agency might help us to carry the added burdens imposed largely by the government's war expansion, but our hopes were not entirely realized. Unfortunately, the United States Public Health Service's organization was limited strictly to activity against the tribe Anophelini. . . . Their program made no provision for the inspection service which is so essential to the success of such a project in urban areas. . . . The public health service and the local mosquito control unit coordinated resources as far as possible. We supplied them with several key field men and some equipment, while they furnished part of the fuel oil larvacide which we applied—but they were not able to contribute as much support as we had anticipated.[10]

8. R. B. Henry of the Medical Corps, U. S. Navy, describes the situation as follows: "The prompt reporting of all cases, with forwarding of contact reports, by civilian physicians and medical officers of the armed forces, was a prime link in the procedure, while the central office maintained a master index of cases of syphilis and gonorrhea in the area, as well as one of delinquencies in the clinic population, and a signal system denoting infectious, potentially infectious, and non-emergency cases, so that these might be followed up in the order named." (*Hearings, op. cit.*, p. 305.)

9. *Annual Report*, Superintendent of Mosquito Control, 1942.

10. *Ibid.*

On the Portsmouth side of the Elizabeth River, the water pressure declined and created a health hazard. There was poor coordination between public housing agencies and the city government in locating new housing projects near the water utility. The Portsmouth city health officer testified:

> There is a definite health problem which has arisen because too many houses have been connected to water mains that are too small. This results in a reduction of water pressure with consequent lack of water on the second floor of many homes in the area in question. . . . Without previous consultation with officials of the water department, the Federal Public Housing Authority now has projected large housing projects—some have actually been started, it is said—and proposes to utilize water from these already inadequate mains. The health hazard will, of course, be made more acute.[11]

There were some physical gains in public health facilities as a result of the war. The city of Newport News was the most fortunate in that regard. This city obtained, as a result of substantial federal assistance, a public welfare and health center housed in a modern building equipped with the newest facilities for carrying on an effective public health program.

One of the notable contributions of the war emergency was the way federal, state, and local agencies cooperated in controlling communicable disease and in protecting public health under conditions that could have been extremely hazardous to health. One of the reasons for this successful operation was the recognition of local responsibility and ability to handle the problems, if provided technical and financial assistance.

Satisfactory cooperative arrangements were made between the state health department and the United States Public Health Service. Grants were made by the Public Health Service directly to the state, which in turn allocated funds and staff among the localities. The city's health department was responsible for the use of money and personnel. Reports, of course, were made to the state department, and occasional inspections were made by federal and state officers to check on conditions. During the war, the activities of the United States Public Health Service increased, especially in venereal disease, malaria, and typhus control. During that emergency, the Public Health Service made available to the state, on a loan basis, doctors, nurses, sanitarians

11. *Hearings, op. cit.*, p. 318.

and engineers, bacteriologists, and medical technicians. The state, in turn, assigned these specialists to the Hampton Roads area, where they worked under the local health officers.

Impact of the War on Vital Statistics

The war increased the hazards to public health because of congested population, inadequate housing, and sanitary facilities, and over-taxed hospitals and medical facilities. Communicable diseases were kept under control as a result of the greatly intensified and cooperative efforts of the United States Public Health Service, the State Department of Health, and the local health services. The health commissioner of the city of Norfolk in his 1944 annual report declared, "Norfolk has the lowest death rate in its history and the birth rate is one of the highest in the country." The birth rate increased sharply from 1940 to 1942 but dropped the following year. At the end of 1945, the death rate had increased to the point where it stood in 1940. The health department's mortality report for 1945 indicated an increase in death rate for degenerative diseases and in death by accident and violence. The tuberculosis death rate in 1945 was approximately 100 per cent over that of 1944.

The health of the inhabitants of the Lower Peninsula on the north side of Hampton Roads was good, although the area was crowded by in-migrant war workers and military personnel. The mortality statistics reveal an actual decrease from 1940 to the end of the war, except in York County which showed a slight increase from 1940 to 1943 and in Newport News where the rate rose sharply from 1943 to 1944. The movement of population during that time, especially the out-migration of those ages most likely to have a higher disease resistance, is a probable cause of the city's increased death rate during this mid-war year.

Water Supply

The impact of defense activities on water supply of the Hampton Roads area began to be felt in 1940. In that year more than $1,000,000 was spent in the Norfolk area either in projects completed or put under construction. About one-third of this amount went for replacing a worn out wooden-stave line with a concrete pipe line from Norfolk to Lake Prince. The water utility in the city of Portsmouth, which also supplies the inhabitants of Suffolk, was sufficiently expanded, with federal assistance, to care for the community's normal water needs for the next twenty-five years. As indicated in Table 29, water consumption in the Hampton Roads area increased approximately 150 per cent from 1939 to 1944. The pressure on the Newport News water supply system, which serves the entire Lower Peninsula necessitated an extension of the water supply by establishing a pumping station on the Chickahominy River and piping water for a distance of about fifty miles. The cost of the water extension (1941-1945) was more than $4,000,000, with the federal government paying the larger part. The result has been a water supply sufficient to take care of the Lower Peninsula's normal needs for years to come.

All three water utilities just mentioned are publicly owned and operated with the aim of supplying good water at a profit.

Sewage and Pollution

Portsmouth's city manager described the sanitation problem in the area as "appalling and dangerous" and called attention to the fact that Portsmouth's normal sewer facilities, geared to 50,000 people, were taxed to capacity by the swollen population.[12]

As stated by Admiral Taussig:

> Lack of sanitation facilities is one of the worst conditions existing in this area. . . . Pollution, recognized as a menace to the health of the community for a number of years, has greatly increased with the large influx of population; this menace is a war emergency measure. . . . The absence of proper sewage disposal facilities has . . . a harmful effect on the housing situation. . . . Pollution of the tidal waters in this area has had a very deleterious effect on the oyster and fishing industry and on the recreational features. . . . We have in this area many thousands of men in uniform and many thousands of war workers who are not in uniform. The tidal waters of this area which comprise Hampton Roads and the many tributaries have become so polluted that bathing is not permitted inside a line from the eastward of Old Point Comfort and Willoughby Spit.[13]

The formation of the Hampton Roads Sanitation District Commission was the result of investigations over a period of years into the problem of reducing pollution in the tidal waters of the Hampton Roads area. While this important area-wide sewage disposal system was not started by the war, its completion was greatly facilitated by the pressure of this emergency and by substantial federal grants.

12. *Hearings, op. cit.*, p. 310.
13. *Ibid.*, pp. 112-13.

The Hampton Roads Sanitation District includes both the north and south sides of the Hampton Roads area with the exception of York County on the north and the cities of Portsmouth and South Norfolk on the south side. The latter cities withdrew because they believed that the city could provide its own system at less cost. The district's area comprised 1,160 square miles and an estimated population of 420,852.

The commission, created by law as a "body politic and corporate and a political subdivision of the Commonwealth," is composed of five resident members of the district appointed by the governor. It employs managerial and technical personnel. Its construction program includes sewage treatment plants, trunk sewers, force mains, and pumping stations. The sewage treatment plant opened in 1948 at the boat harbor in Newport News will serve the entire north side of the Hampton Roads area for the next fifteen to twenty years.

Garbage and Refuse Collections

Garbage and refuse collection, like water consumption, provides a quantitative measure of the war's impact. The extent of this impact on the cities of Norfolk, Portsmouth, and Newport News is indicated in Table 42.

TABLE 42. GARBAGE AND REFUSE COLLECTIONS, NORFOLK, PORTSMOUTH AND NEWPORT NEWS, 1940–1946

Place	1940	1942	1944	1946
	(in thousands of cubic yards)			
Norfolk	270	384	383	362
Portsmouth	143	213	255	260
Newport News*	21	36	31	31

*Garbage only.

Source: Official Records, Departments of Public Works of the respective cities.

Portsmouth's city manager described the difficulties incident to garbage disposal as follows:

Our garbage incinerator was constructed in 1918, and is at an age where continual taxing will cause its complete breakdown. A new incinerator has been approved by the Federal Works Agency in a participating grant with the city, but it still has to go through the board's surveys, priorities, experts, and investigators before we receive priority from the

War Production Board. Therefore, it appears to me that the old incinerator, in spite of its wheezy condition, must continue to function.[14]

The greatly increased garbage collection and sewage disposal in Newport News taxed the local services beyond the limit of safety. For about one year, beginning the middle of 1942, the city was forced to dump a considerable part of the combustible refuse. As a result of the greatly increased pressure on the city's garbage and refuse, federal assistance was granted to double the incinerator's capacity.

PUBLIC HOUSING

Local housing authorities were created in the late thirties, under authorization of state enabling laws, by the councils of the principal cities in the Hampton Roads area. They are public corporations, designated by the state laws as political subdivisions of the state, and are composed of local citizens, usually businessmen, appointed by the mayor. The cities assume none of the authority's financial obligations, but provide the usual municipal services for the housing projects and exempt them from taxes. The authorities, however, make payments in lieu of taxes.

Their original purpose of constructing and operating houses for low income families[15] was diverted by the war to providing houses for civilian war workers and military personnel.

Wartime Developments

The wartime experience of the Norfolk authority was typical. Admiral Taussig in 1940 requested its assistance in housing the families of soldiers and sailors. At that time there were 96 ships and 38,000 men stationed at Norfolk, a slight forecast of what was to come. One month after this request, the housing authority obtained federal approval for a loan of $1,800,000 to build 500 dwellings for naval personnel.[16] Norfolk's architects pooled their resources and housing projects for white and Negro tenants were constructed or leased.

The wartime experience of the Norfolk Housing Auothority has been summarized as follows:

14. *Ibid.*, p. 310.

15. "Persons of low income," as defined by the state enabling act, "are persons or families who lack the amount of income necessary to enable them, without financial assistance, to live in decent, safe and sanitary dwellings, without overcrowding." (Acts of Assembly, Ch. 310, 1938, p. 448.)

16. Norfolk Housing Authority, *This Is It*, p. 6.

An indication of the mushroom expansion of Norfolk as one of the country's chief naval bases was that in contrast to the $8,300,000 spent for government construction in 1941, the work scheduled for the first four months of 1942 cost $69,000,000. One sample of the problem created by the swarming in of migrant workers and naval personnel was an estimate in February 1942 that nursery care was needed for 2,760 children, while Norfolk's three day nurseries could accommodate only 150. . . . Had it not been for the joint action of the Federal Public Housing Authority and the Norfolk Authority, the housing crisis might have become a disaster. Together the two agencies supplied 3,462 dwellings for families and single workers....

The authority entered the hotel business because enlisted men with wives in other cities were up against a problem that produced general frustration. Anticipating a few days of leave, they would try to reserve hotel space so their wives could visit them in Norfolk. Getting a room was as easy as chartering a train of pullman cars. So, with the approval of the Federal Public Housing Authority, the Authority designated 144 units in the Commonwealth Hotel for the exclusive use of servicemen and their families. Family rates were set at $2.50 a night or $15 a week, another boon. Preference was given to families of hospitalized personnel and of men returning from combat. The hotel's popularity is shown by the fact that 45,000 guests registered for a total of 280,000 bed nights from August 1943 to January 1946. The count does not include babies in the 50 cribs provided free.[17]

The Housing Authority of the City of Portsmouth in meeting the housing shortage provided 10,751 units, most of which were classed as temporary, in 1941, 1942, and 1943. Four-fifths of these units were for white residents and one-fifth for Negroes.

Postwar Aspects

While public and private agencies were pressed into service to meet the insistent demand for more housing, at the same time attention was given to the effect that surplus housing would have on real-estate values after the emergency had passed. The city manager of Newport News declared that "permanent housing beyond the normal requirements of the community will after the war result in a very drastic and unnecessary depreciation of real-estate values throughout this entire area."[18] He urged, accordingly, that all future housing should be of a temporary construction and that assurance should be given that the houses would be removed after they had

17. *Ibid.*
18. *Hearings, op. cit.*, p. 250.

served their purpose. The city manager was interested in protecting the real-estate market against surplus housing, but he missed by a long mark the community's postwar needs for housing. As a matter of fact, all the Hampton Roads housing authorities have found that the postwar housing problem has been much greater than during the war.

Among the factors that account for this situation, according to an official of the Norfolk Housing Authority,[19] are the following: (1) the importance of Norfolk as the base of the Atlantic fleet; (2) the resumption of the navy's policy of employing civilian workers for civilian jobs which had been disrupted during the war because of manpower shortage; (3) the fact that such large naval establishments as the amphibious base at Little Creek were made permanent; (4) the filling of many jobs in private business which could not be filled during the war; (5) the opening of new businesses; and (6) an increase in the number of families.

A survey by a committee of the Lower Peninsula Planning Commission which is summarized in Table 43, showed the number of dwelling units in this area in 1944 and the estimated number of dwellings needed in 1950. There was greater progress made in housing the white than the colored population. Practically all the construction undertaken for colored people was by public authorities. The Planning Commission estimated that by 1950 there would be a surplus of white dwelling units and a deficit for colored.

On the basis of this survey the commission made recommendations for disposal of the various housing projects. Ferguson Park, for example, was classified by the housing report as temporary on a

TABLE 43. DWELLINGS IN 1944 AND ESTIMATED HOUSING SURPLUS AND DEFICIT, LOWER PENINSULA AREA, 1950

	Dwellings 1944	Number Permanent Dwellings Needed 1950	Surplus	Deficit
Total	36,352	32,800	3,552	
White	26,367	22,400	3,967	
Colored	9,985	10,400		415

Source: Committee on Housing and Slum Clearance of the Lower Peninsula Planning Commission, *Survey, Study and Recommendations on Housing for the Lower Peninsula of Virginia*, March, 1946, pp. 25–26.

19. Personal interview with George Price, Assistant Executive Director, Norfolk Housing Authority, July, 1948.

permanent site, and should be "removed at the earliest practical date, so that this highly desirable and much needed site will be available for individual home construction for people of middle income." The unexpected postwar housing shortage developed an interesting controversy over this recommendation. The Ferguson Park people resisted the idea and organized to promote a cooperative association to purchase the units.[20] At the time of writing the controversy was still unsettled.

The philosophy of public housing is that public low-rent housing must not compete with the private building industry. The clients of public housing must therefore be drawn from those whose income is so low that they cannot afford to pay the rentals that would bring a profit to the private builder and operator of "decent" dwelling places. On the other hand, public housing must, as a practical matter, exclude families at the lowest income levels because of the necessity of balancing its books and the limited amount of subsidy.

This means that in the city of Norfolk, 7,000, or 54 per cent, of the lowest income families living in substandard houses must continue to live there and that the Norfolk Housing Authority's program will not eliminate the slums because the causes of bad housing will still remain.

Planned Communities

In some instances wartime housing projects can make a contribution in the form of permanent planned neighborhoods. Hilton Village in Warwick County and Craddock in Norfolk County, for example, were the result of World War I housing and today are stable and pleasant communities. Examples of well-planned neighborhoods, resulting from the late war which have promise of future permanence, are Stuart Gardens, Marshall Courts, and Orcutt Homes in the city of Newport News, and Merrimac Park and several other projects in the Norfolk-Portsmouth area.

The Newport News Redevelopment and Housing Authority supervised the construction and now operates and manages the following permanent projects:

Marshall Courts	353 dwelling units
Harbor Homes	252 dwelling units
Orcutt Homes	148 dwelling units
Lassiter Courts	350 dwelling units

20. As of 1947 the 1200 dwelling units were occupied by shipyard workers, veterans, and active service men.

The Marshall Courts project is described by the Executive Director of the housing authority, as follows:

> The Marshall Courts Project . . . was built . . . in 1940-41. It was constructed for the most part on vacant land with compartively few improved properties, necessitating extensive site improvements. . . .
>
> The total site area is 880,703 square feet of which 19.6 per cent is covered by buildings. The buildings are of masonry construction in cinder block and brick veneer consisting of two story multiple unit row buildings and one story duplex buildings generally facing east and west. The streets conform with those of the existing city pattern.
>
> A separate community and recreation building is provided for the use of all tenants in the project and surrounding area. A fully equipped playground is provided for children's recreation. A community council, elected by the residents of the project, sponsors and supervises all activities within the project. . . .
>
> During the war the project was used to house war workers only but as soon as housing becomes less acute on the peninsula, only families of low income living under sub-standard conditions will be eligible for admission.[21]

Stuart Gardens, a war housing project constructed by the Defense Homes Corporation, is a permanent and well-planned neighborhood located on the north side of Hampton Roads. The government corporation sold Stuart Gardens in 1947 to a private corporation. The latter has retained ownership of the apartment units but has sold the single dwellings to private individuals at a price of $6,000 to $7,850 each. About 13 per cent of the purchasers were the original occupants. The apartment units rented, as of October, 1948, from $37.50 to $54 a month.

The project consists of 501 well-designed apartment units and 479 single residence houses of four, five, and six rooms each. A shopping center, a theater, community center, recreation facilities, and a site for a school and church provide means for a well-rounded community life. The playground facilities in the apartment area have deteriorated and are not being replaced. The private corporation which owns the apartment units believes that the expense is not justified.

SUMMARY

Public welfare is something like the proverbial definition of equity, "as long and as broad as the Chancellor's foot." The scope of

21. Correspondence, September 18, 1948.

public welfare is about as broad as the governing boards choose to make it. In the Hampton Roads area, as we have seen, it is used to include the social services, health and sanitation, and recreation. The writer has extended the label to public water supplies and to public housing.

Public assistance case loads dropped during the war except for dependent children. Total expenditures, however, increased because budgetary standards were improved. The war emergency, which swelled the population of the area to such an extent, featured family counseling as a function of the public welfare staff.

Recreational facilities were totally inadequate to care for the needs of the people. Public recreational services were almost non-existent. The combined efforts of both public and private agencies were necessary to meet this problem. This extraordinary experience has resulted in increasing the status of recreation as a public function.

The emergency brought the federal, state, and local governments together in a cooperative effort which bore important results in the control of disease. Problems allied to health, such as food, water supply, and sanitation and housing pressed for attention. Here the localities profited immensely by federal support. The state government was greatly overshadowed by the federal-local effort during the war emergency.

CHAPTER XV

FEDERAL MOBILIZATION OF THE AREA'S RESOURCES*

THE PRINCIPAL federal activities for mobilizing the resources of the Hampton Roads area for war were mobilizing manpower and production, rationing and price controls, and supporting community facilities by federal expenditures under the Lanham Act.

MOBILIZING MANPOWER[1]

The principal claimants to manpower in the Hampton Roads area were the armed services, the naval establishments, the shipbuilding industry, the producers and processors of food, transportation, businesses making and selling essential civilian goods, and certain trades and services essential to the health, safety and welfare of the local inhabitants. The Hampton Roads area office of the War Manpower Commission was opened January 5, 1943, and the area defined in terms of "commuting accessibility" to include the cities of Norfolk, Portsmouth, Newport News, South Norfolk, Suffolk, Williamsburg and Hampton, and the counties of Norfolk, Nansemond, Isle of Wight, Princess Anne, Elizabeth City, Warwick, James City, and York.

The initial staff of the Hampton Roads office included the area director, a stenographer, and a United States Employment Service supervisor. When fully staffed the office personnel numbered fourteen. Two important arms of the area office were the management-labor committee and the area manpower priorities committee. The latter was set up February 15, 1944, to achieve a balance between the demand and the supply of labor, after it had become clear that the program in operation had failed to distribute the insufficient labor supply among the essential employers. An important operating arm for handling manpower problems was the employment service,

*By James E. Pate, Professor of Political Science, College of William and Mary.

1. This section is based largely on *History War Manpower Commission, World War II, Hampton Roads Area* by John W. Stephens, Jr., Area Director, (mimeographed, 1945).

which was nationalized on January 1, 1942, and placed under the War Manpower Commission. Local employment service offices in the Hampton Roads area were located at Norfolk, Portsmouth, Newport News, Suffolk, Hampton and several smaller communities. A staff of 136 was employed by these offices at the peak of their activities.

The principal problems handled by the area office included manpower priorities, manpower utilization and training, stabilization, reemployment, and compliance.

Manpower Priorities

The manpower priorities committee gathered and interpreted statistics on the urgency of need for workers to maintain activities in the area essential to the war effort. Following this, employers were notified by the committee that they should apply for priority ratings upon which workers would be referred. After some hesitation the War Manpower Commission's regional office approved the plan, which in effect was a device for the controlled referral of workers. By the middle of the year 1944, priority ratings and employment ceilings were established for 393 establishments employing 143,000 workers in the area. The results of the priority referral plan, as stated by the area director, were as follows:

> . . . Actual operating of the priority referral system had proved that a more equitable system would have to be initiated; rather than attempting to obtain results by channeling labor from less essential to essential industry, labor had to be channeled, even among essential industries, to those of the industries whose production was at that time most urgently needed in the War Program. It had become apparent that in some instances priority referral hindered smaller establishments in securing the small numbers of workers needed by them, the skills of whom were of such nature that total production suffered as a consequence of inability to obtain same.[2]

A further review of the priority rating system resulted in reducing the number of firms in the higher priority categories. Then, on November 29, 1944, the regional office sent out instructions to establish priority ratings on an "employer order" rather than on an individual establishment basis. This plan had some merits. As described by the area director: "Job shopping was greatly reduced, referrals were more promptly verified, turnover problems and causes of same could be more clearly brought to the attention of the employer."[3]

2. *Ibid.*, p. 15. 3. *Ibid.*, p. 16.

In the early spring of 1945 those employers who had the highest priority on orders were allowed the privilege of "gate-hiring." As stated by the area director: "While results obtained under this procedure were not as satisfactory as had been hoped they might be, the number of workers lost between point of referral and the point of the job was considerably reduced, resulting in a saving in man-hours to the employer."[4]

Manpower Utilization and Training

Manpower shortages called for the maximum utilization of the number available. Among the various practices for attaining such utilization were: inventorying the available supply of manpower in light of production needs; occupational and plant analyses; routing labor to places where most needed; manning tables; job simplification; up-grading and training; control of absenteeism; and removal of employment discrimination because of sex or race.[5]

Occupational surveys were made which located persons with occupational skills in places where such skills were not used. Examples included a machinist working as a butcher, an organic chemist employed as a shoe repairman, a mechanic operating a gas station pump, and an electrician clerking in a grocery store. Some of these occupational maladjustments were the result of the depression, when unemployed men got jobs wherever they could be found. Utilization surveys, or plant analyses, were made to discover causes of manpower waste and to suggest better ways of using the available labor skills.

Training programs were installed in order to brush up rusty skills and to train those without experience. To meet this need of getting the maximum manpower by training, the U. S. Department of Education cooperated with the local school boards and colleges in the area to start vocational training courses. A training within industry program was begun which relieved some critical shortages by permitting workers to be "upgraded" or advanced to a more skilled occupational category.

Manning tables were prepared which listed each kind of job in the plant, the number of employees, and their classification as to age, sex, dependents, and selective service status. Their primary purpose was to provide an accurate basis for deferment of critical workers, a

4. *Ibid.*, p. 17.

5. James E. Pate, "Mobilizing Manpower," *Social Forces,* 22 (December, 1943), p. 161.

schedule of orderly withdrawals for military service, and to indicate the training program required to replace those inducted.[6]

A serious manpower problem during the war was absenteeism. The percentage of workers who were willfully and without excuse absent from their jobs was small. While epidemics fortunately were controlled, there were many factors in congested war areas like Hampton Roads that caused absenteeism: poor housing; inadequate eating facilities; lack of transportation facilities; general discontent; and limited community facilities, such as schools, recreation, hospitals, and child care. Federal expenditures under the Lanham Act, in cooperation with the local governments, provided many community facilities both of a temporary and a permanent nature which thus indirectly lessened absenteeism.

Mention should be made of the day nursery, which released women from the home and enabled them to take jobs. A survey was made of the problem by the U.S.E.S. and cooperating agencies. Local welfare agencies, assisted by the Children's Bureau of the U. S. Department of Labor and the War Manpower Commission, opened nurseries in schools, churches, and in housing centers. These facilities were administered locally. The War Manpower Commission certified those persons who by reason of employment were eligible for use of the nurseries.

Some time was lost by essential war workers taking off time during the week to tend to their shopping and other personal business. The situation was somewhat relieved where the stores and banks remained open one day a week until 9 P.M. Neighborhood shopping centers built in connection with housing projects afforded some relief both to the shopping and transportation problems. Transportation, as noted elsewhere in this report, was a serious problem in the Hampton Roads area. Car pools, rescheduling and rerouting buses and streetcar lines, and assistance of military establishments in transporting enlisted personnel and civilian workers helped a bad situation. "While the transportation system in the area was never ideal," said the area War Manpower director, "it was considerably improved and weathered the storm."

Minimum Wartime Week

A minimum wartime week of forty-eight hours was established by an executive order of the President on April 1, 1943. Certain ex-

6. *Ibid.*, p. 162.

emptions were granted by the order and the area manpower office was authorized to grant others. For example, trades and services, banks, retail stores, and theaters were excepted. Compliance with the order was not a serious problem since the covered firms were largely federal agencies and federal contractors. Most of the violations were among the less essential businesses.

Ceilings

Blanket ceilings were placed on all employers in the area, as of April 20, 1944. Such ceilings were placed at the highest level of employment as of January, 1944, which meant, of course, that no employer could hire more than that number, unless satisfactory evidence was given for exceeding the ceilings. Compliance with this policy should have been relatively easy, as failure could be penalized by having the local U.S.E.S. officer refuse orders for labor. The less essential employers, however, generally disregarded the ceiling order because there was no record of their January employment level on file in the local employment office.

The chief benefit from required ceiling declarations, according to the area manpower director, was to "enhance the normal movement of workers from less-essential to essential industry."[7]

Following this statement, it is somewhat disconcerting to read the area director's remarks that the "intended follow-up on all employers who failed to file employment ceilings was discontinued because of there being no approved form which could be distributed. . . . By April 1945, it was evident that the effectiveness of the ceiling program had been greatly limited due to lack of coordination as well as the inadequacy of information submitted."[8]

Prisoners of War

Higher wages and pressure to get workers into those activities that had a direct bearing on the conduct of the war created acute shortage of labor in many important local enterprises such as fertilizer manufacture, food processing, agriculture, and the lumber businesses. A partial answer to this labor crisis was to employ prisoners of war. At one time, June, 1945, approximately 1700 prisoners of war were employed by forty-six business establishments and the farmers of six counties in the Hampton Roads area.

7. John W. Stephens, *op. cit.*, p. 28.
8. *Ibid.*, p. 29.

Employment Stabilization Program

The Hampton Roads stabilization program, put into force April 19, 1943, and supplemented on July 1, 1944, by the War Manpower Commission regional office program, proposed to stabilize employment by correcting such manpower problems as pirating workers, maximum utilization of local labor supply, absenteeism, and transfer of workers from nonessential to essential war industries. Certain hiring practices were put into effect as a means of stabilizing employment, namely: (1) workers were to be referred to jobs which would utilize their skills most effectively in the war effort; (2) priority was to be accorded to employers engaged in essential activities in the order of the urgency of their activities, (3) a worker engaged in an essential activity could not transfer except to another essential activity, and only then by obtaining a statement of availability from his previous employer, and (4) occupational qualifications and not discrimination for any reason were to be the basis for hiring workers.[9]

Comments by the area director on the experience of Hampton Roads with the stabilization program were as follows:

> The results of the Stabilization Program, although quite favorable, did not completely solve the problems. Hiring of workers in non-compliance continued, as did a large volume of job-shifting and migration to other areas, with little or no difficulty experienced in being hired in other areas without Statements of Availability, due to inconsistencies between the Hampton Roads Stabilization Program and other stabilization programs in the region.[10]

Compliance

An intensive compliance program was not started in the Hampton Roads area until February 1, 1945. Before that time the principal method of securing compliance was by inspections. The records are not adequate enough to provide a basis for conclusions as to their effectiveness. The result of the compliance drive, which began February 1, 1945, found that 556 firms out of a total of 922 checked were violating some of the programs. The most common violation was that of employing workers "without proper referral by the U.S.E.S. or accredited referral agencies." Most of the violating firms pleaded ignorance, which was quite understandable in "view of the various

9. James E. Pate, *op. cit.*, pp. 159-160.
10. John W. Stephens, *op. cit.*, p. 39.

changes" made in the manpower control programs.[11] In only a few cases of violation was it necessary to invoke sanctions. An explanation was usually all that was needed. Although started almost at the end of the war, the compliance program, in the opinion of the area director, was satisfactory.

As to recruiting manpower, the local employment offices were apparently successful. As the area manpower director remarked:

> A summing up of the results of our recruitment efforts during the emergency period indicates that there were 600,000 contacts with applicants and approximately 321,000 of them referred to jobs; resulting in 200,000 persons placed in employment. . . . In concluding operations, we feel in view of the many difficulties encountered in operations prior to March of 1945, it is appropriate to mention that our files do not disclose one single instance where we failed to meet an emergency in ample time to maintain production schedule throughout the area.[12]

WAR PRICE AND RATIONING CONTROLS

The organizational framework for price and rationing controls reached from the Washington office down through regional, district, and local war price and rationing boards. Principal control policies, as well as organizational and procedural problems, were worked out in the national office. Suggestions, of course, for change in policy could come from local and district offices. But O.P.A.'s normal line of communication was from the Washington office to the regional, from there to the district, and from the latter to the local war price and rationing boards. The Norfolk office, for instance, reported to the district office in Richmond, which in turn routed the report to the Atlanta headquarters of the regional office and Atlanta reported to Washington.

Enforcement activities had to be decentralized to a considerable extent. This was done by a process of delegating and redelegating authority. Redelegation of authority to fix prices stopped with the district office. The local war price and rationing boards administered the rules. They did not make them. Probably the nearest thing to price fixing by local boards was in the case of new restaurants opening for the sale of meals. In this case the restaurant owner was required by his local board to adopt the prices of his nearest competitor.

The local boards were the point of contact with the people. They

11. *Ibid.*, p. 24.
12. *Ibid.*, p. 40.

were on the line. They received and acted upon the application of their neighbors for ration currency. As President Roosevelt said: "It seems to me that the local ration boards all over the country have reasserted something very profound in our American tradition—the tradition of the American town meeting. They sit down around a table, view every case on its merits and settle it, not as officials of government, but as understanding neighbors."

The organization and procedure of all war price and rationing boards were similar. All had a policy board, several different kinds of panels and a staff of both paid and volunteer workers.

Adjudicative action, such as determining the eligibility of an applicant for rationed goods, could only be exercised by panels and not by individual employees. Issuing the basic ration books involved no exercise of judgment but was handled by the applicant filing proper forms, a check by the clerk, and the issuing of the book.

Adjudicative procedures were also seen in such matters as suspension or revoking of ration currency. This procedure originated at the local board level. A hearing was given, a decision made and appeals allowed. Ration currency was liable to be suspended or revoked if the applicant made a false statement or misrepresented the facts. One prevalent gas racket in the Hampton Roads area was to get signatures of riders in order to get an extra gas ration. Traffic violations were sufficient cause for suspension or for revoking a gas ration. Driving while drunk was sufficient cause to revoke a gas ration for one year. The Virginia State Highway Department provided the local board with names of speeders or other traffic violators who were called before the board for a hearing.

The work of the price panel consisted primarily of law enforcement. These panels provided a democratic basis for price controls and local dissemination of price control information, and secured better compliance with the program. The compliance techniques were to inform merchants about the price control program, to remind them periodically of their obligations to observe the program, and to persuade them to comply. The panel would meet once a week to review the compliance program. First violators were merely given a reminder. In many cases, adjustments were made merely by calling to the merchant's attention that he was not complying with O.P.A. regulations. A stronger method of securing compliance was to summon a violator to appear before the price panel for a conference. The panel could recommend to violators that they make corrections either by refunding the overcharge to the buyer or by making a refund to the U. S. Treasury. The case was referred to the district office if the retailer refused to accept the panel's decision or if the panel determined that the violation was flagrant. The panel was not a court but a committee of local citizens which secured, if possible, compliance with price ceilings by noncoercive means. The sanctions of law could only be applied by an action in the courts.

The Norfolk Price and Rationing Board

The experience of the Norfolk Price and Rationing Board was typical of others in the Hampton Roads area. The local war price and rationing board consisted of the policy board, a price panel, and panels for the principal categories of rationed articles, namely: gas, fuel oil, tires, stoves, sugar, foods, meats, and fats. Besides the policy board and panels, there was a staff consisting of a chief clerk, paid clerks for the different panels, and any number of volunteer workers. The board and panels, as can be seen from the names on the Norfolk board, (Figure 29), were local citizens usually drawn from the business community. In many cases the paid workers were wives of service men. This accounts for the rather large turnover in the clerical staff.

O.P.A. regulations provided for the appointment of a chief clerk by the local board chairman with approval of the district office. The chief clerk was in charge of the local office. In the Norfolk local board his title was manager. O.P.A. regulations defined his qualifications as well as his chief duties. Besides the chief clerk, other paid employees were the full-time panel clerks. These varied in number and title. A small community used only a general clerk, a price panel clerk, and a food panel clerk.

The paid clerical staff was selected by civil service procedure. The U. S. Civil Service Commission relaxed their written examining procedures in order to expedite the hiring of the clerical staff. For instance, the usual assembled examinations for this type of personnel were not given. During the emergency when time was short and personnel was limited, a person filed his application on a form which stated his background and general and special experience. His application was then certified to the O.P.A. district office which in turn secured approval of the civil service district office at Winston-Salem, North Carolina.

It was O.P.A.'s policy "to enlist the aid of uncompensated volun-

FIGURE 29. LIST OF MEMBERS OF POLICY BOARDS AND PANELS, OFFICE OF PRICE ADMINISTRATION
Norfolk, Virginia

Policy Board—February, 1943

Col. W. B. Rodman—Ret. General Counsel, Norfolk Southern Railroad
James G. Madden—Shoe merchant
I. B. Kline—Auto dealer
R. C. Mackay—U.S. Department of State (on leave)
Hampton Sewall—Manager, Penny's Department Store
I. F. Truitt—Real estate dealer
E. M. Moore—Labor leader
G. L. Hall—Optical business
E. V. Griffin—Auto dealer

Policy Board—March 12, 1945

R. C. Mackay—Director, U.S. Veterans Information Service
E. V. Griffin—Auto dealer
E. M. Moore—Labor leader
J. C. Madden—Shoe merchant
I. F. Truitt—Real estate dealer
I. B. Kline—Auto dealer
G. L. Hall—Optical business
Hampton Sewall—Manager, Penny's Department Store

Price Panel

R. T. Griffin—Owner of coal yard
J. M. Reynolds—Hardware store
I. T. Marshall—Occupation not listed
R. I. Willis—Furniture store owner
A. R. Thompson—Plumbing contractor (owner)
G. R. Brown—Restaurant owner
J. E. Harry—Chain store buyer
J. R. Burton—Department store manager
James McPhillips—Grocery store owner
J. W. Brownly—Department store owner
D. P. Paul—Jewelry store owner
F. A. Johnson—Retired army officer
M. I. Duckworth—Auto dealer
I. Perry—Auto dealer
R. A. Cathey—Coca-Cola manager

Gas Panel

P. M. Felts—Real estate salesman
B. R. Wrenn—Auto manager
R. I. Ashburn—Auto manager
Charles Cacace—Stevedoring
J. W. Amory—Electrical Company
M. L. Stewart—Coal yard owner
E. T. Burdill—Optical company manager
G. I. Shepherd—Coordinator Electric Company
J. W. Barlow—Engineer
J. C. Councill—Real estate owner
S. V. Dame—Railroad commercial agent
H. C. Brigman—Newspaper advertising solicitor
R. S. Hopkins—Restaurant owner
W. C. Kutz—Real estate partner
S. M. Jones—Fertilizer
W. M. Hitt—Engineer
M. Cherry—Occupation not listed
L. M. Saunders—Contractor
E. H. Barker—Fertilizer

Tire Panel

I. T. Timmons—A.A.A. (automobile)
M. F. Aspenwall—Storage and Security Company, Manager

Fuel Oil Panel

J. R. Councill—Wagon merchant
J. F. Moore—Cotton broker

Stove Panel

D. Fowler—Stove and Roofing Company
R. Long—Stoves and Home Supplies

*Policy Board: Negro**

H. G. Christopher—Y.M.C.A. secretary
E. F. Corbett—JOURNAL & GUIDE, Circulation Manager
R. Alston—Labor leader
D. Longley—Insurance
F. Lewis—Coal dealer

*Practically continuous. Only one man replaced during the whole period.

teers to assist in carrying out its rationing, price and rent control activities." These volunteers, said O.P.A., were to be "representative of the community as a whole, and selected without regard to religion, politics, race, sex, economic or social level or occupation."

A volunteer supervisor, appointed by the board, served as a staff aid to the board chairman, and was responsible for recruiting, training, supervising, and scheduling all types of volunteers. All volunteers were given orientation or "basic" training in their job assignments. The chief clerk also saw that volunteer workers had specific on-the-job training. Volunteers were required to take the oath of office. Their work was recognized by various types of awards depending on the length of service. The Norfolk board's volunteer workers had service records that varied from one-half hour to as many as 4041 hours.

Two local war price and rationing boards served the city of Norfolk. The Negro board was unusually stable. Its members served continuously with only one or two exceptions from the time of their appointment until the end of the war. The white board, on the other hand, was renewed several times. The first white board lasted only a few months. The second board was broken on February 6, 1943, when Mr. Caravati, the State Organization Director, dismissed three members of the board for reasons that were never fully investigated. Apparently the dismissal was because of different attitudes and interpretations of O.P.A. policies. For a while the situation was acute and Norfolk faced the prospect of going without rationed goods. Resentment was strong at what appeared to be an arbitrary action by the state district office. Congressman Winder Harris suggested a Congressional investigation of the matter. Colonel Borland, the city manager, stepped into the controversy and acted as chairman of a temporary board. A new board (February 20, 1943) was nominated by the local director of civilian defense to the State Coordinator of Civilian Defense which was confirmed by General Bright, the Director of O.P.A.'s District Office. The new ration board worked smoothly. One year after its appointment (February 20, 1944), a writer in the *Virginian-Pilot* described it under the newspaper title: "From Chaos to Perfection." The board at the peak of its work was operating with 37 paid employees and as many as 40 to 120 daily volunteer workers. The latter spent thirty-five to forty hours a week at work with the board.

The Norfolk War Price and Rationing Board was located in the

Old Municipal Building. When operating at full force, there were stalls for: application forms and information; tires, automobiles and bicycles; fuel oil; gas; foods; boots, shoes, and typewriters. The principal rationing problems were generally evidenced visually by the longest lines. One ordinarily saw the longest queue before the stall of the gas panel clerk. The size of the gas panel and the number of clerks for this panel also indicated that gas was the biggest rationing problem. On V-J Day, gas rationing was stopped. The staff of the local board declined as one rationing program after another was lifted. Shoes and sugar were the last to go. After the rationing let up, O.P.A.'s activities were concentrated on holding the price line. As O.P.A.'s functions declined its staff dropped off and its quarters were reduced. Carpenters setting up partitioning walls in the Old Municipal Building added to the general let down in morale that marked the local board's last days in rationing.

Problems similar to those encountered on the southside of Hampton Roads were also present on the north or Newport News side of the Roads. As summarized by the Newport News War History Commission:

> There were many problems in connection with the equitable distribution of limited supplies. Inexperienced and insufficient help, as well as a large turn-over in employees throughout the war, interfered with efficient administration. An overwhelming amount of "paper" work required by the system and crowds of people, unaccustomed to filling out forms in detail, yet with needs to be met, at times, literally "swamped" Ration Board headquarters. When pressure became too great the doors of the offices were closed to the public until the necessary routine could be cared for.[13]

WAR PRODUCTION

The Norfolk district office of the War Production Board was opened on March 23, 1942. It served seventeen counties and all the cities in Tidewater Virginia. The office was under the direction of a district manager and an assistant district manager. There were three principal units: (1) priorities, (2) the production urgency committee, and (3) the production service unit.

War Production Board district offices were described as the "backyard" relationship between W.P.B., industry, and the public.

13. World War II History Commission, *Newport News During the Second World War*, 1948, p. 139.

The Norfolk district office was one of the smaller offices of W.P.B. Region III, which had its regional headquarters located in Philadelphia. An important activity of the Norfolk office was processing applications for priority assistance. The yearly average volume of such applications processed, as stated by the district manager, were 5,500.[14] The Norfolk district office, which had a total personnel of ten in 1945, experienced frequent changes. In this respect, the experience of local W.P.B. offices was not unlike that of W.P.B.'s general experience in setting up an adequate organization; in devising workable relations between the national, regional, and field offices; and in finding and using methods for expediting production and controlling strategic materials.

FEDERAL SUPPORT OF MUNICIPAL FACILITIES

Action by local governments supported by the federal and state governments kept the municipal services going during the war years. Among supporting activities of the federal government three stand out: (1) the hearings conducted in the Hampton Roads area by the House of Representatives subcommittee (Izac) on Naval Affairs; (2) the work of the President's Committee on Congested Production areas which established operations in the Hampton Roads area on May 20, 1943; and (3) federal expenditures for community facilities under the Lanham Act.

The Izac subcommittee went to the area, held public hearings, and got direct information about the most pressing community problems. The C.C.P.A. followed up the Izac Committee's hearings and by its "on the spot" relation with municipal officials, civic leaders, businessmen, and labor leaders kept close contact with community needs and expedited action on essential community facilities and services. As soon as community facilities were brought up to "minimum wartime standards of adequacy," the C.C.P.A.'s local office was closed and its representative withdrawn. C.C.P.A. was a coordinative and expeditive agency. It broke the jam of red tape and shortened considerably the distance between the community and the war agencies in Washington. Before the C.C.P.A. came into the area, the city manager of Portsmouth complained that his formal applications to W.P.B. for a priority rating crossed thirty desks before final action. The city manager of Newport News was likewise grateful for C.C.P.A.'s help. He

14. Correspondence, Harry C. Ritter, District Manager, Norfolk Office, War Production Board, August 23, 1945.

wrote the area director as follows: "I would like to say that had it not been for the splendid assistance and cooperation from your office, and from that of your representatives, very little could have been accomplished."[15]

C.C.P.A. cleared the way for approval of needed community facilities. Congress, in the Lanham Act, provided the funds that implemented or built the facilities which were essential to meet the emergency conditions caused by war.

Lanham Act Expenditures

The Lanham Act, which furnished federal funds for community facilities, provides a monetary and physical expansion measure of the war's impact on essential municipal services most directly and seriously affected by war activities. Table 44 gives the total expenditures, local

TABLE 44. LANHAM ACT EXPENDITURES, BY CONSTRUCTION AND MAINTENANCE, HAMPTON ROADS–PENINSULA AREA

	Federal Expenditures	Local Expenditures	Total Expenditures
Construction	$31,729,546	$ 5,970,538	$37,700,084
Maintenance and operation	1,630,407	5,997,256	7,627,663
Total	33,359,953	11,967,794	45,327,747

Source: Correspondence from Division Engineer of Bureau of Community Facilities, Federal Works Agency, January 21, 1947.

and federal, including both construction and maintenance. Figures 30 and 31 show the percentage distribution of these expenditures for construction by locality and by type of facility. It is seen from the volume of these expenditures that there was great pressure on municipal water, sewage, sanitation, and school facilities. It is also seen by the table that federal expenditures constituted 83 per cent of the total spent under the Lanham Act for community facilities. As one observer expressed it:

> The opportunistic attitude of the City Council is very significant in its relation to the social life of the community and it reflects the isolationist attitude of the old Norfolk citizenry. They generally do not feel responsibility for alleviating any problems due to the war in this area. . . . The official position is that the Government is responsible for these prob-

15. G. R. Parker, Regional Director, Defense Health and Welfare Services (Confidential Memorandum, December 24, 1941).

lems and should finance facilities to take care of the needs. . . . In contrast, the Council is eager to take advantage of the City's increased income due to war industry, et cetera. The stand has been that since the City debt had so materially increased through the past depression they are attempt-

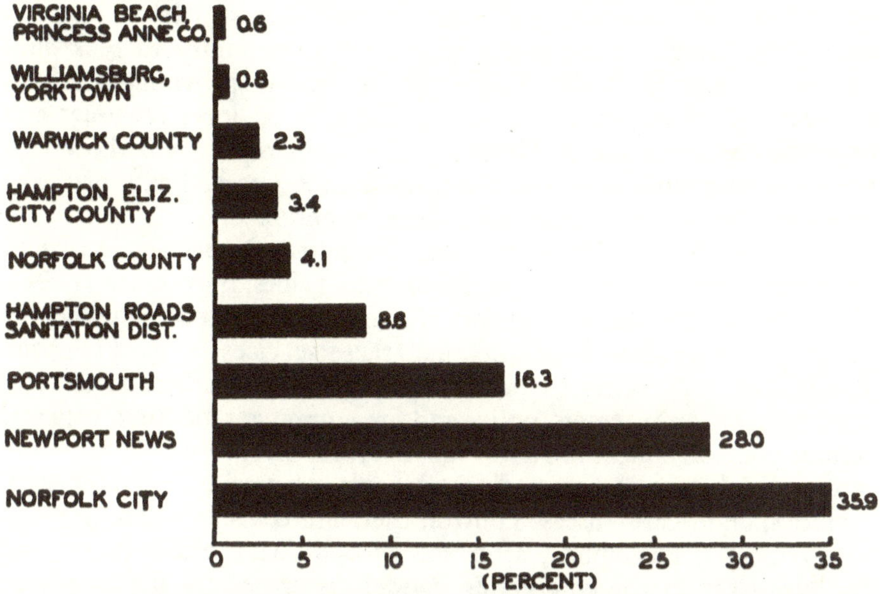

FIGURE 30. PERCENTAGE DISTRIBUTION OF LANHAM ACT FEDERAL EXPENDITURES FOR WAR PUBLIC WORKS (CONSTRUCTION), BY LOCALITY, HAMPTON ROADS-PENINSULA AREA

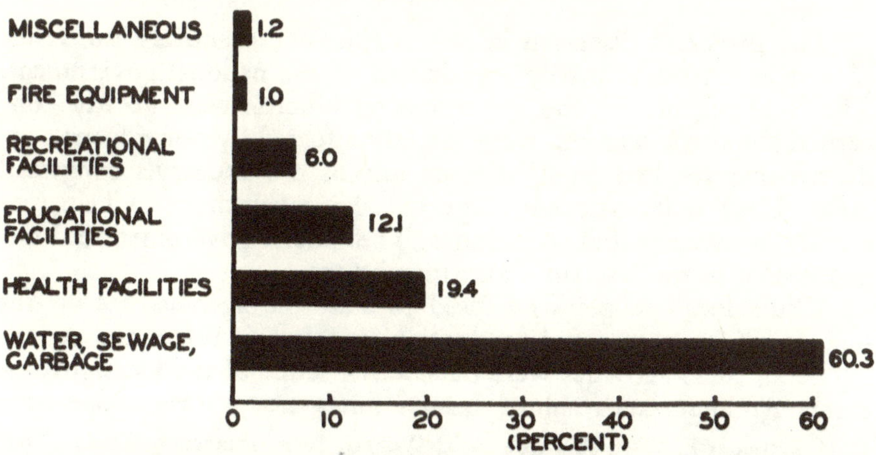

FIGURE 31. PERCENTAGE DISTRIBUTION OF LANHAM ACT FEDERAL EXPENDITURES FOR WAR PUBLIC WORKS (CONSTRUCTION), BY TYPE OF PROJECT, HAMPTON ROADS-PENINSULA AREA

ing to liquidate it during this World War II prosperity and are holding down the total city expenditures in all bureaus regardless of needs.[16]

In reply to such statements one might say that it is not an unnatural reaction for a community to take. Extraordinary conditions created by national and international circumstances over which the city has no control should quite naturally cause a community to seek substantial support from the federal government in providing facilities to meet this situation. Reference to the data on local revenues and expenditures presented in Chapter XII of this report will show that the local communities of the Hampton Roads area had extraordinary expenditures commensurate with their revenues.

A rating by the Committee on Congested Production Areas of the adequacy of community facilities and services, November 1, 1944, about six months before the end of the war in Europe, showed the progress at that time in maintaining these services in the Hampton Roads area. According to this rating (Figure 32), adequate services were water supply, streets, police and fire equipment, housing, venereal disease control, education, and food. Services that were only fair were sewage, garbage and refuse disposal, rents, medical care, commercial facilities, child care, disease control, fuel, and transportation. Services that remained inadequate, after the extraordinary effort to provide facilities to meet the emergency conditions caused by the war were manpower supply and recreation facilities.[17]

SUMMARY

The problems discussed in this chapter were entirely the result of war and were primarily of concern to the national government. The local inhabitants and governmental officials were greatly concerned about the war and were directly affected by home front conditions that resulted from being in one of the country's congested areas. They quite naturally expected the government to help materially in meeting these conditions. The federal government did this generously in the Lanham Act expenditures.

While local people were used to staff the agencies set up for mobilizing manpower and production, controlling prices and rationing food, these activities were outside the scope of the local governments. An important result of the war emergency was the cooperative

16. Margaret F. West, Principal Social Worker, Social Protection Division, State Department of Public Welfare, Field Report, July 16, 1945.

17. C. C. P. A. Final Report, December, 1944, p. 24.

FIGURE 32.

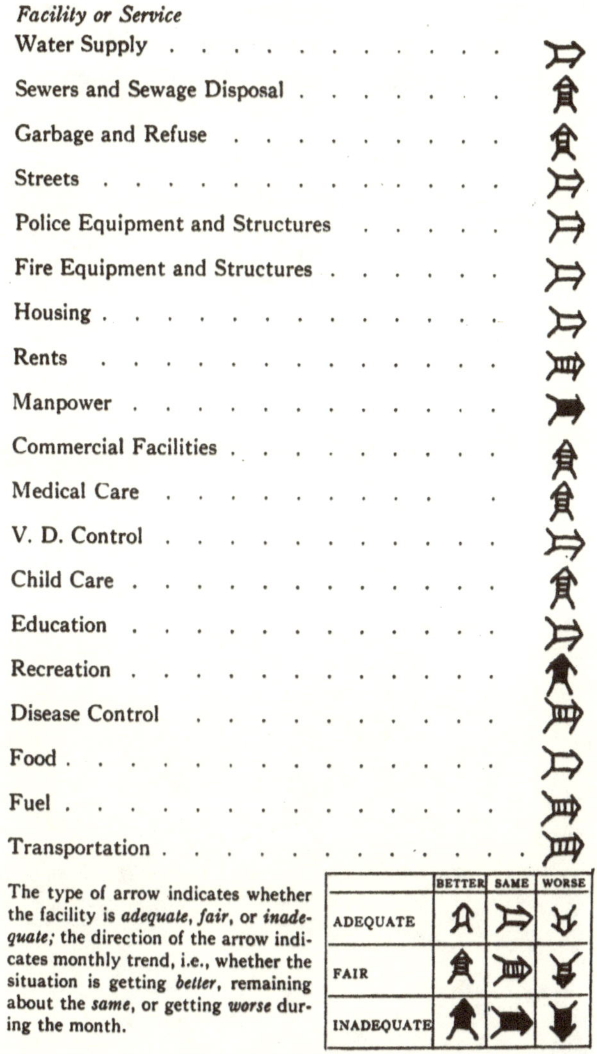

Source: Executive Office of the President, Committee for Congested Production Areas, November 1, 1944.

RATING OF ADEQUACY OF COMMUNITY FACILITIES AND SERVICES IN THE HAMPTON ROADS AREA

effort it evoked among the people and between the local and national governments. The state was overshadowed by the more important relations between the federal and local governments. These were the principals in the large home front activities. When the officials of the national government stopped at the state capitol, it was largely out of respect to the legal superior of the local governments.

CHAPTER XVI

POLITICS: WARTIME SUSPENSION, POSTWAR RESURGENCE*

THE HAMPTON ROADS area is of great political importance in the state of Virginia both because of the large population concentrated there and because the area is a growing point of political change. A fifth of the state's population lives in the neighborhood of Norfolk and Newport News. The area casts about 15 per cent of the state's presidential vote and about 18 to 20 per cent of the Democratic primary vote. Together with the metropolitan regions of Richmond and Arlington, and the partially industrialized western portions of the state, the Hampton Roads area has been a source of New Deal strength and opposition to the dominant machine faction of the Democratic Party led by Senator Byrd. The area contributed 25 per cent of President Truman's Virginia support in 1948. Anti-machine candidates polled respectively 25, 30, and 36 per cent of their total vote in this area in the primaries of 1945, 1946, and 1949. Hutcheson in the senatorial primary of 1946 and Miller in the gubernatorial primary of 1949 carried the more urban sections against the machine faction and came very close to winning a majority in the total area.[1]

The "impact of the war" on politics is not readily identifiable nor measurable. The politically significant factors to be brought under the heading of war are numerous and are not to be clearly differentiated from those associated with the early development of the war crisis and the sequels to war. Indeed, many features of the New Deal policies, such as public works, price inflation, and the social reorganization classified by many as "regimentation," had a political impact comparable to extensive rearmament, the raising of wage levels and increasing of government purchases, and mobilization. In some cases the transition from New Deal policies to war policies was hardly perceptible. The merging of the New Deal and war influences is to

*By W. Warner Moss, Professor of Government, College of William and Mary.

1. The setting of state and sectional politics within which the politics of the area take place is described by V. O. Key in *Southern Politics* (New York: Knopf, 1949) especially in Chapter II.

be seen in the increased participation of Negroes in politics. This increased participation commenced in the 1930's partly because improved income provided an opportunity for participation and partly because of the encouragement given the Negro under the New Deal. The war continued and accelerated both these factors. The identification of purely war factors is further complicated by the peacetime existence of many defense establishments in the area.

Nor is it possible to study the impact of the war upon politics by analyzing the events during hostilities only, or during the peak years of population change and economic activity. The immediate impact of the war appears to have been a suspension of politics as the term is usually understood. There was a general diversion of attention from affairs that were local and personal to wider horizons. The return of attention to local and personal affairs came after hostilities and wartime economic activity had ceased. The residual effects of the war then became factors in politics. Consequently the period of a decade, from 1939 to 1949, has been selected for study.

VOTER PARTICIPATION DURING THE WAR YEARS

The most striking political phenomenon of the war years in the Hampton Roads area was the contrast between voter participation in presidential elections on the one hand and state and local elections on the other. As in the state as a whole, an increased number of Hampton Roads voters went to the polls to select a president but the number interested in state and local elections declined.

The diversion of interest away from state and local affairs appears to be the most obvious explanation for these trends. However, one must also take into account the cycles of revolt and consolidation in politics. The 1937 victory of Governor Price represented something of a revolt just before the war but the rout of the Price supporters in the legislature of 1939 made necessary a period of recuperation for the anti-machine forces. The war may have prolonged that period but it did not create it.

There was a similar situation in regard to local elections. In Newport News all three incumbents in the city council were defeated in 1936[2] and it was not to be expected that another political upset would occur for a few years.

In Elizabeth City County a revolt took place in 1935[3] but peace

2. Newport News *Daily Press*, April 8, 1936.
3. Newport News *Daily Press*, August 6, 7, 8, 1935.

was established in 1939[4] and lasted until 1947. The new conflict culminated in the defeat of the Speaker of the House of Delegates in 1949.

TABLE 45. SIZE OF VOTE IN ELECTIONS, 1932–1949

	Hampton Roads Area		City Elections		Statewide Vote	
Year	Presidential	State Primary	Newport News Council	Norfolk Council	Presidential	State Primary
1932	39,676		2,707		297,943	
1933		34,046				189,623
1934			2,698			
1936	44,045		3,512	6,656	333,316	
1937		40,565				193,274
1938			4,021	10,270		
1940	43,568		4,006	10,230	343,607	
1941		24,163				137,974
1942			2,347	4,805		
1944	55,509		3,802	6,166	388,485	
1945		26,550				138,788
1946		39,431	3,098	16,984		223,528
1948	61,459	16,343	3,866	10,185	419,256	114,269
1949		52,679				316,312

Sources: The presidential and state primary election results are published in the annual report of the Secretary of the Commonwealth. The State Board of Elections also issues the results of the canvass in a bulletin. The Newport News results are published in the Newport News *Daily Press* the day following each election in April. The Norfolk results are similarly to be obtained from the *Norfolk Virginian-Pilot*. The date of the election is early in June.

In both Norfolk and Portsmouth the political climate is moderated by the overwhelming importance of the navy in the life of those cities. There is a widespread belief that many of the local problems which elsewhere are the citizen's business are there the affair of the navy. Nevertheless, in Norfolk the election of 1938 gave expression to a widespread discontent. A rather dramatic and effective revolt appeared in 1946 but it was to be explained chiefly by a division in the ranks of those accustomed to dominate the affairs of the city rather than to war influences.[5]

In the counties, local elections do not stir voters to participation except when personalities are involved. The boards of supervisors possess little power. The judges are chosen by the legislature. The clerks, treasurers, and attorneys serve relatively long terms and the

4. *Ibid.*, August 1, 2, 1939.

5. The Norfolk papers of May and June of 1938 and 1946 describe the political climate of these elections.

duties of their offices are not such as to excite widespread interest except when scandal and crime arouse the public. In 1941 there were no contests in Norfolk County, a fact which the *Norfolk Virginian-Pilot* explained by the unprecedented building boom and business activity.[6]

As the war and its problems receded into the background of time the voter's interest in local affairs returned and the number of votes cast reached record peaks locally and in the state primaries of 1946 and 1949. The city councils of Norfolk and Williamsburg were drastically altered by a heavy turnout of voters in 1946 and in 1948 respectively. The clearest influence of the war is seen in the participation of new voters and in the development of issues concerning the expansion of local government services and the possible consolidation of local governments, which were in turn caused chiefly by the influx of population and by heightened economic activity. On January 1, 1948, Portsmouth annexed a portion of Norfolk County. South Norfolk took another piece of this county in 1949. Leaders in Elizabeth City and Warwick counties prepared to block annexation moves while Newport News prepared to carry the matter to the courts. Such questions created much public interest in a proposal to consolidate the governments of the area north of Hampton Roads.

The identity of the new voters is a matter of interest but the information is not at hand for a conclusive answer. They are probably drawn both from the recent migrants into the area and from the long-term residents who have not previously participated. The political activity of recent migrants was noticeable to observers of the gubernatorial primary in 1949. On the other hand the area has had such a low level of participation in the past that it is certain that some of the new voters have been drawn from this great reservoir of non-participants. There has been a general trend toward a larger electorate in Virginia since 1932 and this trend has been evident in areas with a stable population as well as in the Hampton Roads area. Most of this increased participation has come from the lower income brackets and from Negroes as can be seen by examining the precinct returns of Richmond and Norfolk where Negroes are more or less segregated.[7]

Aided by gains in education, and by wartime gains in economic status, and encouraged by the National Association for the Advance-

6. June 5, 1941.

7. See the *Recreation Survey* prepared for the Norfolk City Council (1946) for maps showing the distribution of Negro population and "economic levels" in Norfolk.

ment of Colored People the Negroes have qualified as voters in ever increasing numbers. From 1939 to 1949 the proportion of Negroes as compared with whites on the poll tax list increased from 3 per cent to 17 per cent in Norfolk County, from 16 per cent to 28 per cent in Newport News, and from 12 per cent to 21 per cent in Portsmouth.[8]

The poll tax lists are inadequate as an index to the number of persons qualified to vote but the lists are relied upon generally by politicians and the trends are often significant. It is interesting that in Newport News the poll tax payments rose steadily to a peak in 1944 while in Portsmouth there was a marked drop from the 1938 peak to a very low level in 1942 and then in 1949 the level reached was the highest on record.

Since the cities had a limited capacity for absorbing increased population a very large proportion of the recent migrants settled in the adjoining counties, particularly Norfolk and Warwick counties, which consequently gained greatly in political importance. Lack of detailed information about the age, sex, and race characteristics of the population makes it difficult to reach conclusions concerning what proportion of the adults voted but the percentage of the total population that voted declined between 1939 and 1949 in Norfolk and Warwick counties while it increased in Nansemond and Isle of Wight, both being counties but slightly affected by wartime migration.

PERSONNEL CHANGES

Politics is largely concerned with the staffing of public offices. The impact of the war was naturally felt in some degree in the loss of personnel to war services but this may have been less in the Hampton Roads area than elsewhere because the governmental functions of the area were an essential part of the war effort. The men withdrawn for military service were usually not of the age group most active in politics, especially as office holders. This was particularly true of the offices which form the basis of machine strength in Virginia—the offices of judge, treasurer, county clerk, and prosecutor. An examination of the lists of local officeholders in the reports of the Secretary of the Commonwealth from 1939 to 1949 indicates no dramatic changes in the decade. In Norfolk County new faces appeared but there was nothing like a clean sweep. In 1944 Warwick voted for a county manager form of government which has reduced the power

8. Poll tax lists may be obtained in the office of the county or city treasurer. The figures for whites and Negroes are sometimes published in the local newspapers.

of the group about the courthouse but the ancient offices are still held by the men who held them a decade previously. An examination of the lists of precinct committeemen of the Democratic Party in Norfolk showed no significant turnover and in 1941 there were only three contests for the thirty-four positions; in many precincts no candidates appeared.[9] The greatest measure of change took place in the Negro and low income areas and coincides with the increased political participation of these groups whether because of the war or the New Deal or the two together.

Since city councils possess some measure of power and since a portion of their membership is elected each two years in Norfolk and Newport News, the change in membership should reflect the impact of the war in some degree if that impact had immediate political consequences. However, there seems to have been little change in the war years. None of the members of the Norfolk Council of 1939 remained in office in 1949 but the year of dramatic change came in 1946 after the war was over. In that year the organization was divided. The delayed impact of the war is perhaps seen in the ability of the opposition in bringing to the polls large numbers of new voters. In Newport News only one member of the 1939 council remained in office but there was not even the kind of dramatic change which took place in Norfolk in 1946.

In neither Norfolk nor Newport News is there any significant difference in the councils of 1939 and 1949 as to the social, political, and economic status of their membership. Negroes have been candidates in both places but have failed of election. The major difference is that the council members are acutely aware of the role of the new voters in the Negro and lower income groups.

POLITICAL SIGNIFICANCE OF SHIFTS IN THE DISTRIBUTION OF WEALTH

The distribution of wealth is a factor in political power. There is little evidence as to just how the new distribution following upon the war has influenced politics, however. There is widespread agreement that the improved position of persons at the foot of the economic ladder has led many of them to take a more active part in elections. This is particularly true of the Negroes and of organized labor where the leadership is bent upon making substantial gains for these minorities.

In the area there was also some indication that men with recently

9. *Norfolk Virginian-Pilot*, June 10, 1941.

acquired wealth were interested in making their weight felt in politics. In other cases men already possessing power found that prosperity provided them with a larger purse to finance political ventures. No previous election in Virginia was accompanied by so large an expenditure in behalf of the candidates as was the gubernatorial primary of 1949.

THE POSTWAR RESURGENCE IN POLITICS

In the postwar period the most significant political development in Virginia was the challenge offered to the established political organization in the elections of 1945, 1946, and 1949.

The climax to this challenge came in the Democratic Gubernatorial Primary of August 2, 1949. Senator Battle, endorsed by the organization and Senator Byrd, was unsuccessfully opposed by Mr. Remmie Arnold, Mr. Horace Edwards, and Colonel Francis P. Miller. Miller, who led the opposition to the organization, was generally regarded as the candidate most acceptable to organized labor, the Negroes, and most other minorities, but his education and social and economic status made him acceptable to many persons of high economic status and social prestige. Mr. Arnold fell heir to some of the support given Governor Thurmond in the presidential race. Mr. Edwards appealed to the urban voters and proponents of the sales tax, and had the support of numerous persons formerly associated with the organization. The turnout of voters was probably the maximum to be expected and the campaign was waged aggressively by all the candidates. The results are summarized in Table 46.

Battle won by a plurality after collecting every vote the organization could influence, including a considerable number of Republican votes. Miller probably won every vote which opponents of the organization could muster. While the votes cast for Arnold and Edwards came from precincts which had not shown strong anti-organization tendencies they were votes which could neither be induced nor coerced into the Battle column. Contrary to the numerous editorials in Virginia signaling Battle's victory as an assurance of continued organization rule in Virginia, the election was a narrow escape for the machine and the future will be determined not only by the actions of the Arnold and Edwards supporters but also by the political affiliation of voters who die and new voters who qualify. Under these circumstances the voting trends of the Hampton Roads area, an area of population change, becomes particularly significant.

TABLE 46. VOTES CAST IN THE DEMOCRATIC GUBERNATORIAL PRIMARY, AUGUST 2, 1949

	Arnold		Battle		Edwards		Miller		
	Number	%	Number	%	Number	%	Number	%	Total
Virginia	22,054	7	135,426	43	47,435	15	111,697	35	316,612
Hampton Roads	3,745	7	17,870	33	10,135	19	22,205	41	53,955
Newport News	324	7	831	18	1,577	34	1,900	41	4,632
Warwick Co.	322	12	724	26	841	30	915	33	2,802
Hampton	65	5	408	31	291	22	557	42	1,321
Elizabeth City Co.	241	5	1,524	30	821	17	2,424	48	5,010
Williamsburg	92	13	213	28	89	17	376	49	770
James City Co.	84	22	131	35	74	19	92	24	381
York Co.	107	7	378	25	435	28	605	40	1,525
Norfolk City	977	8	5,042	39	1,487	12	5,261	41	12,767
Portsmouth	244	4	1,515	26	691	12	3,321	58	5,771
South Norfolk	130	13	280	28	103	10	497	49	1,010
Norfolk Co.	503	6	2,131	27	831	10	4,580	57	8,045
Princess Anne Co.	202	5	2,437	68	310	9	636	18	3,585
Nansemond Co.	135	6	654	31	851	40	472	23	2,112
Suffolk	275	11	1,165	45	732	28	402	16	2,574
Isle of Wight	44	3	437	26	1,002	61	167	10	1,650

Source: Bulletin of the State Board of Elections, August 1949 (dittoed).

In the Hampton Roads area Miller ran ahead of the rest of his anti-machine ticket by three thousand votes but Plunkett, the next strongest anti-machine candidate, ran behind Hutcheson who was the anti-machine candidate in 1946. It is to be concluded then that the anti-machine movement was not much stronger in 1949 than it had been in 1946 in the Hampton Roads area. Battle won by depending upon Republicans to partially replace the defection of Arnold and Edwards supporters from the machine. Edwards also took some votes from the anti-machine candidates by appealing to Newport News people as a "home-town boy" and appealing to the people of Isle of Wight and Nansemond as a native son.

Miller's 1949 vote was significantly smaller than Hutcheson's 1946 vote in Isle of Wight, Nansemond, and Suffolk. It was also somewhat smaller in Norfolk City and Princess Anne. Miller's 1949 vote was significantly larger in Elizabeth City, Norfolk County, Warwick, Hampton, Portsmouth, Williamsburg, and particularly York—all areas of wartime population gain. Even in Newport News, where Edwards was strong, Miller exceeded the Hutcheson vote. In terms of the percentage of votes cast Miller did better than Hutcheson only in Williamsburg, York, and Hampton. The comparison was least favorable to Miller in Norfolk County, Portsmouth, and South Norfolk, areas which must be regarded as anti-machine strongholds regardless of the candidate since the second and third position candidates on the anti-machine ticket showed considerable strength.

In Norfolk City, Miller gained but a single precinct which had been lost by Hutcheson in 1946 but he lost another. In both cases the margin was small and the vote light. The only districts which showed a significant decline in voting went to Battle. The largest increases in voting between 1946 and 1949 took place in Negro districts, which voted overwhelmingly for Miller, with the exception of the wealthiest white area which greatly increased its vote and voted for Battle. On the north side of the James River the increase in voting between the two elections was very large and tended to favor Miller though Phoebus and Hilton Village showed very large increases and voted for Battle. In Elizabeth City, Hampton, Warwick, and Newport News, Miller carried six precincts which had not voted for Hutcheson and lost none that were carried by the earlier anti-machine candidate.

It is to be concluded that Miller brought out the maximum of the anti-machine vote south of the James and if any gains are to be made they must come from increased voting on the part of Negroes and persons with lower incomes. Appeals to middle-class and upper-class whites in this area did not show significant results.

North of the James there is a different picture. Here Miller appears to have gained votes on a personal basis in addition to those normally to be polled by anti-machine forces. Moreover, exciting local contests, such as the fight for the House of Delegates seat for Elizabeth City and Hampton, brought out a large vote, much of which Miller captured. The incumbent in this fight was the speaker of the House of Delegates and chairman of the State Committee of the Democratic Party.

Since the wartime and postwar population gain in the area has been largely of the economic level reached by the anti-machine appeals there is prospect that an aggressive campaign to bring more voters to the polls will profit the anti-machine forces more than those of the state organization. Moreover, governmental consolidation may help emphasize the special interests of the area as opposed to the rural and up-country interests which dominate the machine faction of the Democratic party. The trend is towards an increasingly important role of the Hampton Roads area in the politics of Virginia.

V

SUMMARY AND APPRAISAL

U. S. Army Signal Corps

"Is it possible that the Hampton Roads-Peninsula area may have a destiny which may be less dependent upon national defense needs and policies?" (Soldiers debarking at Newport News with the shipyards in the background.)

CHAPTER XVII

THE POSTWAR PICTURE, FUTURE OUTLOOK, AND BROADER IMPLICATIONS*

PREVIOUS CHAPTERS have dealt with the manner in which the Hampton Roads-Peninsula area of Virginia played its traditional roles of shipbuilding, army and navy training, and embarking and debarking men and material during World War II.[1] Detailed consideration has been given, similarly, to the more direct and immediate effects of these activities upon the social, economic, and governmental structure of the area. Here and there the possible longer-run impacts of the war upon the region and its people have been suggested.

It is appropriate in this final chapter to develop somewhat further these suggestions as to the more fundamental ways in which this historic region may have been affected by its varied experiences during and immediately after the 1939-1945 conflict, to appraise its future outlook, and to consider the applicability of the basic conclusions of this study to the broad problem of local community adjustments to war activities. Were the wartime pains and progress merely fleeting accompaniments of the vast expansion of military establishments, shipbuilding and related activities which faded away as V-J Day became a memory? Were the prewar social, economic, and governmental characteristics of the region[2] so deeply rooted that the war's end found them basically unchanged, or was the very anatomy of the Hampton Roads community shaken and reshaped by war experiences? Is the area's future to be determined largely by considerations of war and peace? If so, how will it be affected by the apparent shift in national defense policy away from a big navy to one subordinated to air power as atomic warfare looms larger in military thinking? Is it possible that the Hampton Roads-Peninsula area may have a destiny which may be less dependent upon national defense needs and policies than has previously been the case? To what extent do the basic social,

*By Charles F. Marsh, Professor of Economics and Business Administration, College of William and Mary.

1. Chapter IV discusses the channels through which World War II came to the area.

2. See Chapters I, II, and III for an analysis of the prewar setting.

economic, and governmental effects of the Second World War upon the Hampton Roads communities constitute a pattern more or less typical of the effects of any war upon any American community in which military establishments and war industry are located?

A summary of the major postwar developments may help to answer such questions and thus shed light on what lies ahead for the area and perhaps for other war-affected communities.

THE POSTWAR PICTURE

Postwar developments may be outlined most effectively in terms of changes in population and other societal aspects, economic conditions, and government and politics.

Population and Other Societal Aspects

In contrast to the period following the First World War, the civilian population of the Hampton Roads-Peninsula localities not only did not fall off after V-J Day but actually rose above the wartime peak. According to the best available estimates,[3] these communities contained 623,132 persons in 1950, 624,227 in 1947, 567,075 in 1943, and 408,624 in 1940. Hampton Roads gained more in population than the rest of Virginia as it accounted for 19.3 per cent of the state's total in 1950 and 20.4 per cent in 1947 as compared with only 15.3 per cent in 1940. Preliminary census returns for 1950 show that its population rose approximately 50 per cent since 1940 while Virginia as a whole had only 21 per cent more people. While most of this growth was centered around the cities of Norfolk, Portsmouth, and Newport News, the counties surrounding these cities rather than the cities themselves experienced the greatest increase. Warwick County's growth of 323.6 per cent exceeded that of any other county or city in Virginia between 1940 and 1950,[4] and Norfolk County, with an increase of 177.3 per cent, was surpassed only by Warwick County and the city of Falls Church, a Washington, D. C., suburb. Negroes, who had comprised a relatively small portion of the wartime inmigrants, dropped from 35.8 per cent of the Hampton Roads-Peninsula population in 1940 to 28.9 per cent in 1947, though this region's in-

3. War and postwar population changes are analyzed in Chapter V. Postwar figures are derived largely from estimates by the Bureau of Population and Economic Research of the University of Virginia and from preliminary figures from the Census of 1950.

4. See Richmond *News-Leader*, June 23, 1950, for an analysis of preliminary returns from the Census of 1950.

crease in non-whites during these years exceeded that for the rest of the state. Of Virginia's colored population, Hampton Roads Negroes comprised 26 per cent in 1947 as compared with only 21 per cent before the war.

The return from military service of many prewar residents, the postwar influx of such new residents as navy wives and children[5] and veterans who married Hampton Roads girls, a large crop of war and postwar babies, and the many civilian in-migrants who remained even after their war jobs ended[6] apparently more than offset the outflow of war workers and families of service men. In other words, the Hampton Roads region escaped during the first four years after V-J Day the serious population shrinkage which occurred after the First World War.[7]

In addition to continued population pressure, postwar social developments included a steady decline in the number of marriages,[8] a meteoric rise in school enrollment, continued housing shortage and accentuation of prewar slums, and increased dependency upon relief.

The high wartime marriage rates and the continued large population have presented the schools of the region with crisis conditions. Norfolk County, for example, expected a net increase of approximately 1,800 pupils in September, 1949. Enrollment in Warwick County schools in 1949 was almost three times that for 1940. Other localities also experienced substantial increases. Space in 1948 and 1949 was at a premium everywhere, especially for the first two grades, where the war babies were concentrated.[9]

While by the summer of 1949 there was a slight surplus of higher priced housing in the private rental market in Norfolk and vicinity, the assignment of additional naval forces at that time promised to push

5. The Commandant of the Fifth Naval District attributed a part of the "mystery" of Norfolk's postwar congestion to the fact that the greatly increased number of navy dependents actually put more navy people in Norfolk in the summer of 1949 than during the war years, in spite of the smaller number of men stationed there. *Norfolk Virginian-Pilot*, July 15, 1949.

6. In reporting the only moderate declines in 1947 and 1948 of real-estate sales and marriage licenses, the Norfolk County Clerk noted that the county had retained "a tremendous proportion of its war-inflated population and business." *Ibid.*, January 2, 1949.

7. Population changes in the area between 1890 and 1940 are shown in Chapter I.

8. In Elizabeth City County and Hampton, for example, marriage licenses dropped each year from 902 in 1943 to only 555 in 1948. See Chapters VI and VII for analysis of war marriages and family relationships.

9. See *Ibid.*, May 15, 1949, and Newport News *Daily Press*, May 13 and July 31, 1949.

the demand for low-income accommodations beyond the World War II high point. More than 3,300 families were on the waiting list for various housing projects operated by the navy and by the Norfolk Redevelopment and Housing Authority, with more families scheduled to enter the market as they reached Norfolk.[10] Both Norfolk and Newport News have taken definite steps to use the Federal Housing Act of 1949 to get rid of slums which had deteriorated under wartime pressures even below their bad prewar condition. Norfolk's Representative Porter Hardy testified that the distressing situation whereby Norfolk slums cost the city for essential municipal services considerably more than the property taxes levied on these slums and bred the worst possible type of social conditions had caused him to favor the new legislation even though he opposed the principle of federal participation in local housing.[11] The presence of war housing units appeared to offer Hampton Roads communities a golden opportunity to overcome the traditional obstacle to slum clearance—finding shelter for the dispossessed slum dwellers while the new housing is under construction. Newport News officials planned to use the federal act, not only to eradicate 1,071 dwelling units which could not "be rehabilitated so as to make for sanitary and wholesome living"[12] and to provide modern low-cost housing elsewhere in the city, but also to make the slum areas available for industrial sites.

The end of the war brought sharp increases in use of public relief. For the whole Hampton Roads-Peninsula region, relief costs increased more than 50 per cent from 1945 to 1947 and case loads rose almost 40 per cent.[13] For Norfolk alone, relief costs increased 123 per cent and the case load rose 71 per cent during the five years 1944-1948. The Director of Public Welfare ascribed the heavier load chiefly to increased unemployment and decreased overtime compensation, a "sharp increase in divorces, separations and desertions which tended to throw women and children on public assistance," and higher living costs.[14] Hasty war marriages have apparently begun to reap their harvest of broken homes and recourse to public relief. That the postwar years have brought some lessening of personal and social disorganization,

10. *Norfolk Virginian-Pilot*, June 3, 1949.

11. *Ibid.*, June 28 and July 22 and 27, 1949.

12. Newport News *Daily Press*, July 5, 1949. The city health department has already ordered a considerable number of Negro families and twelve white families to evacuate some of the worst of these units.

13. See Table 41, Chapter XIV, for data on the war's impact upon welfare.

14. *Norfolk Virginian-Pilot*, July 27, 1949.

however, is indicated by a decline in juvenile delinquency in Newport News as measured by the number of youngsters under eighteen years of age who were in court. The number of adults in domestic relations court, however, in the same city has tended to rise.[15]

Economic Conditions

As with population, economic conditions in the Hampton Roads-Peninsula area after the Second World War remained at a relatively high level in spite of the termination or drastic reduction of most war activities.[16] The type of slump which followed World War I simply did not develop during the first four years after Japan surrendered. Even the general business decline experienced throughout the United States in 1949 was less serious in this area than in many sections of the country. Only 5 per cent of the Norfolk-Portsmouth district's population was unemployed in August as compared with approximately 6 per cent for the country as a whole. The decline in employment, however, resulting from the cancellation in the summer of 1949 of the contract for the navy supercarrier already on the ways of the Newport News Shipyard and the shearing from civilian payrolls at Hampton Roads military establishments of approximately 1,700 persons through the Defense Department's order firing 135,000 throughout the country brought considerable uneasiness as to the future trend of economic conditions in the region.[17]

Strangely enough, the layoff of more than 2,500 shipyard workers at Newport News late in 1948 and early in 1949 was accompanied by an increase in retail sales in that community. Effective buying income for 1948 was estimated by *Sales Management* at $4,900 per family for Newport News, $4,500 for the entire Lower Peninsula, and $4,541 for the Norfolk-Portsmouth district. These income figures compare with an average for Virginia of $4,044, of $3,939 for the Southeastern States, and $4,531 for the entire country. Newport News, with only .033 per cent of the nation's population, in 1948, accounted for .0553 of the country's retail sales.[18]

Several explanations may be offered for this paradox of continued postwar prosperity in a region dominated by shipbuilding and military employment even after the end of hostilities curtailed these activities.

15. Newport News *Daily Press*, August 7, 1949.

16. Chapters IV, IX, X, and XI describe these activities and their impact upon the Hampton Roads-Peninsula economy.

17. *Norfolk Virginian-Pilot*, August 25, 1949.

18. *Sales Management*, May, 1949.

In the first place, several permanent military establishments were expanded or came to the area for the first time after the war. The Army Ground Forces, now called the Army Field Forces, moved to Fort Monroe, and Fort Eustis became the headquarters of the Army Transportation Corps.[19] Norfolk was established as the major supply base and home port for most of the naval vessels operating in the Atlantic, with resultant movement of many naval families to that city.[20] The Armed Forces Staff College was also set up at Norfolk. Most significant of all, if the trend toward emphasizing air power in contrast to naval and land forces continues, is the considerable expansion at Langley Field of the Air Corps and the National Advisory Committee on Aeronautics.[21]

Secondly, the determined efforts of the Peninsula Industrial Committee, the Norfolk Industrial Commission, and the Portsmouth Chamber of Commerce to bring new industries to the Hampton Roads area have met with moderate success. The PIC has invested approximately $1,000,000 in buildings and land for industrial locations, has been directly responsible for bringing in nine new manufacturing plants and perhaps influenced the location of seven other firms in and around Newport News since the war.[22] The Norfolk Industrial Commission reported that 295 plants in that locality produced in 1948 $338,000,000 worth of products with 25,152 workers as compared with 285 plants, $250,000,000 in value of products, and 24,073 workers in 1947.[23]

The continued upswing of the tourist and resort business was a further factor in keeping the Hampton Roads economy in high gear. Virginia Beach handled approximately two million tourists and guests who spent approximately $10,000,000 from May to September, 1948, and probably equalled or bettered these figures in 1949. More than 500,000 tourists visited Williamsburg in 1948 and more than 292,000 out-of-state automobiles entered that historic city that year. The entire Hampton Roads-Peninsula area has benefited economically from these visitors to these focal points.[24]

19. The Peninsula Association of Commerce estimated that the total Army, Navy, and Air Corps population north of Hampton Roads, as of January 1, 1949, was 11,489. Newport News *Daily Press*, September 4, 1949.

20. *Norfolk Virginian-Pilot*, December 19, 1947, and May 17 and July 15, 1949.

21. Newport News *Daily Press*, July 10, 1946.

22. *Ibid.*, July 17, 1949.

23. *Norfolk Virginian-Pilot*, July 14, 1949.

24. See sales promotion pages prepared by Reuben H. Donnelley Corporation in connection with its sale of advertising for the 1949 Classified Directory of the Chesapeake & Potomac Telephone Company of Virginia.

On the debit side, however, has been the continued decline in employment at the two major shipyards and at navy posts; the failure of the Port of Hampton Roads to reach its full potentialities, not only in relation to other ports, but also because of the disastrous nationwide slump in shipping in 1949; and the continued dependence of the region's economy upon the Navy and coal shipments. The National Maritime Union reported late in the summer of 1949 that 1,350 seamen were beached at Norfolk and Newport News because of 100 idle ships which had nothing to haul. Coal dumpings, because of lowered export demand and John L. Lewis' three-day week, dropped from more than 17 million tons during the first seven months of 1948 to 14,700,000 tons in the same period in 1949.[25] Cuts in employment by the major railroads serving the port were unavoidable. The "no-day work week" in the coal mines later in the summer, of course, accentuated these difficulties.

Government and Politics

Postwar population growth, wartime inability because of manpower and material shortages to maintain essential services, and the provision of new services or expansion of government functions during the war through federal financial aid resulted in considerable postwar expansion of local government activities in most Hampton Roads communities.[26] This was particularly evident in Warwick and Norfolk counties, where the greatest population growth occurred. Education, recreation,[27] and public welfare were the most rapidly expanding services but others grew apace. Public health, slum clearance, and community planning received increasing attention. New ground was broken in 1948 when the City of Norfolk established the Norfolk Port Authority and assigned E. O. Jewell, fresh from a successful job of port expansion at New Orleans, the direction of this body in its attempt to develop the Port of Hampton Roads. Because of rising price and wage levels, government expenditures increased even more than services. The year 1948 for Norfolk has been termed "one of inventory-taking by a city which experienced the high tensions of the war years, whose wealth was vastly increased, but whose

25. *Norfolk Virginian-Pilot*, August 2 and 4, 1949.

26. Chapters XII-XIV analyze war and postwar expansion of local functions. The federal role in providing support for local services is indicated in Chapter XV.

27. Chapter XIV notes that Newport News appropriated $48,441 for recreation in 1946 and nothing in 1938 and that Norfolk and Portsmouth also expanded this function many times its prewar level. Federal funds provided the initial stimulus.

facilities and plant showed signs of wear and tear."[28] Governmental problems of other Hampton Roads communities in the postwar years could be similarly characterized.

Expanding services and expenditures by local government during the war and its aftermath led to changes and proposals for change in government organization and structure. Not only have particular departments and certain governmental units themselves been reorganized with an eye to greater efficiency and economy[29] but vigorous efforts have also been made to combine cities and their rapidly growing environs. North of Hampton Roads, such efforts have taken the form of an intensive study by the Lower Peninsula Planning Commission[30] of possible plans for consolidating the counties of Warwick and Elizabeth City, the cities of Newport News and Hampton, and the town of Phoebus; formal transmittal to the five governments of the study committee's recommendation for consolidation into one new city and passage of the necessary enabling act by the 1950 General Assembly; a referendum March 21, 1950, after widespread discussion by civic groups and spirited campaigning, in which voters of Newport News and Warwick County favored consolidation into one city and those of Elizabeth City County, Hampton, and the town of Phoebus failed to give favorable majorities; and certain legal steps by the city of Newport News toward annexation of parts of the surrounding territory as a possible alternative to consolidation.[31] The cities of Portsmouth, Norfolk, and South Norfolk, south of Hampton Roads, have each initiated proceedings for annexing parts of the adjacent suburbs without considering the broader consolidation approach. Considerable controversy and confusion among the affected communities have developed over these annexation proposals.[32]

Special mention should be made of functional consolidation, an increasingly popular type of joint government action in the Hampton Roads-Peninsula region. The Hampton Roads Sanitary District, a joint attempt by most of the governmental units on both sides of

28. Statement by City Manager of Norfolk, as reported in the *Norfolk Virginian-Pilot*, December 31, 1948.

29. Chapter XII analyzes these modifications in governmental structure.

30. The underlying study was made by Professor Pate, author of Chapters XII-XV and the present writer.

31. See *Report of Study Committee of the Lower Peninsula Planning Commission on Consolidation of Local Governments* (mimeographed), May 19, 1949, and Newport News *Daily Press*, May 20, July 7 and 14, and August 9, 1949, and March 22, 1950, and previous March issues.

32. *Norfolk Virginian-Pilot*, July 7 and 9, 1949.

Hampton Roads to promote public health and to redeem the waters of Hampton Roads for recreational and seafood purposes through eliminating most of the pollution of those waters, is the most elaborate example. While initiated before World War II, operation of the sewage disposal program was not begun until 1948.[33]

Increased political awareness and participation, particularly among Negroes and other groups whose economic status improved greatly during the war years[34] and among the many newcomers to the area, have been a major postwar development.[35] This has been evidenced, not only in the intense interest shown in such local matters as the improvement of schools and other services, annexation and consolidation plans, the bringing of new blood into the various local governing bodies, but also in increased participation in state and national elections. Hampton Roads voters have shown an increasing tendency in recent senatorial and gubernatorial primaries to favor candidates opposed to the dominant faction of the Democratic Party led by Senator Harry Byrd. While this tendency was apparent in the New Deal days of the late thirties, it was accentuated by such wartime developments as the influx of population from other sections—much of it in the younger age groups—, urbanization, changes in distribution of income, and increased political influence of Negroes and organized labor.

WHAT DOES THE FUTURE HOLD?

The "refiner's fire" of the Second World War and the postwar period has made the basic characteristics of the Hampton Roads-Peninsula area stand out more clearly and thus has facilitated appraisal of its future outlook. The capacity of its strategic location, excellent harbor, favorable climate, level topography, and farm, forest, and seafood resources to provide support for an expanding population at a high level of economic and social well being has been emphasized by the developments of the forties. In spite of a shortage of fresh water, and absence of such basic industrial resources as coal, iron, and petroleum, Nature's balance sheet for the area has continued to show a distinct surplus.

33. See Chapter XV.

34. Increasing unionization of workers was a factor in improving the economic status of many persons in the area. Chapter XI discusses this and other phases of the war's impact on labor relations.

35. Chapter XVI analyses underlying political developments and trends in the area from the 1930's to the present.

The region's rich history similarly provides an asset which, though inherently intangible, has become increasingly tangible as hundreds of thousands of visitors have come to renew and enlarge their understanding of events and places which helped to shape the destiny of this country. This historical appeal, combined with the natural advantages, the skillful development of these resources by Colonial Williamsburg, the National Park Service, the Jamestown Corporation[36] and other agencies, and the growing reputation of the College of William and Mary and Hampton Institute provide the basis for a continuing influx of new permanent residents, tourists, and students which should strengthen the region's economy in the years to come. The fact that World War II brought thousands of members of the armed forces to the region for the first time, many of whom have already returned or will return in the future, provides further ground for confidence in the region's continuing ability to attract new residents and visitors.

Also on the asset side are the vast government enterprises—largely military—which are apparently permanently established in the Hampton Roads area. Military personnel and civilian workers, with their families, should continue to furnish the basic purchasing power to support a variety of trades, services, and public utilities. In the Newport News Shipbuilding and Drydock Company, the fertilizer companies of the Norfolk-Portsmouth district, and varied groups of smaller manufacturers, the Hampton Roads-Peninsula communities should have substantial sources of industrial employment in the future as in the past. Finally, its railroad and port facilities should continue to attract a considerable volume of foreign trade and keep the Port of Hampton Roads among the nation's leaders.

With all these prospects for a healthy economy, an undertone of insecurity and even defeatism pervades the thinking of many of the region's residents. Chief among the factors responsible for this uneasiness is the dominance in the Hampton Roads economy of the navy and the current shift away from a "big navy" policy in Washington. A recent statement that "the biggest thing in life continues to be the seafaring man, source of so many troubles and triumphs, to whom the city's fortunes have so long been wedded for better and for

36. The presentation each summer since 1947, in Williamsburg, by this corporation, in cooperation with the Virginia Department of Conservation and Development, of Paul Green's historical drama *The Common Glory* has attracted increasing crowds. Almost 80,000 persons paid admission in 1949.

worse"[37] would probably be accepted as correct by most Norfolk people. The shock to Newport News' economy and to that city's confidence in its own future from Secretary Johnson's cancellation of the supercarrier contract in the summer of 1949 emphasized the dependence of the area upon navy policy. The dwindling role of the navy in future military planning poses a severe problem for those concerned with the future of Hampton Roads. While the tendency for the navy to concentrate an increasing portion of its shrinking Atlantic coast activities in Hampton Roads gives some ground for optimism, it is clear that this can provide only temporary security.

A corollary of this dependence on the navy is the tendency for the presence of large government agencies, especially in Portsmouth and Norfolk, to inhibit the development of vigorous business leadership and individual initiative. Too many businessmen and other civic leaders are inclined to say, "What's the use of trying to do anything on our own? Washington will make the major decisions affecting employment in the area and, hence, our business volume and profits anyway." Local leaders who have attempted to develop an economy less dependent upon the navy have made relatively little headway. While this has been less true in Newport News, where the Newport News Shipbuilding and Drydock Company has built a vigorous tradition of private enterprise and used modern business principles effectively, yet adherence to this tradition and application of these principles are necessarily circumscribed by government policies with respect to the construction of ships for the navy and the merchant marine.

A second major factor responsible for the widespread feeling of insecurity and defeatism is the general recognition of the fact that the Port of Hampton Roads is not only underdeveloped today but that the forces which keep it from realizing its full potentialities are too strong to make its full development possible within the reasonably near future. Such conditions as a local population too small to attract large and varied imports, less frequent steamship arrivals and departures than the larger Atlantic ports, absentee ownership of steamship lines serving Hampton Roads with consequent slight interest in and ofttimes downright opposition to developing this port when this might be at the expense of New York or other home ports, and lack of intra-port coordination of shipping facilities are looked upon by

37. Richard Tregaskis, "Norfolk," *Saturday Evening Post*, July 9, 1949.

many shipping people as insuperable barriers to the attainment of front rank among the country's ports.

The unfortunate separation by water and by years of misguided traditional rivalry of the ports of Hampton Roads into separate and distinct communities has constituted a third obstacle to the development of a feeling of security and optimism as to the region's future. The mutual distrust and hostility between citizens of these communities, especially between the shipping interests of Norfolk and Newport News, has consistently caused them to shy away from cooperating in promoting their larger interest. Few regions in the United States have so much in common economically and socially; yet longstanding petty rivalries with each other have tended to keep the larger goals submerged.

Recurrent stoppages in coal mining and consequent declines in coal dumpings at Hampton Roads and uneasiness as to the future competitive position of coal have helped develop this feeling of insecurity. The possibility of the coal industry's pricing itself out of the competitive fuels market, as concessions to John L. Lewis and his union bring higher costs and the demand for other fuels rises, is a serious threat to the continued prosperity of a port which depends so heavily on coal shipments for a substantial proportion of its trade.

Are these depressants inevitable and unavoidable, or are there possible ways of containing them and of building an economy in the Hampton Roads-Peninsula area which can rise above them? A "yes" or "no" answer cannot be given to this question but at least one thing is clear. While naval and other military activities are too completely interwoven with the economic fabric of the area to be eliminated even if local residents desired and had the power to do so, it is obvious that its future growth requires the development of types of economic activity which are less dependent upon considerations of war and peace, especially naval policy. At least three possibilities exist through which this may be accomplished.

More diversified industrial development is one promising approach. The efforts of the Peninsula Industrial Committee, the Norfolk Industrial Commission, and the Portsmouth Chamber of Commerce in their brief span of activity have been sufficiently successful in attracting industries which are adapted to the area to warrant the belief that much more can be accomplished. In addition, if recent speculation as to the possible location of a giant steel plant in the Hampton Roads section should be fulfilled, a major step will have been taken down the road toward economic independence from fluctuations in naval policy. Favorable consideration has apparently been given to such a location because of the imminent exhaustion of high-grade ores in the Lake Superior region and the ease with which ores from the vast Labrador and South American deposits could be combined with West Virginia and Virginia coking coal and limestone.[38] Lack of fresh water, the vulnerability of Hampton Roads to atom bombs,[39] and the attractions of other sites may, of course, prevent such a plant from coming to Hampton Roads.[40] Moreover, it is possible that the coming of such a heavy industry to this area would create so many economic and social problems that it would not be an unmitigated blessing.

A second possibility of developing a more balanced economy is the elevation of the Port of Hampton Roads into a truly top-flight port. As suggested earlier in this chapter, certain difficulties must be overcome if this is to occur. Chief among them is the lack of sufficient population in the hinterland as well as locally to attract a volume of imports and diversified exports large enough to result in the steamship sailings and other facilities essential for a first class port. Greater industrialization would be the most effective way of building up this trade, not only because of the raw materials which would be imported and the manufactured products to be exported, but also because it would increase the size of the local market for imported consumers goods through bringing a larger population to the region.

A second obstacle, as previously noted, to building up the port is the lack of locally owned steamship lines. The only effective way of meeting this difficulty is the building up of a sufficient volume of shipments to encourage the growth of locally owned lines or to force the recognition by the absentee owners that their Hampton Roads operations are sufficiently important to warrant their being pushed.

The most baffling obstacle, and yet the one which superficially should be simplest to remove, is the unwillingness of shipping leaders of the region to think in terms of the Port of Hampton Roads rather than of the Port of Norfolk, the Port of Portsmouth, and the Port of Newport News. Only when these leaders look beyond their smaller

38. See *Norfolk Virginian-Pilot*, February 28 and March 1, 1949.

39. See reports of National Security Resources Board.

40. The United States Steel Corporation did in fact decide against a Hampton Roads location late in 1949 when it selected a Delaware River site for its new Atlantic seaboard plant. It is still possible, however, that one of the other steel companies might build a new plant in the Hampton Roads area. See J. B. Blackford, "Steel Industry Eyes Virginia as Mill Site," Richmond *Times-Dispatch*, January 15, 1950.

local interest and unite to further the Port of Hampton Roads as an entity can much progress be made. They might well follow the example of the Port of New York into which the separate interests and rivalries of New York City and the various New Jersey ports have long since been submerged.[41]

A third possibility of lessening the dependence of the Hampton Roads communities upon the whims of defense policy is the further development of their historical, recreational, and residential assets into a travel trade many times greater than now exists. While Williamsburg and Virginia Beach have been the focal points of attraction and have made good progress in capitalizing their resources, many other points in the area have scarcely made a beginning in exploiting their opportunities in this important field.

What does the future hold as to the social and governmental aspects of the Hampton Roads-Peninsula communities? Will the dimming of the memories of World War II and its immediate aftermath bring a return to prewar social and governmental conditions and attitudes? Probably not, though certain prewar characteristics and tendencies have merely been accentuated by the war rather than changed in nature. Expanding population, the urbanization of rural communities adjacent to the Hampton Roads cities, congestion in the cities, high divorce rates, poor housing, and high rates of crime and delinquency provide examples of prewar conditions in the area which were intensified during the war years. Similarly the spread of unionization of labor and increases in the incomes and educational status of the Negroes and low-income white workers which had begun in the late thirties were accelerated by war and postwar developments. The resulting tendency toward more equal distribution of income and higher living standards of formerly underprivileged groups, not only in Hampton Roads, but in other centers of war activity probably constitute a permanent result of the Second World War, the full economic, social, and political implications of which will not be clear for some years.

One outstanding impact of the war upon the region has been the substitution of "ferment" for inertia on the part of many citizens. The need for action in meeting the various types of wartime emergencies in such a congested area as Hampton Roads in housing, education,

41. For further discussion of the potentialities and limitations of the Port of Hampton Roads, see *Norfolk Virginian-Pilot*, August 5-8, 1949.

water supply and sanitation, recreation, and other fields forced local citizens to take many types of joint action, both governmental and non-governmental, which were new to them. The return of veterans, torn from their prewar habits of thought and action by their wartime experiences, emphasized still more the fact that an aroused citizenry had taken the place of the relatively placid prewar population. Insistence upon better government services and upon more effective local government became increasingly evident. While voters in only two of the five local governments of the Lower Peninsula area favored consolidation into one city, the strenuous campaign before the March, 1950, referendum invigorated the political atmosphere of the entire area. It also provided widespread public education in local government problems and probably laid the foundation for ultimate consolidation under one government of the Lower Peninsula communities. It has also stimulated greater attention on the part of the southside cities of Norfolk, Portsmouth, and South Norfolk to the possibilities of consolidation as an alternative to the less satisfactory, piecemeal annexation approach. Certain it is that the increasingly complex economic and social problems will cause citizens to force their local governments into more economical and efficient types of organization than those now in effect.

BROADER IMPLICATIONS OF THE STUDY

The experience of the Hampton Roads communities in World War II suggests that any community which may be assigned heavy military or industrial duties in any future war may expect a rather definite pattern of developments. It may expect, in the first instance, to find its population doubled or trebled almost overnight, particularly in the rural areas adjacent to the older centers of population. And it will be confronted with all the social, economic, and governmental effects of this in-migration of workers seeking employment in war industries, of military personnel seeking recreation and release from the discipline of the camp, and of a host of dependents and camp followers.

The social effects of this vast in-migration tend to be particularly obvious. Not only is the total population increased but its structure tends to be distorted. Men in the productive twenties, thirties, and forties, women in these and somewhat younger age groups, and white people instead of Negroes tend to dominate the in-migrant population and thus become relatively more important in the total population. Crowded living quarters, disrupted home ties, hasty marriages, abnormal relations between the sexes both within and without the marriage relation, neglect of children by working parents, and inadequate recreational opportunities take their toll in various types of personal and social disorganization both during and after the war. Rising divorce rates and increased crime are indexes of these social maladjustments.

The prime economic effects of expanded war activity center around the sharply increased demand for most types of labor and for most consumer goods and services. While war agencies are the main source of demand for labor, civilian businesses serving the swollen population soon experience acute needs for workers. Ordinarily the latter are at a severe disadvantage in competing for labor because of the preferred legal position of the essential industries and their greater capacity to pay high wages. Labor shortages in nonessential businesses provide a strong impetus for them to use labor-saving devices, to form personnel departments, and to improve managerial practices in other ways. The Hampton Roads experience indicates that many of these war-induced managerial improvements tend to continue in effect even after the war needs have disappeared. The recruiting of additions to the labor force from housewives, school children, and the aged is another effect of labor shortage which tends to remain to some degree even after the war emergency has passed.

The intense labor demand tends itself to increase wage rates. It also encourages unionization of workers, which creates further pressure upon the wage structure. Increased wages combined with full employment of a vastly increased labor force result in substantially higher incomes for most of the population, especially of such traditionally low-paid workers as Negroes. These higher incomes and rising standards of living increase the demand for goods and services of all types. To the degree that businessmen selling them can obtain adequate supplies of goods and labor and keep costs below selling prices, greatly increased profits are realized, even after excess profits and other taxes. In the midst of this song of plenty and prosperity, however, attention should be called to the "forgotten men" of the war-affected community—manufacturers of nonessential goods who find it next to impossible to shift to war production and retailers of goods which war requirements prevent from being supplied. They must tighten their belts, shift to other lines of business, or perhaps close up and accept employment in war enterprises. Perhaps the most far-reaching economic and social effect of war activity is the rise in incomes and living standards and changes in consumption habits and social attitudes on the part of Negroes and other underprivileged classes. To the degree that these changes tend to be relatively permanent, and there is considerable evidence to support this, the implications for the future are almost revolutionary in nature.

If the wartime experience of the Hampton Roads congested area is typical, public action will be required in any war community to provide housing, recreational, hospital, and school facilities. Action by local government will also be required to expand local facilities for water, garbage collection and disposal, sewage disposal, and police and fire protection. Local governments faced by war pressures in the future are likely to find, as the Hampton Roads governing bodies have found, that they alone are quite incapable of meeting those demands for new and expanded public services. They will see the federal government supplying a large part of the cost of the necessary facilities as well as technical assistance to meet local situations. At the same time local issues are intensified, participation in local politics is reduced. Consequently, the programs initiated by the federal government have more potency than in more normal times and are subjected to less local criticism. This study of the Second World War's impact on the Hampton Roads-Peninsula area of Virginia supports the hypothesis that in an emergency, whether of war or of economic depression, the governments that stand out in the American federal system are the federal and local governments. These are actually in the front lines of the civilian war effort and their activities tend to push the state government into the background. In view of this situation, it would appear that the indiscriminate assertion of the legal dominance of state governments over municipal affairs conflicts with the important role of municipalities as units for the satisfaction of local needs. A sound redistribution of state and local powers on the order of the federal principle would afford state supremacy on general issues and would encourage the maintenance and development of local self-government strong enough to meet local problems.

Infiltration of new elements in the population during and immediately after the war period plus improvement of the economic status of Negroes and other low-income groups under war conditions tend to lay the foundation for increased political participation and desire for change in the postwar years. Absorption with war problems during the war period itself actually tends to lessen political activity and participation rather than to stimulate it.

It may be asked whether the methods used in this study—largely case studies based upon field interviews aimed at obtaining qualitative information at the local or "grass-roots" level—justify the making of the type of generalizations outlined in the foregoing pages. The danger that such methods, which are comparable to what the social anthropologist terms the "participant observer" method, can degenerate into the collection of unrelated fragments of information which have little scientific value is real. The authors of this volume, however, believe that "grass-roots" studies have greater value than most social scientists admit. The findings of such studies, if checked and evaluated with caution, can help to test the generalizations of "armchair" economists, political scientists, sociologists, and historians as well as make their own contributions in the form of statements of principles as to how people act under various types of pressure. It is the hope of the writers of this volume that this study of the impact of World War II upon the Hampton Roads communities of Virginia will not only help them as parts of a traditional war area to understand more clearly their perennial problems and discover possible solutions to them, but will also shed light on the broad problem of community adjustments to wartime pressures wherever and whenever these pressures may occur.

INDEX

INDEX

www.ingramcontent.com/pod-product-compliance
Lightning Source LLC
LaVergne TN
LVHW090307210926
848480LV00001B/163

* 9 7 8 0 8 0 7 8 6 8 2 5 6 *